Praise for *The Pen and the People*

'Every historian carries with them a list of the books they wish they had written, and *The Pen and the People* features high in mine.'

David Vincent, Professor of Social History, The Open University

'The study is probing and provocative: the result is a book that stimulates and reminds us that, when all is said and done, history should be about people and seeking to describe, understand, and explain their thought processes and behavior. It also demonstrates how very readable history can and should be ... This is a fascinating social history Susan Whyman is to be applauded for following one excellent social hist another.'

Rosemary O'Day, *Journal of British Studies*

'Th studies of *The Pen and the People*, as well as the substantial archival boo hey emerge, will certainly require a revision of the history of eig iteracy.'

Betty A. Schellenberg, *Huntington Library Quarterly*

Im significant new ground ... This is a thoroughly researched sch h will undoubtedly have considerable impact on the field wh case studies will appeal to the more general reader.'

James Daybell, *History Today*

'Th s an important work that overturns the accepted view that lite century England was rare, confined to the small elite who hac education.'

Wendy Jones Nakanishi, *English Studies*

'Th dy, written with verve and learning, shows convincingly tha new postal services encouraged an expansive culture of lett h rich and poor-with improved communications then, as tod ocial changes.'

Corfield, Professor of History, Royal Holloway, University of London

Th d ground-breaking book. Dr Whyman's research, largely dra r-used resources of local record offices, radically extends the for exploring the uses and effects of literacy in the long eig y the working and middle classes.'

John Barnard, Emeritus Professor of English Literature, University of Leeds

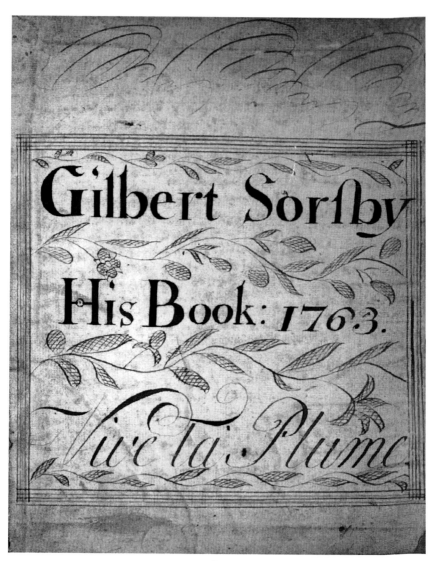

Notebook of Gilbert Sorsby Jr, a Derbyshire farmer, 1763.

THE PEN AND THE PEOPLE

ENGLISH LETTER WRITERS 1660–1800

SUSAN E. WHYMAN

OXFORD
UNIVERSITY PRESS

OXFORD

UNIVERSITY PRESS

Great Clarendon Street, Oxford OX2 6DP

Oxford University Press is a department of the University of Oxford.
It furthers the University's objective of excellence in research, scholarship,
and education by publishing worldwide in

Oxford New York

Auckland Cape Town Dar es Salaam Hong Kong Karachi
Kuala Lumpur Madrid Melbourne Mexico City Nairobi
New Delhi Shanghai Taipei Toronto

With offices in

Argentina Austria Brazil Chile Czech Republic France Greece
Guatemala Hungary Italy Japan Poland Portugal Singapore
South Korea Switzerland Thailand Turkey Ukraine Vietnam

Oxford is a registered trade mark of Oxford University Press
in the UK and in certain other countries

Published in the United States
by Oxford University Press Inc., New York

British Library Cataloguing in Publication Data

Data available

Library of Congress Cataloging in Publication Data

Whyman, Susan E., 1937–
The pen and the people : English letter writers 1660–1800 / Susan E. Whyman.
p. cm.
Includes bibliographical references and index.
ISBN 978–0–19–953244–5
1. English letters—History and criticism. 2. Letter writing—History—18th century.
3. England—Social life and customs—18th century. 4. England—Civilization—18th century.
I. Title.
PR915.W49 2009
826′.509—dc22
2009019291

Typeset by Laserwords Private Limited, Chennai, India
Printed in Great Britain
on acid-free paper by
MPG Books Group, Bodmin and King's Lynn

ISBN 978–0–19–953244–5 (Hbk.)
ISBN 978–0–19–960218–6 (Pbk.)

1 3 5 7 9 10 8 6 4 2

TO FRANK

Contents

Acknowledgements

My first book, *Sociability and Power: The Cultural Worlds of the Verneys* left me with unfinished business. The Verney Archive had demonstrated how rich letters could be as sources of historical evidence. Still, I wanted to hear the voices of people lower down the social scale than those of the Verneys. I also wished to look at lives and letters from the viewpoint of a historian, using the innovative pathways of the Internet in tandem with the deep, timeless, but often silent riches of English archives. Both, I believe, are needed for discovering and understanding unknown people of the past.

Letters, by definition, expose the intellectual, friendship, and kinship networks of every writer. I wish to thank the people in these three tiers of my own personal networks. Without their aid my ten-year project would never have been completed.

First, I wish to pay tribute to the archivists in English Record Offices and libraries. With their varied backgrounds and personal erudition they form the first rung of my intellectual network. At Duke Humfrey's Library at the Bodleian Library, I thank the present staff, as well as Mary Clapinson, Greg Colley, and William Hodges. Bruce Barker Benfield, Patricia Buckingham, Clive Hurst, Josie Lister, Richard Ovenden, and Mike Webb also rendered assistance. Helen Dafter and the reference librarians at the Royal Mail Archive helped me over many years. I also owe debts to Colin Harris, Frances Harris, Margaret O'Sullivan, David Wykes, David Powell, Joan McKillop, Elizabeth Knight, Elizabeth L. Johnson, Mary George, Charles Greene, and Andrea Immel.

I thank the following for permission to reproduce copyright material: Beinecke Rare Book and Manuscript Library, Yale University; Bodleian Library, University of Oxford; British Library; Chetham Society; Cumbria Record Office, Kendal; Derbyshire Record Office, Matlock; Trustees of Dr Williams's Library and Trustees of the Congregational Memorial Hall; Hull City Archives; Library of the Society of Friends, London; Trustees of the National Library of Scotland; Oxford University Press; North Yorkshire County Record Office, Northallerton; Princeton University Press; Royal Mail Archive; and Joan Wilkinson, Derbyshire. I thank the Henry E. Huntington Library and the University of California Press for permission to include matter published in 'Letter writing and the rise of the novel: The epistolary literacy of Jane Johnson and Samuel Richardson', *Huntington Library Quarterly*, 70 (2007), 577–606 and the British Library for permission to include matter in 'Advice to letter writers: Evidence from four generations of Evelyns' in Frances Harris and Michael Hunter (eds.), *John Evelyn and His Milieu* (2003), 255–66. I thank Mike Burt, Seth Cayley, Rupert Cousens, Kate Hind, and Hannah McGuffie Oxford University Press for their commitment to this book.

Intellectual support and social enjoyment came from academic networks that included Evelyn Arizpe, Hannah Barker, Alastair Bellany, Clyde Binfield, Arthur Burns, Elaine Chalus, Elizabeth Clarke, Mary Clayton, Michelle Cohen, Robert Darnton, Kristin Gager, Jonathan Gibson, Anthony Grafton, Leonie Hannan, Bob Harris, Karen Harvey, Uriel Heyd, Rab Houston, Ann Hughes, Jane Humphries, Kathryn Gleadle, Terttu Nevalainen, Dianne Payne, Jonathan Rose, Gil Skidmore, Nigel Smith, Morag Styles, Alison Wall, and the members of the British Studies seminars at Yale and Princeton Universities, the Restoration and Reform and the Eighteenth-Century seminars at Oxford University, and the Long Eighteenth-Century seminar at the Institute for Historical Research, London, which has been my academic home away from home.

The following people gave me long-term help, stimulating conversations, and read my chapters. I am grateful to Sonia Anderson, Michelle Cohen, Margot Finn, Peter Lake, and Anne Stott for doing so. Sylvia Stevens shared her deep knowledge about Quakers, whilst Keith Wrightson brought sense and clarity to my early attempts to explore popular literacy. Clare Brant has been a constant epistolary companion over many years, whilst Amanda Vickery provided helpful perspectives about letter-writers and common interests. Tim Hitchcock, Julian Hoppit, and Perry Gauci offered invaluable recommendations during key periods of this project. Joanna Innis's suggestions throughout the entire period were, as usual, incisive and invaluable. Pene Corfield's contributions to all aspects of this book are too numerous to itemize, but all are gratefully accepted. Finally, Moshe Sluhovsky and Betsy Brown read almost everything I wrote over a ten-year period. Their loyal support says everything about the unique importance of friendship networks.

Hospitality networks were also significant and appreciated. Thanks go to Jose Patterson, Harriet and Harold Montefiore, Kathy Woodhouse and Peter Watts, and the Huckvale family.

Lastly, no author could ever complete a project of this breadth and duration without the unqualified support and love from family. It brings me great joy to thank my daughter, Jennifer Whyman and her husband, David Greene, my son, Bill and his wife Paula and my sister Ellen Messing. I cannot, however, adequately repay them for their patience and love. I also want to recognize my four grandsons, who may someday write books of their own. They, above all, have provided the inspiration for my work: Benjamin and Evan Greene; David and Eric Whyman.

This book owes everything, as do I, to my husband, Frank. Nothing has yet been said about the powerful efficacy of a sense of humour, without which any undertaking is found wanting. This he has amply provided, along with love and constant support. For all of my priceless networks, I am grateful.

Oxford, England
January 2009

List of Illustrations

PART
I

Creating a culture
of letters

Introduction

The pen, the post, and the people

During the eighteenth-century, the pen, the post, and the people became permanently connected to each other. This fact made a difference in the lives of individuals described in this book. The experiences of Joseph Morton neatly illustrate this point. In 1765, he left his family in Kelso Scotland to settle in a Westmorland village, where he hoped to find work as a gardener. Throughout his 124-mile journey to Kendal, he distributed letters to friends in return for much appreciated dinners. Morton's first two letters to his family gave detailed instructions on how to address his mail, so as not to incur double postage. One letter was sent part way by the carrier, the other wholly by post. 'Let me know', he wrote, with a wise concern for cost, 'whither this or the other was Dearest'.[1]

Morton's deep knowledge of postal practices was not unusual for his time and class. Though he was often jobless, he never stopped writing to his parents in phonetically spelt prose. Letter-writing was a normal and indispensable part of the way he coped with life. In fact, Morton adjusted his own routines to mesh with rhythms of the post. Even in times of real poverty, he, and others like him, found makeshift ways to send letters—using friends, servants, porters, newsmen, hawkers, itinerants, or carriers. When Morton's life descended into bitter failure, his letters, written from 1765–99, brought emotional comfort and family assistance. In better times, they helped him to find stable employment.

Why should we care about a gardener and his letters? Filled with mundane details and commonplace language, why have ordinary letters captivated readers for centuries? Chapter 3 demonstrates why Morton, himself, regarded writing them important. But current-day readers can instantly see that his letters reveal two vital features of eighteenth-century society—features that may, at first, appear surprising: the structural presence of the Royal Mail, and the existence of literate workers, who knew how to use it. Before 1660, the English postal system remained undeveloped. Naturally, only a small group of writers penned epistles on a daily basis. By 1800, high-speed coaches crammed with letters and newspapers, sped to every corner of the land.

Yet this is not the traditional story. The Royal Mail is normally described as a backward institution, burdened by inefficiency before 1840. Chapter 2 maintains, however, that by the eighteenth century, basic routines for collecting and sending mail had already been established.[2] In the 1680s, the London Penny Post was the envy of other nations, with deliveries by bonded carriers up to ten times a day.[3] From 1720–60, Ralph Allen of Bath created a national network of post roads and offices, thus transforming a structure that had centred mainly upon London. Numbers of letters carried surged dramatically, but the expansion of the post's physical configuration was even more important.[4] In the 1780s, a further leap was made by John Palmer, whose coaches replaced the post boy and produced 'the mail coach era'.[5] Hence in 1776, when a spinster, Barbara Johnson needed money, she was happy to have it sent by mail. 'The best method of conveyance', she advised her brother, 'will be in a Draught by the Post.'[6]

Since letters and literature were so tightly linked in this period, we should not be surprised to find similar comments in contemporary novels. It was only natural, therefore, for Jane Fairfax to remark in Jane Austen's *Emma*: 'The post-office is a wonderful establishment... So seldom that a letter, among the thousands that are constantly passing about the Kingdom, is ever carried wrong—and not one in a million, I suppose actually lost! And when one considers the variety of hands, and of bad hands too, that are to be deciphered, it increases the wonder.'[7] In the eyes of middling-sort people like Jane Fairfax and lower-sort workers like Joseph Morton, the post office was, indeed, a wonder of the world.

This book addresses the question of how the pen, the post, and the people became linked to each other during the eighteenth century. Who was included in the group of possible letter-writers that might use the Royal Mail? How and why did they learn to write letters? What roles did letters play in the lives of ordinary people? Finally, what kind of impact did these developments have on eighteenth-century culture? This book suggests that the letters of Joseph Morton are characteristic of a popular epistolary tradition that welcomed and absorbed untrained writers. It was built on the foundations of an older tradition, but during the eighteenth century it shed many of its formalities and adopted aspects of merchant culture. By 1800, all ranks of society were participating in a vibrant culture of letters.

Of course, the mere existence of a Post Office, and makeshift ways around it, says little about its actual use. But institutions do not arise in a vacuum. They anticipate, as well as follow, social and economic trends. This, I believe, was the case in regard to the Post Office. As we shall see, medieval, renaissance, and early-modern letter-writers provided a solid foundation for the expansion of the Royal Mail. In every century, moreover, the commercial and diplomatic classes lobbied hard for postal improvements. Surely, no institution could prosper and expand without a critical mass of people to use it, or to provide brokers for that function.

Yet historians insist that literacy rates did not rise significantly until the mid nineteenth century. Only then did the advent of state schooling finally generate a rise in popular literacy. Paradoxically, at the time of the post's great structural growth from 1750–1840, studies show literacy was stagnating or declining. A goal of this book is to use large caches of correspondence to suggest how villages without schools could produce letter-writers like Morton.

As this volume was researched, three findings based on the ubiquitous presence of letters offered clues to this problem. The first piece of evidence has already been discussed—the structural existence of a postal system, whose ways were understood by local people, even in isolated northern areas. The fact that letters permeated factual and fictional genres[8] was another indication that there were plenty of models to aid writers and that usage was widespread. Of course, this statement could be made about other times and places. Nonetheless, there was an epistolary moment in the eighteenth century when letters and literature were unusually intertwined. The rise of the epistolary format throughout Europe, and its culmination in the epistolary novel was not, I believe, an accident. Nor was the fact that the eighteenth century has been called the 'golden age of letters'—a time when 'the familiar letter was the chosen medium of the age'.[9] It is evident that eighteenth-century readers imitated epistolary models that they found in printed literature. What is less clear is whether letters, themselves, had a significant impact on literary culture. This query is answered positively in Part III of this book.

The third, and most important, finding was the discovery of thousands of manuscript letters written by people below the rank of gentry in archives and local record offices. These letters were found in over sixty collections during a ten-year period. Though that number is surely sufficient for one researcher's lifetime, I believe the surface has only been scratched. The existence of these letters in family archives was, in itself, unsurprising. What was unexpected was the ordinary backgrounds and extraordinary literacy of the people that wrote them. A Derbyshire wheelwright and a domestic female servant discussed Milton, Swift, and Addison in the early eighteenth century. At its end, the son of a poor basket maker found work as a shopkeeper's apprentice, because he could 'write well'. The boy's intense pride in his writing was revealed in a family letter: 'It was a mistake of Mother thinking that my Master Indited my Letters', he complained. 'They are all my own works.'[10] The pride of this boy and the presence of so many correspondences support a key theme of this book. They suggest that letter-writing helped promote literacy further down the social structure than we have imagined.

Discovering unknown letter-writers

In order to understand how Morton acquired epistolary skills, it is necessary to suspend usual ways of thinking about historical evidence. Because something does not appear in the normal place in records, this does not mean it does not exist. The absence of a school, for example, in lists of licensed institutions does not indicate an educational vacuum in a particular village. It took only one literate person to produce a great deal of learning in a cottage or on the porch of a church. Even when scholars find records for which they search, they do not always turn out as expected. A letter from a nobleman may be a hurriedly scrawled note or a formulaic epistle merely signed by the peer. On the other hand, the phonetically written letters of untrained women can reveal hours of dedication and startling confidence.

The unexpected evidence that underpins this book was first discovered in the Derbyshire Record Office. It offered clues as to how people like Joseph Morton learnt to write letters. Years ago in Matlock, I was shown a thumb-worn rectangular volume bound in decaying leather. My hands, I later discovered, were holding the first copybook printed in

English, dated 1571: *A Booke Containing Divers Sortes of hands* by John de Beauchesne. (See Plate 1, 1602 edition.) Originally published on the continent, it was filled with alphabets for its owner to copy in numerous scripts. Like other copybooks, it offered advice on how to make ink and hold a pen. The third folio entitled 'Rules Made by E. B. for his Children to learne to write bye' contained annotations by former owners.[11] (See Plate 2.) One of them was, most likely, a small-scale farmer, and a member of the local Soresbie family. How that precious book reached their tiny village of Brailsford, we will probably never know.

In itself, however, the book offered little more than a mystery. What finally produced some answers to questions about popular literacy was the cornucopia of handmade imitations that cascaded onto my desk. In every generation, from the late 1600s to the mid nineteenth century, the Soresbies filled handmade notebooks with writing exercises, including simple letters. (See Frontispiece and Plates 17 and 20.) What is more, the family preserved each volume as part of their family history, for they knew the value of personal writing. As Chapter 1 shows, these books were examples of how reading and writing could be learnt outside the walls of a licensed school. They suggest that literacy might be acquired in isolated areas by using homemade copybooks. The discovery of other large family letter collections in the same record office leant credence to this idea. Three of them are used as case studies in Chapter 3.

This book has emerged from the experience of reading letter collections of unknown middling- and lower-sort people. Their stories will be told in their own words, just as families who preserved them had hoped. Perhaps the best way for readers to get a sense of the letters is to provide some extracts from them. The five examples below are arranged chronologically from the 1680s to the early 1800s. Each of them highlights a different level of epistolary expertise and asks why they were important to their writers and to us. Together they reflect both the diversity and common patterns that exemplify family letters.

* * * *

For untutored Dorothy Soresbie, letter-writing took place in a rural Derbyshire hamlet in 1689. 'I am troubled that I cane not heare frum you', she wrote her 'Deare cosen'. 'Houe you all do...pray sen mee word what cums of oure flocke of shepe...let mee heare of your helth and hop ines which I love.'[12] It must have taken Dorothy hours to sound out each syllable and shape each letter. Yet Dorothy knew letter-writing conventions, expressed herself confidently, and demanded a swift response. How did she learn to write her letter in an isolated farming community? Was she one of a kind, or were there other women like her? If there were other writers, why are female letters of this period found less frequently than those of males?

By 1733, the daughter of a Hull merchant, 11-year-old Esther Pease penned a more formal letter. Esther had to write more deferentially than Dorothy, for her letters were monitored by her father: 'Tis so long since I writ, that I begin to fear your anger', wrote this 'Dutiful Daughter' to her 'Dear Good Papa'. 'Pardon omissions', she begged, 'and let me have a Letter.'[13] By the 1730s, the daughters of the Pease family, as well as sons, were given early epistolary training. In fact, letter-writing was vitally important to the entire family. This fact is confirmed in six generations of their carefully preserved correspondence.

By 1760, 8-year-old Joseph Robinson Pease wrote home from boarding school. His letters, though still respectful, were filled with intimate nicknames and high spirits, for epistolary conventions had become more informal. 'Honour'd Grand-Papp', wrote Joseph lovingly, 'I thank you for continuing your regard for my wellfare & happyness & am your dutifull Grand-son Joe Robinson.'[14] As Chapter 1 shows, children's letters may be compared effectively with those written as adults. They also reveal varied reasons for writing them. Were Joe's motives for writing purely functional? Or was he, perhaps, discovering the joy of expressing his thoughts through written language? Joe's later correspondence suggests that this early letter was written for both reasons.

At the same time, but in sharp contrast, Merey Williams, wrote an angry letter to a group of London churchwardens asking poor relief for her illiterate friend, Catherine Jones. 'Gentelmen of the parch', she proclaimed, 'you sid in your letter that you had tackun her case into consederrason but did forget the pour crettor I doe see that you have not forget to fed your one gugetsis [guts?] and it is as lowfull for you to tack as much car of heer as your selfs.'[15] Though Merey and Catherine were probably unrelated, they were kindred in their common poverty and part of an informal support network through which the literate helped the illiterate. Merey may have preferred to plead Catherine's case orally, but the geographic mobility of writers that marked this period made this impossible. Her favour to a friend shows how people from the lowest strata engaged in mainstream epistolary culture, even if they could not read or write.

Finally, the first letters of the Pease children may be compared with the last letter of Ruth Follows of Castle Donington, which she sent to her grandchildren in 1804. Ruth, a Quaker preacher, knew death was imminent, so it was critical to advise her loved ones about their souls. 'I am set down as in the depth of poverty', she admitted, 'but I felt willing to salute my dear grandchildren once more.' If they were faithful, they would have 'the joyful sentence of coming blessed of my Father . . . I conclude in that love which changeth not, and am your very aged, infirm, and much reduced grandmother.'[16] Unlike the other letters, Ruth's was motivated by deep religious faith. Yet though she was a basket-maker's wife, her letters show little trace of the awkward construction and phonetic spelling used by earlier women writers. As Chapter 4 confirms, her religion demanded, and also helped her to acquire, superior epistolary skills.

Letter-writing and epistolary literacy

These five unpublished letters give hints of the diversity of letters that are contained in this book. They also forewarn readers that a wide range of literacy skills will be found in its pages. Like David Vincent and R. A. Houston, I suggest that literacy is best examined on the basis of actual use—in this case in personal letters.[17] To harness letter-writing practices to the service of studying literacy, I introduce a new cultural category: 'epistolary literacy'. I have used it to observe the literacy of particular people in specific situations. When a long series of letters exists, one can also see changes and continuities over time.

A first step in determining writers' levels of epistolary literacy is to look at both material and intellectual aspects of their correspondence. Similar factors found in all types of letters can helpfully be assessed. They range from layout, spelling, and grammar to content, originality, and literary techniques. When these universal aspects of letters are compared, the relative literacy of individuals becomes more apparent. Without counting letters, therefore, a range of competencies can be established. Even brief extracts from the letters cited above immediately display differences: Merey Williams and Dorothy Soresbie, for example, might be on one end of the literacy spectrum, the Peases and Follows at the other.

Further information about basic literacy and epistolary literacy can easily be gleaned from long runs of letters. So that findings applied to all case studies, I asked three general questions of each collection: why were these letters written, for what purposes were they used, and what kind of impact did they have on the lives of writers and their families? It is hoped that by focusing on one ubiquitous format, it will be possible to glimpse what literacy meant to a range of people.

Of course, epistolary literacy, as a level of expertise, involved far more than writing one's name. Those who possessed it could read and write coherent sentences, like those in a simple letter. At this level, people wrote with a command of the vernacular that could be understood by a reader. Messages were received and sent routinely, and the writer was at ease with epistolary conventions, equipment, and language. This included at least a rudimentary knowledge of sentence structure and composition (but not spelling), and the mastery of material artefacts—pen, ink, paper, and seals.

For those who persevered, epistolary literacy brought significant rewards. They were able to engage in a dynamic set of practices that involved letter-writing, reading, interpretation, and response by networks of individuals with shared conventions and norms. Epistolary literacy offered a narrative template to lay over random events, giving order and, sometimes, meaning to life. A specific location on a broad literacy continuum, it lay mid-way between mere name signing and the Latin epistles of classically trained males. Long runs of letters show writers making qualitative leaps in epistolary literacy. As their confidence mounts, they move along the spectrum almost before our eyes. Sometimes we observe them thinking out loud—crossing out words and replacing them with better ones. Replies to letters are rare forms of readers' responses. Consequently, actual dialogues of real people can be reconstructed.

As we shall see, the uses of epistolary literacy were extremely diverse. Case studies move from the beginners' end of the spectrum with children's letters in Chapter 1 to the use of letter-writing to satisfy literary objectives in Chapters 5 and 6. Letters might start off being merely functional; then they helped new writers to fulfil psychological needs and cultural aspirations. Writers with epistolary literacy usually made a commitment to be literate on a regular basis. Few people wrote just one letter, because they expected an answer that would be answered in turn. This also made them readers, who reread letters to ensure they said what they meant. Epistolary literacy was thus a cumulative self-generated technology. It provided the glue that cemented connections between the pen, the post, and the people.

The epistolary tradition in English culture

The growth of the Post Office and numbers of people with skills to use it did not take place suddenly. In fact, the Royal Mail and epistolary literacy rose from centuries of dependence on letters. The central place of letter-writing in English culture and the particular influence of the letter-form cannot be overestimated. Without knowledge of this foundation, and the rich historiography it inspired, eighteenth-century letters cannot be understood.

Letter-writing played an important role in ancient, classical, medieval, and Renaissance cultures.[18] Moreover, the forms and conventions of earlier periods continued to influence early-modern writers. During the middle ages, the *ars dictaminis* applied classical rhetoric to letter-writing. According to its rules, a set order was established for all parts of different types of letters.[19] The influence of the *ars dictaminis* grew in importance during the Renaissance, when classical sources and rhetoric were revived. The letter soon replaced the oration as the way that humanists and scholars disseminated ideas and conducted controversies.

In *De Conscribendis Epistolis* (1522), Erasmus provided a guide to epistolary practices, including the writing of 'familiar' letters. Every seventeenth-century grammar-school boy would have memorized his definition of a letter: 'A letter, as the comic poet Turpilius skillfully put it, is a mutual conversation between absent friends, which should be neither unpolished, rough, or artificial, nor confined to a single topic, nor tediously long.'[20] Erasmus wished to teach students how to write logically in a highly polished form, no matter what the topic. But the rules of classical rhetoric clashed with his ideal of the open-hearted, familiar letter. His model letters, which were provided for emulation, would also be emulated in epistolary manuals.[21] Erasmus's teachings remained significant for elite eighteenth-century school boys. For the Soresbies, Follows, and paupers, they were not as relevant.

It is important to understand how elite letter-writers learned their craft, in order to compare this with experiences of lower- and middling-sort writers. In fact, traditional methods of instruction changed little from the sixteenth to the nineteenth centuries. Elite boys and girls learned their ABC's from a parent, private tutor, governess, or perhaps at a local school. Then boys entered an endowed grammar school, or one of the great public schools, before attending university. The first formal exercise in composition that male scholars experienced was the imitation of Cicero's letters. Clearly, letter-writing lay at the heart of the humanist grammar-school curriculum.[22]

In 1612, John Brinsley's *Ludus Literarius* explained 'how to make Epistles that are short, pithy, full of... good matter, sweet Latin and familiar.'[23] He and his pupils read simple Latin letters; then they summarized their contents in both Latin and English. When easy epistles were mastered, they composed answers and proceeded to harder ones.[24] English schoolmasters, like Roger Ascham, William Mulcaster, and William Kempe, followed this double-translation system between Latin and English letters in endless editions of their published guides.[25] The significance of a classical education for a lifetime of polished letter-writing cannot be overemphasized. Under its iron grip, it produced grammar-school boys with superior skills, who wrote and spoke elegantly. Their sisters, however, remained at home—a fact confirmed by their phonetic spelling.

English letter-writing manuals emerged after 1568, and their impact is questioned in Chapter 1.[26] By the 1650s, the *précieux* style of Jean Puget de la Serre became fashionable. His extravagant language, found in French manuals and real letters, caused a backlash among English writers and readers. By 1700, there was a movement to re-examine the English language, for some authors thought it was coarse and corrupted. Suggestions were made for the founding of an English academy that might set higher standards. More important, there arose a longing for plainly written prose that could be clearly understood.[27] All of these trends affected epistolary composition. By Morton's time, the art of letter-writing had dominated English education for centuries. Yet the classical tradition was based on knowledge of Latin, and it excluded women and all who lacked a university education—the majority of the population. It did, however, offer a stable foundation, from which a popular version could emerge.

The eighteenth-century context

As we have seen, postal histories, epistolary literature, and masses of letters in archives suggest a democratization of letter-writing during the eighteenth century. If this is true, why did the base of letter-writers expand at this time? What specific factors contributed to an outburst of epistolary literacy? It is helpful to think of epistolary culture as having different overlapping layers. Of course, upper-class males with university training wrote in different ways from those lower down the social scale. The letters of Joseph Morton represent a newer mode of epistolary practice that evolved from the classical tradition. Before we can grasp what was distinctive about it, we must briefly review the historical and literary factors that encouraged it.

Improvements in transport and communications were particularly important, for letters could not be carried without them. Turnpikes were established throughout the century and upgraded with toll income. Even in the North of England, local roads were improving. Thus when Morton's employer asked him to travel from Kendal to Bristol, he 'had no objackson to the Journay thinking it a good opertunity of Seeding the Country'.[28] From 1660–1750 there were scores of river navigation acts and new canals enhanced water transport. By the 1770s, Robert Johnson of Bath found the Duke of Bridgewater's works 'really surprising', with canals extending 'thirty miles above the ground . . . and six miles into the bowels of the earth'.[29] In addition, carriers and stagecoach services were visible proof, often on a daily basis, that metropolitan and provincial cultures were increasingly connected. Indeed, all households discussed in this book had relatives living in London. Martin Daunton has documented the integration of different types of transport and the fall in journey times that went with it. Reduced transaction costs and increased efficiency, he argues, may have been more significant than improvements in industrial or agricultural productivity.[30]

These developments were preconditions for the postal services that already have been discussed. But the rise of the Royal Mail was part of a wider movement to assert human control over space and time. The growth of empire in the eighteenth-century made letter-writing a necessity, not just a pleasure. Letters show that the 'dimension of distance' had a huge impact on families.[31] Those described in the case studies had at least one member who was either travelling abroad or living in the colonies. Of course, Morton was, himself, an immigrant, and he keenly felt the pangs caused by distance from his family.

Improved roads and new canals tied hamlets to a wider world marked by another cluster of developments: urbanization, economic growth, and a swelling tide of trade and industry. The negative aspects of these trends on literacy are often cited. But our letter-writers also saw them as evidence of national progress in which families, like themselves, might participate. Despite hardships, Joseph Morton expected to 'Rays in the worald'.[32] Robert Johnson, in the same period, visited Matthew Boulton's workshop in Soho, where he noted hundreds of people who 'chiefly work by the great and appear to do it with a spirit and industry I never saw in any other place'.[33] Johnson was well aware that Birmingham's canals had already reduced the price of coals from 7–8d. to 4d. a hundred.[34] Mines and factories might not require literate workers, but there was a crying need and great opportunity for entrepreneurs, inventors, accountants, and clerks who wrote well. Joseph Morton, as we shall see, became a member of this group.

Economic progress, in turn, brought wealth, leisure, and education to the middling sort, whose voluminous letter collections are explored in this book, especially in Chapter 4. Studies in every geographic location in this period show high rates of middling-sort literacy. It was needed to succeed in a wide range of occupations and businesses. Moreover, reading and writing were integral parts of a middling-sort culture that encouraged education and literary pursuits. All types of schooling increased throughout the eighteenth century, not just the reputable institutions frequented by children of merchants and Dissenters. Local country schools taught poor children basic skills, before they were forced to work. Parents liked the way they complemented rhythms of working life.[35] As Chapter 3 argues, intermittent informal education was likely the norm for children in rural villages. Basic skills might be further developed in later years.

In practice, education and literacy often led to upward social mobility. Parents of letter-writers in every chapter saw letter-writing as a skill that might enhance one's chances in life. Whilst desperately looking for employment, Morton made sure that his children attended the local school. He was as proud of his eldest son's academic progress as any nobleman. Joseph's relative, James Morton, used his epistolary literacy to become a well-paid teacher in a Scottish school in 1805.[36] The letters of the Soresbie, Pease, and Langton families record their rise in social status over the generations. Though letter-writing was not responsible for this advancement, it was an integral part of each family's respect for literacy and education over many generations.

We must add to these historical factors a related cluster of literary developments that encouraged epistolary literacy. Chapters 5 and 6 describe how new literary genres and the dramatic rise of print culture created a tempting world of popular literature that was accessible to new audiences. William St Clair has documented the growing numbers of authors, booksellers, readers, and libraries over the eighteenth century. More people were reading more texts on a wider range of subjects. This applied to all social strata, regardless of income, occupation, education, age, or gender.[37] Changes in readership were accompanied by changes in the public role of authors, including that of letter-writers. Before the Restoration, most women preferred to publish anonymously. After 1700 women writers began to gain respectability. Letters, however, were usually printed by both sexes only after an author's death. In 1735, Alexander Pope contrived to publish his correspondence, while still living, by blaming this on the perfidious acts of the publisher, Edmund Curll. Pope's example opened the floodgates for other collections of published letters.[38]

Finally, the epistolary novel had an impact on letter-writing by offering model letters in an alluring format. Epistolary forms of literature had, of course, pre-dated the novel. They flooded the English market in the late seventeenth century, especially from France.[39] Not surprisingly, many of the causes for the rise of the novel suggested by Ian Watt's *The Rise of the Novel* were closely linked to letter-writing: interest in the daily lives of ordinary people, a concern with introspection and privacy, and an increased acceptance of secular individualism.[40] The convergence of all of these literary and historical factors encouraged the spread of letters.

The importance of letter-writing

People have written about the importance of letters in every period. Therefore, the historiography is unusually rich. This book, however, speaks of letter-writing in an uncommon register. Its distinctiveness lies in the low social backgrounds of its subjects and the large numbers of new manuscript collections that have been discovered and interpreted. Thus it introduces readers to an unknown group of ordinary writers, who are missed in other studies. Their letters are analysed from a historical point of view, by using other types of documents to place them in context. Finally, their particular experiences are related to wider issues of eighteenth-century culture. This broad view is possible because letter-writing is both intimate and also spans the disciplines. It therefore can tell stories about dissimilar subjects that are joined in correspondence—emotion and economics, identity and industrialization, literacy and literature, the pen and the people.

It was difficult to choose this book's case studies, for there was far more material than could be used in one volume. To present as representative a sample as possible, a mix of collections spans the long eighteenth century (1660–1800) and incorporates different geographical regions, occupations, religions, and types of letters. Both sexes are included in both country and urban settings. On the other hand, gentry and titled families have been generally excluded.[41]

The basic selection criteria for reading family letters were a substantial unbroken series that spanned at least two consecutive generations and normally included replies. Additional materials, which provided background for letter-writers, were also required. These might include birth records, marriage settlements, wills, genealogical sources, account books, diaries, journals, school books, copybooks, and writing exercises. The presence of these documents made it possible to reconstruct mini-biographies of specific letter-writers. A full description of the book's research strategy and selection criteria is located in Appendix I. Tables in Appendices II–IV analyse selected archives, letter collections, and writers that were consulted for this book.

This study has profited from works about letter-writing that have increased in recent decades. Their major accomplishment has been to undermine stereotypes of the simple transparent letter and to suggest new methods of interpretation. Recent books depict a challenging genre with rhetorical conventions and ideological assumptions. Three examples of nuanced readings for an earlier period are James Daybell's *Women Letter-Writers in Tudor England* (2006), Lynne Magnusson's *Shakespeare and Social Dialogue* (1999), and Alan Stewart's *Shakespeare's Letters* (2008).[42] Essay collections[43] and special issues of periodicals offer some of the best work on letters,[44] along with feminist writing,[45] works on letter-writing in France,[46] and book history,[47] which examines material aspects of texts. Readers may also refer to my previous work on letters for bibliographies of secondary sources.[48]

Studies of eighteenth-century letters have been dominated by literary and linguistic scholars. Clare Brant's *Eighteenth Century Letters and British Culture* (2006) and Susan Fitzmaurice's *The Familiar Letter* (2002) are two excellent examples. Few of these works are based on manuscript letters, whose advantages for assessing literacy are discussed in Appendix I. Yet the greatest gap in studies about all periods of letter-writing is the lack of letters written by ordinary people. Most books concentrate on the gentry or aristocracy, with a sprinkling of mercantile and middling-sort writers. Illustrations tend to show elegantly dressed writers behind fashionable desks.[49] Standard works highlight letters of famous literary figures, such as Pope, Swift, Johnson, and Walpole.[50] Local archives include hundreds of lesser-known letter-writers who imitated these luminaries—graduates of Oxford and Cambridge, men of letters, the clergy, and professional men. A few are used here for comparative purposes, but their writings generally emulate those of elites.[51]

This book claims that the literate nation included more than gentlemen and scholars. It suggests a culture of letters that embraced lower- and middling-sort writers had developed in England by 1800. The following chapters trace the rise of a popular epistolary tradition that emerged from its classical foundations. It demonstrated its flexibility by discarding rigid rules and adopting aspects of middling-sort culture. Eventually it matured into an accessible model that favoured plainly written language and the merchant's round hand. Part I explains how a culture of letter-writing was created—how children and untrained adults learned to write letters, and how the Royal Mail distributed them. Part II contains case studies of northern farmers and workers and compares their epistolary literacy with that of middling-sort writers, especially writing clerks, merchants, and Dissenters. Part III considers how letters became 'literary'. It reveals their potent effects on travelogues, the language of sensibility, and literary criticism. Finally, it claims that epistolary literacy was a major influence on the rise of the novel. The conclusion suggests that links between the pen, the post, and the people not only affected individuals. The democratization of letter-writing had social, economic, and political impacts on eighteenth-century culture.

These claims are supported by common patterns found in every type of letter. One of the most significant is that all writers talked endlessly about the Post Office and letter-writing, itself. They did so in every emotional mode—hilarity, disgust, anticipation, anxiety, affection, and anger. In truth, it is rare to find personal letters that do not refer to the two topics. These comments are generally found in the first and last paragraphs of letters, which are often deleted by editors of printed collections. Yet without knowing how contemporaries viewed letter-writing itself, we lose a crucial layer of interpretation.

To recover this 'talk' about letters, a huge database of writers' remarks was used to write each chapter. For example, limitless excuses for *not* writing letters reveal how important they were to both parties. In a similar fashion, intense demands for more letters disclose an overwhelming dependence upon mail. When, people asked, would their letters arrive? Why had they been delayed? Had the writer forgotten the person who desperately waited for mail? The reason for this intense focus was that letter-writing was important to both senders and receivers.

This epistolary 'conversation' shows that letters had become an established genre with a commonly accepted language. Apparently, 'talking about letters' was an ordinary form of daily discourse. This conversation was enthusiastically adopted by the gardener, Joseph Morton. His letters, and those of others of his class, have been used to show the rise of epistolary literacy for an expanding group of users.

Yet the spread of letters would never have occurred without the services of the Royal Mail. Letter-writers like Morton not only used it, they regarded its comings and goings with intense desire. 'I was as Impationed for Writting as you Were for Receiveing', he told his brother, Thomas, who grew angry when Joseph did not write.[52] This book's introduction opened with Morton's directions to his family about how they should send his mail. It closes with the unhappy admission that they did not always follow his instructions. 'When you Derect your Letters to me', he *again* had to remind them, 'write at the Bottom (Single Sheet) as you, see I have Done for Last Letter was Cherged Double postage.' Morton urged their compliance, not only to lessen costs, but because he could not afford to live without letters. Despite this incident of double postage, he continued to write and enjoy his epistolary literacy. Like people around him, he had become permanently connected to the pen and the post.

I

Creating the letter

How to acquire epistolary literacy

Let us observe a young man as he writes a letter in the early eighteenth century. (See Plate 3.) There is no letter-writing manual at hand—just a pen made from the third left feather of the wing of a goose, and a pot filled with ink. We will assume we are watching the son of an artisan or merchant. He has not had a grammar-school education, but he knows how to read and write. Later we will consider how he became literate; for now, we will view his actions and examine the letter as a material object.

Our composite letter-writer has been created by carefully piecing together data from letters, diaries, pedagogical works, letter-writing manuals, grammars, copybooks, hornbooks, prints, portraits, museum exhibits, and contemporary literature. Calligraphers, who delight in using a quill pen, have also contributed their knowledge. This technique uncovers hidden aspects of epistolary practice through a systematic reading of dozens of varied sources. It allows us to reconstruct the step-by-step process of how letters were composed and read. This section is thus presented in a narrative format, in order to describe the experience of a writer.

First our young man must find a space in which to write, but he does not expect privacy. He may work in a tiny room called a closet[1] or in the midst of a crowded household. He sits at a table or writes with a board on his knees, but here the casualness ends. The youth's pose may appear natural, but it requires coordination of eye, hand, and body at just the correct angles. Without a sloped surface to relieve pressure on his neck and shoulders, he must constantly hold himself erect. Our youth will grow weary and lean forward with a drooping head.[2] Yet he knows that 'mind, hand, and eye, must altogether go'.[3] If he attends school, his master may advise him to 'let your hand move with an easy motion and without hurry'.[4] If there is no school available, he may learn at home and practice writing in a hand-made copybook. By the eighteenth century, he will be encouraged to produce 'a clean smooth stroke, perform'd with a Masterly *Boldness* and *Freedom*'.[5] Like his country, which is growing more confident, he will try to 'hold the head high' and write 'with grace and freedome' with his arm 'at liberty'.[6]

Our writer checks his equipment to see that all is ready: 'paper, incke, pen, penknife, ruler...and dust box'.[7] His quill is responsive once he knows how to use it, but hard to manage at first. If our youth works with his hands, perhaps as an artisan or apprentice, manipulating a pen will come naturally. His quills wear down quickly and need constant repair, so he makes a few at a time, and places a spare at his side. He chooses one made from the left wing of a goose, because it fits his right hand well.[8] He could buy quills from the stationer's shop, ready-cut and hardened, but he heats and shapes his own to save money.

When the youth cuts his nib, he uses a steel knife that can make curved and straight cuts. Yet producing a good pen is not easy. If his slit in the nib is too short, the ink will not flow; if too long, it may leak out in blots.[9] Moreover, he must shape his nib differently for different scripts. (See Plate 4.)[10] Unsurprisingly, he fiddles with his quill to get the right effect. Soon he will cut and use his quill automatically. At this point, writing will have become a normal practice of everyday life.

Now our youth picks up his pen with his fingers closed 'round about the neb, like unto a cats foote'.[11] His copybook may have an illustration showing the right and wrong way to hold it.[12] (See Plate 5.) After each stroke, he dips his pen in the pot and cleans the quill's edge. As the ink thickens, he refreshes it with vinegar or wine. If his supply runs out, he can burn and beat wool into a powder. He can also buy ink powder ready-made, or purchase it from a seller, who cries his wares at six pence for two ounces. (See Plate 6.) The ink is a mix of galls from oak leaves and iron salt or copperas laced with gum Arabic.[13] Later, his inkwell may be part of a stand with matching sander and penholder.[14] Some day he may even own a steel pen in a metal penner.[15] By 1680, for example, Mary Hatton had already sent one to her brother, whilst Roger North claimed proudly in 1700, 'I write with a steel pen. It is a device come out of France.'[16]

Our young man uses a cream-coloured hand-made sheet of paper made from rags and pressed into flat sheets.[17] He buys it from the stationers in a quire of four large leaves. He folds one sheet in half, and again in half, and cuts or tears the top edges to produce eight pages. The paper used to be imported from France or Italy, but by 1700 there are a hundred English mills.[18] A quire of paper costs about 8d. and from 1–8d. postage will be due, depending on the distance. This is costly, for six to ten shillings is a day's wage for a craftsman or a week's wage for a labourer.[19] As we shall see, there are widespread ways of diminishing costs by sharing or borrowing resources, or avoiding postage altogether. Still, our writer must also possess light, space, and leisure. These challenges are not insurmountable, but our writer must be highly motivated.

Before he begins, our youth will decide what script to use. His choice will depend on his gender, skill, type of letter, and time period in which he writes. By 1700, he will choose the italic hand if he wishes to be in fashion, not the older secretary hand which is harder to read. Later in the century, his hand will shift gracefully into a larger round 'copperplate' hand (See Plate 24). We will find that different scripts tell different stories about gender, class, and national identity.

Now our youth considers letter-writing conventions. Before he can write a proper letter, he must understand the genre: how it works, its social role, and the situations that give rise to it. At first, the boy grasps only its formal features—layout, design, appropriate length, and forms of address. His letter resembles spoken language and is filled with compliments. Later his letters will lose their stilted tone and contain more original content. As he masters grammar, expands vocabulary, and organizes his material, the boy is becoming an author.[20]

Next, our writer must yoke epistolary conventions to the personality of the reader. So too historians must link letter-writing with reading, for they are seamless parts of one process. In early-modern England, the rank, gender, kinship, and relationship of the writer and reader had a material impact on every part of the letter. These factors affected format and spacing, width of margins, quality and number of sheets of paper, forms of address, amount of space dividing parts of the letter, and even the number of lines filled with 'humble services'.[21] A seventeenth-century letter to a patron, for example, would have wide margins and several lines of space before and after the addressee's title.

During the eighteenth century, letters became more informal, though there was always a tension between the form's conventions and the impulse of the writer. Age, gender, rank, and kinship, still affected the degree of artifice, flattery, and deference. By 1800, however, parents and children, as well as husbands and wives, wrote more naturally to each other. While the basic framework and conventions were retained, the formulaic aspects of structure and content diminished. As our case studies show, the epistolary balance between self-expression and controlled use of norms tipped towards more freedom. We find a gradual contraction of elaborate forms of address, such as 'My Honoured Lord' to the simpler 'Sir' or 'Madam'. Eventually these terms also gave way, especially amongst kin, to 'dearest papa' and endearing nicknames. Thus in 1781, Jacob Pattison tellingly begged his father not write so formally. The term, 'Sir', he insisted, 'appears cold, & seems to place one at an uncomfortable distance'.[22] Elaborate 'humble services' and fawning politeness also declined as authorship broadened to include new writers. Rank was still important, especially outside the family. But though servants deferred to masters and clients to their patrons, they wrote directly to each other, some for the first time, in less obsequious ways. These trends will be illustrated in later chapters.

When our writer is ready, he enters date and place in the upper-right corner or below his signature. Normally he starts and concludes his letters with apologies or references to letter-writing and the post office. He answers questions arising from previous letters and presents topics and himself with the reader in mind. Whether the letter is one of friendship, duty, or patronage will depend on his relationship with the addressee. After he has said all that is on his mind, he slides artfully into a closing, as he has observed others do. He may then add a bold ornament directly below his signature. This proud flourish shows the world that he is a well-trained individual, who has acquired epistolary literacy.

If he is wise, our youth rereads his letter and corrects errors. Then he sprinkles sand mixed with gum from North Africa to stop the spread of ink. This is expensive, so he uses it with care.[23] He folds his paper carefully reserving its blank back side for the address. This is the public part of the letter, for it will be seen by the postman and, perhaps, a government censor. Then he seals the paper with wax to avoid tampering and confirm authorship.[24] The key moment in the life of the letter occurs as it is given away, and it is too late to recall its secrets or to decide not to send it. Indeed, posting a letter by giving it to a stranger has been called 'the quintessential example of a social act'.[25]

Now we must change our location, and conjure up an image of a letter reader. (See Plate 7.) Let us assume she is a female friend of our young man. Even before she reads his letter, she is actively engaging with him. She inspects the handwriting, notes date and time of postmarks, and opens the letter with anticipation or dread. As the seal is broken and the paper is unfolded, a material artefact lies beckoning in her hand. On the outside, ink, paper, stamps, and address greet the reader; on the inside, salutation, layout, spaces, and signature form a pattern. Her reading of the letter is anything but passive, for she interprets its contents in light of her own ties with the sender. Their relationship is confirmed through the quality of the paper, neatness of the penmanship, and choice of script. She reads between the lines for hidden nuances and brings her own unique experience to this act. Her interpretation of the contents may differ from that intended by the author, but one thing is certain: both our reader and writer possess epistolary literacy.

Next she may read the letter aloud to one or more people. Their interpretations of the same text will be different from hers. Perhaps she will pass it on to others, in its original form or by making a copy. The copy is now in her handwriting and is a new version of the text. She will likely docket it by endorsing the back with the name and date of the sender and a note about its contents. Then she will perform the most amazing act of all. She will preserve it! Even if a postscript says 'burn this letter' she may paste it in a letter book, file it in a larger correspondence, or hide it under her mattress. The afterlife of the letter is now in process.

Learning to read and write

The letter-writing and reading depicted above was more informal than that of classical scholars, described in the introduction. Yet it owed its ethos and conventions to the centuries of epistolary education that had preceded it. The older tradition provided a stable foundation for all types of eighteenth-century letters. By 1700, however, the imitation of Roman authors formed only one strand of epistolary education and practice. The rest of this chapter compares the classical epistle with the middling-sort letters that flowed out from and coexisted with it. Later, this more informal model would dominate business and personal correspondence. To understand how this progression took place, we must ask how our boy and girl first learned to read and write, so they could apply these skills to letters.

For answers to this question we must look for unofficial sites and methods of acquiring literacy. The ecclesiastical licensing system was supposed to embrace all local schools, but complaints about ignorant teachers indicate there was much unlicensed instruction.[26] Teachers ranged from curates or parish clergy to neighbours, shopkeepers, craftsmen, or 'any literate person with time and patience'.[27] Since school attendance by non-elites was often irregular, strong motivation and parental support were needed.[28] When schools were not available, reading and writing were sometimes taught at home.[29] Families that possessed these skills prized them and passed them on to children. In addition, local brokers wrote and read letters or taught for a fee. It was thus possible to learn basic skills, which were low-cost or free.

The bulk of the population took their first steps toward literacy in a local petty, ABC, dame, or parish school between ages 4 and 8. The petty school taught 'the first principles of all religion and learning',[30] including reading and writing English, as well as numbers and arithmetic.[31] Educational treatises show the same methods were used to teach literacy for over 300 years. Since material in early editions was simply recopied into later ones, they remain useful guides.[32]

Some masters stated it took several years to teach reading and writing,[33] but bright pupils learned to read in a few months.[34] Kempe believed the age of 5 was the best time to start.[35] Hoole thought 6 or 7 the proper age for country pupils, but city children might begin at 4 or 5.[36] G. D. encouraged pupils to write daily for an hour or two for a period of six months.[37] Brinsley recommended writing every day at 'about one of the clocke' when 'hands are warmest and nimblest'.[38] Generally, by the time students reached 7, they would have some knowledge of reading, and by 8 they might know how to write. Yet writing was taught separately at the time when children were of work age or admitted into workhouses.[39] Therefore many boys and girls in charity schools were taught to read but not write.[40]

Students began by memorizing the alphabet, a letter at a time, with the aid of a hornbook. This was a paper sheet pasted on a board covered with horn and fixed in a frame.[41] The alphabet was displayed in lower and upper case, often in different typefaces, followed by sober texts from scripture and prayer book.[42] After memorizing vowels and consonants, pupils combined them into syllables; then they joined syllables into words.[43] Words were first sounded out; then written down.[44] The basis of all teaching was repetition. Students progressed through drills in a sing-song chant, moving forwards, backwards, and crossways through the alphabet or text.[45]

Some teachers were more inventive, when it came to teaching writing. Kempe taught pupils to draw their pens over each letter, then to imitate the original, and finally to draw a letter with no original in sight.[46] Others had students write with broad pen tips in large letters with spaces in between for corrections.[47] Teachers ruled sheets and placed them under thin paper so that the lines showed through. Some pupils used wires, instrument strings, or glued threads as rulers.[48] Masters often walked among students[49] and games were played. Rivals judged each other's writing and winners might receive a pen or apple.[50] Rare illustrations show visual aids like writing boards, picture alphabets, or flash cards.[51] Brinsley wanted each boy to have his own copybook made of good paper to encourage pride.[52] As we shall see, the copybook was of critical importance.

Copybooks, handwriting, and national identity

There were two basic kinds of copybooks for students: printed volumes published by writing masters; and blank homemade books in which pupils practised writing. The survival of both types in family archives indicates they were basic tools for acquiring literacy. By the late sixteenth century, the invention of the rolling press and copperplate engraving stimulated the growth of British copybooks.[53] The first English translation in 1571 fixed a pattern[54] in which masters 'set the copy' by displaying alphabets in different scripts, as well as simple texts.[55] Copybooks taught self-discipline along with literacy—a skill needed for success in other areas.[56]

At the same time, many educational treatises were published. Their prefaces disclose a tradition of teaching common people to write as early as the sixteenth century.[57] Though *A Nevv Booke of Spelling with Syllables* (1621) was 'devised chiefly for children', it was also directed to 'the ignorant to teach them to write'.[58] Edmund Coote addressed his book to 'both men and women that now . . . are ashamed to write to their best friends'. If there is 'none present to help thee', he advised, 'make a mark thereat with thy pen or pin, untill thou meetest with thy Minister'.[59] G. D. claimed that his book was for pupils' use 'at such times as they are at home . . . the learner hath no Copy . . . or the waies may be foul, the Scholler sick or lame'.[60] Others provided instruction for 'even the meanest teachers and learners' such as 'Tailors, Weavers, Shop-keepers, and Semsters', who might then teach others to write.[61]

Treatises and copybooks give tantalizing glimpses of an interactive community of readers, writers, and middlemen. Handwritten decorations, doodles, and alphabets fill their pages. (See Plates 16 and 20.) Thus Margaret Grill added two alphabets of crude letters on the last page of Coote's *English School Master* (1687).[62] Letitia Walsall used blank pages of a printed advice book to practice writing. Walsall's work shows the steps she took in order to learn the alphabet; she lined her paper, wrote her name, and began copying letters. At first they were large and ill formed; then they became smaller. Next she combined capital and small letters from the beginning to the end of the alphabet. The improvement that came with practice is evident in her book.[63]

By the 1680s, new copybooks linked to business and trade emerged. Their authors were ambitious writing masters, who taught at schools or in merchants' homes. By the 1750s they actively promoted writing schools in London and large towns, whilst itinerants charged small fees in rural areas.[64] Printed copybooks now served two main groups: men and women without access to instruction and students studying to become government or business clerks. In 1698 Ayres claimed that '*good Writing* is expected and desired among all Ranks and Degrees'. When 'Merchants . . . and Men of . . . Considerable *Offices*' sought apprentices, Ayres insisted, the first question asked was 'is he anything of a *Penman*?'[65] Eighteenth-century copybooks used examples and texts from commercial documents. Thus letters of credit soon replaced scripture as set texts to copy. John Clark dedicated his manual to the Lord Mayor of London, noting the 'natural Dependance' of writing and trade.[66] All masters credited writing with invigorating the economy. In short, 'good penmanship and national prosperity became identical'.[67]

The varied scripts featured in copybooks arose from the need for speed and changes in materials and tools. Specialized hands that were difficult to learn betrayed occupation and conferred status on lawyers, diplomats, and scribes.[68] The secretary hand, a derivative of Gothic black letter, was used for business and in hornbooks well into the seventeenth century.[69] With the spread of humanism, shipping, and trade, the roman hand was transformed into the faster, less formal, inclined italic script. Popular in England by 1650, its adoption was, in part, a European reaction against ornate hands used in France.[70] There was a widespread yearning to lay 'aside the starch'd affected Flourishes and illiterate Copies that senseless Pretenders have impos'd on the World'.[71] The shift from secretary to italic also had gender implications. It was identified with women because it was fashionable and easy to master. Hence Billingsley recommended it for ladies—they '(hauing not the patience to take any great paines, besides phantasticall and humorsome) must be taught that which they instantly learne'.[72]

Italic, in turn, developed into the round hand—a clear, all-purpose cursive whose slope encouraged speed in one flowing movement. (See Plate 24.) We see it in merchants' bills of lading, shopkeepers' accounts, and eighteenth-century family letters.[73] (See Plate 25.) As Aileen Douglas notes, 'Eighteenth-century England occupies a particular place in the history of handwriting, because it is here that the multiple hands of the Renaissance . . . gradually gave way to the English round hand.'[74] By the mid eighteenth century, it began to dominate general and commercial writing.[75] 'It cannot be denied', wrote an admirer, 'that the English have excelled the other nations in this class of cursive hand . . . doing so because it suits them for the use of commerce.'[76] George Bickham agreed in 1754, 'It's natural tendency to . . . despatch business [became] universally . . . practiced by all degrees of men, in all employments.' Prior to this time, handwriting categorized a person by gender, class, and occupation. It was therefore a remarkable change to have one accessible hand for every writer that was easy to learn. This, I suggest, had a levelling effect that was quite revolutionary—an effect evident in George Bickham's *Universal Penman* (1741).[77] Though it contains alphabets of many writing masters, they appear similar. The highly legible 'copperplate' hand has been called 'thoroughly unromantic, and dull'.[78] Yet it captured the values of its English writers and helped them to acquire epistolary literacy.

The round hand of the merchant also became an expression of national pride for people without a classical education. Students destined to be clerks saw 'their accomplished penmanship as a particularly English quality' that gave status, dignity, and respect. This was evident in the letters of John Fawdington, a Yorkshire bridle maker, as we will see in Chapter 3. Ayres pleaded for 'free writing-schools in our Country Towns, because where ye Grammar school sends forth one scholar for Divinity, Law or Physick, forty if not a hundred are sent out to Trades & other Imployment'.[79] By the mid eighteenth century, England was establishing an empire of handwriting. As her ships ruled the seas, her clear copperplate hand was also influencing commercial correspondence.

Letter-writing manuals and epistolary literacy

With this background in mind, let us return to our young man, who was writing a letter at the beginning of this chapter. Local schools and copybooks might teach him how to read and write. Yet once basic skills were attained, how was the leap to epistolary literacy actually made? Were there models for emulation in our youth's mind that he could call upon to construct a letter? A wide range of cultural prototypes and local sources are highlighted throughout this book. Nevertheless, the analysis of letter-writing manuals has been the favoured approach to understanding how all classes learned to write letters.

Eve Bannet has claimed that manuals produced 'a single standard language, method, and culture of polite communication'. Still this statement conflicts with the diversity of writing found in real letters. Bannet admits that 'eighteenth-century letter manuals were vocal about their usefulness, silent about how a reader–writer was supposed to use them'.[80] Why, we must ask, did these guides decline to do so? Some answers emerge when the sources of their texts and the social backgrounds of their authors are examined. They suggest that the typical manual rooted in French politeness may have had less impact on lower- and middling-sort writers than publishers admitted. Yet manuals were reissued in France, England, and America for over 300 years. A lucrative market was evidently foreseen, for if purchases declined, editions would have ceased.[81] Interestingly, Dublin booksellers, often the first to find new markets, generally ignored letter manuals.[82] As Bannet indicates, the actual use of manuals is difficult to understand.

One way to approach this problem is to compare the models suggested for use in manuals with actual letters. In truth, few letters were found in family archives that resembled those in published guides. Nor were there references to using manuals in real letters, though examples sometimes appear in personal book lists. Because highly educated families had little need for French or commercial models, we would expect people lower down the social scale to purchase them. Yet it is doubtful that many of these writers actually copied and sent model letters.

As Roger Chartier has shown, there was a mismatch between manuals and their intended audiences. Their prefaces claimed they served the same audiences as those addressed in copybooks—women, children, servants, untrained adults, and foreigners. Yet manuals often employed language, formats, and model letters from the world of high society and the court. Even later guides for clerks and merchants, with a few exceptions, re-published courtly letters. John Hill's *The Young Secretary's Guide* (1696) is usually cited as a new type of guide for the commercial classes. Tellingly, his model letters were still based on Jean Puget de la Serre's *Secretary in Fashion* (1687). Though he gave them a more utilitarian slant, they were written and categorized according to rules of classical rhetoric. Thomas Goodman's *The Experienc'd Secretary: or, Citizen and countryman's Companion* (1707) relentlessly retained the language of the court.[83] If used as a model, its gushing prose would have exposed the writer as an outsider. Few manuals included plain, informal letters, like those found in archives.

Manuals might have been purchased by the socially ambitious to help with patronage letters. Chartier suggests they may have been read for more impractical reasons: to enter a restricted social world, for romantic entertainment, or for literary interest.[84] This hypothesis gains credibility when we analyse the motives and social backgrounds of their authors. One would expect them to move in the politest circles and to socialize amongst people with exquisite manners. In fact, few, if any, were from titled families; some were younger sons or men from junior branches of the elite; more were self-styled 'gents', teachers, or clergymen. Some were ejected from their positions or had failed in their careers, and were experiencing downward social mobility. What they all had in common was a classical education, spare time for writing, and a need for funds. They also wrote other types of publications, as if searching for a market. The many editions of earlier manuals were heaven-sent models, which they might duplicate or adapt. Hovering on the fringe of society and encouraged by Grub Street, authors of manuals tried to make money from previously learned skills. Few of them travelled in elite circles.[85] Nevertheless, they were well-equipped to create alluring worlds for readers, even if their model letters were not actually used.

For the English, the love–hate relationship they felt for France was probably entwined with manual-buying habits. Because of English cultural insecurity and the desire for French refinement, people might have bought them in the late seventeenth century. But by the 1760s, the tables had turned. A more confident English public was now focusing on its own language and the gentrification of its prose.[86] Instead of French models, the British epistolary ideal embraced an easy natural style of writing. The critic,

Thomas Edwards, for example, refused to use 'all rules of Ceremonial' in letters.[87] In 1748, he reluctantly sent friends 'complements (though I do not like that french word, where I mean profession of Friendship and respect)'.[88] By 1800, James Hogg declined to start his letter 'with a great many fine compliments such as wishing you joy of your young son, enquiring after your health, with a thousand pretences to love and friendship'. He was, he declared, 'a sworn enemy to all ceremony'.[89]

Yet if Cicero's letters and French manuals were not used by our youth, Chapter 3 shows that there were other models to emulate. Society was awash with letters ranging from those in royal proclamations to letters in cheap pamphlets. Most important, as writers themselves regularly admitted, their primary models lay in real letters that were sent and received. Those written as a child set indelible patterns of epistolary composition for the rest of one's life. The following case studies compare elite and non-elite children's letters and explain why they were so important.

Elite and non-elite children's letters

Letter-writing was a valuable skill that parents passed on to their children. The same epistolary patterns in every generation document this claim: similar forms of address, terms of endearment, vocabulary, docketing, and dating structures. Children acquired epistolary literacy by writing regularly to family and friends. Hundreds of their letters to watchful kin are found in local archives, along with samples from parents to guide them. (See Plates 8, 9, and 31.) At first youngsters ruled their paper, painstakingly formed separate letters, and struggled to maintain even lines. Spelling was phonetic, crossed-out words flourished, and margins were violated by unexpected lengths of words. Since these letters usually contained only compliments, they may seem formulaic and uninteresting. In fact, their regular appearance tells us that we are witnessing something central to eighteenth-century culture. A case study of four generations of Evelyns is presented as a foil to show how a well-educated, elite family encouraged epistolary literacy.[90] It is then compared with letter-writing activities of children in merchant families. Children's letters are significant, because they document when, how, and why epistolary literacy was acquired. They also serve as a foundation for analysing adult letters in later chapters.

The Evelyn family

The huge Evelyn archive offers stunning evidence of the epistolary expertise of an educated elite family. Even so, the letters of 15-year-old John Evelyn, the diarist (1620–1706) left much to be desired. 'My father being... extreamely displeased at my Writing so ill a Character', he admitted, 'I put my selfe to the Writing Schoole for a Moneth or two, till I had redressed that in some measure.'[91] Evelyn's act revealed both accessibility of instruction and awareness that he must improve his scrawled secretary hand. Scores of letters to and from his son Jack (1655–99)[92] and grandson John (1682–1763) show continued concern about their letters.[93] The first from Jack at the age of 10 was in Latin with a note from his tutor: '[Jack] presents you with his duty & a distick of verses... They are according to yr desire, wholy his own.'[94] A triumvirate of father, tutor, and son cooperated to ensure that the son mastered letter-writing in Latin, French, and English, first at home, then at Eton, and later at Oxford. On the back of a precocious letter filled with verses labelled 'the Oxford Gazette', the diarist noted: 'Jack was but 12 years when he writ this.'[95] After Jack matured, he still signed himself 'your dutifull son', but dropped the adjectives 'most humble' and 'obedient'.[96] His Latin epistles were typical of an elite boy with a classical education, whose family was passionate about letter-writing.

Though Jack's sisters were also ordered to write letters, Susan's were still filled with apologies and inkblots at the age of 18. When told to describe her travels to the coronation in a letter, she was overwhelmed: 'It is to[o] hard a task for me to undertake. All I can say is it was very fine.'[97] This remark reveals gender differences that arose from the impact of a university education that was given to sons. Yet both Jack and Susan were assigned epistolary tasks and monitored at home. Though Jack's sister Mary (1665–85) was a more willing correspondent, at the age of 11 she confessed: 'I wish I could writt better.'[98] By the age of 19 she composed elegant epistles, but she still lacked Jack's epistolary confidence: 'I wish you could see how uneasy I am', she wrote her brother, 'when real favours must be repaid with complement and formality.' To show him respect, she placed one-inch deferential spaces around her closing words and signature—a custom that merchants' offspring would soon discard.[99] Mary had little need to imitate model letters from manuals. Better examples were found in real letters that she and other young ladies copied into albums. In 1730 Mary's own letters written in the 1660s were transcribed into books by her great-granddaughter.[100] As she copied them, she observed elegant models of how to write politely.

Naturally, once elite boys acquired a classical education, they had epistolary advantages over their sisters.[101] Women's phonetic spelling, poor grammar, and awkward presentation thus persisted until the mid eighteenth century, when more girls were sent to school. Still, if university widened the epistolary gender gap, training at home gave Evelyn girls an epistolary foundation for life. Their adult letters were carefully constructed and often reached high standards. In contrast, Jack's wife, Martha (c.1661–1726), the daughter of a Levant merchant, still used phonetics and crossed out mistakes as an adult.[102] Gender and class were both significant factors in regard to female epistolary literacy.

In the next generation of Evelyns, the diarist continued to mentor his grandchildren's correspondence. 'Pray forget not to write Latine letters', he warned John, 'til you have gotten a style: [Pliny] and Cicero...are excellent',[103] as are 'admirable examples in Erasmus'.[104] John vowed to send his grandfather at least one Latin letter per month 'follow[ing] strictly the method of composition prescribed by you'.[105] In 1698 Evelyn composed a letter for John to copy to congratulate Francis Godolphin on his marriage. I know 'of no more acceptable & proper method of you expressing yr gratitude', wrote Evelyn, 'than by Epistles.'[106] John's letter to Godolphin was proudly showed to Evelyn's friends. 'That it was all yr owne', he reported, 'some...would hardly believe.'[107] Similar epistles were ordered and sent to John's Uncle Evelyn, Oxford officials, and Samuel Pepys.[108]

John's Latin letters were not merely academic exercises. They helped to fulfil the goal of his education, as articulated by his grandfather: 'an intire conquest of the two learned Languages: [and] an Easy & Natural style of writing'.[109] The constant translating of words between Latin and English produced a deep intimacy with language at the most formative time of life. The adult letters of Evelyn's children were thus recognizable symbols of their elite education and status. They also became valuable passports into a world of patronage and power.

Epistolary mentoring was still forcefully administered to Evelyn's great-grandchildren.[110] In 1726, Charles Evelyn was ordered to write a letter in French to Lord Godolphin.[111] He did so, however, in rounded letters, not in angular italic. A family member now underlined and corrected Charles's mistakes, for spelling and punctuation were becoming standardized.[112] The tight secretary hand of the diarist bore little resemblance to the flowing writing of his descendants.

The Evelyn study documents the importance of epistolary literacy to elite parents. In every generation, early letter-writing was encouraged, for it was a measurable prerequisite for entering adult society. Elders set high standards and reinforced them through mentoring. At the age of 13 the diarist's grandson remarked: 'Tell [my sister] that I shall be very glad when she can write, that I may hold correspondence with her.'[113] This comment indicates that at the first moment of written self-expression, entering epistolary networks was an expected right. When children became parents, they offered similar advice and the pattern was repeated. Elite families hoped letter-writing would help children to function in a society based on social networks. This was also true of non-elite parents, especially merchants, who are highlighted in the next case studies.

The Pease family of Hull

Letters between parents and children in three merchant families—the Peases of Hull, the Cotesworths of Newcastle, and the Langtons of Kirkham, Lancashire—survive in abundance. They have been chosen as case studies to provide a detailed framework for understanding how epistolary literacy was, in fact, acquired. Like the Evelyns, our merchant families had close family relationships and carefully mentored children's letter-writing. Yet there were also differences.

The Pease family papers in the Hull City Archives contain six generations of letters between parents and children, often with both sides intact. They are especially helpful in showing shifts by both sexes in hands, format, and style. The Peases left Holland for England in the seventeenth century, and by 1800 they were merchants, manufacturers, and bankers. The Puritan, Robert Pease (b. 1607) returned to Amsterdam after the Restoration because he sought more religious freedom as a Dissenter. Another Robert Pease (1643–1720) sent two sons back to Britain, one of whom, Joseph (1688–1778) settled in Hull in 1709.[114] (See Plates 10 and 11.) There he established a flourishing linseed and oil-processing business. In 1754 he founded a private country bank, over which the family, at first, lived.[115]

Joseph preserved the letters of his children Esther (1720–97), Robert (1717–70), and Mary (1727–57), along with drafts of his own letters, written in a small cramped italic hand.[116] At the age of 14, Robert wrote from school in Kirkstead, Lincolnshire in large round letters, but crossed out words and left dreaded ink blots. He saluted his 'Ever Honoured Sr' and closed with 'Your dutifull son'. 'We are all very well Blessed by God', he noted repeatedly, and sent 'humble services' to relations. 'Sir in ye morning & afternoons I learn bookkeeping ... and 7 nights I get a Catechism against popery.'[117] As in the Evelyn family, letters were reread by Pease kin and checked for errors.[118] Over time, Robert's hand became smaller so as to fit as much as possible onto costly paper. By the age of 21 his writing improved, along with the regularity of habits that he would need as a merchant. This is shown in letters 'dated 15, 22, 29'.[119] No longer childish presentation pieces, they contained independent ideas. Robert was better trained than his father, whose cramped scrawl was hard to read.

Letters of Robert's sister, Esther from a school in York, reveal both her epistolary skill and her tense relationship with her father. He ordered her to write each Friday, but 'between schooling abroad and schooling at home' and 'the necessary part of work, call'd Visiting', she often forgot her duty. At the age of 11 she wrote with dread to her 'Dear Good Papa': 'Tis so long since I writ, that I begin to fear your anger; and so long since I was favour'd with one from you, that I am uneasy.'[120] When she was 13 years old, Joseph asked Esther to write an original letter without first making a copy. 'Sir at your command', she responded in 1733, 'I write to you without a coppy, and therefore I hope you will sooner excuse my mistakes. I wish I was as loveing a daughter as you are a loveing Father.' This letter showed Esther's erratic spacing, lack of punctuation, crossed out words, and spelling mistakes. It proves how hard a child had to practice to learn to write conventionally.[121] Yet smooth-flowing cursive correspondence by Pease women in the 1750s and 1760s[122] show they now wrote far better than their fathers—a situation common in other middling-sort families. There was also less difference in epistolary skills between Pease sisters and brothers than in the Evelyn family. This was a sign of the care taken to train women writers.

Esther's epistolary apologies demonstrate how women learned as children to use deferential rhetoric—a skill that would help them as adults to cope with men. We see this strategy again in the correspondence of Esther's sister Mary (1717–57) to her husband Robert Robinson (1720–56).[123] In 1752, Mary sent greetings to 'My Dear Bobby' from 'your Loveing & affec: wife'. But her professions of loneliness and apologies for not writing were soon followed by her decision to remain away for another month. Her descriptions of social activities clearly indicate she was having exhilarating experiences.[124] Mary had learned to use letter-writing, first to express obedience, then to claim the right to do as she pleased.

When Mary's son Joseph Robinson (1752–1807) inherited the family fortune, he changed his name to Joseph Robinson Pease.[125] His letters, written from the ages of 8 to 17, show the epistolary development of a typical schoolboy.[126] The earliest, at 8 years, from a school in Stockton-on-Tees, contained only one sentence in large printed letters: 'Honour'd Grand-Papp, I thank you for continuing your regard for my wellfare & happyness & am your dutifull Grand-son Joe Robinson.'[127] The letter, written in the large flowing hand that we often call merchant 'copperplate', differed from the italic of earlier generations. At the age of 10, Joe gave thanks for 'the Plumbs & the copybook' in a smaller cursive hand. 'Print me the Alphabet', he begged, '(two or three times over) on cards, to spell by, these long Evenings.'[128] Then he promised 'to make all the Improvement I can' in writing. His success with this method was evident in letters at the age of 12.[129]

This progress was crucial, for Joseph soon entered Warrington Academy, where the Dissenters John Aiken and Joseph Priestley were establishing a challenging curriculum. Joseph liked both his 'Latin & writing Master who behave very well'.[130] In 1764 he received an hour of daily instruction in writing,[131] but in 1766 the school was 'without a writing master' for five months.[132] This might account for the arrival of a writing tutor, apparently paid for by Joseph's father.[133] Joseph also studied geography, arithmetic, and read Erasmus, thriving under a blend of classical and modern instruction. It is unclear how long he stayed at Warrington, but in 1769, prior to leaving for business in Amsterdam, he was 'learning French, accompts & geography with Mr Astley'.[134] By the age of 17, Joseph wrote elegant letters in a small cursive hand.

When we compare them to those of his grandparents' generation, we find a shift had taken place by the 1740s and 1750s in handwriting and presentation. Pease children's letters by both sexes now bore signs of regular instruction by writing masters. Before mid century, children's penmanship and formats had remained unique to the writer; now round letters dominated. By the end of the century, the round hand itself had become standardized. Letters of children in different families and ranks tended to look more alike.[135] This reflected the homogenization of physical aspects of the English letter, which adopted the hand and style of the merchant.

On the other hand, Pease siblings used more informal prose filled with intimate nicknames, for the urge to write naturally overrode stultifying conventions. Moreover their epistolary training was focused on commercial skills for sons and equal competence for daughters. Gender differences were minimal, for it was crucial for merchant fathers to equip every child to function in a world that required frequent writing. Indeed, economic survival might later depend on it.

Nonetheless, there was no attempt by the Peases to use elaborately written letters as tools to rise above their rank. Though they bought a country house near Hull, for its chalk quarry as well as its status, sons remained in business and retained an urban focus.[136] The family occupied a place at the highest social level in Hull and their stress on children's education in every generation helped to make this happen.[137] Letter-writing, in turn, was an important part of their schooling that might later become an asset in both business and social life.

The Cotesworths of Newcastle

Children's letters of the Cotesworths of Newcastle and the Langtons of Kirkham, Lancashire reveal similar shifts in letter-writing, though sadly girls' letters do not survive. The Cotesworths corresponded in the beginning of the eighteenth century, whilst the Langtons of Kirkham did so at its end. Instead of stressing physical aspects of letters, these two cases show *why* epistolary literacy was encouraged and *how* it was linked to the business and social mobility of two merchant families. Both William Cotesworth and Thomas Langton spent inordinate amounts of time, energy, and ink tirelessly prodding their sons to write letters. Why, we may ask, did they do so?

The reasons, I suggest, rose from the backgrounds of the two fathers, pride in their own achievements, and high aspirations for their offspring. Children's letters were thus linked to concerns about schooling, careers, family finances, and dynastic survival. The Evelyn children were born into leisured circumstances. In contrast, William Cotesworth and Thomas Langton had to focus on the future of their businesses. If a merchant had money, however, there were educational and employment choices for the next generation. Whether sons should remain in business or pursue different goals was a key question. Proper letter-writing skills were crucial for both eventualities.

William Cotesworth of Newcastle, the second son of a Teesdale yeoman, (*c.*1688–1725), made the most of his marriage and entrepreneurial skills. He became a mine owner and trader, supplying London with salt, lead, hemp, flax, wines, and tobacco, as well as coal.[138] Cotesworth was perhaps the most colourful of a group of grasping men, who bought up estates of northern gentry at the end of the seventeenth century. By 1716 he claimed the status of a gentleman,[139] though his enemies thought him 'too little a man' to become Lord of the Manor. They believed 'Black Cotesworth' was 'not an honest man, but a rogue and a black devil'.[140] His servants plotted to poison him, and he was the subject of threatening letters.[141] Cotesworth's own letters lacked proper grammar, punctuation, and spelling. After the Jacobite rebellion of 1714, he became a government spy with the help of local postmasters. This experience showed him how important letters could be.[142]

Cotesworth's concerns about the epistolary literacy of his sons, William (d. 1721?) and Robert (d. 1729?) were shaped by this background. His two daughters entered boarding school in Chelsea, London,[143] but though he apprenticed William and Robert, this was a formality. Cotesworth wished to offer them a 'more Polite Way of living'. William was intended for the law; Robert for the highest echelons of commerce.[144] The boys briefly attended the Royal Grammar School in Newcastle,[145] but Cotesworth found it wanting. They then entered the respected Sedbergh School in Yorkshire, founded in 1525.[146] Cotesworth demanded long letters about every detail of their schooling, though he could not understand their references to classical authors or poetry.[147]

Their correspondence became a tense three-way conversation in which Cotesworth tried desperately, without proper training, to improve their letter-writing skills. Like Evelyn, he composed a letter for the boys to copy, this time for a widowed Aunt. Yet its overblown politeness and misspellings made it inappropriate for the occasion. When William wrote a good letter after many failures, Cotesworth reacted like Evelyn. 'It was writ with judgement in an easie style', he responded. 'Mr. Baker carried it to the Mayor [of Newcastle] and Mr Ellison would needs carry it to Hebburn; the original went last post to Mr [Henry] Liddell who it is likely will read it to my Ld Chancellor.'[148] Cotesworth and Evelyn, two most unlikely bedfellows, were guilty of the same paternal boasting. Like Evelyn's son Jack, William sent his father an epistle that he had 'translated out of Horace, which, with several other such like pieces serve to divert me at my leisure hours'.[149] William was also forced to send letters while travelling, though his 'arms ake[d] very sore' from riding.[150]

Though William grew to cherish letters, his brother, Robert was 'indifferent' to writing.[151] 'I had not sent you to Sedbergh but for your improvement', Cotesworth warned him, 'wch my dim sight cannot discern at this distance any other ways than by your letters.'[152] Cotesworth quickly understood that letters revealed a writer's character and accomplishments. Later in life, they would help to indicate whether his sons had become members of polite society. Cotesworth was never accepted into this world, but he hoped his sons would rise above his own status. In his mind, I suggest, epistolary literacy was a skill that might help them attain upward mobility.

In 1717, Robert was sent to London to study writing, French, geography, and arithmetic;[153] then to a writing master at the Hand and Pen in St Mary Axe for High German and Spanish.[154] At the same time, William entered Trinity College, Cambridge,[155] where he developed a love of language. He thus pleaded with Robert to spend more time composing letters:

> If you have nobody to write to, invent someone . . . Never be weary nor think you compose too slowly, but if you write one letter in the week, if you do it nicely, think you have done enough. To read all the letters that you can lay your hands upon is the best way to stock you with subjects, and to read letters wch you meet with by chance wou'd please me better than any Collection that is printed for there is always something aim'd at wch often runs the author into . . . being bombast, whereas between Friends a letter is commonly free and unconfined.

'I shall expect to hear from you very frequently', he concluded, 'and you may depend upon a constant correspondence on my side.' 'We are all young and at a great distance from our Friends', he added poignantly. 'We need all the comfort and advice we can give one another.'[156] This was a confirmation of the importance of letter-writing from a young man's point of view, not that of his father. It shows the impact of real letters, unlike those in printed collections or manuals.

After studying at Oxford and the Middle Temple, William died suddenly, and Robert returned from his firm in Holland to study law in London.[157] After Robert's early death in 1729, his sisters inherited Cotesworth's estate. Their descendants became 'comfortable country gentlemen',[158] and by the

1750s, Cotesworth's grandson, Robert Ellison was attending Eton. Yet his family grew anxious about 'what advancement he has made in writing and arithmetic ... as such are not much regarded at Eton'. After leaving Eton, he needed further instruction in London to become apprenticed to a London banker. In the end, the boy succeeded in banking, but left it with his father's approval, because it was too risky. He retired to Switzerland to write poetry and died in 1783.[159] Cotesworth's social aspirations were partly fulfilled by his descendants, but only a return to commerce made this possible. Despite careful planning, death denied him the joy of seeing his sons live as gentlemen.

The Cotesworth case study describes a middling-sort father, who encouraged his sons to leave his business and rise above his social rank. Thus he chided them when they failed to see the importance of letter-writing and how it related to their future. For Cotesworth, children's letters played a role that transcended their use in business—a role that had satisfied the Peases. Letters were part of the advantages of a privileged grammar-school education, which he hoped might contribute to his sons' upward mobility. Their presence in archives reveals the hopes and dreams of parents at a time when social advancement was possible for sons of first-generation entrepreneurs.

The Langtons of Kirkham, Lancashire

The records of five generations of Langtons show how a father strove to perpetuate a commercial dynasty, in contrast to Robert Cotesworth. Once again we find a parent prodding his sons to write letters, but for different ends. The Langtons were merchant-manufacturers who both produced and sold linen, unlike those who merely finished and distributed goods. Cloth was dressed, spun, and woven in their workshops and sheds, where the family at first lived amongst the workers.[160] In the late seventeenth century, Cornelius Langton (1691–1762) settled in the market town of Kirkham,[161] which provided the navy with sailcloth.[162] Protection from continental imports and the growth of colonial trade contributed to a flowering of the linen industry from 1740–90. The Langtons participated in the spoils of this trade.[163] They were consequently large fish in a small pond and quickly became prominent in local affairs.[164] Originally known as drapers in records, they eventually called themselves 'merchants' and 'gents'.[165]

In the third generation under Thomas Langton (1724–94) the family's business and status were at its zenith. When he married upward,[166] Thomas was called a social climber for 'giving [dinner]...parties without the correct staff'.[167] A 'shrewd, hard-headed, and single-minded business man', he guided the firm through the American War and won contracts with the Royal Navy.[168] His father's will left him money for a 'university education or some laudable trade or employment'. After learning Greek and Latin at Clitheroe Grammar School,[169] Thomas made a conscious decision to enter his father's firm.[170] He shrewdly concentrated on the sale of flax, iron, timber, rum, sugar, and tobacco in American and Baltic markets, as well as dealing in slaves.[171] In the 1780s, he visited the Lake District and Bristol's Hotwells, placed two sons as his agents in London and Riga, and built a house for his eldest son in Kirkham.[172] Despite his grammar school education, he chose to be a trader and pressed his sons to do the same.[173] Though he was careful to consult them, there was one point on which he would not compromise: his sons' duty to write letters.

We observe his obsession in his correspondence with his schoolboy sons John (1756–1807) and William (1758–1814) from 1771–88.[174] Scorning elegant letters marked by compliments, Langton's were succinct and to the point. The closest that he ever came to politeness was to sign off 'in haste with proper respects to everybody'.[175] Langton rarely wrote a letter without some reference to letter-writing itself—for example, who wrote last, when letters were (or were not) received, and the time of the next post. Those to his sons were peppered with questions about 'how you improve in your writing'. Langton's obsession, I suggest, stemmed, in part, from his desire to perpetuate a firm that depended on letter-writing. All of his sons, except one who was blind, joined his business. None of them, however, remained there.

To help his children acquire epistolary literacy, Thomas commanded the eldest, John and Will to 'engage in a copious correspondence'.[176] In 1771, Will was ordered to send letters to his Aunt Rigby, his Mamma, his sister, and Aunt Tabby. Not only must he write to Mr Bolton,[177] he was responsible for seeing that Bolton's son wrote home 'once in a fortnight'.[178] As soon as the boys' letters were written, Langton issued new commands.[179] In fact, the entire family was in a constant state of writing, reading, or awaiting a letter. Langton's fixation was motivated in part by his sons' future business needs. Yet his deep love for Will and John was another reason for concern. 'We daily remember you', he wrote, 'and are uneasy unless we often hear from you.'[180] Then he appended another list of people to whom the boys must write.

John and Will posted their letters from Woolton Academy near Liverpool, run by a graduate of Manchester Grammar School and Brasenose College, Oxford.[181] It advertised itself as 'an Academy for the instruction of youth in the . . . useful and polite branches of learning and teaching'. Instruction in Latin and Greek was offered along with foreign languages, mathematics, and bookkeeping.[182] When the writing master resigned, Langton wrote impatiently: 'I should be glad you were kept pretty duly to your writing, and to see you make good proficiency therein.'[183] When the school moved to Waltham, Essex, Langton considered withdrawing his sons. Eventually he relented, though the new school fee was forty guineas a year.[184] Langton's younger sons at home were sent regularly to writing masters for periods of intense instruction. Indeed, the family's travels were planned to take advantage of their presence. In October 1771 the Langtons journeyed to Liverpool as it was 'the season scholars are instructed in writing'.[185] Zachary's writing improved so much that in 1776 he was placed at a school in Hampstead, London.[186]

Langton continuously articulated how epistolary literacy was linked to commercial success. 'Good writing is a fine and very useful accomplishment in business', he insisted.[187] French and other languages were helpful, but 'writing and accounts . . . are what is chiefly to be regarded'.[188] 'I have always particularly recommended to you to endeavour to improve in your writing', he remarked, 'which is a great advantage to a person in trade, and may be of future service to you. Let me therefore remind you of it, and do not scribble.'[189] These comments about letter-writing had a moral undertone, for their stress on personal improvement invoked middling-sort virtue.[190] In fact Langton obsessively compared his sons' letters with those of other children: 'Mr Hornby', he declared, 'tells me that his son Thomas is very much improved in his writing and accounts. I would not have him surpass you therein.'[191] Yet Langton was not interested in writing for show. Nor did he wish to enter high society. Instead he demanded clear purposeful letters, which were crucial to success in business.

As he built his firm, Thomas, nevertheless, achieved a measure of upward mobility. He moved out of rooms above the shop and into his own house.[192] Moreover, there was 'an increasing pretension to elegant standards' by his sons.[193] John and Will left the firm in 1804 and tried to lead a life of leisure, unconnected to commerce.[194] Will became interested in antiquarian studies and preserved the family papers. Later, financial problems forced him back into a Liverpool business with his brother Tom.[195] Tom had prospered in a merchant firm in Riga, but returned to England in the 1780s. He educated his children in Switzerland, and his European pleasure jaunts vexed his father. When his Liverpool business failed, he emigrated to Canada.[196]

Zachary thrived in London and joined the firm of Pickfords.[197] He rose to master of the Skinner's Company and was a member of London Common Council.[198] Cecily married into the Hornby family and bequeathed three cases of books at her death. None of the sons remained in the family business. Langton's grandchildren became solid members of the middle class, holding prominent positions in banking, education, and literary institutions.[199] Of course, children's letters were not the cause of this success, but they were part of the family's stress on education and self-discipline in every generation. A child with epistolary literacy possessed a skill that could be applied to business or leisure—whichever fate, health, and talent ordained.

Letter-writing of non-elite daughters

The Pease family archive shows that there was little difference between epistolary skills of their sons and daughters. Yet in most collections, including that of the Peases, we find fewer letters written by women as children *or* adults. This is, of course, a product of lower female rates of literacy. Though percentages changed over time, women's skills always lagged behind those of men. Lack of financial resources is usually cited as the main reason for this fact. But later chapters will suggest other reasons for the lack of survival of female letters.

Many families preserved only sons' writings for legal and financial reasons, or because of patriarchal attitudes. Another explanation for the paucity of sources is that girls did not go to boarding schools until later in the eighteenth century. Yet both parents and daughters left home for other reasons and needed to correspond. As geographic mobility grew, friends and families were increasingly apart. Untrained women, who learned to write as adults, often wrote fewer letters, and none as children. Chapters 5 and 6 suggest another cause for low survival rates of women's letters: their wilful destruction by modest women, who purged intimate revelations and the slightest hint of scandal.

Nevertheless, there are rich caches of letters from both young and adult women in the archives examined for this book. Long series arose out of women's friendships, for example; others from travels. After the 1760s, letters from girls at school survive. Quaker merchant families, such as the Lloyds and Farmers gave children the same epistolary supervision found in previous case studies. In the 1760s, Priscilla Farmer monitored her daughter Mary's letters as diligently as Thomas Langton. 'Thy hand is run too small for a learner', Priscilla complained, 'and it does not improve as might be expected.' Like letters of Will Langton, Mary's were compared with those of other children. John Freeth's 9-year-old daughter, for example, was highly accomplished. 'I saw a letter from her', Mary was informed, 'and indeed... she writes much better than thee... I intreat thee', Mrs. Farmer pressed, 'to acquire a better Hand.'

Like William Cotesworth, Mary's mother had not been taught to write properly. 'Don't be contented with writing as well as I do', she insisted, 'because I never lerned so young nor so long as thou... To be able to read and write thy own mother tongue in a Beautiful correct manner is a... desireable accomplishment and... distinguishes Persons of a superior education, therefore spare no pains to arrive at some perfection.'[200] The words 'correct', 'desirable', and 'perfection' reveal Mrs Farmer's attempts to enforce social norms. Epistolary supervision was part of a larger effort to discipline girls that was increasingly evident by 1800. This development shows the Janus-faced elements of epistolary literacy—both the liberating effects it had on self-expression and the pressure it placed on women to conform to conventions.

Like Mary Farmer, the Strutt girls of Derby became anxious when letters were monitored by parents. In 1774 Elizabeth feared she would never learn to 'speak & write elegantly'.[201] When commanded to describe a journey, her sister Martha grew even more nervous. 'I wish I could leave behind me those awkwardnesses you tell me of', she wrote her father. As Chapter 3 will show, his lack of education was linked to his obsession with epistolary literacy. Yet Strutt's plan to 'improve' his children by focusing on their letters worked well. Adult epistles of his daughters were written with impeccable manners.[202] Letter-writing was a critical part of their education at home.

Finally, two generations of the Batemans of Manchester, preserved their daughters' letters from school—once in the 1770s, and again at the turn of the century. Like the Pease girls, Rebekah Bateman at the age of 11 composed 'a short sensible letter' on ruled paper. 'You should remember', she wrote her brother, 'I am not as old as you therefore you ought not to expect too much.'[203] Yet her adult letters equalled, if not excelled, those of her brothers.

These few examples of letters of merchant's daughters could be greatly multiplied. Here, they serve as an introduction to the topic of how epistolary literacy was gendered. They stimulate questions that will reappear throughout this book, and provide a framework for studying adult women's letters. Nonetheless, some patterns in epistolary training given to young women have already become evident. Before the mid seventeenth century both elite and non-elite girls had less formal education than their brothers. Their letters often display phonetic spelling, awkward presentation, and lack of self-confidence. This was as true for Lady Catherine Fairfax as it was for Mary Bowrey, the wife of a London sea captain.[204] Class did not override inferior gender skills during this early period. Yet as education became available for middling-sort daughters, the situation changed. Apologies were still present in young girl's letters, but now they were often a sign of strategy, instead of weakness. Mentoring and practise created accomplished female letter-writers in both elite and merchant families. Their letters as children are all we have to indicate how this happened.

Conclusion

Children's letters have been highlighted in this chapter, because they illuminate how reading and writing skills were acquired. Though the learning process was not easy, challenges could be met with family support. The parents in our case studies were obsessed with the epistolary skills of their offspring. Early writing specimens are also important to eighteenth-century scholars. Because this was a period when letters became standardized, end-products often look similar. Yet by comparing those written at different ages and analysing their material aspects, we can start to reconstruct the letter-writing experience. Since proud parents not only saved letters, but wrote about the mentoring process, we get their side of the story too. Epistolary literacy, I suggest, was a well-mentored rite of passage that provided entry into the adult world for both sexes. It offered practise in using written language, often for the first time. Letter-writing additionally strengthened family relationships and social networks.

The eighteenth century was also a time when letter-writing became a practice of everyday life for more non-elite families. Elite children continued to write artful letters, as they had done for centuries. But as Chapters 3 and 4 illustrate, more lower- and middling-sort letter-writers acquired epistolary literacy. Instead of classical models and Latin epistles, they found commonplace texts to emulate: bibles, popular literature, business records, copybooks, and, especially, real letters.

Parents in our merchant case studies knew the importance of epistolary literacy. Unlike John Evelyn, they did not take this skill for granted. They treated it as a precious possession and hounded both sexes into writing well. Merchants had pressing reasons for encouraging epistolary excellence, for economic survival depended on constant communication. 'An Epistolary Correspondance may be of great service to you', William Smith advised his son in 1769. 'Your future destination...is for Trade, but Learning is not incompatible with it, on the contrary it facilitates the conducting of it.' Once attained, he added, 'it gives a person a superiority in his Sphere of action'.[205] After letter-writing helped families with their business affairs, the next generation might use it to gain that cultural 'superiority'. For some it might even contribute to upward social mobility.

The beautifully formed round hands of merchant children, embellished with shading and flourishes, are found in more collections than can be dealt with here. But in keeping with their mixed functions that integrated business with pleasure, merchants' letters retained an informal style. The British epistolary ideal espoused an easy natural way of writing, rather than the ornate ceremonial manner of the French. Witty letters with classical allusions were still sent by boys, who were steeped in the classics. Yet merchants' letters written in a 'copperplate' hand, not those of the elite, would become ubiquitous emblems of English culture. The writing master and his copybooks, not Cicero and his epistles, haunted the pages of lower- and middling-sort letters. Those written by children reveal how epistolary literacy contributed to the rise of a literate public.

2

Sending the letter

The Post Office and the politics of the mail

Light be the earth on their heads, and easy rest their bones, who first invented writing, and who establish'd the Post-Office: thus ought I to wish, since to them I owe a great deal of the pleasure of my life, a correspondence with my absent friends.[1]

There is nothing more sacred than letters, and the very existence of a Post Office depends upon its fidelity and dispatch.[2]

The possession of epistolary literacy by a new group of letter-writers would have had little effect without a Post Office. The quotations above—one at the beginning of the eighteenth century, the other at its end—show how attitudes to the Post Office had changed over time. In the 1730s, Thomas Edwards of Buckinghamshire called letters 'the pleasure of my life'. By the century's end, letter-writing had become more than just enjoyable. As an ordinary writer told the Secretary of the Post Office, letters had become 'sacred' objects. These personal responses should not surprise us for, from its inception, the Post Office and its many functions aroused strong feelings. There were early hopes that it would provide intelligence, support foreign policy, raise revenue, and become a bureaucratic arm of the state. The main concern was to establish a monopoly to gather and censor information.[3] Yet during the eighteenth century, popular demand for reliable news and mail became a driving force for change. By 1800, a service that was created to censor mail had become a valued political right for English men and women.

In comparison with continental posts, however, it was late in coming. Until civil war ended and the monarchy was restored, stable mail service was impossible. Yet once the Post Office reorganized in the 1660s, public demand for services never flagged. As the introduction noted, by 1800, the post boy was replaced with high-speed coaches crammed with newspapers and letters. They linked every hamlet to a wider world marked by urbanization, migration, trade, wars, and empire. The Post Office was thus part of a wider movement to assert human control over space and time. A culture of letters could not have spread throughout the nation, without the services of the Royal Mail.

A firm knowledge of postal practices is, therefore, essential for understanding the topic of letter-writing. Yet the British Post Office in the eighteenth century has received less attention than that of other periods. It rarely appears in basic histories or their indexes, and the major work by Kenneth Ellis is about administration, not actual use. Martin Daunton's fine study of the nineteenth-century Post Office ignores its eighteenth-century roots. Postal reforms of the 1840s are seen as suddenly modernizing an ailing, corrupt institution.[4] The sources used here tell a different earlier story. Comments from thirty-four letter collections reveal what people thought about the post, and why it was important to their lives. We see the problems they encountered and the solutions they developed to obtain postal service. Letter-writers' remarks reveal how different ranks of people adjusted to changes in communication and found ways to avoid paying postage. They tell the story of how a national institution emerged out of resistance to, and pressure from, the public. These views are supported by local postal histories and the Royal Mail Archive (RMA) in London.

With the help of these sources, the first section of this chapter describes how the Post Office developed historically and how letters were sent and received. The second part examines comments about the mail that are found in every collection. These personal reflections, which are often deleted in printed letters, describe how the Post Office was actually used. Their prevalence confirms that letters were a familiar genre and postal practices were well known. These private views are merged with institutional records. Together they show how the Royal Mail encouraged a culture of letters and literacy.

This story is significant for several reasons. It describes the rise of a national institution with agents throughout the land. By offering an institutional frame for a cultural topic like letter-writing, it links literature about the self to economic issues. It also connects the history of communication, especially the work of Harold Innis, to the political world. As Innis, Richard Kieblowicz, and Wolfgang Behringer show, the Post Office in every age and place has been linked to culture and power. When the Royal Mail connected levels of city, country, and empire, tensions were created. The Post Office became 'an agent of modernization' from outside the community that unblocked and constructed a circular communications system.[5] At all points in time, it was a contested site. In this chapter we witness negotiations that arose between an evolving bureaucracy in a commercial society and a growing number of people who possessed epistolary literacy.

The Post Office in the seventeenth century

The Royal Mail started later than on the continent, where posts were more decentralized and accessible to merchants. It emerged in England on an ad hoc basis to meet government needs.[6] By the sixteenth century, only the Dover Road had settled posts. Indeed the horses provided for the king's messengers were often taken from plows or carts.[7] Henry VIII's first Master of the Posts, Brian Tuke (1516–45) chose postmasters and divided roads into stages.[8] By 1584, some public service was offered, but rival posts were suppressed in 1591.[9] From the start, the state's obsession with monopoly was challenged by illegal services.[10] At the same time, fear of free communication produced postal censorship.

In the early seventeenth century, increased literacy, trade,[11] and an interest in news[12] led merchants and the public to demand better service. Finally, in 1635, Thomas Witherings offered a proposal to reorganize the 'Letter-Office' for public use. A central London office coordinated mails on six main post roads and charged 2d. per letter.[13] But his plans foundered during the Civil War in the 1640s, when Parliamentary and Royalist mail services engaged in wild competition.[14] At that time, opposition pamphlets claimed the postal monopoly violated Magna Carta. The right to carry mail, they insisted, was a right of freeborn Englishmen.[15]

In 1653, the mail was 'farmed' out for £10,000. This meant that a bidder paid a fee to provide service and pocketed incoming revenues.[16] John Thurloe, Cromwell's Secretary of State (1655–60) created a secret room for opening letters that would continue in some form and place until 1844. The Royal Mail now became 'the pulse of all political movements, the deputy postmasters in the country serving as a hydra-headed agency for the State—seeing, hearing, and reporting everything of importance'.[17] In 1657, Witherings's plan was re-enacted and rival posts were shut down.[18] This act turned a 'rudimentary means of State communication over limited routes, and showing no signs of improvement' into a 'self-supporting service available to the general public'.[19] Due to rapid expansion of the Royal Mail, by 1667 the privilege of providing postal services cost 'farmers' £25,000.[20]

Charles II and his Secretaries of State intensified intelligence activities within the Post Office. They closely monitored post routes and channelled them through London, where the mail could be carefully supervised. The Postmasters General worked closely with the principal Secretaries of State to enforce state policies.[21] During the 1660s, Secretary of State, Henry Bennet, Lord Arlington (1618–85) and his deputy Sir Joseph Williamson (1633–1701) reorganized the flow of information in and out of the Post Office.[22] They searched and bribed carriers and foot posts, whilst spies informed on those 'subtil and sly fellowes in and about the Citty...laden with intelligence'.[23] Though there was no statutory precedent, state documents provided customary language that no employee should detain or open a letter 'except by express warrant of the Secretaries [of State]'.[24] In a secret room adjoining the General Letter Office with its own private entrance, John Wallis,[25] Isaac Dorislaus,[26] and Sir Samuel Morland[27] opened, copied, and resealed letters from 11 p.m. until 3 or 4 a.m.[28] Charles II was shown the room, filled with machines.[29] It was said employees could open letters, take impressions of seals, imitate writing perfectly, and copy a letter in one minute, using an 'offset process of pressing damp tissue paper against the ink'.[30]

In response, the state and the public resorted to the 'science' of ciphers and cryptology.[31] Not surprisingly, the letter in this period was viewed in plays and prose as a 'disguised tightly folded form of communication' in a milieu 'thick with informers...skilled in creating crafty letters, and unpicking and inventing codes'.[32] In 1665, the French Ambassador thought the English Post Office had 'tricks to open letters more skillfully than anywhere in the world'.[33]

Williamson also forged links between the Royal Mail and the newspaper. He used the Post Office to gather news from domestic informers[34] and foreign contacts, who reported on shipping, trade, and military affairs.[35] Then he circulated what he wished in the government's official newspaper, *The London Gazette* (1666–88).[36] Williamson ordered a postal employee, James Hickes,[37] to save the best information for his own private newsletters. In return for intelligence, these handwritten news-sheets were sent postage-free to a special list of fifty informers, half of whom were postmasters in 1674.[38] London postal clerks wrote so many newsletters 'that if some of them were not prepaired the preceding night, we could not compass them'.[39] The local postmasters who received them were often poorly paid innkeepers, who provided drink, gossip, and horses. In 1667, John Lisle promised that if he became postmaster he 'would... give large intelligence, especially through foreigners who resort to the post'.[40] In practice, postmasters were put in and out of office as power changed hands.

Under Witherings's plan, the post grew quickly and by 1677 centralized procedures were established. The General Letter Office in London had an inland office with forty-three employees, including a comptroller and accomptant, cashiers, an alphabet man, window men, sorters, receivers, and letter carriers. Six Clerks of the Road supervised mails carried three times a week on the six main post roads to Kent, Yarmouth, Chester, Bristol, Plymouth, and the North, and to Dublin and Edinburgh. There were also weekly deliveries to Dover, Harwich, and the continental pacquet boats.[41] Domestic rates were 2d., 4d., or 6d. for one sheet carried up to 80, 140, or more miles. The office received ship letters, maintained government expresses, and provided horses for travellers riding post. London mail was collected and delivered to the 'infinite number of little offices abroad... receiving letters in the streetes'.[42]

It is helpful to reconstruct the journey of a letter after it was handed into the General Letter Office, first in Bishopsgate, then in Lombard Street.[43] Patrons entered a large courtyard filled with merchants clamouring for mail, some clutching ship data from Lloyd's coffeehouse next door. The building contained residences for top officials, a boardroom, sorting office, and carriers' work area in the basement.[44] The staff enjoyed Irish beef and small beer, whilst officers attended dinners to celebrate the passing of the annual accounts.[45] Customers approached two windows, where a clerk and an alphabet keeper sorted London letters into pigeonholes. Paid and unpaid letters were put into different boxes. Country letters that passed through London were sorted into the six roads. Postage due at delivery was written across the address.[46] The fact that the recipient had to pay was important.

Consequently some writers asked permission before starting an ongoing correspondence.

To maintain control in the 1670s, the treasurer and the comptroller, Thomas Gardiner attended the opening and closing of each mail. Porters manned the doors 'to prevent the going out of Letter Carriers' until the king's mail was sent.[47] This gave officers in the secret room time to open and reseal letters. As postal forms show, the key event lay in the 'recconing' of accounts when the mail was 'sum'd up' and subjected to standardized checks. Letters were put into as many baize-lined leather bags as there were post towns and placed 'into one great Maile, buckled and sealed'. Each bag was tied with packthread and affixed with a way-label 'upon which . . . every Postmaster writes the hour he receives the Maile and the houre he sends it away'.[48] Outgoing mail left on Tuesday, Thursday, and Saturday nights. When it reached the first receiving house or Post Town, the postmaster took out his bag. At every step, the letter was marked for postage. Mail from York to a branch on the Chester road was hence marked in York, in London, and perhaps in Chester, depending on its destination. This was a time-consuming and expensive process.

From the start, people wrote letters demanding better service. Many of them complained about the amount of postage due. If more than one sheet was suspected, the letter was held up to a candle and charged double or triple rates. Gardiner advised postmasters not to 'exasperate turbulent spirits and potent men; who may put forward to complaine in Parliament'.[49] He also worried about indifferent postmasters, who let letters be diverted to 'coaches, carriers, heglers etc'.[50] Rather than force the public to use the post, Deputy Postmaster General, Colonel Roger Whitley (1672–77) advised: 'They are to be brought to it by degrees, by ye benefitt they find and ye diligence and ingenuity of ye persons imployed.' He believed the public would soon see 'the usefullnesse of this office to their commerce and how wee worke and travaile night and day for them . . . and how cheape and easy their correspondence is to them'.[51] One wonders how local employees did so well under constant pressure in a highly politicized situation.

Whitley's intimate letters to local postmasters show a department struggling for stability amidst public pressure. Salaries were so low that postmasters could 'not . . . live upon their employments'.[52] In return for intelligence, Williamson rewarded them with *London Gazettes* that sold for a penny. Postmasters used them to attract customers, or loaned or sold them for profit. By the 1670s, this practice had become so common, that

some postmasters received *Gazettes* instead of salaries.[53] The circulation of
Gazettes proved so successful that the Six Clerks of the Road were informally given the privilege of 'franking' other newspapers to postmasters—that
is sending them postage-free. They negotiated rates with publishers then
charged postmasters only 2–3d. a paper. Though rates varied with time,
postmasters received a percentage of about 2.5–5 per cent on sales of
franked newspapers.[54]

A privilege formerly restricted to MPs, who were able to send letters
postage-free, was now extended to newspapers for the Six Clerks of the
Road.[55] Not surprisingly, the Royal Mail's franking allowance rose from
£4,000 to £7,200 from 1670–7.[56] Williamson's 'perk' had a profound
impact on the spread of news. Postmasters placed papers in coffeehouses,
taverns, and alehouses with lower-sort customers, thereby encouraging
reading and public opinion. Though there was no legal basis for franking
newspapers, it became a hallowed right. As we shall see, this postal
development had later unintended consequences for the freedom of the
press.

During the Exclusion Crisis in 1680, London's postal monopoly was
temporarily shattered by the Whigs.[57] William Dockwra announced 'the
New and Useful Invention, commonly term'd the PENNY POST' that
delivered letters for a penny.[58] They were stamped with the hour, day,
and office and then carried through town six to ten times a day. Bonded
messengers rushed to and from seven central offices and 500 receiving-
houses. A letter brought in at 8 a.m., would be stamped by 9 a.m., and
delivered at or near 10 a.m.[59] Expensive advertisements and handbills, likely
financed by the Whigs, targeted a broad public, including shopkeepers,
tradesmen, and workmen. These occupations indicate the breadth and
depth of London letter-writers.[60]

The public now saw the benefits of an efficient low-cost postal system.
'Letters are delivered at the remotest Corners of the Town', wrote Defoe,
'almost as soon as they can be sent by a Messenger, and that Four, Five, Six
to Eight Times a Day.' 'We see nothing of this', he added proudly, 'at Paris,
at Amsterdam, at Hamburgh or any other City.'[61] Since licensing laws had
temporarily lapsed, the press and the Penny Post became allies. They were
called 'two incomparable twins of the Liberty of the Subject! One may
Write, Print, publish and disperse ingenious Libels', noted a pamphlet, 'and
no body the ... wiser for it.'[62] With the fall of the Whigs, the Penny Post
was absorbed into the Royal Mail.[63] Yet a later political poem glorified

'Mighty Dockwra' and pamphlets insisted that citizens had a birthright to use whomever they pleased to deliver letters.[64] Dockwra's Penny Post would become a model for future services when political rivalries cooled.

The Glorious Revolution led to freer communications and a surge in postal revenues from £65,000 in 1682, to £148,000 in 1700.[65] In 1698 the Penny Post carried 792,080 London letters and packets, whilst the letters it sent to the country numbered 77,530. By 1703, it carried more than a million items.[66] Now Londoners could write and meet in the same day. 'Please to send by the penny post when you will be there', wrote an expectant trader, 'that I may waite on you.'[67] It was claimed that 'every 24 hours, a Post goest 120 miles; and in five days, an Answer of a Letter may be had from a Place 300 Miles distant'.[68]

Still, five days was a long time to wait, and though gross revenues grew, the speed of mail remained constant at three to four miles per hour.[69] By 1700, the Post Office had established basic procedures, but letters of complaint showed reform was sorely needed. Only after the Hanoverian succession (1714), and the failure of the Jacobite Rebellion (1715), would a more confident government be ready to expand postal services for the public.

The state of the eighteenth-century post office

In 1711, a Post Office Act that embraced Scotland set the stage for major advances in the eighteenth century.[70] To discourage private ventures, it empowered the Post Office to erect and set up cross stages, connecting one main post road with another, short of London.[71] This crucial provision laid the groundwork for a new nationwide postal network. Postage was increased to 3d. for a single sheet carried eighty miles. This enabled His Majesty 'to conduct and finish the present war', but not to improve public service.[72] To support Britain's status as a growing world power, the Royal Mail became 'the centre of imperial communications, controlling a large fleet of packets; a propaganda and intelligence organ, serving as the government's mouthpiece, eyes, and ears; and an important source of patronage, employing hundreds of officials, postmasters, and sailors'.[73] The dramatic effects of imperial distances and constant war are revealed in Treasury Letter Books and private letters.[74] In 1714, for example, the North family was unable to receive mail. 'Tis impossible to help it till ye paquett boat is settled', wrote Lady Alice North, 'for I've try'd all ways.'[75]

'Here is people wch have now received letters dated a year ago & which have all lain this while by ye way.'[76] Postal treaties with foreign powers improved this situation along with a fleet of expensive packet boats that drained Treasury coffers.[77]

The eighteenth-century Post Office was composed of the Inland and Foreign Offices, the Penny Post, and the Bye-and-Cross Post departments. It was overseen by the Treasury, and run by a small, dedicated staff in London. Its two appointed Postmasters General, one from each party, were landed politicians with little ministerial experience, whose duties were 'occasional and light'.[78] Their letters add human interest to postal history. In 1708, for example, Sir John Evelyn was congratulated by friends 'on her majestie's honoring you with so considerable a place of trust and proffit'.[79] Yet his work in London when 'the deputations of the Postmasters [had] to be ready' caused family conflict.[80] Once rooms were fitted up for him at the General Letter Office, harmony was restored.[81] Yet Evelyn still had trouble receiving mail from the country. 'I was very uneasy in my mind & ill', he wrote, when his wife's letters were delayed.[82] Though Sir Francis Dashwood was appointed Postmaster for political reasons in 1766, his personal papers show early reform efforts to replace boys on horses with carts.[83] The letters of William Pitt, 1st Earl of Chatham, reveal how mail from abroad was disinfected and how officials in the secret office were paid in the 1760s.[84]

Postmasters General enjoyed patronage for vacancies in the London office and Lord Walsingham intervened in the 1780s. Mr Harbridge, he noted, on a document labelled 'Specimens of handwriting', was 'genteel' and could 'write quick & well'. More important, his father supplied the Post Office at a time when it had 'few such Contractors'.[85] Patronage for country postmasters was less significant, since they earned so little and local MPS interfered. 'Morris the postmaster is dead', reported MP John Tucker in 1775, 'but I hear of nobody who wants to succeed.' Though the job was 'not worth ten pounds a year', he struggled with a rival to put his own man in place.[86] In 1782, Jeffrey Aldcroft of Knutsford was appointed postmaster, though he did not live inside the town.[87] These examples could be multiplied up and down the century and officials were put in and out according to local rivalries. The political value of controlling postmasters far surpassed its monetary worth, and their ousting and resettling affected local politics. Postmasters were, however, forced to take oaths not to use their position to 'meddle in ye elections'.[88]

In 1750, there were 350 local postmasters, one-fifth of them women, who followed their husbands into office. By 1800, there were over 500 postmasters, many of whom were innkeepers. They were exempt from local office, billeting troops, and the land tax, and received allowances for riding work.[89] Yet from 1711–63 central staff grew very little. In 1788 the Post Office asked for raises for forty-six carriers whose salaries were £30–60. Since London's population was over half a million by mid century, and there were over seven million people in the nation, the Royal Mail's accomplishments were no mean feat.[90]

Estimates of postal revenue vary with sources and are particularly misleading from 1718–61, when pensions and secret service payments were omitted.[91] In brief, though gross receipts rose with trade and industry, net profits remained static at about £100,000 in the 1720s, £95,000 in the 1730s, and £85,000 in the 1740s. A peak of £102,015 in 1755 was followed by a trough of £73,730 in 1758.[92] Net figures may be contrasted with gross receipts: for 1726, £178,000; 1736, £188,000; 1746, £201,000; 1756, £238,000; and 1766, £265,000.[93] The gap between gross and net revenue was caused by rising operating costs, external raids on revenue, and systemic problems like franking.

A national network: The postal reforms of Ralph Allen and John Palmer

Increases in gross revenue after the 1720s were built on reforms of Ralph Allen, a former post boy, later postmaster of Bath. From 1720–64, he created a new system of bye and cross routes that turned the six roads into a national network.[94] (See Plates 12 and 13.) To assess his reforms, we must grasp the distinctions between four types of letters: a letter from Plymouth to London was a London letter; a country letter went from one part of the country to another, always passing through London; a bye letter travelled between two towns on a post road, stopping short of London; a cross-post letter passed between two different post roads.[95] From the start, mail had flowed chiefly through London—a fact that made censorship easy.[96] Since postage was based on mileage, the customer paid twice: first for the journey to London; then outward to the addressee.

Before Allen's reforms, bye and cross letters 'were thrown promiscuously, together in to one large bagg, which was to be opened at every stage . . . to pick out of the whole heap'. Not surprisingly, 'great quantitys...by clandestine and private agreements' were unaccounted for or destroyed.[97] Complaints from the public and the decline of Jacobitism led a more secure government to accept Allen's offer to run all bye and cross posts for £6,000.[98] His personal letters, some with incredibly bad handwriting, show his commitment to rationalize mail delivery.[99] Allen appointed well-paid surveyors 'to Inspect all the Maine roads, Cross Roads & Branches'[100] and to inform the Post Office 'in a clear & methodical manner'.[101] Letters to Mr Lumley and Mr Carter, for example, show his insistence on reform. 'Whatever office you may...pass thro, always examine into the Conduct of the Deputy...and redress the abuses etc which...have crept into the management.'[102] Allen became the go-between with London for all country matters and his quarterly system of post bills and vouchers reduced fraud and disorder. He set up daily posts from London and tri-weekly bye routes, increased some speeds to five miles per hour, and created a postal network for the common good.

These reforms had major benefits for merchants, who begged Allen for mail service to their towns. In 1748, for example, John Tucker of Weymouth had news that 'the Post Office have at last of themselves done what we have been so long soliciting for and made a new branch from Salisbury to Axminster'. This meant that Tucker now received letters at 9 a.m. and was able to send a same-day reply at 2 or 3 p.m.[103] By mid century most market towns had a daily service and northern regions were integrated into trading and manufacturing networks.[104] Allen's claim that in 1735 mail arrived four days sooner in Manchester, Chester, Liverpool, York, Hull, and Beverley[105] is confirmed by letter-writers in these places.[106] The letters of Derbyshire workmen examined in Chapter 3 were served by a new branch from Manchester to Chesterfield and another from Nottingham to Derby.[107]

Though Allen saved the Royal Mail a great deal of money,[108] his greatest achievement was his transformation of the post's physical structure. Increased public confidence led to the demise of rivals and the awareness that a well-run service could be beneficial to the public.[109] In 1726, a foreign traveller reported from London: 'You may...write twice a day to anyone living in the town and once a day to about 150 small towns and villages...Whatever is sent by the 1d. post is well cared for.'[110] By 1756, Maitland listed over 200 towns with Post Offices,[111] and by 1764, important places had delivery six days week. By 1775 there were 444 English post towns, 132 in Scotland, 195 in Ireland, more in the West Indies and America. By 1800 there were over 783 post towns in England.[112]

The Treasury admitted that despite previous fears of competition, 'the Country letters and the Bye way & Cross road letters, seem rather to have aided and improved each other'.[113] Postage due per letter decreased, whilst speed and geographic coverage grew along with bureaucratic oversight. Mail was hence spread socially and geographically to a greater number of people in a faster way. The dominance of London as a hub for all mail was broken. By 1764 Allen was the owner of Prior Park in Bath, a trusted friend of politicians, and the supposed model for Squire Allworthy in Henry Fielding's Tom Jones.[114] In 1755, Sir John Evelyn noted on a letter received from Allen: 'Farmer of the cross post by which he has gott a great estate, built a palace near Bath, where he lives like a Prince.'[115]

Yet as Allen's new routes slashed travel times for flying coaches, post boys on horses still used country lanes. The difference was noted by John Fawdington, a Yorkshire saddle maker: 'Most of these towns that I visit', he wrote with disgust, 'are only supply'd . . . by a bit of a lad upon Horseback.'[116] Still, road transport was getting better, even in the North. By 1750 there were 418 turnpike trusts covering 15,000 miles,[117] whilst John Metcalf, Thomas Telford, and James McAdam were engineering road improvements.[118] Mail was nonetheless delivered using antiquated methods. Merchants argued that trade suffered because of the backwardness of the Royal Mail.

Into this situation stepped John Palmer of Bath. He saw the Post Office needed to provide public services that were timely, safe, and reliable. With William Pitt's help, he changed the way mail was delivered by replacing the post boy with new high-speed coaches.[119] (See Plates 14 and 15.) A trial run in 1784 delivered mail from Bristol to London in sixteen hours.[120] Within a year Palmer's coaches sped on roads in East Anglia and the south-east. By 1786 they serviced the Great North Road, where they 'outran every conveyance'.[121] Now many letters sent on Monday had an answer by Wednesday.[122] By 1790, all major post routes had daily coach delivery.[123] Robert Johnson of Bath quickly noticed the difference: 'Palmer's plan of the mail coaches is now established and the expedition they travel with is astonishing. We have the evening papers here, the morning after they are printed.'[124]

Palmer's French-made post coach weighed three-quarters of a ton, carried six passengers, a driver, and an armed guard with a clock. Time bills recorded mail delivery at every stage so that the public knew exact times of arrival. As the mail coach drew near, traffic gave way, tollgates opened, and horses stood waiting. But institutional change rarely comes easily. Postal officials feared that branches would not connect, that timetables must change, and that they would lose control to coach subcontractors.[125] After heated political disputes, Palmer was dismissed in 1792, but he received compensation later.[126] Nonetheless, his vision for swifter mail delivery was gradually fulfilled.

In defending his coaches Palmer affirmed a radical notion. They were, he claimed, based on a 'plain and simple idea that the business of the Post-Office was merely a branch of the carrying trade of the country, monopolized by Government, for the advantage of the public'.[127] This focus on public service was a revolutionary change. Later William Pitt noted as he talked about Palmer's coaches: 'The real advantage is convenience to the public, rather than profit.'[128] In truth, a mix of higher rates and volume along with the use of coaches eventually increased net income from £196,000 in 1784 to £391,000 in 1793. By the early nineteenth century, revenue was over £1 million.[129] Mail delivery now became more reliable and safe, whilst speeds increased to eight to nine miles per hour.[130] Coaches grew so essential that the period from 1785 to 1835 has been called 'the mail coach era'.[131] Of course additional reforms were still needed. Yet by 1800, a foundation was laid upon which a more modern system could be built. This situation is confirmed by the personal comments about the post that are analysed below.

The importance of the Post Office to letter-writers

What impact did postal improvements have on individual letter-writers? Though relations between the post and the public were not always positive, they were deeply felt. At the opening and close of letters, all classes stated that they needed the Royal Mail for practical and emotional reasons. When high costs and slow speeds thwarted letter-writing, people created alternative methods, many of them illegal, to ensure mail was received. Because most writers' comments are deleted in printed collections, historians have underestimated the significance of the Post Office. Yet it must have seemed astonishing to people whose parents had lived without it. Despite its flaws, the Royal Mail performed 'a great public service'.[132]

We can test this claim by observing the deep connections of the post to the personal rhythms of daily life. As society became more commercial and postal services expanded, the public subjected its own routines to those of the Royal Mail. People of all ranks wrote at particular hours on specific days, so as to make optimal use of the post. The fact that its changing functions and schedules were known to paupers, middling sorts, and professionals, was, in itself, important.

People accommodated themselves to the post because they needed it to cope with practical concerns. When messages were harnessed to the beat of the mail, affairs would go smoothly. Conversely when communication failed, frustration set in. In 1695 Oliver Le Neve grew testy when no mail arrived 'on Saturday, the usual daie of Letters comeing from Norwich'.[133] Complaints about delivery show that people knew when each post was due. 'You are not so kind to keepe your promis with me in writing every post', claimed Catherine Clavering of Lamesley, after awaiting each one expectantly.[134] Some people worried that the mail might leave before letters were completed. 'I am asham'd', wrote Frances Cottrell, 'to send such a scral as this, but fearing the post will be gon I dare not write it again.'[135] In 1762, Mary Robinson wrote considerately to 'Dear Bobbey': 'I thought it better to defer yours till this post then to write two by one post, so that you might hear oftener from us.'[136] The importance of mail was constantly affirmed in personal comments.

Moreover, people understood the cadence of its routines. 'The middle Post is a long one here', observed Anne Evelyn, 'the letters not coming in till Thursday.' 'I shall not disappoint', wrote her mother, 'of one always by Monday's post.'[137] In an increasingly market-based society, time became more valuable. Thus in 1748, the merchant John Tucker ordered every movement to coincide with the mail: 'My exertions are all timed in what I call the long post between fryday night and Tuesday night, that no letters may remain unanswered that of necessity require it.'[138] Necessity is the key word to notice, but the post also brought luxuries. Tucker's 'packets of the middle part of [Pope's] Dunciad' were kept back one post, because they were not sealed by 9 a.m.[139] The serial nature of literature was surely encouraged by the routines of the Post Office.

People also relied on mail for impractical reasons that were related to their anxieties. How psychological dependence upon letters affected the emotional lives of people is an important, overlooked topic. The use of intensely felt language was a sure sign of this addiction. In 1695, for example,

Cary Stewkeley had 'a thousand frights and fears' about her sick mother. 'I live in hopes of a letter', she moaned, 'by Monday's post.'[140] Without an expected letter, wrote John Tucker in 1748, 'anxious thoughts will not be any way alleviated'.[141] In 1789, Rebekah Bateman of Manchester wrote fearfully to her angry husband about his failure to get her letter. She begged him not to be 'displeased . . . because the post time here is different. I did not forget your request & I felt very uneasy when I found my error.'[142] In another letter, Rebekah admitted: 'Spirits low . . . since you left & till I hear from you.'[143] The opposite was true for another worried wife: 'I am much happyer since the post came in for you know I am the grandest cowerd in the wourld.'[144] These heartfelt remarks suggest the emotional impact of receiving, or not receiving, mail.

This was not only true for the middling-sort families cited above. More unexpected were the sentiments of four lower-class letter-writers. George Follows, a poor Quaker basket maker, tried desperately to support his family, whilst his wife Ruth preached throughout England. When their children left home, Ruth was afraid they would discard their Quaker faith. After long expectation in 1769, she finally received a letter, which allayed her 'uneasey fearing something was amiss'.[145] 'Many fears & doubts had Passed our poor minds', she responded, 'but thy saying that no Accident had befallen thee: was A means of Removing . . . those painful Apprehentions that had troubled us concerning thee.'[146] The psychological upset caused by not receiving mail was a sign of how much it was valued.

John Fawdington, a Yorkshire bridle-maker, discussed the Post Office as he made love to Jenny Jefferson in the 1780s: 'How gratifying to my affections will it be to know that I am not utterly forgotten of you, or as a Dead man, out of Mind.'[147] If he received no letter, he swore, he should 'be ready to scold the Post boy for not driving as if he had a design against his neck'.[148] When two letters came at last, he thanked Jenny 'gain & gain . . . for tho (by some neglect I suppose in the Post Offices) I received them both at one and the same time'. 'They were accompanyed', he added, 'with a double degree of love.'

Sailors and their wives were also dependent on the Royal Mail. Indeed the Post Office paid 1d. for each 'ship letter' received. In 1708, letters and news were lifelines for John Starke in Virginia, stranded far from home. 'I am gott into a Tag end of the world', he complained, 'where little of the English Transactions appear, at least very late when they doe comme.'[149] Women left at home knew how to contact their men on ships. In 1697,

Thomas Bowrey's wife wrote to him 'on Board/ye St George Gally/riding In ye downs/If ye ship be gone, to be returned to Mrs Mary Bowrey/att Mr Gardiners an apothecary'. 'Pray my dear let me hear from you', Mary wrote, 'for that [is] the only cumfor I have now.'[150] Bowrey's mother likewise sent him letters full of news: 'Hear was A womon that hath a Coz: A Board ye Mary Gally', she reported, who 'sayeth that thear came a letter from Hollone: from one of her frind: that sayeth ye Mary Gally and All ye Shipts Company was well at ye Cape Jeanary ye 8.'[151] Letters from Bowrey's wife and mother show how two unlettered women depended on the Post Office.

How people coped with problems of the Royal Mail

Personal comments demonstrate the benefits of the Post Office. But how did people handle its problems caused by slow posts, lost letters, uncertain deliveries, and high costs? Complaints about the mail's slowness were received regularly by postmasters. In 1748, Thomas Edwards 'thought every post as tedious as a tired horse'.[152] In 1760, four innkeepers in Yorkshire and Derby were so disgruntled that they started a short-lived coach service.[153] Paying more for faster delivery was a strategy used by George Fitzherbert in Derbyshire. 'My letter', he wrote his wife, comes 'by an express as it will get to you a day sooner & much safer.'[154] A sample of dated letters in the 1720s and 30s, which also have postmarks and dates received, suggest that towns on good roads in the central or southern part of the country might receive mail from London in two days. If answered immediately, the entire round trip might be done in four.[155] The Legards in York received London letters in three days by the 1760s.[156] The journey to Sheffield took four days in 1760; after Palmer's reforms it might take as little as twenty-six hours.[157] Despite wars and bad weather, the speed of foreign mail also improved. In 1706 Thomas Bowrey's mail from Barbados to London took nine months.[158] By 1730, Tucker had a reply from St Helena in six.[159] Mail from Venice reached the Johnsons in Bath in two and a half weeks in 1779.[160] In 1803, their letters from Paris took nine days.[161] Of course, these were optimum times, and letters often took longer, but they show what was possible.

Constant waiting caused anxiety, but theft of mail was worse. Post Office records cite prosecutions for armed robbery, overcharging for postage, forging franks, wilful destruction of letters, and embezzlement of enclosed bills or money. Tales of robberies described post boys tied to trees.[162] But by 1776, Barbara Johnson was happy to have her money sent by the Royal Mail. Though accidents might happen, she could still assert with confidence: 'I believe the Post is pretty secure.'[163] This statement suggests people trusted the Post Office, but not all were convinced. In 1787, John Fawdington still sent his wife separately 'the other half of the Bank of England Post Bill for £10'.[164]

Over the century people learnt to address letters in ways that enhanced delivery. Before streets were numbered in London in 1767, houses were identified as being near landmarks. Thus the Bowreys' mail was sent at different times to Wellclose Square, Marine Square, and 'near the tower'.[165] After many losses, Pen Pendarves in Cornwall told friends to direct letters 'by Helstone Bagg'.[166] The poor took the most pains and were highly informed about postal practices.[167] 'Dirct to Armin nigh Rawcliff by Doncaster bag', wrote a London pauper phonetically.[168] Poor Ann Clark of Bermondsey was even more thorough: 'Plees to Derect/For me to bee Left at the son/in Wite street/neer sant gorges/church in the Boorow/Sourthwork/Pray send an answar/By the next post.' At a Norfolk Post Office, Samuel Follows inquired for 'the Best way and how to Direct' to his brother in Nova Scotia.[169] When his mother Ruth preached, she left a trail of detailed directions, so as to reach her as she travelled.[170]

There were also strengths in the postal system that encouraged safe delivery. Mail could be collected at any Post Office, and their hours were well known to the public. Hence Ruth Follows 'got up erly to write' so that friends could 'put ... this into the Post Office'.[171] Mail could also be left at coffeehouses or shops, and was forwarded if requested.[172] The Langtons of Lancashire arranged to collect their letters at Oxford, as they travelled to Bristol Spa.[173] Increased mobility made delivery harder for the Post Office, but more important to its clients.

In addition, there were close personal contacts between postmaster and the community when the addressee paid for mail. 'The postman has waited', wrote a merchant in 1733, 'ever since I began this letter.'[174] Mr Hughes of Twford reported that the postman called 'at my gate'.[175] 'Often when the postman has passed the door', wrote Mary Wilson, 'I have wished a letter to you.'[176] These comments show that though payment by addressees caused problems, it fostered positive relationships between individuals and the Post Office. Though the system was prone to undelivered mail, it may have been in some ways more flexible than today's post.

The problem of high postage costs, however, presented a more difficult problem than slow delivery of mail. At the end of the eighteenth century, costs rose abruptly to 3d. for a single sheet for only 15 miles; 4d. for 30 miles; and up to 8d. for 150 miles just inside England.[177] Even the rich kept detailed records of amounts of postage paid.[178] All ranks developed strategies to avoid postage, because mail had become a necessity. Though it is often assumed that letters were 'a forbidden luxury' for the poor, they still found ways to send them.[179]

If letters were most commonly called 'favours',[180] receiving one brought a heavy obligation to pay its postage. Therefore letter-writers commonly apologized for the expense. Harriet Dalrymple was 'ashamed' that her friend must pay 'for so shabby & hurried a letter'.[181] Not surprisingly, there was a taboo against letters of more than one sheet. Robert Johnson of Bath wrote wistfully that he could not 'find any body that will ever put one to the immense expense of paying for a double letter'.[182] Letters with multiple sheets were of most concern to merchants, who had to enclose bills and other items, thus increasing postage due. They wrote angry letters to the Post Office demanding relief. By mid century, the northern commercial lobby was becoming increasingly vocal. In 1753 postal officials reported that: 'the Merchants or Manufacturers of several Trading Towns have disputed this charge of double postage' when patterns or samples were enclosed in them. Only if they were over one ounce would they pay.[183] Manchester merchant, Thomas Bateman summed up traders' views in a taciturn comment: 'I have no reply to make worth postage.'[184] Yet his father-in-law, a timber merchant gladly prepaid letters to his daughters at boarding school. Middling-sort writers were often wealthy enough to choose when to pay.[185]

For the lower orders, this was not possible, and they paid only when necessary. As we have seen, the letters of Joseph Morton, an unemployed Kendal gardener, displayed a keen knowledge of the post.[186] Because he 'fered of the postages', Morton omitted an enclosure in 1779.[187] Paupers benefited from the post even if they could not write themselves. In 1758, authorities in Catherine Jones place of residence prepaid 4d. for her letters. They did this in hopes that London churchwardens would send her money for poor relief.[188] Escalating charges affected everyone, not just the poor. Consequently, ways were found to evade paying postal charges.

Alternatives to using the post

People of all ranks developed ingenious strategies to reduce or avoid postage. Alternative modes of conveyance included friends, carriers, agents, servants, porters, newsmen, and hawkers. Letters to merchants were sent to the continent, for forwarding back to England. Others hid them in loads of books, butter, or clothes. In practice, the nature and effect of these strategies varied by class. A range of transport options now leant themselves to this deception: the wealthy carried letters in private coaches; traders might use canal barges and coastal vessels; and there were bumpy, but large, wagons for lower-sort people and their letters. A government report acknowledged the problem: 'Whatever penalties are held out to Coachmen, &c. carrying Parcels, the Public . . . will send by the safest and most expeditious conveyance, to the very great loss of the revenue of the Post Office.'[189] Though rival services were suppressed, the authorities could do little to enforce the monopoly envisaged by the Royal Mail.

Tobias Smollett's *The Expedition of Humphry Clinker* reveals a hierarchy of ways to send letters that varied by gender and class. In the novel, who and how one could send a letter reflected the presence or lack of power. At the bottom of the ladder, Win, a female servant, watched for chances to slip her letters into other people's mail, whilst Jarvis had to see that his master's letters were delivered, often in illegal ways.[190] In real life, families used several methods simultaneously, sending duplicates by messenger, carrier, and coach.[191] The point is that there were choices. In 1712, Anne Evelyn opted for 'the letter caryer if messenger be scarse'.[192] When Henry Godolphin's letters went missing in 1725, he wished he had sent them by coach.[193] Within a ten-mile radius of the General Letter Office, mail still cost 1d. Hence in 1749, Thomas Edwards forwarded letters to a friend near London, who then put them in the cheaper penny post.[194]

Sending letters by carrier cost less than the Royal Mail.[195] 'Ye Carrier comes Every weeke', noted the Quaker George Taylor, '& I shall have as much brought me for 2d. as I pay to post 2 or 3s.'[196] When Francis Wise earned his diploma, it was to be sent by post, but Wise crossed out 'post' and inserted 'carrier' instead.[197] Provincial newsmen who delivered papers were also ready to help. Barbara Johnson used one in 1777, thinking him 'a very safe conveyance for anything'.[198] Wealthy people had their own messengers and loaned their services to others. 'Lord Craven's custom of permitting everyone in the house to have their letters enclosed to him', was appreciated by his friends.[199] In 1714, Anne North received a message from abroad, 'brought by a gentleman met on the way going to England'.[200]

At the other end of the social scale, Joseph Morton carried letters for friends 'as Derichted' whenever he went to Kendal. In 1779, Alice Rigg received one of them, for 'that Day ... there was some Dent peaple in town'.[201] Morton sent letters by hand whenever he could. If not, he waited 'till Friday ... as the Cartmell carrier Goes of then ... Which is the only opertunity I have for Letters'.[202] The Follows family saved money by sending letters to kin, who passed them by hand, adding news at the bottom.[203]

Merchants, chafing under what they saw as unfair treatment, also found ways to cut costs. In 1731 Robert Pease advised his father, Joseph: 'whenever you send me a parcell you had better put the Letter in it.' Joseph later slipped a letter into one for I Bance & Co.[204] 'If you would post yr letters for me under cover to your uncle', wrote Richard Tucker to his son Edward, 'I would save postage.'[205] William Spencer received a packet of letters from Mr Fossick, which opened at the bottom. He cut off those for Fossick's wife and made sure the others were delivered.[206] William Strutt, put letters that 'pass[ed] between Derby and London in carriers' bags of the hosiery business'.[207]

Sending letters free of charge by using an MP's frank was a widespread practice for all but the lower sort.[208] Nancy Nicholas employed them carefully in 1699: 'Tis not proper when the Parliament men are in London', she wrote, 'to frank papers out of the country.'[209] Elizabeth Adams had special 'frank cases to put my letters in', apparently signed paper covers that were wrapped around letters.[210] In 1779, Edmund Rack of Bath waited to use his until he had several to mail. 'It's a waste', he confided, 'to send a single Letter in a Frank.'[211] When the Johnson family received gifts of franks in 1777, they were expected to write many packets in return. William Strutt tersely summed up the situation: 'A letter sent by post is a subject of apology, a relative's frank a rare gift.'[212] Franking created more mail by encouraging people to write more often without paying postage.

Conflicting roles of the Post Office: Distribution of newspapers and censorship of mail

In the 1760s the practice of franking took an unexpected turn. The Post Office began to frank huge amounts of newspapers to a broad swathe of the population. This was an egalitarian project that ran counter to its role as censor. In effect, by the end of the eighteenth century the Royal Mail had become a commercial newsagent spreading papers throughout the nation. At the same time, the Janus-faced Post Office continued to open letters in hopes of restraining the government's opponents. This created tensions between the Royal Mail and the people that used it. A powerful circular system of communication had been gradually created.[213] Once it gathered momentum, its effects were impossible to control.

It is helpful to recall that in the seventeenth century, Secretary of State Williamson ensured that the newspaper and the Post Office would remain tightly connected. In his day, however, there were few news-sheets. By the first half of the eighteenth century, provincial newspapers had spread throughout the provinces. In 1740, over forty papers supported dense networks of agents, usually booksellers in towns and newsmen or carriers in the countryside.[214] Not surprisingly the government rewarded newspaper publishers that supported its goals. In the 1730s, Walpole spent £5,000 per year distributing friendly papers.[215] Postmasters were told to 'make these papers as public as [you] can, and to send...names of persons...who keep coffeehouses, that they might be furnished with them gratis'.[216] Postal employees, who owned shares in loyal papers, sometimes failed to deliver the opposition press.[217] Hence when *Applebee's Journal* arrived at Weymouth's Post Office instead of *Mist's*, readers were incensed.[218] They also demanded '*The London & St James G[a]Z[ette]* instead of the *Westminster Journall*, all once a week'.[219] In the 1770s, the *General Evening Post* linked its printing schedules to the departure of mail. Postal clerks were paid 'for their extra trouble' in holding back posts when papers were delayed, or sending mail ahead of the main delivery.[220] In England, as in most nations, the newspaper was 'regarded as a natural adjunct of a Post Office'.[221]

After the Restoration, Secretary of State Williamson had allowed the Six Clerks of the Road to frank newspapers from London at discounted prices.[222] Over time this practice led to wild abuses. From 1711–61, franked letters increased 700 per cent, while paid letters only grew by 50 per cent.

These numbers reveal sharp increases in the amount of letter-writing that were masked by the post's net revenue figures.[223] Rising circulation led to huge profits for postal employees. Some estimated them at £3,000–4,000 a year, others at £6,000–8,000.[224] By the 1760s, the Clerks franked almost 60 per cent of newspapers sent through London.[225]

In 1764, a loophole in a Postal Act established to reduce franking, allowed MPS to let others sign their franks. The Post Office was quickly flooded with newspaper orders from printers, booksellers, and politicians. Franked papers were now sent direct to clients at prices that undercut those charged by postal clerks.[226] In 1765, franks actually rose from 51,818 to 97,048![227] Newspapers franked from London grew from 1 million copies in 1764 to over 8.5 million in 1796.[228] In practice, the free circulation of newspapers was thrown open to the public.[229] By the 1790s, the Royal Mail proudly stated: 'Not only clerks in the Post Office, but also every other person is at liberty to circulate in any part of the Kingdom any quantity of newspapers free of postage.'[230] The Post Office had solved the pressing problem of how the public could obtain affordable news. Unless papers were franked, they could never have circulated en masse. The consumer would have had to pay for the newspaper, the stamp tax, and at least 2–6d. per sheet for postage.[231] This right to receive newspapers at a discounted rate arose from a statute to restrict franking.

Ironically, the privileges of a few postal clerks had profound effects on the spread of news. They also had an impact on the reading and writing experiences of people throughout the nation. Newspapers were not only read in London inns and taverns, but appeared over the doorsteps of provincial men and women. People who could read a newspaper, then circulate their opinions in letters, were empowered in new ways. The dangers of this politically explosive development were not lost on the authorities. This made some officials more determined than ever to use the Post Office to censor mail.[232]

Over the century, the secret office was expanded, and it established close ties to European Black Chambers.[233] Huge volumes of intercepted letters in The National Archives and British Library are evidence of the office's effectiveness.[234] Due to an opened letter, Bishop Atterbury was arrested in the 1720s.[235] Writers were also targeted. Hence, John Gay warned a correspondent that 'those dirty fellows of the Post Office do read my letters'.[236] By 1735 this custom was derided in the House of Commons: 'The practice of breaking open letters was become so frequent ... it was certain that no man would carry on any treasonable correspondence by means of the Post Office.' After the Jacobite rising of 1745, general, instead of express, warrants were used to stop 'all letters, packets, or papers' considered dangerous. This abuse, claimed, the *Craftsman*, was done by leaving 'a Blank . . . Warrant to be fill'ed in by the Postmaster General'.[237]

Ordinary people were not usually affected. Yet in 1774, Elizabeth Strutt in Derby chose not to write a letter for it was 'liable to be opened by others'.[238] Elizabeth observed this with no opinion. In contrast, Richard Follows, who left England to make his fortune, believed that postal privacy was a public right. In 1776, he feared officials had stopped his letters from North America: 'Surely there is somebody that opens what they have to convey', he wrote, 'which I think is very wrong.'[239] In the 1790s, the Post Office increasingly spied on radicals and the letters it opened helped compromise men like Horn Tooke and Thomas Paine.[240]

Yet the opening of letters was not disclosed publicly by parliament until 1844.[241] The Postmasters General were then forced to admit that 'there was no sufficient authority for this practice'.[242] Henceforth, they promised, 'it would be 'discontinued . . . altogether'.[243] *The Sun* reacted angrily: 'When a man puts a letter into the post-office here, he confidently believes [it] . . . will not be read either by Postmaster-General, or penny postman, or Secretary of State, and that no human being will venture to break a seal which has hitherto, in this free country, been regarded as sacred as the door of his own private residence.'[244]

Intercepting, opening, and then closing letters were subtle acts. They encouraged free speech through letter-writing; then took it away by surveillance. People could avoid the post by using other alternatives, but none of them had the reach of the Royal Mail. Its double-faced character was evident as it simultaneously distributed newspapers and opened people's letters. Regardless of this ambivalence, by 1800, postal service had become a necessity to the nation.[245]

Conclusion

The public's use of letter-writing is best understood by placing it in the context of postal practices of the period. This chapter has shown how people utilized the Post Office and how it contributed to a growing culture of letters. In the seventeenth century, basic postal routines were established and the quantity of letters carried surged dramatically. In the eighteenth century, a national network grew out of the old six roads. Coaches improved speeds, yet costs remained high. Franking and creative strategies helped to mitigate problems, but use still differed by class. Though the poor found ways to send mail and were not totally excluded, the middling sort gained most from postal improvements. Overburdened postmasters worked well on low salaries, but inertia, corruption, and obsolete practices hindered reforms. There were no failed postal Bills from 1711–90. This vacuum may have occurred because the Treasury controlled finances and resisted costly plans put forth by postal officials.[246] Even so, many nineteenth-century reforms, including universal penny postage, were conceived and discussed by postal officials in the 1790s.[247] They could not be enacted until economic, social, and political pressures reached a critical mass.

By 1800, however, the public was finally becoming a driving force for change. Because people regarded mail service as essential to their lives, demand for cheap, reliable service grew more intense. Yet because this pressure was fragmented, it is difficult to find. Personal letters and postal records offer different kinds of evidence that document popular demands. Individuals wrote passionate letters clamouring for better service. Towns sent mass petitions for new routes and Post Offices.[248] In 1792, for example, Secretary Freeling of the Post Office received an angry letter from Mr Ga[nn]att of Dudley. He had had to leave a letter 'with bills totaling a large amount at an Alehouse in the care of a common Servant; there being no regular appointment of Post-master'. This was contrary, he noted, 'to the improved regulations which have taken place in the . . . Post Office'. Ga[nn]at proudly wrote of his town's 'manufactories, navigable canals, and excise revenue of £43,000 a year'. Because 'great numbers of the inhabitants' were 'sending their letters by private hands', Ga[nn]att implored Freeling to appoint a postmaster in Dudley.[249] It is significant that Freeling read and commented on the letter. The Royal Mail not only supported trade, it listened to the pleas of an ordinary midlands merchant.

In 1792, another ardent letter signed by 'inhabitants' and 'gentlemen of the neighbourhood' was sent to Anthony Todd, the most powerful man in the Post Office. It contained a petition for a new postal route from St Andrews to Ansthruther. St Andrews was nine miles from Anstruther across country, but residents had to send mail there by way of Edinburgh, a circuit of 100 miles. 'I concur', wrote Todd, though he did not 'expect any great addition to the Revenue . . . on account of the general accommodation

it will afford to that part of the country'.[250] Further letters show individual
requests were passed on to Lord Walsingham, the Postmaster General,
who was advocating reform.[251] Because the Post Office now 'worked',
people wanted it. Most important, their letters were infused with a sense
of entitlement. A debate was being waged about the function of the Royal
Mail—about how to balance its many roles with the duty to provide
public service. This duty was expressed in a letter from a Mr Miles that was
quoted at the opening of this chapter. His idea that a letter was a 'sacred'
object was a new phenomenon, which had developed with the institution
that carried it.[252]

   The debate about the role of the Royal Mail reached a crisis after 1774.
Courts had ruled that the Post Office could no longer charge an extra
penny for carrying letters directly to homes inside post towns. Officials had
to find ways to finance home delivery and soothe an insistent public. 'The
mode of receiving & of transmitting letters', townspeople complained, 'is
at once irregular and insecure.'[253] Citizens, however, resisted paying more
postage. Documents reveal the difficult situation in which officials were
placed. Parliament, advised Lord Mansfield, should 'not leave it to every
Postmaster to exact what Sum he shall think fit and persuade People to give
him'. Yet it was evident that not every one could come to the Post Office.
This was especially true for women and the poor, who did not have daily
contact with the commercial world.[254]

   The decision, in fact, left many problems. It remained unclear where
town lines were to be drawn, who would carry, who would pay, and
if this rule might extend to rural areas.[255] We are 'much at loss what
directions to give', a document concluded.[256] As Holdsworth observed:
'Central control over the machinery of the posts was small...It was
for a long time uncertain whether postmasters were obliged to deliver
letters...without charge, or whether they could charge for delivery.'[257] A
King's Bench opinion in 1774 showed a profound shift had taken place
regarding public service. 'It is better that the Post Master that undertakes
this Office should undergo Inconveniences', it declared, 'than all the
people should.' This new way of thinking stoked fears about universal
carriage, especially in manufacturing towns.[258] Postmasters might soon be
forced to carry letters 'to every Hole and Courner of the country'.[259] 'If a
postmaster was obliged to send a person with the letters to all the Villages
within his delivery', wrote an official, 'I do not know who would be a
postm^r.'[260]

This inclusiveness was a democratic concept that was remarkable for its time. So were the high emotions that were evident on both sides of the debate. In 1777, Secretary Anthony Todd received a complaint from a postal employee about extensive franking by merchants. 'Nay if I class'd with them almost every little pretty Miss capable of joining her Letters, I should not exaggerate the abuse: for either a Father, a Brother, A friend or a Lover is to be found to avoid the Act, however dissimilar the Hand Writing... without... any Credit for the great advantages they derive from the... Post Office.'[261] In addition to describing franking abuse, the letter disclosed the existence of a vast nation of letter-writers. The experience of correspondents included in this chapter confirms the truth of this view.

The levelling aspect of letter-writing had political implications. Because a personal letter was enclosed and paid for, it became private property outside the supervision of the state. As postal service became more commonplace, letters offered convenient venues for individual expression of critical views. On a wider level, a non-elite group of writers and readers were participating in a nationwide institution, which linked them to the world of public opinion. The newspaper, novel, and coffeehouse are often cited in regard to the rise of the public sphere, but the letter and the Post Office are rarely mentioned. Yet the Post Office created a public space for private conversations of people ranging from paupers to professionals. As it did so, it offered shared experiences to a nation of letter-writers. The Royal Mail not only circulated newspapers throughout the nation, it carried the letters in which private judgements were expressed. This arena of unrestricted discourse was as provocative to the state as any coffeehouse.[262] By 1800, a service created to censor mail had become a private necessity and a public right.

PART II

Creating a culture of literacy

3

Letters and literacy

Farmers and workers in northern England

The Post Office served the entire nation, but writers far from London had a special need for its service. One such correspondent was a wheelwright's apprentice in rural Derbyshire. His courtship letters with a domestic servant make fascinating reading. In the 1740s, they were filled with references to Shakespeare, Milton, Addison, and Swift. Yet how could two servants in isolated villages have read these authors and written these letters?

Northern England, we are told, was a secluded backwater with few schools and little literacy in the 1740s.[1] It was inhabited by humble farming folk, who rarely travelled beyond their villages. Mud-soaked roads and poor communications created insurmountable barriers to the wider world. Not until the nineteenth century would educational reforms bring schools and literacy to the North. It would be fruitless, therefore, to look for a literary letter written by a love-sick apprentice. Yet the existence of this letter, and of others like it, raises questions about the extent of eighteenth-century literacy.

This chapter shows how persons with little formal education acquired and used letter-writing in their daily lives. Drawing on rich unexpected archives in the North of England, it depicts the inner worlds of farmers and workers. Our letter-writers started life as small husbandmen or low-status craftsmen, but their livelihoods changed in response to life cycles and economic conditions. They occupied the upper layer of the working class in rural areas that were undergoing change. In contrast to the middling sort described in Chapter 4, they worked with their hands, followed a trade, and were dependent on others. Naturally, their social relationships and lifestyles also differed. Letters show their families in stages of downward and upward mobility. The most successful became members of the middling sort, but the focus here is on their early lives.

At present, quantitative methods are used to determine rates of popular literacy. The standard practice is to count signatures in parish records and compare them with marks made by those who could not write. Data is then subdivided by age, gender, occupation, and other factors and converted into percentages of literate and illiterate people. Quantitative methods have produced valuable comparisons of literacy for a range of people, periods, and locations.

This book introduces a complementary qualitative method, in the hope that it can add to our understanding of literacy. In fact, the unexpected discovery of so many non-elite correspondences inexorably propelled this book's direction toward the topic of popular literacy. The sheer numbers and depth of letters written by people below the rank of gentry, offered an opportunity to look at literacy at the moment of actual use—in this case in writing letters. A plan was devised to use long runs of correspondence as a basis for case studies of lower-sort writers (see Appendix I).

To link letter-writing practices to the study of literacy, a new cultural category—'epistolary literacy'—has been introduced. The possession of epistolary literacy meant far more than signing one's name. Those who enjoyed it could write coherent prose and engage in accepted epistolary conventions. With practice, they were able to conduct business and construct personal relationships. Epistolary literacy was thus a valuable skill, which gave its owner a certain standing in the community.

In order to evaluate a writer's level of epistolary literacy, groups of factors that appear in all types of letters were analysed in each case study. They included visible elements of the material letter, such as layout, spelling, and epistolary conventions. Intellectual aspects of letters were also evaluated: for example, scope of contents; use of language; presence of imaginative inputs; and development of literary strategies. Without counting letters, therefore, the literacy of farmers and workers was analysed and compared.

Northern archives were used as a test case to see if letters written by people below the rank of gentry could be found. The high level of literacy in Scotland and the porous nature of northern boundaries suggested that non-elite letter collections might have survived in northern England. Once located, it was hoped that letters might show changes that were transforming the North into a place of economic vitality. This was indeed the finding of the case studies. They dovetail nicely with those of current works about the North/South divide in the eighteenth century. Hence, Mark Billinge, Neville Kirk, and Dave Russell suggest the presence of 'a growing North and a stagnant (later even a declining) South'.[2]

Before proceeding, a word about selection criteria is in order. Historians have used a range of definitions to describe 'the North', although highland topography and early industrial development are constant factors.[3] Some restrict their definitions to the six or seven counties closest to Scotland (Cumberland, Westmorland, Lancashire, Northumberland, Durham, Yorkshire, and sometimes Cheshire) which they label the 'far North'. Others include northern midland counties and call this the 'near North'.[4] Chapters 1, 3, and 4 describe letter-writers from Cumberland, Westmorland, Lancashire, Northumberland, Yorkshire, and Derbyshire. The latter seemed important to include in this period, since shifts in its economy made it 'a southern partner in an increasingly northern enterprise'. Its wild rugged terrain also linked it to the 'broader regional stereotype, which defined the North of England as an industrial "Land of the Working Class"'.[5]

Four case studies are arranged in chronological order and analysed thematically. The fifth spans the entire century and integrates previous topics. All the letter-writers worked in rural areas, which have been less studied with regard to literacy than urban locations. None of them had to wait until the nineteenth century to acquire epistolary literacy. How they did so is explained in the rest of the chapter.

The Wheatcrofts of Ashover: Discovering preconditions for epistolary literacy

The lives of Leonard Wheatcroft, 'the Black Poet of Ashover' (1627–1706) and his son, Titus (1679–1762) shed light on a key question: was it possible to acquire reading and writing skills in rural areas like Derbyshire? Without these basic competencies, a more specialized epistolary literacy could not have developed. The Wheatcroft papers demonstrate that by the early eighteenth century, three preconditions for epistolary literacy existed in rural Ashover: access to informal schooling, availability of local scribes, and the growing need for all forms of writing. The Wheatcrofts were well aware of the value of written records and immersed themselves in reading, copying, adapting, and composing narratives about their lives. They grasped every chance to use their reading and writing skills, and passed them on to others.

The son of a country tailor, Leonard worked at various occupations. At different seasons and stages of life, he was a tailor, small-scale farmer, gardener, virginal tuner, carpenter, soldier, water-works craftsman, parish clerk, and schoolteacher. But the leisure activity that pleased him most was his personal writing. He authored a long autobiography, a courtship narrative filled with letters, and other unpublished manuscripts.[6]

Leonard's home lay four miles east of Matlock and seven miles south of Chesterfield. By the late seventeenth century, Ashover claimed almost 800 inhabitants in 190 households.[7] Yet Wheatcroft's horizons stretched far beyond its fields, and his life was marked by change. He roamed across northern England, partly for reasons of trade, and partly for the sheer delight of visiting fairs, markets, and friends. In one year, he claimed, he journeyed 550 miles. His brother moved to London, where he became a draper and employed three of Leonard's sons as apprentices. Though Wheatcroft's daughters eventually went into service, their training was not neglected. 'I put Leo and Ester to Darby to learne sum better worke and breeding', he noted in 1675, 'after that to Nottingham.'[8] As we shall see, geographic mobility that included sending kin to London was common to families featured in this book.

Wheatcroft was called a 'yeoman' as early as 1658. But after three periods of imprisonment for debt, he lost his house and had to pawn his goods. His wife helped out by selling ale—an indication of their low status. By 1680, however, his son reclaimed part of the property and Leonard resumed his position as parish clerk and registrar.[9] For literate people like Wheatcroft, parish posts offered opportunities for training and advancement. In 1680, he began 'to teach scoole and had many schollers for the space of two years'. Another period of teaching took place in 1683, 'being perswaded by my neighbours that I would take upon me to teach a scoole'.[10] His early teaching was done in informal meeting places that do not appear in lists of licensed schools. They help to explain the presence of hidden rural literacy.

Though work and parish activities filled his busy life, Leonard found time for creative writing in his secretary hand. Into a long autobiography entitled 'A history of my birth parantage and pilgrimage',[11] he pasted letters and local documents.[12] Leonard's handwritten literary miscellany was entitled: 'The Art of Poetry, or Come you gallants, Looke and buy, Heare is mirth and melody'. It imitated popular miscellanies from London and showcased verses drawn from printed and oral sources.[13] Addressed 'To the Reader',[14] the manuscript adopted features of published books, such as title page and layout.[15] As he filled it with drinking songs, anagrams, and poetry, Leonard wove popular literature into his work.[16]

Wheatcroft's skill in letter-writing was revealed in a narrative about his courtship with his future wife, Elizabeth. A long series of love letters—probably a blend of fact and fiction—were inserted into the text and presented as real dated correspondence. Wheatcroft defined the letter 'as a messenger of my thoughts' sent 'to kiss your hand... but heart also'.[17] 'O my dearest Love', he moaned, 'How loung must I waite at the pool of your Bethesda?' (John 5:2) 'I pray you accept of this letter as a token of my unchangeable love.'[18] Elizabeth asked if Leonard's letters were 'serious or feigned'[19] and wondered where he 'learned all these fine compliments'?[20]

As Cedric Brown has shown, he found them in romances, chivalric tales, and the bible. Then he altered what he read to reflect his own natural speech. Aware of literary rhetoric, he self-consciously shaped his narrative by blending life experience with printed material.[21] Because Wheatcroft steeped himself in reading and writing, he was known as a local author. At a public competition against a rival poet, he was 'decked with lorill branches' before 'a great company' at Ashover hill. Leonard claimed his work was read by a network of local luminaries that included the Duke of Rutland.[22] Not surprisingly, he bequeathed his passion for writing to his eldest son Titus.

Titus began 'to work of the tayler trade in the yeare 1690'.[23] He finished his father's autobiography, and inherited Leonard's post as parish clerk, serving from 1706–52. Titus's voluminous manuscript collections and commonplace books include youthful writing exercises. (See Plate 16.) His Church and School or the Young Clarks Instructor describes Ashover's school and its library.[24] This institution gave students a basic literacy that provided a foundation for writing letters.[25] Like his father, Titus was asked to informally teach local children. 'I [had] begun to teach school', he noted, 'in thate house which is called Twitchbanks and was there a year 1699. Then I taught in Solomon parlor 1 year and a halfe, then at Towndrow house in Ashover hill 2 years and a halfe.' Houses and parlours in rural towns and villages offered makeshift venues for learning.

By 1704, a school was endowed by William Hodgkinson for the use of poor children.[26] After it opened, Titus stated proudly, 'I taught in it a quarter of a year before any other schoolmaster came.' William Heald,

who had taught at Darley for eight years, soon became master at £20 per
year. Titus, however, seemed pleased with his own £5, 'which money
was raised by subscription'. Later he spoke of teaching for '24 years and
at £4 per year is £96'.[27] In 1712, the town attracted two singing masters
from Leicester who 'taught halfe a yeare above 50 schollers'.[28] Thus, early
in the century and far from London, Ashover was supporting educational
amenities.

We can picture the endowed school built 'North from the church...on
a very pleasant hill side' with its face standing 'near the twelve a clock
sun'.[29] A spring in the courtyard brought water 'for the use of ye Mr and
Schollers to quench their thirst and to clean their hands that they may not
sulley their books'. Over the school door, a motto in Latin claimed 'an
unruly or untoward youth, by the care and pains of a diligent master, may
become more pliable and dutifull (or to that effect)'. Built of 'very good
free stone' with five windows and a fireplace, the school was over ten yards
long, 'the breadth...five yards...very well paved wth great stone'. The
chamber was 'almost halfe compas of the school with a good Large writing
table, and a writing-desk fitted very conveniently for the writing boys and
girls'. This comment shows that some girls in rural Derbyshire were trained
to write, as well as read. The building could accommodate 120 scholars,
a large number for a rural area. Yet there was still 'good room for the
Master to walk amongst them to instruct them in the rules of writing, and
arithmatick'.

Titus also wrote about the school's surroundings. Students looked out
onto 'a very pritty Court, or garden...and at every corner...there is
placed a birch-tree, that ye mr may not want Rodds for the moderate
correction of his unruly schollers'. Between every birch there were '2
handsome spreading Sycamores for to sit under'. Around several trees there
was 'placed a good and handome stone bench for boys to sit and play
at and get their dinners in summer time'. In inclement weather, 'a good
[causey?]' between church and school ensured that 'Mr and Schollers may
go to church decently and in order'. This rare portrait of a country school
shows its careful construction and central place in the cultural life of the
community.

The school's broad range of reading material is described in 'A Catalogue or Roll. Of the names of All the Books that I Titus Wheatcroft
have Feb. 16. 1722. With the Number and price of them.'[30] This is a

38-page list of 384 books valued at £32. It cites other manuscripts by Titus including: 'The Clerk and his Companions...a book of my own composing in question and answer, valued at 16s'. Maureen Bell has prepared an analysis of Titus's book catalogue. Her preliminary work indicates it contains 50 per cent religious titles, 20 per cent school books and texts (including language and spelling, oratory, rhetoric, penmanship, shorthand, dictionaries, and copybooks), and 30 per cent literature, the humanities, and sciences.[31] With one exception, there are no Latin authors.[32] Most titles are old ones, acquired second hand and valued at under 2s., with only 7 per cent worth more than 4s. There were at least seven booksellers in Derby from 1675–1722. Others might be found in Chesterfield and Ashborne by 1700, and in nearby Winksworth by the 1720s. Titus could therefore buy low-cost school books without making a long journey.[33]

Ashover's school and library were not unique in Derbyshire. In addition to its ancient grammar schools, there were small schools like the one in Tideswell. As early as the 1570s, it operated with the help of pupil teachers. Every Friday, the upper forms had exercises 'only in writing until they c[ould] write handsomely their own Lattins and lessons'.[34] A nineteenth-century survey documented seventy-four endowed charity schools in Derbyshire, which likely represents the tip of the educational iceberg. Most of them taught reading and writing to the poor free of charge. Some were later housed in purpose-built schools, others in teachers' homes or churches.[35] As a map by Marion Johnson shows, by the 1730s there were free schools in most Derbyshire villages, as well as bookshops and printers in main towns.[36] Yet the Victoria County History of Derbyshire cites only sixty-four schools by 1800.[37] These facts raise questions about the assumption that northern literacy was stagnant before 1800.

Ashover, in fact, offered access to local schools and books. Moreover, all forms of writing were becoming increasingly important, even to people who could not write themselves. We know that Leonard was paid for writing verses to commemorate local events and landowners. Perhaps he also composed letters for illiterate neighbours. Unpublished local manuscripts record the work of village scribes, who earned fees for writing letters and deeds, or did so free of charge for friends. Their existence in rural areas was another precondition for the rise of epistolary literacy.[38]

Three scribes of this period are likely to be representative of other brokers. Roger Lowe (d. 1679), who minded shop in Ashton, Lancashire, kept accounts of the writing he did for others in the 1660s and 1670s. Lowe acted as a notary in tandem with shopkeeping and was 'regarded as somewhat of a scholar'. Wallace Notestein believed 'his education and his utilitarian knowledge gave him an authority that came just short of elevating his position'. Writing, he suggested, offered Lowe the freedom of self-expression that he lacked in his job of minding someone else's store.[39] Along with writing wills, presentments, and indentures, he was paid to teach youths 'to endite letters and to cast accounts up'. Lowe proudly remarked he was often 'sent for' to write letters. Sometimes they had practical objectives; other times they concerned the heart. When a client told him 'he loved a wench in Ireland...the day after I writ a love letter for him'.[40] Roger received 1s. from Widow Low for copying a sermon, 6d. for a bond, and a whopping 11s. 9d. from old Jenkins for drafting a will and other papers.[41]

Like Lowe, John Cannon (1684–1743), a former excise man and parish official in Somerset, acted as community scribe and recorded his fees. He was self-taught in maths, read widely, collected grammars, and instructed others in a local school. Writing his autobiography became his most pleasurable avocation. Like the Wheatcrofts, Cannon inserted letters and manuscripts into his writing.[42]

In his spare time, Sussex shopkeeper, Thomas Turner (1729–93) wrote documents and letters for neighbours in the 1750s and 1760s. In 1756, he composed a letter for Mr Piper, then sent it by carrier with other papers. Unfortunately, 'the poor old wretch sneaked away without ever offering to pay for paper etc., though all of it together, to wit, paper, sealing-wax and thread amount[ed] to 1d.'[43] Turner's low costs suggest his services were available to ordinary people.

Like the Wheatcrofts, Turner kept school for a bit, then quit when it bored him. He charged 3–6d. per week for instruction and was able to use the late schoolmaster's library. David Vaisey's account of Turner's reading reveals a well-versed man in touch with current affairs. Turner's experience confirms the prevalence of intermittent teaching in rural locales. His students entered and left school in different seasons, depending on their work and the state of family finances. None of the people cited in this chapter discussed their own education. It is likely that they learned their skills from someone like themselves.

The Soresbies of Brailsford: 'Vive la plume'

Teachers and scribes reveal glimpses of rural landscapes where it was possible to acquire epistolary literacy. This was certainly true for the Soresbie family of Darley and Brailsford, Derbyshire.[44] Their stunning archive, which has lain unnoticed by scholars, was shaped by seven generations from the 1670s–1840s. It contains deeds, bonds, wills, marriage settlements, financial accounts, legal documents, genealogical material, writing exercises, copybooks, school records, and religious books, as well as correspondence. These surrounding documents offer a rich context for interpreting lives and letters. They uncover patterns in the preservation of family papers, which are normally associated with the gentry. Soresbie records mark life's passages: births and deaths, courtships and marriages, and financial and legal landmarks. They prove that once the family became literate, they passed on writing skills to their children. Descendants, in turn, added new documents in premeditated ways.[45]

The archive provides a foundation for the case studies that follow by allowing us to analyse a family's records, generation by generation. As we do so we can tease out hidden pathways that led to literacy and letter-writing. Letters from 1677–1829 reveal different levels of literacy, as well as changes in handwriting from secretary and italic to a flowing, round hand. (See Plates 17–20.) There are more in-coming than out-going letters, for copies required twice the amount of costly paper. Drafts were hence routinely made on the backs of other records. Letters of rural workers were usually brief and direct. Some were written for practical ends and specific to local farmers; others met social and psychological needs. They lessened loneliness, relieved fears of illness, expressed love, sought patronage, and provided lewd entertainment. Often, writers divulged problems of economic survival. They also articulated how the ability to write letters helped farmers to cope with life. Unlike some husbandmen, whose fortunes declined with enclosure and industrialization, the Soresbies became substantial yeomen.[46] Their letters not only reflected changing economic conditions, their epistolary literacy likely contributed to their later prosperity.

The earliest document in the archive, cited in the introduction, is the first engraved copybook published in England: *A Booke Containing Divers Sortes of hands* by John de Beauchesne published in 1571. (See Plate 1, 1602

edition.) Its presence in a tiny northern hamlet offers powerful evidence
of how rural literacy spread. This thumb-worn volume not only taught
writing, it showed how to cut quills, mix ink, and hold a pen. It was not
surprising to find a homemade copybook nestled nearby. Its owner had
proudly endorsed it: 'Charles Soosby ... His Book ... Learning is bether
then ether house or Land ... 1678.' (See Plate 17.) Inside he printed a
rough country poem, which offered a 'chalinge' to the rival 'stout ~~contons~~
comptons boys'. The book also contained copies of jokes and verses,
for example: 'They killed or: king with Staves & Axes/For w.ch Greatt
Brittan—Now Payes Taxes. Liber nos domine.'[47] This volume was one of
many generations of copybooks preserved by the Soresbies. It is a perfect
example of collections of popular literature—local lore, proverbs, puzzles,
jokes, songs, and poetry—found in archives of rural families. Without
them, we would be unable to see how the technology of writing was
acquired through acts of copying. When youngsters proceeded to original
composition, they often turned to letters—a well- known, accessible genre.

The earliest Soresbie letters written from 1677–89 belonged to Roger,
husbandman of Darley (d. 1693).[48] In 1677 his 'cosen' Dorothy used letters
to remind loved ones of her presence. 'These are to let you cnow', she
wrote phonetically, 'that I gate well to Kneeton.'[49] (See Plate 18.) Of
course spelling at this time was a free-for-all for both sexes. But though
it took a long time for Dorothy to compose letters, her opinions were
forcefully stated. In another message, she chided Roger for neglect and
noted reproachfully: 'I heard my cosen eliner had bene veri ill and ... yo
ws sum case of ... her ill nes.'[50] Though Dorothy lacked skill, she knew
epistolary rules and never apologized for her work.

In the next generation Edward (1665–1729),[51] a Darley husbandman,
married Jane Moseley of Brailsford, where the family now farmed.[52] Edward's wills, inventories, marriage settlement, and business letters survive.[53]
In addition, a love letter to Jane contains apologies for 'bad writing &
inditeing'.[54] Her sister's homemade copybook[55] lies near elegant printed
editions of French and Latin copybooks owned by the Ferrars and Shirley
families.[56] Different ranks simultaneously used copybooks to acquire distinct
levels of literacy.

The bulk of the archive belonged to Gilbert Soresbie Sr (d. 1775), who
probably assembled the collection.[57] In 1732 he gave 'poor people of our
parish ... ye meal dish full of corn'. He was also able to hire a servant.
Later in life he served as churchwarden, grand juryman, constable, tax

collector, and joined the Brailsford Society for the Prosecution of Felons.[58] To hold these jobs that marked his rising status, he needed good writing skills. They are found in abundance in his handmade copybook, adorned with geometric designs.[59] Gilbert also left notebooks, arithmetic exercises, a hand-ruled stitched booklet containing 'Meditations for Christians', a valentine, and phonetically written country poems.[60] He saved coarse letters about sex,[61] letters about property for legal evidence,[62] and one to a daughter praising her 'Extraordinary Improvement in those necessary Accomplishments of writing and accompt'.[63]

On the other side of this letter is a draft seeking employment from a 'Most Honoured Sir'. 'If your worship please to Honour so mean a Man', he wrote, 'I hope... I shall gain your Favour: for Having gott some learning... Especially Accounts... would willing Increase it.' Gilbert wished to be 'serviceable to my Master & for ye Creditt of both hi[s] [hon]or and me.' This last pronoun suggests that though Gilbert was deferential, he was also proud. 'An accont of my Breeding & behavior... would Re-comend me to your service', he insisted. He concluded with hopes that his reader 'will never here no worse a Carrector then is here present' and begged 'Leave to Subs[cribe]/My Self Sir yr Humble & obed[ient]/Servant'.[64] (See Plate 19.) Though Gilbert's epistolary skills lacked polish, he knew that a convincing letter could open doors to employment. It was crucial for him to read, write, and keep accounts of his farming and parish activities. Much has been written about the merchant's need for writing skills. They were also necessary to maintain a farmer's status in a changing agricultural world.

Gilbert Sr's son, Gilbert Jr (1750–c.1836) was the family's first trained calligrapher. At the age of 13, he tooled his initials on the cover of his book of math problems. The title page adorned with leaves in red and black ink announced the owner: GILBERT SORSBY, His Book: 1763, Vive la Plume. (See frontispiece.) Gilbert Jr's joy in writing well is found on every ornamented page: headings are flourished, tables are ruled, and answers are shaded with his pen—a product worthy of the writing master, who must have taught him. Another volume shared with his sisters is a long elaborately copied manuscript, 'The Church Catechism Explained', with many signatures on the back page claiming this was 'his' or 'her' book.[65] 'An ingenious Person is an Ornament to the Nation', wrote Gilbert Jr over and over in one of his many writing books.[66] (See Plate 20.) But though his round 'copperplate' hand resembled those of highly trained merchants, Gilbert Jr copied texts and maths problems about corn, cattle, and land.[67] He also printed verses about country girls in agricultural settings, such as 'The Reconcilement', 'The Birth of Kisses', and 'The Lasses Lamentation'.[68] His books and letters were rural variants of those penned by merchants' sons. Like them, Gilbert Jr was steeped in a culture that required excellent writing skills.

Late eighteenth- and nineteenth-century copybooks were added to the archive by Maria Jane Soresbie (1843–72). She also preserved *The Parents' Best Gift containing Catechism and Prayers* and *The English Language Grammatically Written in all the Usual Hands AND The True Italian Method of Book keeping*.[69] Her forebear, Mary Soresbie (b. 1738), daughter of Roger Soresbie (d. 1762) had married William Cox (b. 1742), a descendant of the late seventeenth-century tutor to Earl Ferrars. By 1821, Mary's son Edward Soresbie Cox owned land in nearby Culland and in Brailsford. In contrast, Roger's brother, Gilbert Sr (d. 1775), who had held high-status parish offices, found his resources 'stretched thinly' late in life. His son, Gilbert Jr (1750–c.1836) had to sell his farm and become a tenant. When it was sold again to a rival kinsman, he moved away, rather than pay rent to his competitor. In 1846, other Soresbies in the village were listed as carriers, farmers, and lead merchants.[70] The upward and downward mobility of rural life is sharply exposed in family letters.

Why did the Soresbies spend hours copying alphabets, exercises, and poetry into homemade books? Why were these volumes saved for posterity in every generation? Did this have something to do with the family's upward social mobility? And what can we learn from the presence of these books? I believe copybooks offer evidence that rural literacy was needed and valued. They reveal how skills might be acquired, within and without institutions, in a culture that prized writing. They also show the educational aspirations of rural farmers. Copybooks gave precious evidence of family literacy and were proudly saved for that reason, like the portraits and plate of aristocrats. They were foundational documents for the development of epistolary literacy and, sometimes, economic success.

Copybooks that mixed bawdy verses with religious meditations contributed to the development of popular culture. This culture owed a debt to the process of copying, which was regarded differently than it is today.[71] By the late seventeenth century, it was deemed a valuable skill, which was 'almost universal among the educated'.[72] Indeed, copying had 'richer connotations than mere reproduction, imitation, or mimicry in our modern, generally derogatory sense'. When used in personal copybooks, it became an 'attempt to give meaning to the scattered incidents of an individual life'.[73] The Soresbies, I believe, had this high sense of the copyist. Their notebooks not only encouraged regular writing habits, they led onward to familiarity with mathematics, law, poetry, and other branches of knowledge. Though the Soresbies were, at first imitators, the passages they copied marked their entry into a world of original composition. This was an example of a culture rising upwards from the crucible of local experience.

The principal message of the Soresbie archive was that literacy and writing were prized in every generation. Though we know of no endowed school in Brailsford, the family owned books and spent money on informal schooling for sons *and* daughters.[74] In a bundle of Gilbert Sr's papers, an undated letter in an eighteenth-century hand speaks of hiring someone as a village teacher: 'Tell him my father and mother is well pleased and freely willinge to Allowe him his Diet Lodginge and what other necessaries may be thought Conveinent... There are severall in this our towne and Parrish of Brelsforth who will Come to be Instructed by him and give him A Reasonable Allowance for his service.'[75] Groups of parents thus banded together to find teachers for their children. They hired local residents, often women, who charged by the week and might be paid with local produce. Thus in 1752, Gilbert Sr sent Lydy Evans a cheese and butter, in addition to 2s. 2d. for nineteen weeks of Ann's tuition.

Running balances for teaching fees were reckoned at Christmas, Easter, and in the summer. Gilbert Sr's records of tuition money paid from May 1748–October 1752 are revealing. During that time, four different women taught his daughters, Ann, Jane, and Elinor. The girls studied for a bit, dropped out, and then returned. Over a four year period, Gilbert Sr spent a total of £1 11s. 2d. for the three girls. Ann was the most regular scholar, studying most of the year, whilst Jane and Elinor had less instruction. Fees averaged about 1–3d. a week. In addition to normal teaching, in 1748 Mrs Johnson was paid an extra 6d. at Christmas 'for Ann going now and then to read'. For the brightest Soresbie girl, extra education was evidently available. Gilbert Sr's accounts start again in 1756, when he paid Lettis Britain 6s. 3d. for twenty-five weeks of school for Gilbert Jr. Once he reached the age of six, Gilbert Jr attended regularly. Ester and Frances joined their brother from 1756–9. Their combined tuition was 14s. 6d. in 1756, 14s. 1d. in 1758, and 9s. 2d. in 1759.[76]

These accounts demonstrate that interested parents found and shared teachers in rural villages. But though fees were not large, they were constant, and a large family's expenses mounted. Poor families surely could not afford these costs. Nevertheless, the Soresbies' archive tells us that rural literacy was both possible and valued. We see this most tellingly in a series of Gilbert Sr's letters about a disputed will of his brother Charles (c.1700–63). Because no one had witnessed his signature, a lawsuit threatened.[77] This was important because Gilbert Sr might inherit a silver porringer, spoons, cups, buttons, clothes, linen, and books.[78] This commonplace tale found in letters suggests what the Soresbies had known for centuries: a person's handwriting was an extension of the individual and a precious possession. That is why seven generations cultivated it so assiduously and saved their writings for posterity.[79]

Joseph Morton of Scotland, Cumberland, and Westmorland

The Wheatcrofts and Soresbies enjoyed a settled way of life. This was not the case for unskilled labourers, who wandered about England seeking stable employment in the second half of the eighteenth century. Most worked at several occupations trying to make ends meet. As shown in the introduction, some, like Joseph Morton, had hopes to 'Rays in the Worald'. Yet his letters disclose how hard it was for landless workers to secure a livelihood.[80] They capture the restless migration and economic fragility of workers in north-west England. Transportation and communications were improving in places with trade and industry. But in Cumberland and Westmorland, where Morton wandered, the independent yeoman farmer was threatened by changing economic conditions. By 1800, the number of these landholders had declined.[81] A literate population would certainly be needed, if the region was to attract trade and industry.

The phonetically written letters of Joseph Morton from 1765–99 were the popular equivalent of elite memoirs and travel writing.[82] Morton used them to gain employment, maintain family ties, and to meet psychological needs of an immigrant, who was lonely and insecure. The son of weavers, Joseph had left Kelso in Scotland to find stable employment. In 1765, he arrived in Kendal, a town noted for its small workshops and textiles.[83] He planned to do gardening for large farmers or absentee landlords, whilst earning money from raising vegetables on his own plot. He would also sell pieces of cloth made by his Scottish family and send them some of the profits. This was not an unusual career path for the place and period. There were strong economic ties between southern Scotland and northern England and they shared high rates of literacy.[84] Kelso was a centre for weavers, who supplemented work at the loom with small-scale farming. In the 1760s, Kendal traders imported wool from Scotland; then returned finished cloth to Glasgow for colonial export.[85] On his 124-mile journey to Kendal, Morton visited Scottish emigrés with ambitions like his own. One of them, James Stalker, took him to an iron forge, 'all going by the Stress of watter both hammer and Bellows'. He thus witnessed the effects of the new industrial ventures that would transform northern England.[86]

Morton's letters to his Scottish family were written in a large italic hand. Spelling was erratic, but there was an attempt at punctuation. Joseph's limited vocabulary was repeated over and over and was specific to his personality. For example, he used 'thank God' on all occasions and wrote the word 'garding' for 'garden' or 'gardening'. Well aware of epistolary conventions, he addressed his 'Honnored Parrants' and 'Dear Brother'. He described himself as 'Your Ever Dutifull and affectinat Jos: Morton' and carefully noted dates and places. Joseph's claim to fame, however, was his intimate knowledge of postal practices. As we have seen previously, when messengers were unavailable he wrote 'Single Sheet' on the envelope to avoid a double charge.[87]

Despite technical flaws, Morton wrote openly with loving affection. Yet this freshness was accompanied by a rhetorical strategy aimed at presenting himself in the best possible light. This tactic was especially useful when things went wrong. Letters to his family revealed recurring patterns. Some were written to announce successful life passages; others to admit failures. Letters of disappointment always generated requests for gifts of cloth and money. They also showed his longing for emotional support. Yet Morton learned to phrase delicate subjects positively. His optimism boosted his spirits and enabled him to save face, for he deeply loved his family. Because he craved their respect, Morton used letters to report the praise of others. This habit grew stronger with each failure. Consequently his letters must not be seen not as crude missives, but as artful constructions that confirmed the value of his life.

In fact, Joseph's years in England were marked by constant struggle. He went from one ill-paid gardening job to another and lost the small plot he had cultivated himself. Yet no matter how bad things were, he continued to write optimistically. From his first job in Cartmell, near Kendal, he reported that his diet was 'the Best I Ever Dide in my Life'.[88] Two years later, he was working for an absentee landlord Mr Jacob Morland,[89] where he had the 'management of the Garding myself'. I 'Dous as I think proper', he wrote, and 'nobody to find fallt with me'.[90] This was Morton's first reference to the master/servant relationship—a topic that filled later letters.

Morton married a local girl, Augness Tennant. Though 'winter stockings is...turning thin',[91] he wrote cheerfully, 'I hope that we Shall Lead a happy and a greeable Life to the Glory of God and our own Interest, in this Life and that Which is to Come...Now I think myself Settled in the Worald and hopes to make a Very Good Liveing'[92] 'I am Lookit on Very Well', he insisted, and 'Exspect to Rays in the Worald as Well as you have Done.'[93]

In 1770, he took a fourteen-year lease on a property called the Farmery. He hoped it would yield £20 a year in seeds and vegetables.[94] 'I am Very well beloved in this place', he claimed, 'and several Genttleman [are] Going to Drop there owen Gardings for they think they can heave them Better from me.'[95] At first, Morton sold cloth sent by his brother, but illness and bad weather brought hardship. He soon owed his family £17.[96] To deal with this failure, he used heightened exaggeration as an epistolary tactic: 'I believe Money [was] never more Scarch in this Cuntry this 20 or 30 years', he moaned, unable to repay his debts. His wife bore 'a Son thought to be as Large a Child as Ever Was born', but 'no body Exspected She would see next morning'.[97] 'I is in the place to which I belong', he maintained, 'so if there be any neadeseetity I...may Get the parash to Stand my friend...I and my familey will become a Charge upon them untill I be outherways provieded for.'[98]

To avoid poor relief, Morton took a gardening job at Levens Hall, a seat of the absent Earl of Suffolk. As a result, he gave up his independence. Not only did he lose his land and dreams, he could only see his family one night per week. Nor could he travel, for he 'must not be off the place unless bussiness requires'. After thirteen years in England, Joseph had little freedom. But he was thankful to be employed,[99] with '£10 wadges and £10..8..0 Bourd' and 'a Deal of parkesets or Vails, as no families is hear but the stured'.[100]

Because of his lack of freedom, Morton used letter-writing to express his longing for independence. He chafed against the steward's authority, who 'rules all in this place...and...doss as he pleases'.[101] Though he could 'live at a very modret Exspence', having 'got unto a noublemans familie', he 'must apear Clean and Deacent'.[102] As Winchester notes of the region, 'even in this comparatively gentry-free environment, the impact of large landowners is visible'.[103] Suddenly, after receiving only partial wages, Morton lost his place. 'They wanted a young man', he claimed, 'a thing which has never been for fiftey years for they have all been Married Gardiners that has lived hear that any Man Can tell of.'[104]

After his dismissal, Morton was 'Seldom with out Some Sort of work'.[105] Happily, his three children attended 'the free School, of which hear is a Very Good one'. In fact the school at Heversham was well known as the best in the area. 'I have kept them all [there]', Morton bragged, 'Ever Since they were able to Go to one.'[106] 'I allways thought they were Better there then in the Streets.'[107] William had 'got to be the Best Scholler', wrote Joseph. 'The M^r says he neaver had a Better of his age in Schole for tho he is only 5 years old he Reads with Some that is 17.'[108] As in the Soresbie family, there was a tradition of literacy. Morton therefore strove to educate his children.

It took a year to find another place at Abbot Hall near Kendall. Even then, he was 'neaver certen whither I was to Stay the year or not'.[109] But Morton soon had a piece of luck. He was asked to ride to Bristol for his employer—a six-day mission of trust that he could never afford himself, and 'a good opertunity of seeing the Country'. In the tradition of elite tourists, Joseph wrote an epistolary travel account, faithfully observing all he saw. He must have read printed travel guides, for he followed their model of observing climate, mileage, and local attractions. He compiled a table of distances between each town visited and observed that Bristol had '19 Parash Churches besides Chappels of eas'. The town, he remarked, 'is Reconed the next City to London for Largeness'.[110]

On the journey home, Morton visited his own network of friends. At Wigan, for example, Mr William Pinkerton treated him to 'Bothe Brickfast and Dinner'.[111] In the end, he travelled 286 miles without rain until the last six miles of the trip.[112] Only a literate man could have delivered such a detailed account to his master. Morton's literacy and numeracy skills qualified him for the journey, whilst his letters became vehicles for self-expression, information, and independent opinions. Their many uses served him well, as he embraced the joys of travel.

Morton's last letter, written after a five-year silence, comes as a shock. It shows how literacy could help an insecure family improve their economic status. From Cake Row, Ryton in County Durham, Joseph suddenly reported: 'I have again Entered into Mr-Lamb's servece But in a Differant Way to What I was befor.' Lamb had 'begun to work a Colliery both for Land and Watter sale. My office', he noted, was 'to atend the pitts for the Land Sale to take pay, and Keep the Accompts for what is Sold for Ready monny or Creedet.' For this he was paid 8s. a week with 'house and fireing free'. This came to over £20 a year, or twice his former pay. His son also worked at the forge for 5s. a week. Why Joseph was chosen for this job was soon revealed. 'It takes pritty Closs atendence', he assured his reader, 'But I have Little or nothing to du But *Writting*.'[113] After twenty-one years of wandering, Joseph's literacy helped him to earn more money than he had ever known. Though he had to relocate his family, his writing job lifted him out of the lower classes and brought him the stability he craved. Morton's letters provide a rare example of how the industrial revolution affected the life of a rural worker and his family. Joseph was inexorably drawn towards an area where mining offered economic opportunities.

Literacy and letter-writing, I suggest, became increasingly important as small farmers and labourers faced economic change. Morton's letters helped him in a number of ways. They were his only link to his Scottish family and ensured they would not forget him—a desire common to emigrants. As he read their messages, he obtained emotional support. Family letters gave concrete evidence that he was not alone in the world. Yet if epistolary literacy brought psychological benefits, it also helped Morton to 'Rays in the Woarld'. When all else failed, his literacy ensured that he would work above, not inside, the mine.

John and Jenny Fawdington of Asenby

John Fawdington (1757–1817) of Asenby in the north riding of Yorkshire was a bridle-maker like his father and grandfather.[114] His letters (1781–1817) record his courtship to Jane Jefferson of Deighton (b. 1766)[115] and his journeys through northern England buying leather and selling saddles. In contrast to the Morton letters, Fawdington family records from the 1690s to the early nineteenth century describe generations of a stable family. Though Fawdington had to travel in order to peddle his wares, he had networks of family and friends in Asenby and nearby villages. Profiting from increased trade and improved transportation, he made a living from his work.

Like the Soresbies, the Fawdingtons preserved records of the births of their children. Jane Jefferson's, for instance, was recorded on a small piece of paper in a beautiful round hand. The bottom half was used to do sums, write lists, and to comment about some walnuts. Paper was expensive in Fawdington's world, and the writing on it was precious.[116]

Again like the Sorebies, the Fawdingtons preserved their copybooks. Inside John's arithmetic book, questions and answers were laboriously copied in a large 'copperplate' hand. Each page, title, and section was decorated with tasteful ornaments. The book contained story-like problems about measuring cloth, calculating inheritances, purchasing stock, and determining debts. In the back was a printed inscription: 'John Fawdington, Bubwith School Anno Domiini 1781', followed by 'J. Fawdington, Finis' and two signatures in a cursive hand.[117] Bubwith, a town of 540 families in 1822, lay 13 miles from York, and 7 from Selby. Unfortunately, we do not know how John came to be there.[118] Its school does not appear in standard lists. Yet it must have been excellent and Fawdington a good student, for his flowing round hand was exemplary.[119]

By the end of the century, John possessed a higher level of epistolary literacy than the Soresbies and Mortons. He used cursive, flourished his initials, and separated sentences with wavy lines, a fashion of the period. He also indented paragraphs and capitalized words.[120] His letters reflect the fact that spelling, punctuation, and grammar had become more standardized. John probably learned these skills at school or imitated texts in printed books. Another new element was the use of quotation marks to surround his epistolary conversations. Gone were most, but not all, phonetic spellings; present was his trademark—a flourished number eight, lying on its side beneath his signature.[121]

Fawdington's courtship letters of 1786–7 were addressed to Jenny Jefferson of Deighton, 'whose amiable and peaceful disposition . . . endeared her to all who knew her'.[122] They were filled with epistolary references: when would she write, what would she say, would the post be on time? 'How . . . gratifying to my affections', he mooned, 'to know that I am not utterly forgotten of you, or as a Dead man, out of Mind.'[123] Jenny responded to this with 'tender affection'.

Both writers were aware of polite epistolary standards and were self-conscious about how they wrote. 'I woud begin (according to the example set me by a certain amiable Female Correspondent)', John wrote teasingly, 'about half way down the first side . . . the Intervals, between every Word about an Inch & a half . . . But this foolish Pen of mine was determined to get forward in its own Stile.'[124] When writing as a lover, John wished to write without fashionable constraints.

Yet he was also aware of the language of sensibility that was sweeping the country. As his courtship progressed, therefore, he was often caught up in passionate hyperbole. 'Ah Jenny', he moaned poetically, 'when will the long wish'd for Morn appear that brings you to those Longeing Arms.'[125] 'Many a time have I wander'd alone in the Fields by Moonlight & in my usual Romantic Way whisper'd to the Passing Breaze the tender tale—Oh my Dearest Jenny Loves me.'[126] He hoped for 'Smileing Infants, Prattling on the Knee—and all the Gay luxuriancy of Wedded Bliss'.[127]

John had read romantic literature, and he emulated it in letters through reversed verbs, poignant questions, inflated language, and intimate revelations. His own poetry survives in 'Lines by the late Mr Fawdington of Asenby (on the death of a friend)'.[128] It places him within the culture of sensibility that we usually associate with elite writers.[129] Thus Jenny's letter made him 'shed ten thousand Tears . . . I cannot look at it but my eyes burst to water. What a luxery it is to weep in this Manner.'[130] By the 1780s, romanticism had found a comfortable home in the letters of a Yorkshire bridle-maker. John saw that he could play with language, and he used it in different ways for different purposes. His letters, in effect, became a training ground for expressing emotion in a literary manner. Hitherto, he had had vague amorphous feelings. Letters gave him a space for the concrete expression of falling in love.

John and Jenny finally wed in the summer of 1787, buying used furniture 'very little worse for wear', though he 'wish[ed] to purchase new'.[131] After their marriage and birth of their children, John hated to leave his family. Yet he had to travel on horseback to buy leather and sell saddles.[132] His letters from Cockermouth, Carlisle, Lancaster, Kendal, Penrith, Ulverston, Whitehaven, and Newcastle show the geographic mobility that now characterized north-east England. Letters to Jenny provided a place where he could retreat into a dream world, though he was sad when he awoke: 'I have fancied my self sleeping with my love . . . nursing my little [son]', he confessed, '& thought I saw him run away.'[133] The dream revealed his fears for his family as he rode alone through a 'wild country'.[134] During a terrifying thunder storm in 1796, Fawdington struggled to describe abstract emotions: 'I imagined the Rocks woud have been cleft asunder. I cannot give you any idea of its grandeur & sublimity. I am not apt to be much alarmed at these things, but really I felt my self agitated as I had never felt before.'[135]

John's language likely reflected passages that he had enjoyed in books, though he left no traces of his reading. 'Oh my Jenny', he sighed, 'that I coud but ... take the Wings of Tomorrow Morning & fly to thy bosom for a few short Hours and return by the same conveyance to the prosecution of this my tedious Pilgrimage.'[136] John lived in similar surroundings at the same time as romantic poets like Wordsworth, and he too communed with nature. Letters allowed him to express a range of emotions, from melancholy to the sublime. He fits the model of masculine sensibility that is often attributed to elite writers of the late eighteenth century. His letters not only expressed his inner thoughts, they helped him to fulfil literary aspirations.

Yet like every good letter-writer, John also used correspondence in practical ways. He provides an interesting view of northern commerce in letters written on the road. This different type of travel account, related to the world of work, is rarely revealed. His letters uncover a network of saddlers and bridlers, whom he met on travels or called on to collect mail. In Penrith, for example, he stayed with a Mr Brathwaite, with whom he also dined. At times he travelled with other riders as 'several stage[d] together'. Once he met 'a very capital saddler from the Isle of Mann who promised me a good order'.[137] Far-flung networks and sociability were not limited to the elite, and mobility was greater than imagined—a point also illustrated in Morton's letters. Like Morton, Fawdington understood postal practices and wrote 'Single sheet' on envelopes.[138] To avoid theft, he sent halves of bank notes and bills in separate letters.[139] John's trips to places like Newcastle fair put him in touch with others in his trade.[140] Travel also kept him abreast of current affairs. Thus in 1803 he admitted: 'All are sadly afraid of Bounap[arte]' on the Lancashire coast.[141] Fawdington's rambles show that north-east England had escaped the isolation of earlier periods.

By the 1780s, John's letters reveal a surge in his region's economic progress. 'I have been pretty successful at one of the cotton Factories', he reported, whilst Mr Merrywether of Yarm promised orders for 'what they want in the leather line' at Hawkshead. In 1787 he found 'trade brisk, orders plentiful, & Money likewise'.[142] In his will he left 'one pound one shilling for my daughter Betty Eland, and if remainder ... my three daughters . . . are to have it amongst them share and share alike'.[143] Glimpses of John's economic independence, as well as Morton's later good fortune, can be found in personal letters.

Finally, early nineteenth-century letters from the West Indies were written by Fawdington's son, John Jr. He hoped to make his fortune with a Mr Playter, who had married a lady 'not quite of the white breed'.[144] Unlike his father and grandfather, who enjoyed stable employment, John Jr chose to live abroad. His career path may have been just as insecure as that of young Joseph Morton. Without additional letters, we can only speculate on his future.

Fawdington's correspondence reveals a complex individual, who worked hard to make a living and was also a romantic writer. They caution us not to stereotype the cultural lives of individuals, by referring to their occupations. John wrote letters for practical purposes. But he also used them to satisfy the romantic side of his nature and to express inner thoughts in aesthetic ways. His epistolary literacy enabled him to develop literary skills, retreat into a dream world, and indulge in a language of sensibility. His emotional world of letters gradually emerged from his schooling, travels, life experience, and cultural aspirations. There must have been others like him.

Jedediah and Elizabeth Strutt of Belper and Derby

The final case study analyses family letters of Jedediah Strutt of Derby (1726–97), 'cotton-spinner and improver of the stocking-frame'. Strutt and his friend, Richard Arkwright (1732–92)[145] are usually remembered as founders of England's 'dark satanic mills'.[146] But their early lives as Derbyshire working men—Strutt as a wheelwright and Arkwright as a wigmaker—are less well known.[147] Strutt's letter-writing had important effects on three distinct periods of his life: during his seven-year courtship; later, as he searched for a career path; and as a widower with five children after the death of his wife, Elizabeth (1729–74).[148] The Strutt papers span the eighteenth and early nineteenth centuries. They contain both sides of long runs of correspondence over several generations, as well as memoirs, journals, and genealogical material.[149]

At first glance, the early lives of Strutt and Fawdington appear similar. Both were educated in country schools and profited from the rise of trade. Both wives were literate and saved their courtship letters.[150] Yet their husbands ended life in opposite circumstances: Fawdington remained a bridle-maker, whilst Strutt became a powerful mill owner. Jedediah's parents were Dissenters—most likely Presbyterians, who worshipped in Alfreton.[151] His stern father, a small farmer, had little interest in schooling. He gave his son a 'narrow & contracted' education, which Strutt rued all his life.[152] His brother fled to London at age 14 and became a draper. In contrast, Jedediah was apprenticed to a wheelwright in the village of Findern, five miles from Derby.[153] In the 1740s, he boarded with the family of his future wife Elizabeth Woollat.

Findern was the site of a Nonconformist academy run by Ebenezer Latham (c.1688–1754), but Strutt could never have afforded its fee of £16 per year.[154] He may have attended the local free school, which taught 'the children of poor people ... whose goods [were] not worth more than £20, in ... reading English perfectly and the Bible, and to write a fair and legible hand'.[155] The academy's students, in contrast, learned logic, mathematics, natural philosophy, anatomy, Hebrew, and theology. Their readings included Locke's *Essay on Human Understanding*, Whiston's *Euclid*, Gravesande's *Natural Philosophy*, Le Clerc's *Physics*, and Keil's *Anatomy*.[156] The school must have been a hotbed of intellectual inquiry, and though Strutt and Woollat were not students, they had close contacts with the academy at the most impressionable time of their lives.

Like most country girls, Elizabeth became a domestic servant—in her case, to the headmaster, Latham. When he moved his academy to Derby she went with him. Eventually she moved to London as housekeeper to another Dissenting minister.[157] Her experience gained through service, which probably included access to books, set her on a path of self-education that is rarely mentioned in literacy studies. Yet motivated women, as well as men, could educate themselves outside of institutions, especially if they were Dissenters.[158] By 1754, Strutt was working as a wheelwright in Blackwell.[159] His relationship with Elizabeth was sustained by seven years of writing courtship letters. After their wedding in 1755, Strutt heard that London friends 'talked in a very taunting Sort of a manner & wondred that you wou'd leave such a place to come & Marry a wheelwright'.[160]

While they were still servants, reading and writing filled the couple's lives. Indeed their letters were studded with references to Shakespeare, Milton, Swift, and the Bible. They each had different epistolary skills and used letters in distinct ways. Elizabeth's lack of training was evident in ink blots, crossed-out phrases, and phonetic spelling. She often printed her letters with spaces between syllables, as if sounding them out as she wrote. Yet she was not afraid to use difficult words and her sentiments were imaginative and fresh. She was clearly more at ease when writing than her earnest lover. Unlike Jedediah, who was sober and introspective, she wrote openly with a gentle humour that added life to her prose. Jedediah's epistolary literacy was at a higher level. His spelling, grammar, and punctuation showed signs of former training.[161] (See Plates 21 and 22.) Nonetheless, he was ill at ease when writing—a fact of some importance, as we shall see.

Like the Fawdingtons, Elizabeth and Jedediah were self-conscious about their letters and discussed how and why they wrote them. Throughout his life Jedediah insisted that he did not enjoy letter-writing. 'I shall . . . learn to do a thing I never lov'd', he promised Elizabeth, 'that is, to write long Letters.' He believed he lacked polish, possessing only 'plain Common Sense Without much Genius'.[162] He knew that, if she 'read with Candor, and the same simplicity with which I write, you will certainly find it Sincere'.[163] Yet his painstaking drafts, which continued in old age, belied this statement. A love letter and its original draft show he omitted intimate sentiments in his final copy. This fact indicated editing and a struggle for self-control.[164] After a long silence, Jedediah warned Elizabeth: 'Letters from me are very rare things; for I can recollect but one or two instances to your Sex.'[165] In later life, his position forced him to produce a large correspondence. Yet his letters still reminded Strutt of his low background, poor manners, and discomfort in polite society.

Elizabeth, however, refused to accept his unwillingness to write: 'When I compare your letters [they] . . . are some what inconsisttant: in ye first you say you are an utter s[tranger?] to writeing, in your next that you [have?] done all you can by Letters.' She praised his efforts and depended on his 'Goodness not to expose my Nonsense'.[166] Her letters were composed, she assured him, 'less to make you thinke I write well, then to learn from you'.[167] This exchange uncovers a common pattern of gendered letter-writing, in which the woman apologizes and makes compliments, so that the correspondence will continue. Yet though Elizabeth deferred to his higher technical skill, it was she who controlled the epistolary relationship, and her ease added grace to her supposedly inferior writing.

Over time, the couple began to use letters in new ways. Jedediah, for example, was in continuous dialogue with himself about what to do with his life. As a wheelwright, he confessed in 1751: 'I am not fully Satisfied, nor perhaps may never be so, for I really don't know what I wou'd wish for next...I am a Servant and perhaps wou'd turn Master, of what or who?'[168] Letters gave him the opportunity to work out his goals safely, in the presence of one who loved him.

On her part, Elizabeth used letter-writing as a tool to examine her own conduct. Though her lack of endearments before marriage revealed characteristic feminine modesty, once marriage was certain, she expressed ideas frankly. She wrote a letter that gave 'a short view of my real temper' so that Jedediah might not be 'ignorant of some Peculiarities in my temper, which if unknown...might have been the foundation of some uneasiness'. Then she presented a list of her strengths and weaknesses, in the same way in which a novelist might describe a character.[169] She admitted, for example, 'that indignities fire my resentment, and lead me to evidence the spirit of my sex'.

The couple not only explained themselves to each other, they did so in a literary manner, inserting references to literature, employing poetic language, and discussing the meaning of words. Thus Elizabeth evaluated one of Jedediah's courtship letters: 'I can't but say it a pears to m[e] a little romantick, (tho there is not a Juba, a portius, [or] a Marcus, yt [stir] ye passions in a more elagant manner).'[170] (See Plate 21.) She was familiar not just with romances, but had read Shakespeare and Addison's *Cato*. Strutt responded by referring to her use of language. She had spoken of a lover who 'with all his puissant power [and] force pierc'd every tender & sympathetick nerve'. Now the word 'puissant', he explained, was 'sometimes used to show the valor or Courage of some great Conquerour but more especially in Knight Erantry and Romances when the Author has occasion to magnifie the Hero of his Fable in Slaying of Dragons [and] Giants'.[171] The Strutts enjoyed using literary language and wove romantic sources into letters.

Wheatcroft and Fawdington also used poetic language, but the Strutts employed more complex techniques, like inserting literary extracts into letters. To encourage Jedediah to visit, for example, Elizabeth made 'youce of Dean Swift's compliment to his friend. I have, says he, but a small house and only one snug appartment it lies on my left side is verry warme, and ye will allways be a welcome guest to it, as long as ye edifis remains in ye tenure and posestion of your humble servant'.[172] The process of reading and inserting quotations into letters indicates a higher level of epistolary literacy than we have seen before. In a similar act, Elizabeth compared the words of a dying neighbour with 'ye advice our late Queen upon her death bed gave our presant Duke William'. Elizabeth first read the Queen's advice, perhaps in a newspaper, then copied it and inserted it into her letter.[173]

In the same manner, Jedediah used Milton's work to coax Elizabeth to return to Derby: 'Here it is you may hear the morning and the evening Song of many a Warbling Lark and Linnet, and as Milton expresses it, The Shrill mattin song of birds on every bough.'[174] 'Who haunts your shades now I'm away, or hears your warblers Sing! Who treads your peaceful walks, or tastes your cooling springs?' First Elizabeth, then Jedediah, placed extracts from their reading into letters. These sophisticated acts did not just integrate writing and reading, they revealed a self-consciousness about how language was used.[175]

Finally, like Fawdington and Wordsworth, Jedediah was moved by nature and expressed his inner feelings in letters. In his garden, he had made a little arbour with 'Jessamine and Woodbine too to twine among the branches. This often puts me in mind', he wrote, 'of Adams Bower [the] Nuptial Bower and Edens Sweets the leaving which gave Eve so much reluctance. There I spend many an Hour in rambling fruitless speculations.'[176] (See Plate 22.) For Jedediah, the natural world was a catalyst to imaginative thinking. Though he said he did not like writing, letters became a place where he could actualize his reading, express his love, and think about the next stage of his life.

After the couple married, Strutt invented the famous 'Derby Patent Rib' in 1756. An 'ingenious attachment' for the stocking frame, it enabled the production of ribbed hosiery. Strutt was one of Derbyshire's mechanically talented 'exact men',[177] whose patents stimulated trade and manufacturing.[178] Derby, Leicester, and Nottingham lay at the centre of a well-known hosiery industry. As early as 1739, Samuel Evelyn noted in a letter: 'There is a Poem lately published at Nottingham on the silk Mills at Derby.' After Strutt obtained his patent, he moved to Derby, where he produced silk stockings for the London market.[179] By 1771, he formed a temporary partnership with Richard Arkwright to build cotton mills in Nottingham and Cromford. Strutt built his own cotton mills near Derby at Belper in 1778, and in Milford in 1789. They employed 400 people, rising to 600 in 1780 and 2,000 by 1832. His cotton-spinning firm would become the largest in England.[180]

The Strutts and their five children lived in the shadow of the mills. In the 1770s, Derby's 7–8,000 people were packed into crowded streets.[181] There were silk mills, a china factory, an iron strip mill, and copper-smelting works. Defoe had called Derby 'a town of gentry rather than trade', and its social structure was still rigid.[182] Country families maintained town houses and held exclusive assemblies. Yet no matter how wealthy Dissenting tradesmen grew, the first generation could not bridge the gap between land and trade. Tellingly in 1774, the Strutts still let rooms for the Derby races.[183] The family attended the Unitarian meeting at Friargate Chapel, where Jedediah was a trustee. They socialized with its members, as well as hosiers and cotton spinners.

Strutt's letters in the 1760s show him wrestling with his transition from a rural wheelwright to an urban businessman in a world of social inequality. His reason for making money, he told Elizabeth, was so that 'we may not have the two great calamities of Human Life, poverty & old Age, Come upon us together'. After seeing freezing London beggars, he admitted: 'I look'd on 'em with pity but did not relieve any of them. They & the Horses seem much in the Same Case, both Hackneyd out of their lives, both are Slaves to the lusts & passions of Man. This Seems to be an evil not to be remedied by Law or magistrates & if it be nessesary to the being of the World how is the providence of god to be Justifyed?' After considering the evils created by an industrializing society, he opted for the answer that God took care of all people, 'but the Virtuous & good are his peculiar Care & Concern'.[184]

Strutt's struggle to reconcile his wealth with his faith, led him to Unitarianism. He hoped that his children would not have to struggle as he had, and this principle, he assured Elizabeth, was not 'irreligious'. To convince her, and perhaps himself, he listed his moral aims: to 'improve ones mind in every moral & Divine, as well as every polite & useful improvement . . . to Spend a life of diligence, honesty, Sobriety, & virtue; to have been the Author of anything great or good whereby mankind are made wiser or better'. He concluded with a summary of his deepest beliefs: to act with 'truth & ones own best reason, & in a firm belief & trust in the existence of god & his providence is truly to be religious'.[185] These reflections, I believe, were an example of how a working man used letters to ponder abstract ideas—an action that took him to a more complex level of literacy than spontaneous speech.[186]

In 1774, while Strutt was in London on business, Elizabeth died. After bouts of depression, he threw himself into raising five children, aged 11–18. Despite his wealth, they were brought up with extreme frugality and stern moral discipline. The eldest, William (1765–1830) was sent to schools run by Mr Gregory in Findern, Mr Lowe in Norton, and Mr Wilkinson in Nottingham. At the age of 14, however, he was put to work in the mill.[187] George (1761–1841) went to Chesterfield at the age of 13 to improve his writing at a school run by Mr Astley, a Unitarian minister. 'I should chuse to wright better', George admitted. He soon returned to the mill to work beside his sisters and uncles.[188]

As his children matured, Strutt grew obsessed with their letter-writing. His fixation was even more intense than that of the merchant fathers cited in Chapter 1. He mercilessly demanded constant letters with correct spelling and grammar. Yet the epistolary achievements of Strutt's children did not come easily. In July 1774, Elizabeth begged her father to point out 'anything you think inelegant in my letters' and promised to improve.[189] George still had epistolary problems at the age of 17. 'I have been so afraid of writing', he admitted in 1778, 'least you should think my letter too trifleing.' He begged to be excused from writing more than once a month.[190] Martha cited anxiety as *her* reason for not corresponding.[191] 'I have defer'd writing (as I always do)...[for] want of courage & resolution which I always want in writing.'[192] As a result of his constant prodding, the adult letters of Strutt's sons and daughters became chillingly standardized by the end of the century. Gone were the idiosyncrasies of individual workers like Morton and Fawdington. This phenomenon, I believe, was related to Strutt's epistolary awkwardness and his focus on improving his children's social skills.[193]

The reason for Strutt's obsession becomes clearer when we read a letter to his son, Billy, which was accompanied by a gift of Lord Chesterfield's *Letters*. Like Chesterfield, Strutt had observed his son's shyness, but he hoped he would achieve 'Manly Eloquence in Speaking & Writeing'.[194] Billy quickly admitted: 'Whenever I...express my Thoughts either in Writing, or in speaking, I am puzzled and at a loss to do it in that easy Elegant manner.' Though he was 'not to be a Nobleman nor prime-minister', Strutt reminded Billy, 'you may possibly be a Tradesman of some eminence'. Billy must thus acquire 'the Manners, the Air, the genteel address, & polite behaviour of a gentleman'. 'You may believe me', Strutt wrote in a telling comment, 'for I now feel the want of them by dear experience.' It was painful for Strutt to describe 'the awkward figure one makes, the confusion & the Embarrasment one is thrown into...from the Consciousness of not knowing how to behave'. As a boy, Strutt had had no one to instruct him in social graces. He was, therefore, unable to teach them to William, 'having never learnt them myself'. He had, instead, marked Chesterfield's volume with a pencil, flagging up useful passages for William to commit to memory.[195]

This incident helps us to understand that Strutt's letters were constant reminders of his lack of education and manners. He had felt a want of confidence in polite society; his children must be different, not just for the sake of status, but to help them get on in life. It was fitting that he found answers to the problems of educating his children in the very letter-form that he had failed to master himself. This analysis is supported by a poignant letter to his daughter, written after his second marriage to a yeoman's widow (perhaps his housekeeper). Strutt confessed that he found himself 'but little known & . . . regarded. Few people imagining that the house at Derby belongs to me, that I have my concern in the business there, or that you are my children.' 'Acquaintances seem not be acquainted', he added, 'nay . . . I think their Eyes wished they did not see me.'

These problems had arisen because he had 'little pride & no ostentation . . . not being fond of finery & dress, not thrusting myself into what is calld Genteel Company, not frequenting Assemblies, Balls, Concerts, plays & shews'. Moreover, he had never wished to acquire 'these great means of popularity' that made entry into society possible.[196] For Strutt, letter-writing was one of 'these great means of popularity' that might help his children to become socially accepted. It was too late for him, but it was not too late for his offspring.

In the end, Strutt's plan for their elevation worked beyond his wildest expectations. As adults, each son ran a part of the business and contributed to Derby's economic and cultural life. William (1756–1830) built the first English fire-resistant mill, founded the Derby Philosophical Society, and was a fellow of the Royal Society. George Benson (1761–1841) managed the Belper mills and later became a banker.[197] Joseph (1765–1844) supervised the commercial side of the business and established Derby's Mechanics' Institute. Martha and Elizabeth married prominent local businessmen. They were avid readers and deeply engaged in liberal politics.[198] In 1775, Elizabeth wrote Strutt about a nostalgic visit to his former home in Findern. 'Everybody is surprised when they consider what we are, & what we have been. I often think of it & . . . my heart & eyes overflow with joy & gratitude.'[199]

In the next generation, William's son Edward attended Trinity College, Cambridge. Other Strutts went to Harrow.[200] Edward Strutt of Belper became the first mill owner to sit in the House of Lords, an event the radical press called 'the surrender of feudalism to industry'.[201] It is unlikely that Jedediah could have imagined this honour.

The Strutt papers suggest the social value of epistolary literacy, but they also reveal its limits. At times it satisfied workers' aspirations, but it also created anxiety and unfulfilled expectations. Strutt scorned gentility until old age; then insisted that his children acquire the manners that had eluded him. But if Strutt lacked polite letter-writing skills, his epistolary literacy brought him other benefits. It enabled him to maintain an intimate relationship with his wife, Elizabeth that survived seven years of separation. As they wrote to each other, they created a literary world that they alone could enter. In the end, a wheelwright and a servant expanded their intellectual horizons through the ordinary act of writing letters.

Conclusion: Letter-writing and literacy

Though Jedediah and Elizabeth discussed letter-writing routinely, they never referred to it as something out of the ordinary. They regarded it as a commonplace activity and took their skills for granted. This was true for all letter-writers described in this chapter. Together they offer evidence of epistolary literacy lower down into the social hierarchy than imagined. The remarkable fluency of these writers complicates notions of a literacy gap between North and South, as well as farm and town.[202] It also adds a qualitative dimension to notions of literacy in this period.

With these case studies as background, it is helpful to review the current state of research on literacy. In the 1980s, literacy became the focal point of interdisciplinary debates. Some scholars viewed it as a positive development that brought progress to society.[203] Others stressed the enduring power of oral culture and criticized the notion that there was one universal form of literacy. Keith Thomas, David Cressy, Keith Wrightson, and W. B. Stephens have shown that literacy takes distinct forms at different times and places, and must be analysed in context. Differences in gender, age, rank, trade, and religion must be taken into account. Furthermore, regional variations produce distinct forms of literacy in agricultural, industrial, and urban populations.[204] Learning clearly takes place in a dynamic environment in which social, economic, and political forces 'push' and 'pull' people into literacy.

Given these complexities, the measurement of literacy presents a daunting task for scholars. Moreover, there is little agreement about what the term means.[205] In practice, the statistical claims of a few respected scholars are quoted in secondary works. Cressy's percentages of *illiteracy* based on name signing have become generally accepted: 90 per cent men, 99 per cent women in 1500; 70 per cent men, 90 per cent women in 1649; 55 per cent men, 75 per cent women in 1714; 40 per cent men and 60 per cent women in 1750. From 1754–1840, Stephens sees little improvement in female illiteracy, with that of males remaining static until 1795. For Cressy, gains in literacy have been 'irregular and halting rather than steady and progressive'. 'The long eighteenth century', he argues, 'saw marginal improvement and some stagnation, the consumer and commercial revolutions notwithstanding.'[206] Yet this view sits oddly for a period of economic expansion, especially after 1750.[207] Moreover, recent studies of the literacy of the poorest groups in society raise questions about this low estimate—for example, new works on pauper letters and prisoners' correspondence.[208]

The more optimistic views of Margaret Spufford and Jonathan Rose for the periods before and after the eighteenth century are more compatible with this book's findings.[209] R. A. Houston, Wrightson, and David Vincent also approach literacy in positive ways, particularly in regard to the sup-posedly backward northern counties.[210] Houston estimates male literacy in the North rose from 58 per cent in the 1720s to 70 per cent by the 1740s.[211] Wrightson and David Levine show increases in a northern coal mining community 'among yeomen and farmers... including many small holders, tenants, and part-time wain or waggon-drivers' as well as craftsmen and tradesmen.[212] Andy Wood's study of mining parishes in the Peak District from 1754–70 finds literacy rates of married couples in keeping with na-tional averages.[213] Norman McCord and Richard Thompson claim that by the end of the eighteenth century, the North 'probably had a higher level of literacy than any other principal region across a wide social range'.[214]

Of course, the same statistics may be interpreted in different ways. For Vincent, male and female literacy rates of 60 per cent and 40 per cent indicated 'how much could be achieved without the presence of the state or even of a widespread system of church education. The patchy efforts of charity schools do not explain how three men in five could sign their names in the 1750s.'[215] This chapter has been influenced by Vincent's point of view and his focus on the *uses* of literacy.[216] It is hoped that the qualitative method of using 'epistolary literacy' will complement and add to previous statistical studies.

The case studies in this chapter suggest that literacy increased gradually in response to local needs. Like the Post Office, it did not emerge suddenly in the 1840s. This unhurried view fits nicely with the accepted opinion that the industrial revolution evolved slowly over time—not in large formal factories, but in small cottage industries and the 'putting out' system.[217] Literacy may have emerged similarly in parts of northern England, creating small informal pockets of literate people. The region's proximity to Scotland, with its high rates of Bible reading, likely contributed to this trend. Houston attributed improvements in northern literacy to demographic and economic factors. They naturally had their greatest impact on groups taking part in commercial growth.[218]

According to this view, the rise of literacy was a patchy affair affecting certain people more than others, depending on local needs. In this chapter, we have met some of these people—inquisitive individuals, who were precursors of a wider literacy. They laid the foundation for a later period when state schools would increase their numbers. Economic conditions that 'pushed' them into literacy have emerged subtly in the case studies. They show how trade and industry inexorably drew workers into acts of writing and national networks. Joseph Morton's sudden removal to a coal mine starkly illustrates this point. His ability to write catapulted his family into a new way of life. Strutt's meteoric rise began with a simple knitting frame—but his literacy helped him to develop it inside a network of hosiers and spinners. England's economy surely benefited from this type of literate worker with entrepreneurial skills.[219]

Letters also reveal how economic growth led to improved communications and transport. Fawdington, Morton, and Strutt used the canals, turnpikes, postal routes, and Post Offices that transformed northern England from 1750–1800. The geographic mobility found in all case studies, undermines the view of an isolated North.[220] Wheatcroft enjoyed visits to friends and fairs, whilst a trip to Bristol for his employer enabled Morton to become a tourist. Fawdington had to travel to sell his bridles; in contrast, Strutt's lobbying forced him to commute to London. Letter-writers depict a vital industrializing area, with kin in London, and people and letters on the move. Upward and downward mobility of rural families is also exposed.

Morton's letters capture the restless migration and economic fragility of workers in north-west England. His desire for freedom and antipathy to stewards were rooted in the insecurity of Westmorland's independent farmers.

Of course, people were not just functionally pushed into literacy; they were also internally motivated to acquire it. For the Methodist, George Newton, a Sheffield ironworker, literacy grew out of a conversion experience and a desire to read the Bible.[221] Strutt's case shows the impact of the Dissenting academy at Findern, even on those who did not attend it. The impact of faith on literacy will be dealt with more fully in Chapter 4. Ultimately, literacy evolved from a mix of internal factors: necessity, dissatisfaction, aptitude, self-discipline, opportunity, and deeply felt ambition, if not for oneself, for one's children. Morton, for example, endured privation, recognized desires, grasped opportunities, and thrived on hope. Unwilling to accept despair, he instead educated his children. Of course, the family lay at the core of rural society and its impact on literacy was immense. Once families became literate, they passed on their skills to children. Parents also gave children a sense of narrative by telling folk tales and stories.[222]

The community helped to support literacy by providing makeshift places of instruction. Naturally, these parlours and porches do not appear in lists of licensed schools. Widespread intermittent teaching, paid for by groups of parents, is another overlooked explanation for hidden rural literacy. Students came and left school in different seasons, depending on their work and the state of family finances. Naturally, access to education depended on financial resources, but perhaps not as exclusively as imagined. Most of our writers were educated informally in ways that escape documentation. In addition, workers' autobiographies usually mention some type of early schooling. Their stories encourage us to reconsider our definitions of education and our bias toward formal institutions.[223] The demands of society often led to a hidden supply of schooling that sidestepped the issue of which children to educate.[224]

Furthermore, in contrast to some perceptions, the North was not bereft of endowed institutions. As we have seen, there were free schools in most Derbyshire villages by the 1730s.[225] These findings are confirmed by Spufford's work in Cambridgeshire; that of Cressy in Norfolk; Derek Robson in Cheshire; Doreen Smith in West Sussex; Stephen Glover, Thomas Noble, and Wood in Derbyshire;[226] and W. P. Baker in East Yorkshire.[227]

Wrightson and Levine describe schooling for workers' children in Ambrose Crowley's northern factory. Crowley told the schoolmaster in Winlaton 'to carry it with an even hand to all his scholars, and not to despise any for their poverty, but to encourage ingenuity and virtue in all of them'. Writing samples of the children of Crowley's workers were periodically shown to the school's governors. An endowed school at Marley Hill and a Society for Promoting Christian Knowledge (SPCK) school formed a network of local institutions.[228] For groups participating in the growth of trade and industry, opportunities for literacy likely grew to meet local demand. This is not to say that literacy was widespread, but that a literate base was created amongst the population.

The case studies in this chapter have shown the epistolary skills of a group of writers in that literate base. Their unexpected literacy warns us not to underestimate the human spirit. By the end of the century, Fawdington possessed a higher level of epistolary literacy than the earlier Soresbies. More schools, dictionaries, and the standardization of language were, in part, responsible, along with the spread of taste and manners. In fact, Fawdington, a bridle-maker, was as aware of epistolary conventions as the mill owner, Strutt.

To more fully understand the literacy of every letter-writer, case studies were analysed in regard to three questions: *Why* did these farmers and workers want to write letters? *How* did they *use* them for specific purposes? What *effects* did letters have on writers' lives? All families used letters to help them make a living. The case of Joseph Morton, whose writing skills led directly to a mining job, illustrates this point most dramatically. As farmers, the Soresbies experienced powerful incentives to read bonds, 'cast an accompte', and write letters wherever credit was used.[229] Gilbert Soresbie used his to showcase his literacy skills to a potential employer. They also helped him to run his business, consult lawyers, and hold local office. Fawdington needed letters to connect to buyers and suppliers, whilst Strutt's business required constant correspondence. Because letters provided legal and financial evidence, all of our families preserved them, often cramming several onto one piece of paper.

Yet practical needs were not the only reasons for writing letters. All of our families needed them to meet psychological, social, and cultural needs. In a changing world marked by separation from loved ones, letters eased loneliness and supported travellers and exiles. They cemented the family ties and social networks on which everyone depended. Letters also helped workers to develop the social relationships that underpinned courtship, marriage, and work. For Morton, letters comforted an immigrant, who was lonely and insecure. Yet those he wrote on his trip to Bristol were also vehicles for independent opinions. Jedediah Strutt employed his to express love, plan a career, and reconcile business and religion. Then he bullied his children into using them as stepping stones into society. On a lighter note, family letters were handy conduits for receiving information, pleasure, and a great deal of entertainment—all of which were appreciated in rural villages. The Soresbies used theirs in all of these ways. Of course, the functional and cultural aspects of epistolary literacy should not be viewed separately. Strutt and Fawdington used letters to develop the romantic *and* practical sides of their characters.

Thus far, this conclusion has been limited to the epistolary literacy of males. Sadly, we have few in-depth case studies that show how rural women learned to write. There is some indirect evidence in the Soresbie's financial accounts, but experiences of girls taught at home are rarely documented.[230] Not surprisingly Elizabeth Strutt's education is unknown. Yet despite inferior training, her letters warn us not to stereotype women as apologetic writers. Dorothy Soresbie, had less training in the 1670s, but she, too, was successful in achieving epistolary goals.

Though it is natural to find fewer women's letters, it is also likely that unknown female writers existed. In his work on Audley, Staffordshire (1650–1770), Robert Mayer speculated as to why female literacy remains hidden. He decided to study probate material, instead of marriage registers. At first, he found only 2 per cent of women were literate. When he expanded his cases to those where women also signed as witnesses, illiteracy levels dropped. In addition, he found older women had higher rates of literacy. Perhaps experiences after marriage stimulated adult literacy, especially if one's partner was literate. Smout's study of Scottish literacy found women who became literate as adults, whilst Smith's work on West Sussex found higher rates of literacy amongst female servants.[231] Research is sorely needed that explains the masking effects of current studies. In contrast, the wilful destruction of women's letters is discussed in Chapters 5 and 6.

Elizabeth Strutt's experience is important, not only as a case study, but because she, more than others, developed literary techniques in letters. This is not to say that other writers were unaware of literary strategies. In every case study, writers read literature and imitated its practices. Leonard Wheatcroft's miscellanies were studded with poetry based on the language of chivalry and the Bible. The Soresbies observed the narrative structures, as well as the texts, of their jokes and bawdy stories. By 1800, Fawdington used words and techniques found in romantic literature to commune with nature.

In contrast, Elizabeth discovered how to turn her letters into literary compositions. Both she and Jedediah assumed the other had read a core set of writings, which were central to their world of literature. Elizabeth alone used letters to construct real characters in the way that published authors did in books. Shortly before her marriage, we recall, she analysed her 'inward temper' for her future husband. It was important, she warned Jedediah, to grasp the 'Blemishes and Defects . . . found in every Individual of the Human Race'. As she listed her virtues and vices, she constructed a well-designed image of a real human being. This epistolary exercise not only enlightened Jedediah, it allowed her to develop a sense of self.[232]

Elizabeth also led the way in constructing premeditated rhetorical strategies to accomplish epistolary goals. We do not know how she learned to do this, but reading works by distinguished authors probably played a part. Her compliments to Jedediah and her efforts to prolong their correspondence were examples of artful writing. This was also true of Morton, who had the least advantages, but used rhetoric and exaggeration as epistolary strategies. Elizabeth took her epistolary literacy to a higher level, and she pulled a resistant Jedediah along with her. Hence an untutored woman tutored a more expert male writer, and dominated their epistolary relationship.

Finally, Elizabeth employed her epistolary literacy to think about language in rational ways. Writers in all case studies used letters to reflect upon abstract ideas, which was different from using spontaneous speech.[233] But Elizabeth and Jedediah took their interest in language a step further. They examined how authors used words in literature, and then placed them in their own letters. This use of quotations was a complex cognitive act that required many sequential actions: reading, preserving, recalling, selecting, copying, and analysing language.[234]

The Strutts' complex acts of writing neatly illustrate Robert Pattison's definition of literacy, which has underpinned this book. Literacy, he maintained, was a cultural process that demanded 'consciousness of the uses of language and the mastery of skills to express them'.[235] The Strutts,

I suggest, fulfilled this definition. In their hands letter-writing became a tool for thought. Vincent explained this process in a similar comment: 'Becoming literate will only transform the way an individual thinks, if literacy is used in order to think. Practice... is the key to change.'[236] Epistolary literacy provided that practice for workers and farmers in the North of England.

4

Letters of the middling sort

Confronting problems of business, religion, gender, and class

L etters of northern workers were part of a popular epistolary tradition that had developed by 1800. This chapter deals with another group of correspondences—that of middling-sort families. By the end of the eighteenth century, their style of writing became the dominant model for expressing epistolary literacy. Yet letters of both groups reveal the personal pride that accompanied using one's voice to chronicle a private life.

Historians have struggled to define the middling sort, notably by wealth, status, occupation, and local associations.[1] Others have classified middling-sort people by their cultural values and lifestyles—their education, careers, leisure pursuits, and consumption.[2] H. R. French has recently stressed the importance of the parish context and the influence of gentility upon the middle classes.[3] This chapter is based on a different philosophy. It questions the benefit of placing such a variegated group of people into fixed categories. Instead, it uses letter-writing to show how middling-sort individuals negotiated their own identities on a daily basis. The result is a messier, intimate, more realistic set of self-portraits drawn by people in the middle of the social structure.

Though the middling sort were, themselves, diverse, they were linked together by a crucial trait that is so obvious, it is often overlooked—the possession of reading and writing skills, especially epistolary literacy. In fact, middling-sort families constantly wrote letters in real life and in fiction. The ability to do so implied that the writer had joined the ranks of an expanding literate nation. Membership required training and practice. Yet in contrast to social prerequisites like pedigrees, breeding, and a classical education, epistolary literacy became an inclusive middling-sort skill. For some, letter-writing grew to be a passion, or even an obsession. Epistolary literacy was thus a unifying attribute and powerful weapon in the business, family, and spiritual lives of middling-sort people.

Twenty-five families were considered as case studies for this chapter, but their number and breadth precluded using all of them.[4] Letters of professionals were consulted, but excluded, due to that group's integration with elites. Final selections were drawn from three overlapping categories: merchants, writing clerks, and Dissenters. A chief characteristic that made them ideal subjects was their common need for epistolary literacy, on which work and well-being depended. The chosen families are the Tuckers of Weymouth, the Follows of East Anglia and the Midlands, the Batemans of Manchester, and the Wilsons of London.

Before analysing these case studies, common aspects of middling-sort correspondence may be observed. In contrast to the limited numbers of workers' letters, there are thousands written by middling-sort males *and* females. Because of their breadth and detail, it is possible to witness the shaping of their writers' identities and relationships. In addition, the wide scope of their contents shows they penetrated all aspects of daily experience. Since their goal was to link personal and business lives, they were markedly multifunctional. News of sick children, church matters, and business affairs happily comingled in their letters.

Another common trait was the level and variety of anxiousness that was constantly expressed in letters. Of course, anxiety is universal, but some of its causes—social, economic, political, and religious—were heightened or, in some ways, distinctive for families in this chapter. No matter how wealthy or powerful they became, they lacked some degree of religious, cultural, or political equality. Moreover, they did not possess the instant, unassailable status that accompanied a landed estate. In this ill-defined social position between gentry and workers, our families owned property, enjoyed leisure, and had relative freedom from clientage. This, I suggest, gave the most successful middling sort a feeling of entitlement to an independent lifestyle. Yet even those with the highest degree of social and economic power, were limited politically. Thus the Tuckers failed to succeed in national politics and were slighted by their patrons. Surprisingly, striving for gentility was not a central concern for families described in this chapter. Instead, there was resistance to imitating elite conduct. Some writers even voiced feelings of moral superiority.

In order to understand middling-sort anxiety, we must recognize the problem of facing unlimited risk with limited amounts of assets. Because banking facilities were undeveloped, most letter-writers lived on a sea of credit. Social relationships were thus sorely needed to weather risks and protect reputation.[5] Unsurprisingly, middling-sort letters reveal deep concerns about upward and downward mobility. These anxieties were linked to family decisions about the education, careers, and marriages of their children. We observe these choices during common rites of passage, often over generations. As letter-writers matured, business, family, and religious priorities jostled for dominance. Yet Dissenters experienced a different type of anxiety centred on the struggle for personal salvation. As we shall see, religious and economic stresses produced different types of letter-writing. Nonetheless, the longing for independence overrode religious differences. Each of our families struggled for autonomy in their political, business, and religious lives.

These anxieties were reflected in the language of middling-sort letter-writers. Studies claim that by the mid eighteenth century, a tripartite language of 'sorts', 'ranks', and 'orders' was giving way to a language of 'class'. It was also a time of expanding vocabulary, and experimental usage. As we have seen, forms of address between family members grew more intimate and less complex. At the same time, the maturing of print culture led to standardization of spelling and grammar.[6] Yet if some elite letter-writing remained eloquent, bookish, and concerned with rhetoric, middling-sort writers preferred plain, practical language. They also employed different types of linguistic strategies. The Tuckers, for example, developed two alternative tactics: a negative 'language of resentments' to resolve worries about rank and power, and a positive 'language of interests' that expressed deeply felt principles. In contrast, our Dissenting families wrote in what one friend called 'the Language of one in the School of Christ'. Their choice of words enabled church members to recognize fellow worshippers by the way a letter was written.[7]

These distinctive 'languages' leap out of letters in the case studies. In every instance they are bound up with concerns about personal identity and social relationships. Though impossible to uncover in most types of sources, these dynamic concepts are revealed in letters that extend over time. Long uninterrupted series with both sides of the conversation reveal two basic functions of every correspondence: the construction of a personal identity, and the creation, not just a reflection, of an interpersonal relationship. In every letter, a sense of self is conveyed for the benefit of writers and readers, who have contracted to share their thoughts. Identity, in this context, signifies how writers imagine themselves, often in ideal terms. It also indicates how writers think others see them.[8] Particular issues of identity that concern each of our families are traced in this chapter: language, power, and class for the Tuckers; gender, family, business, and religion for the Batemans, Wilsons, and Follows.

Interpersonal relations are also analysed. An ongoing correspondence is, by definition, a social relationship that is created and transformed over time. When archives are rich, one can see if the bond is asymmetrical or between equals. In this chapter, we see those being formed between husbands and wives, parents and children, siblings and cousins. In the Tuckers' case, we also observe relations between political patrons and their clients. For Dissenters, letters disclose ties between writers and their churches, co-members of religious communities, and, most importantly, to God. How social relations change over time is a key element of this chapter.

The case studies: Merchants, clerks, and Dissenters

Case studies were drawn from three groups of writers that overlapped with each other. Merchants formed the largest category, but they were closely followed by Dissenters and writing clerks. Archives of other groups were eliminated or used selectively, such as those of a sea captain, mathematical-instrument maker, clerk of the works at St Paul's, ironworker, and printer (see Appendix III). All three groups needed epistolary skills to cope with life.

Merchants have left the largest number of middling-sort correspondences. (See Plate 23.) Obviously, letters have been linked with commerce in every civilization.[9] Merchants needed timely information in order to survive. 'On a normal working day' in an eighteenth-century counting house, 'every available surface would have been littered with large pewter inkstands, sandboxes, [and] rulers.' Double desks fitted with shelves, pigeonholes, and divisions for filing ensured that all letters sent and received were filed and could be retrieved. The term 'correspondence' had a double meaning for people in commerce. It not only meant the exchange of letters, it described an ongoing relationship predicated on trust.[10]

By the late seventeenth century, most Londoners thought literacy was an essential skill. Those who could not read and write, quipped Richard Steele, were 'scarce to be reckoned among rational creatures'.[11] A commercial education became mandatory for anyone entering trade. Though schools taught geography, languages, and maths, writing and accounting were entrenched at the centre of the curriculum. The merchant's round hand became the gold standard for all types of writing and was needed to enter business. (See Plate 24.) Indeed, eighteenth-century ledgers, accounts, and letters have an artistic flair. It is no wonder they became models for the nation's commerce, for they were, and still are, a pleasure to read.[12] (See Plate 25.)

Though merchants were united by their flowing, round hands, they were a particularly diverse group. Some traders, whose archives were examined, were wealthy and prominent; others were not. Some dealt in services; others produced, bought, sold, or financed goods. The Peases of Hull spanned all categories over four generations. Starting off as wode producers and sellers, they later became bankers of Hull.[13] The merchants in Chapter 1 used correspondence chiefly for business. Here we observe their letters meeting social, psychological, and religious needs.

As trade expanded, merchants needed more clerks to write letters and keep accounts. Yet this mass of men is rarely included in middling-sort studies. Perhaps this is because they had no dedicated niche in a specific part of the economy. Instead, like Joseph Morton, they wrote for others, wherever work could be found. The importance of clerks is indicated in the rise of schools that prepared men 'Qualify'd for Trades, Merchandize, the Publick Offices, Clerkships, Stewardships or any other Parts of Business'.[14] In the eighteenth century, hopeful candidates flocked to London seeking tutors and employment. Yorkshire apprentice James Jenkins, for example, petitioned a London businessman, who needed 'a lad who wrote a good hand'. Since 'mine was scarcely middling', Jenkins reported, 'I was placed at an Academy...in Prescot-Street Goodmans Field.'[15] The Spencers of Yorkshire and the Hubbertsys of Westmorland sent young men to London in search of clerical work. Even Edward Baker of New Street Square sought a clerical post, when he could no longer survive making mathematical instruments.[16] Writing skills offered clerks entry into a fluid world of business marked by downward and upward mobility. This point is illustrated by Samuel Follows's experience in one of the case studies.

A high degree of epistolary literacy was unusually prominent in bulging archives of Dissenters. Though not all middling sorts were Dissenters, most Dissenters thought they were middling-sort people, and few aristocrats adopted Nonconformity. They appear in this chapter, because of their special relationship with epistolary expertise. Though letter-writing has been examined in regard to specific faiths, little comparative work is available. This chapter provides a rare opportunity to compare the language, content, and format of letters written by Anglicans, Congregationalists, and Quakers. Eighteenth-century historiography often assumes the decline of religious piety. Yet a serious Christian way of life became a part of middling-sort respectability for many nonconformist and Anglican families.[17] Case studies record the presence or absence of faith in people's lives. They also address the problem of how to uncover hidden beliefs. Nicholas Rogers's contention that 'religion continued to be an important touchstone of political conflict' is confirmed in this chapter.[18]

To understand why Dissenters appear in case studies, it is helpful to assess their influence in regard to literacy and letter-writing. There were, perhaps, only 338,000 Dissenters early in the century, but numbers of congregations grew after the 1750s, especially those of Congregationalists. Despite small numbers, however, the proportion of Nonconformists in the literate population has been estimated as high as 13 per cent.[19] Marjorie Reeves accounts for this by noting: 'the culture of dissenting groups...seem[s] to have made them...unusually articulate, theologically aware, and ready with their pens. Their surprisingly wide vocabulary is often attributed to their reading.'[20]

Dissenting culture was also characterized by a language of enthusiasm that is glaringly present in letters. Indeed, Anglicans, who could agree on very little, were united in their hatred of enthusiasm. Nonconformity also offered lay initiative and a sense of independence for women. Letters of female Dissenters are thus plentiful in numbers and lend themselves to analysis regarding gender. Perhaps because Dissenters lacked equal political rights, they obsessively turned to letters to express personal views. For some, letter-writing became a form of social protest between the saved and the unsaved.[21]

This is clear in papers of the Muggletonians and Quakers, whose movements were sustained by letter-writing in the face of seventeenth-century persecution.[22] Eighteenth-century Dissenters, who have received less attention, include the Quaker Payne, Story, Farmer, and Lloyd families;

the Methodist Newtons; and the Unitarian Smith, Pease, and Strutt families.[23] Anglican letter-writers were often less self-conscious about their faith. The Tucker letters, for example, contain few references to religion. On the other hand, an Anglican case study where religious language is important is examined in Chapter 5

This brief background regarding the epistolary needs of merchants, clerks, and Dissenters provides context for the case studies. The Tuckers, Batemans, Wilsons, and Follows are, intentionally, a diverse group from different geographical regions and religious communities. The Quaker Follows came from small towns in Leicestershire and East Anglia, while the Anglican Tuckers lived further south in Weymouth, Dorset. The Wilsons resided in London, the Batemans in Manchester, and both were Congregationalists. Their social status, wealth, and politics also differed, along with their attitudes to the wider world. The Tuckers of Weymouth were stone merchants with political ambitions. They enjoyed high status locally and longed to extend their power beyond Dorset. Rebekah Bateman and Elizabeth Wilson were sisters, who married cotton and silk dealers. Both families were absorbed in their chapel communities and kept some distance from non-Dissenters. The Follows family of Castle Donington and various towns in Norfolk and Suffolk were Quakers. Though they began life as poor basket makers, the next generation tried to better themselves as apprentices and clerks, whilst a grandson became a shopkeeper. The Follows tried to isolate their children from society, but this was impossible.

All of them left correspondence that spanned several generations and included answers to previous letters. The Tucker papers cover the entire eighteenth century, whilst the Follows's archive runs from the 1740s through the nineteenth century. The Bateman and Wilson letters deal with the last quarter of the eighteenth and the early nineteenth centuries.

These four families were selected with the realization that it is impossible to make generalizations for all middling sorts. Yet the letters that unite them offer portraits of families with common resources, problems, and dreams. Each of them occupied an ambiguous position in the middle of a social structure that was undergoing change. They afford plenty of opportunity to consider larger issues and to make comparisons with each other and those in other chapters. The Tucker letters, for example, shed light on debates about social class, language, patronage, and politics. The Follows's correspondence shows a family contending with problems of economic survival, family break-up, and Quaker spirituality. The Bateman and Wilson letters reveal anxieties about gender, conversion, business, and faith. The purpose of this chapter is to see how their lives and identities were transformed by the possession of epistolary literacy.

The Tuckers of Weymouth, Dorsetshire

Don't let the unruly exclam'ns of a noisy mob or the more secret whispers of malice or envy give you any disturbance. You know it has ever been the fate of men ingaged in popular interests to be maligned.[24]

In 1737 an ambitious Weymouth stone merchant, John Tucker, gave this advice to his brother Richard. Both brothers had just suffered disturbing personal insults during a local election. What annoyed John most was that his adversary 'never had the manners to speak to any of us. You will treat him as you think he deserves', he told Richard, 'which I should advise to be but barely civil.' This resentful defence of status is one of many examples that show how the Tuckers used letter-writing to gain confidence about their personal identities. John contrasted his family's manners and unselfish work for the public, with the vulgar actions of the unruly 'mob'. As he did so, he reminded Richard, and himself, of the Tucker's self-worth. As the brothers wrote to each other, they were creating and transforming a relationship that offered psychological comfort. The language that they employed was an important factor in resolving how the Tuckers viewed their opponents and each other.

In this case study, we observe a new role for letter-writing—the development of a language that shaped personal identity. Letters are used to suggest how the Tuckers viewed their position in the middle of the social structure. We can also speculate how their language contributed to the rise of class-consciousness. John's defensive support of status in the opening quotation is, at first, surprising, for the Tuckers were positioned at the top rung of the middling-sort ladder. But though they possessed local power, they were still dependent on those above them in the wider world. Luckily, the Tuckers obtained relief in anxious situations by confessing in a letter what they could not say to others.

The Tucker archive permits us to construct a picture of the personal identities and relationships of Edward Tucker Sr (1622–1707); Edward

Tucker Jr (d. 1739); his sons John (1701–79) and Richard (1704–77); Richard's children Edward III (1738–61) and Rebecca (d. 1812) and Rebecca's children.[25] Four generations of letters also show changes in handwriting and style over time.[26] Edward Sr's scrawled fragments about God in a cramped secretary hand are far different from the round hand and polite presentation of his great grandchildren, Gabriel and Sarah Steward.[27] In the second generation, Edward Jr strove to attain a genteel style of letter-writing. Family patterns are evident over time in dating techniques and closing services from your 'reall loving son'.[28] The archive contains many types of letters—courtship, advice, condolence, patronage, congratulations, and circular letters to voters.[29] Someone annotated and preserved both sides of the correspondence, as well as legal and financial papers. Records were saved, not just for business reasons, but to create a book of life about family achievements.

The Tuckers established themselves as stone merchants at a time when the construction industry was booming. Hence, their work helped build the infrastructure upon which commerce depended.[30] The breadth of their financial interests was stunning. They bought and sold stone for themselves and the government, traded port wine, whale oil,[31] fish, and flax,[32] invested in copper and lead mines,[33] funded North American enterprises,[34] and were privateers in the Channel Islands in wartime.[35] The founder of the dynasty, Edward Sr was a small Weymouth merchant adventurer.[36] His sons inherited his business and wrote him loving letters, but firmly rejected his Quaker faith.[37] The next three generations of Anglicans wrote thousands of letters without any reference to religion. They integrated themselves into mainstream society and held high public office.

Unlike his father, Edward Jr (d. 1739) tried to improve his letter-writing and sent 'humble services'.[38] In contrast to his private letters, those to people outside the family were overly showy and strained. Edward Jr's epistolary naivety is revealed in a jocular letter from a clergyman. The cleric had called Edward Jr's writing 'a patchy peice full of fragments' by 'a spurious bratt'. Edward Jr corrected the cleric's spelling and warned he would not respond to 'ludicrous epistles'. 'I have business of greater moment', he claimed, 'than to answer letters of no value, inconsistent, impertinent.' His friend's reply implied that Tucker lacked social graces. 'When you send yr reflexions abroad next', the clergyman wrote, 'send 'em out in a more handsom dress; not an antique One, like an old Grephon in a Ruff. . . For to tell you the Truth in plain English, what becomes Porters and Carrmen don't become Scholars and Gentlemen.'[39]

This statement referred to the problem of Tucker's ambiguous middling position, in between the lower and elite classes. The cleric saw himself as a gentleman, but thought Tucker's letters lacked breeding. Nor was Tucker, however, a labourer, like a porter or carman. A bipolar view of society was no longer sufficient, with its supposed line of gentility under which men like Tucker were positioned. Indeed the Tuckers looked down on others and regarded themselves as genteel. Their letters uncover different views about status that normally elude us.

Edward Jr also used letter-writing to acquire literary techniques. This effort is visible in his courtship letters of 1701[40] to his future wife Rebecca Gollop, the daughter of a small landowner.[41] The family proved so satisfactory as in-laws, that both of Edward Jr's sons married Gollop sisters.[42] Like Leonard Wheatcroft in Chapter 3, Edward mimicked language found in literary romances, in his case *Don Quixote* and Samuel Butler's *Hudibras*. Rebecca's 'Ravishing Expressions', he murmured, 'Raise[d his] Groveling Soul to the highest pitch of Terrestiall Tranquillity'. His own words were 'graven too Deeply On the Table of my Heart for Anything But Death Ever to Obliterate'.[43] This exaggerated sensibility showed he was experimenting with literary language. Edward Jr compared his own horse with 'Rosanante the Horse of the famous Don Quixott; Or the admired steed of the Ingenious Hudibras, for (to Use yt Authors Own Words): Att Whipp or Spurr, Noe More he Skip't/Or Mended's pace, then Spaniard Whip't.'[44] Like Jedediah and Elizabeth Strutt in Chapter 3, he inserted extracts from famous authors into letters. All three thought it normal practice to integrate reading and writing.

An inventory of the property of Edward Jr's merchant partner reveals the sources of the quotations. In addition to Cervantes' and Butler's books, it lists two bibles, two prayer books, works by Drs Tillotson and Willis, the *Duty of Man*, 2 volumes of Hales's *Contemplations*, and Leybourn's *Arithmetic*.[45] We see how small provincial merchants shared, read, and incorporated books into letters. Edward Jr's love letters lie in the middle of the epistolary spectrum—correct in conventions, but plagued by exaggerated politeness.

Edward's literary aspirations were in keeping with his political ambitions that soon led to a crisis in his feelings of self-worth. The Tuckers gained high public offices after George I's accession, with the help of two

Whig politicians, George Bubb Dodington (1691–1762)[46] and Sir Robert Walpole (1676–1745).[47] Edward Jr and his sons served as members of Parliament for Weymouth and Melcombe Regis from 1727–78 (with the exception of 1747–54).[48] As we shall see, however, these offices depended on patronage and could be abruptly withdrawn.

Edward Jr and his sons also became Mayors of Weymouth, alternating terms amongst themselves from 1702–70s. Weymouth was the only constituency except London to have four MPs. The town, dominated by the stone trade, was filled with quarrymen and seamen. Due to its type of freehold franchises, votes could easily be manipulated. Walpole and Dodington gave offices to the Tuckers, because they needed them to act as agents and to ensure Whig votes.[49]

Edward Jr became Surveyor of the Crown Quarries in Portland in 1714 but passed the post to his son, Richard, when he entered Parliament in 1727.[50] As quarry surveyor, Tucker controlled government orders and had influence over employment.[51] But fierce competitors in business and politics made his power and status uncertain. In 1735, Dodington gave his place in Parliament to Edward Jr's son, John. In 1737, however, Walpole publicly humiliated Edward Jr and forced him to give up his seat.[52] The Tuckers were, in fact, helpless when they entered national politics, which was run by 'great men' with real power. Their sense of manhood was thus vulnerable to outside forces. They found solace in writing letters that contained written evidence that their problems were not of their own making.

Edward Jr also suffered from economic pressures, which came with high office. His income nowhere matched those of his parliamentary associates. Hence, he found it hard to 'live in town & attend Parliament & great men's Leveys for £20 a day'.[53] When he lacked cash, he tried to reduce expenses, for he was only a merchant with a reputation to guard. 'As I know the Justice I owe to all Mankind', he stated, 'I cannot goe with a Clear conscience into Any Measures that my Narro Circumstances Will not Answer.'[54] Risk was a constant companion for a merchant with a good, but not opulent, income.[55]

The anxiety in Edward Jr's letters mounted noticeably in the 1730s, as Sir Robert Walpole's friendship declined. The 'great man', it seemed, thought the Tuckers too high and mighty. 'Mr T', he remarked, 'made a Bluster of a great interest but had none, but that they (the Treasury) gave him.' Walpole's wounding statement lay at the heart of a dilemma for middling men like Tucker. Once they left their native town, they became political dependents. Letters indicate that Edward Jr found himself over his head when holding national office. Indeed, it caused him sleepless nights. As political competition, contested elections, and lawsuits rose, he became more distressed. 'Rather then be harasd & distresd in body & mind as I had been', he grumbled, 'I would choose to live on bread and water.'[56] In one letter he described what we might call a depression: 'The Consequnces turn my brain and prevent me from doing things materiall relateing to my own affairs.' Edward Sr was in the throes of fear, for he 'kn[ew] not how to Act with Safety'.[57] John's compassionate letters constantly reminded Edward Jr of his own achievements: ''Tis below ye dignity of such a station to ... aske pardon', John wrote regarding Walpole. 'I don't know any obligations you are under to him though I think he owes some to you.'[58] This poignant letter evoked dynastic pride. It must have bolstered Edward's flagging self-image.

Long runs of letters between John and Richard reveal a similar supportive relationship.[59] In the absence of portraits, letters suggest John was a powerful, short, fat man with gout.[60] He liked to hunt, but once had to forego a horse, 'not judging him strong enough for me as I ride now above fourteen stone'.[61] Because his merchant calling demanded constant writing, he 'wanted exercise of a different kind from that I dayly use'.[62] Richard suggested standing when he wrote letters and sent him a tall desk, so he could do so.[63] This small incident is indicative of their larger relationship. John was the dominant brother, and he planned the grand strategies that brought political power. He also helped Richard to extricate himself from political crises. Their letters are thus filled with John's advice and Richard's thanks.

On his part, Richard was good at managing details that made life run smoothly. He wore two responsible hats as quarry supervisor and manager of the Weymouth stone business.[64] Richard sent John intelligence about local politics and enjoyed an active social life. Though his close comrades were traders, he hunted with the parson and attended a local ball.[65] When Ralph Allen recommended Weymouth for sea bathing in the 1750s,[66] Richard received a visit from the Duke of Gloucester. The Duke 'has done my house ye hon'r of a visit to hear your sister play on ye harpsichord', wrote a very proud Richard. 'We shall have something to boast of hereafter.'[67] The Tuckers were at the highest social level of their provincial town. Still, they did not normally socialize with gentry or aristocracy.

John lived in London holding office as MP, and later Navy Cashier. Naturally, he became more accustomed to metropolitan standards. When he hired lodgings for Weymouth men, who were testifying before Parliament, he worried about the quality of accommodation. 'They are not as Polite as some', he told Richard, 'yet . . . the Vicinity of them to the place which will be their scene of action will atone for the want of Ellegance.' John's easy access to print supplied both men with material for quotations in letters. John bought books and periodicals for the whole family, which were passed back and forth between town and country.[68] Both brothers read Fielding,[69] 'ye Dutchess of Marlbourough's late book',[70] and the scandalous memoirs of Teresia Constantia Phillips, who 'lays on very thick' about things 'that were better buried in oblivion'.[71] Pope's *Dunciad* greatly pleased John, especially the fifty last lines,[72] and when his pamphlets accumulated, he chose to 'bind them together', as if starting a family library.[73] The favourite book of both brothers was Edward Young's *Night Thoughts* published in 1742.[74] When an intimate friend lay dying, John quoted from it in letters and recommended its 'consideration' to 'every Rational [man]'.[75] In 1757, Richard advised his profligate son Edward III, 'to read Dr Young's Advice to Lorenzo in his 2nd nights thought or complaint'.[76] The whole family enjoyed reading scandalous pamphlets, as well as a poetry and prose.

It was letters, however, that bound the brothers together. They shared an unspoken agreement to confide in each other and to vent their feelings when anxiety mounted. This epistolary pact brought exquisite relief. The brothers' private communications, therefore, differed from public ones. A proud masculinity underpinned their letters to people outside the family. Indeed, there are hundreds of letters written by men, who dominated business affairs. There are also many letters to and from Tucker women. But because they are not part of a series, it is difficult to generalize from them. A few examples give an indication of their level of epistolary literacy. In 1724, John's sister, Mary wrote in a round, flourished hand. Though she apologized for 'the occasion of my trubling you with this scrole', she knew how to send compliments.[77] In 1742, Martha Tucker wrote well, but with similar apologies.[78] By the 1780s, girl's letters sent from school were accomplished and conventional.[79] Dorothy Tucker enjoyed writing them so much it was 'difficult . . . to lay down the pen'.[80] Epistolary literacy was thus important to Tucker women.

When we return to the letters of John and Richard, we see how carefully they were trained as boys. Their large round hands bedecked with flourishes illustrate the high standards of the commercial community during the eighteenth century.[81] Their endless drafts and copies as adults were a different matter—written without margins and crammed with abbreviations.[82] (See Plate 26.) When one brother was pressed for time, the other took over, for every out-letter had to be duplicated. 'I have not time to take a copy', John told his father, 'therefore I desire and expect R. T. will transmit one.'[83] Letter-writing was needed to stay in business and a key part of the grand duty to keep one's affairs in order. If the Tuckers allowed even one post to go by, an explanation was demanded. 'Although I have not any thing materiall to say', Richard confessed, 'I would not omitt writing.'[84] No matter how hectic life became, letter-writing was a sacred responsibility.[85] Thus John, so tired 'that he c[ould] hardly walk', after twenty-three hours at the House of Commons, trudged home to write a letter. During one hectic period, he hired his brother's scribe.[86] John and Richard wrote to each other every post, which in the 1740s came to four times a week.[87]

Letter-writing manuals miss the gusty flavour of the Tuckers' letters. Standard advice is repeated mechanically from one guide to another. 'A tradesman's letters should be plain, concise, and to the Purpose', notes one, and 'free from quaint studied Expressions'.[88] In contrast, the Tuckers' letters were filled with warmth, intimacy, and local phrases. Their earthy colloquial language is full of punch. Still, hearty thanks for 'favours' and 'services' show traders adhered to epistolary conventions.[89]

Letters to and from John in China in the 1720s show the labyrinthine measures taken to remain in touch. Some were written from London coffee houses; others were passed by friends to sea captains in endless chains of moveable texts. In 1729, Richard received a letter from John, 'but *now* almost despair of hearing until next year'.[90] He would gladly 'pay postage of a letter . . . three times a week, without promise of reimbursement'.[91] Merchants had to have friends in every port to ensure receipt of mail. As they did so, they created social networks at home and abroad.[92] In Weymouth, the Tuckers joined a political 'clubb' where they aired private opinions with men of modest standing.[93]

Though we have no records of what they said at their club meetings, the Tucker letters are so detailed that we can use them to observe local linguistic patterns. We observe how the brothers used specific words to describe themselves and others. As political fortunes rose, language about the 'self' grew positive. As offices were lost, negative remarks about others increased. This language was most visible in the 1740s, when self-interest and 'country' principles placed the Tuckers in opposition to their patrons, Walpole and Dodington. Letters show the Tuckers were ardent country 'patriots', and thoroughly immersed in court/country struggles. During a bitterly fought Weymouth election, they successfully defied Walpole. After his fall, they became disillusioned when political reforms they anticipated failed to materialize.[94]

In response to political and business disappointments, two related linguistic strategies appear in the Tucker letters: a 'language of interests' and a 'language of resentments'. Since these modes of expression grew out of personal relations, we can use John's association with his patron, George Bubb Dodington to explore both strategies. Dodington's ties with John were so intimate, that he left him his Weymouth property.[95] Still, their unequal rank guided John's conduct. As attitudes to each other changed over time, John's sense of identity was affected. The following summary of their relations provides context for this argument.

John sat in Parliament in 1735–47 and 1754–78.[96] He followed Dodington in and out of office, and together they defied Walpole in 1740.[97] John served as secretary to Dodington in the Navy Office (1744–9), as paymaster of the marines (1757–79), and as keeper of the King's Private Roads (1770–9).[98] John was, of course, dependent on his 'lord', and their relations were often stormy. After 'part[ing] in a tif', John remarked: 'Perhaps both our *resentments* will subside, as the nature of our situation requires us constant intercourse.'[99] Tucker's letters reveal a frank relationship with little servility, but unequal power.[100] Later in life, John dined informally at Dodington's estate in Eastbury, where he met literary men and Sir Francis Dashwood, eleventh Baron Le Despencer (1708–81).[101] John was in fact 'gentleman enough' to be a member of Dashwood's Medenham Society or Hell Fire Club.[102] Tucker, alone, left an account of the private chapel, where scandalous meetings took place.[103] This fact warns us not to stereotype all merchants as sober traders.

When Dodington lost office, there was a provision in each re-entry that 'Mr Tucker ... be provided for'.[104] Usually they worked in tandem as in 1750. 'Mr Tucker and I met Mr Pelham', noted Dodington. 'We settled the Weymouth re-election.'[105] In 1752, Dodington admitted that their interest in Weymouth was a joint one.[106] John's self-image was thus closely linked to his dependence on Dodington. Yet John showed the same independent spirit in crossing him as he had demonstrated earlier with Walpole. When

John voted against the Septennial Bill in 1742, he noted: 'Nothing but Annual Parliaments will every stop the Torrent of Corruption or give the Nation a free Representative.' 'Mr Dodington and I', he added, 'were on different sides.'[107] In 1751, Tucker thwarted Dodington's choice of captain for his own ship.[108] He also twice attempted to deal with the Grenvilles behind Dodington's back.[109] In 1762, Dodington wrote bitterly of the 'unexampled as well as unexpected behaviour of a man who owes every thing to me. I am glad Lord Bute', he added cuttingly, 'taught him to behave with the submission which becomes his *rank and situation.*' Though he bitingly noted John's inferior status, he added admiringly: 'Mr Tucker has found the only way (I did not think there had been one) of serving Lord Bute without obliging me.'[110]

But what was John's *rank and situation*? Social status is, of course, a dynamic concept that shifts in the eye of the beholder. It can rarely be seen, but is visible, if imperfectly, in the language of letters like the Tuckers'. In the following sections we will see how language was used to shape personal identities and relationships. Two interrelated linguistic strategies have been mentioned earlier: a negative 'language of resentments', which helped to restrain anger, and a positive 'language of interests', which communicated strongly held principles. This 'language of interests' grew out of the Tucker's positive desire for reputation, dignity, and, especially, independence. It can be detected in the way the Tuckers assigned ideal qualities to themselves and their friends. The 'language of resentments' was a negative strategy. It was based on comparing oneself with others, both above and below one's rank, and attributing negative qualities to one's enemies. There was always an assumption that one's own values were superior in some way, either socially or ethically. In each linguistic mode, one's self-image was strengthened and anxiety was relieved.

Of course, this type of linguistic response was just one of many possibilities, and the Tuckers were hardly typical in regard to political success. Still, their language shows how one middling-sort family used letters to examine their social identity before the advent of class consciousness. We may think of these positive and negative modes of expression as linguistic layers, which flowed with other sources, into a later language of class. In this early period, the term 'class' was rarely used by the Tuckers. Nor did they employ historians' favourite terms, like 'chief inhabitants'.[111] Instead they talked about one's 'station' in life, suggesting a place of advancement that could be maintained or lost. Thus when John did well, he was congratulated on his 'advanced station'.[112] In contrast, when Richard's profligate son overspent, it was clear he had 'run up excess debts...above his station'.[113]

One way of looking at the Tuckers' social identity is to see how others referred to them in wills, deeds, and letters. Whilst Edward Sr had no polite titles, his son, Edward Jr was addressed as Mr Tucker.[114] When his sons, John and Richard, married in 1731 and 1734, they were still called Mr in their marriage settlements, whilst their father-in-law, George Gollop was an 'Esquire'.[115] John was first addressed as Esq in the 1750s, but only in London at his office.[116] By the 1760s he appeared as Esq in local deeds.[117] In the 1770s, wills of both brothers' referred to them as 'Esquire', though both men were called 'merchant' in earlier versions.[118] Richard had come a long way since his comment to John in 1729: 'You guess very right as to my affection for ye title of Esqr.'[119] This rise in status surely contributed to his feelings of self-worth.

The following sections examine ways in which the Tuckers used linguistic strategies in letters. The first step toward developing a language of interests was to acknowledge one's dependence on others. 'I expected nothing less than the resentment you shew in your letter', John wrote Richard, at a time when money was short. 'The greatest Expence cannot ever establish us on any secure foot, in the opinion of Those whom we must rely on to transact...affairs for us.'[120] At the height of office, John admitted he could not solve a problem, since he had 'listed under a L'ds banners, without whom we should be but of little significance'.[121] 'I am...grown weary', he complained, 'of ye little dependance there is on ye truth and Friendship of ye great.'[122] 'Oh how easy and quiet might we sett down, if we had no inclination to push for anybody...There would be no roome for any anxious moments.'[123]

Once dependence was admitted, letters developed the ideal self-images to which the Tuckers aspired. Independence was mentioned most often as a goal. 'I hope I shall be able to conform my mind & method of life to my circumstance', wrote Richard, '& have resolution enough to live (as far as one in my Station of life can do) Independent...rather than to go into any measures yt will...Violate [my] Reputation.'[124] His word choice indicated that he saw himself a man of 'independence' and 'reputation'. When offered a deal to join his political enemies, John found it 'utterly impossible for me either with honour or even common decency' to do so. 'To think of selling my Selfe to the Court', he added, 'is what I cannot...do on any

Consideration.'[125] The 'selfe' was a precious possession when adorned with 'honour' and 'decency'. In the language of the market, it could not be sold.

This was as true for politics as it was for commerce. 'I wish with all my Soul', John wrote in the midst of a local election, that 'strangers' be prevented 'from Intrudeing themselves by dint of money...to ye Prejudice of people, who have a Naturall Right and can't make use of Corrupt measures to secure it'.[126] John was expressing his own positive sense of identity as a 'natural ruler' of Weymouth. He and his brother were natives and had the people's interests at heart, unlike unnamed 'strangers'. Middling-sort men were best suited to run local affairs, not corrupt outsiders like Walpole. As John described this ideal natural ruler, he was constructing an image of his own self-worth.

Another way of detecting how the Tuckers perceived themselves is to examine the positive language they used to describe friends. Members of the Tuckers' local club were called 'our brethren',[127] suggesting an intimacy close to kinship. John and Richard also spoke positively about men 'of honour and honesty'[128] and 'men of worth in Towns'.[129] Positive terms were used to describe men who were 'country' patriots, not court politicians. Thus John longed to support 'Men of Fortune & Figure who want to...oppose the Court Out & Out & keep up the independancy of the Borough at all times'.[130] The terms honesty, worth, independence, reputation, and fortune described the successful merchant, whose wealth and principles made him a natural ruler. These qualities derived from the middling sort themselves—from their superior values and virtues—not from the elite. There was no mention of gentility or politeness in the list of positive characteristics that embodied the Tuckers' ideal self.

At the same time, tensions and disappointments released a 'language of resentments' that was often directed against those with gentility. For H. R. French, 'the concept of gentility had more potential than the category of the "middle sort of people" for an extra parochial collective identity.'[131] This approach, however, downplays the importance of negative feelings against the gentry, as seen in the Tuckers' letters. French's own example, Henry Abbott, an Earls Colne cloth trader, 'resented the gentry as a group, particularly when they claimed legal and social authority of a kind un- available to him. This', French noted, 'was close to "class consciousness"', because it implied 'the social positions and economic interests of "gentle- men" and "tenants" were inevitably and diametrically opposed'.[132] Berry's study of John Marsh, an amateur musician in Chichester, raised a similar point. Berry found the unedited pages of Marsh's manuscript were 'riddled with petty grievances, biased accounts of internecine warfare, and judgments upon his own and others' conduct'.[133] Edmund Rack of Bath voiced similar sentiments as a he tried to 'cut a figure' in Bath's Society for the Encouragement of Agriculture, Arts, Manufactures, and Commerce.[134]

These anecdotal references are conceptually integrated in the work of Vera Nunning. She suggests there was a 'deep-seated middling belief in the basic inferiority of the lower classes'. At the same time, middling sorts called the upper classes 'luxurious, corrupt and immoral'. The result of this 'ingenious combination' was 'a coherent system of values which defined their own social group as the most valuable and virtuous order of society'.[135]

Nunning's ideas are visible in the Tuckers' language of resentments, especially when they looked upwards. The villains of their letters were 'Overbearing Gentry'[136] and 'haughty and insolent' politicians, who were known as 'great men'.[137] Letters decry the undeserved privileges of 'country gentleman'. Thus Dodington talked haughtily of giving Parliament seats 'to country gent'n' rather than 'stock jobbers'. Because of this partiality, Richard feared, the Tuckers would 'make but a pitifull figure after ye Reput'n we have acquired'. Those 'sort of gentlemen', he cautioned, 'always go down worst with our folk'.[138] By contrasting 'our folk' with landed men, Richard excluded himself from the group that was associated with gentility. This left men of 'reputation' in a nebulous category, one that Richard believed was ethically superior.[139]

Men like Walpole, John fumed, enjoyed seeing 'how humble we can be whenever a great man thinks fit to talk big and bully'.[140] In John's view, the 'great man' was a corrupter of government and hostile to 'men of town & Corporation'.[141] 'All great men are alike', summed up John. 'The only difference is that some are less scrupulous to avow themselves than others.'[142] In letters, the Tuckers could look down on those in power and simultaneously praise themselves.

The Tuckers, however, did not reserve their animosity to 'great men' above them. They made negative remarks about 'middling' men, which, again, made them feel superior. When discussing a candidate for mayor, for example, Richard observed 'yt people of that persuasion in the middle station of life [a]re generally more stubborn than others & harder to be wrot upon than people of better educa[tio]n and sense'.[143] Naturally, the Tuckers considered themselves part of the latter exalted category. When evaluating the status of another person, each individual compared it with that of his own imagined rank, which was usually a step up from the one under consideration. Letters were perfect sites for venting emotions in regard to slights about status and power.

Negative language was also used in relation to members of the ill-defined professions. In 1733, 'a young spruce apothecary... asserted very confidently' that writs for a new Parliament would be issued. The Tuckers instantly dismissed his news, for 'he talk'd like an apothecary'. Such a man, it was inferred, was unacquainted, like the Tuckers, with affairs of state.[144] Naturally, the Tuckers had harsh words for competing merchants. By mid century, traders from other towns tried to take business away from the Tuckers. John hoped to 'crush these little pedlars... and put the Trade, though little, on a better foote'. Rivals were called 'interlopers' or 'intruders', signifying their interference in the Tuckers' affairs.[145] Richard labelled them 'new Adventurers', who 'seduce our workmen from us by offers of advantage'.[146] Though merchant networks were often supportive, there were also deep divisions amongst the trading classes.[147]

It is harder to understand the Tuckers' references to the lower orders. Richard told a seaman that he was too grand for a seat in the Weymouth Corporation reserved for those 'among the lowest class'.[148] John spoke of a friend, who was 'every day mixing himself among our people of ye lowest classes'.[149] He also cited 'people in low life' when he discussed 'a woman who once lived a servant with me'.[150] John's account of 'a noisy mob' is easier to grasp.[151] In the main, the Tuckers turned their thoughts and pens to negative comments about the 'great men' that threatened them. Their fluid, negative language stands in contrast to the stable ranks, sorts, and classes with which historians are familiar.

None of this would be apparent without the Tuckers' huge correspondence. Letter-writing is usually seen as valuable to merchants for business reasons. The Tucker archive reveals a more complex use of letters—as a place to develop linguistic strategies that enhanced personal identity and social status. This was not a casual or sporadic process, but a daily application of epistolary literacy. As David Gerber notes, letters provide continuity of identity. They are part of an ongoing narrative we 'compose about ourselves that ensures us that we are knowable persons'.[152]

The Tucker letters help us speculate how language may have contributed to the rise of class-consciousness. As letters were written, ties were constructed between people above, below, or equal to each other in rank. Thus as people corresponded, distinctions of social status were repeatedly made and renegotiated. This two-way dialogue, I suggest, provided preconditions for the construction of power relations—or what E. P. Thompson called 'the making of class'.[153] Since then, scholars have sought new ways to understand social relationships. With the decline of Marxism, the search for a methodology that shows how people interacted socially has become more urgent.[154] Letter-writing, I suggest, can offer new pathways into how ordinary people communicated with each other before the advent of class.

The Batemans of Manchester and the Wilsons of London

A loving letter is all the comfort one has when absent from each other.[155]

One thing was clear in August of 1781, 15-year-old Rebekah Clegg (c.1764–97) was not returning to Mrs Trinder's School in Northampton.[156] Mrs Trinder had told high-spirited Rebekah: 'I had a Mama, pap, & sister going to Heaven & I was going ye broad road to Hell.' As intended, this remark instilled terror in our young Congregational schoolgirl. 'O . . . if it should be true', groaned Rebekah, 'how terrible for me who has had so many priviledges & slighted them.'[157] She refused to stay at school, not even for 'an hundred guineas',[158] but she would be fearful for her salvation for the rest of her life.

Rebekah was the daughter of Sarah (1733–1811)[159] and Arthur Clegg (1732–1818) of Manchester. Clegg was a founder of Moseley Street Congregational Chapel and served as deacon for over fifty years.[160] Rebekah married a cotton merchant, Thomas Bateman (1760–1847) of Manchester, in 1786.[161] He was less interested in his wife's type of evangelical religion that was influenced by George Whitefield, and he immersed himself in his work. Her sister Elizabeth (1762–1847) wed a silk merchant Thomas Wilson of London (1764–1843).[162] When he inherited money, he left commerce and spent his life building Congregational chapels throughout England.

Papers of three generations of the Batemans and Wilsons from the 1760s–1840s show how epistolary literacy and evangelical religion shaped a family's lives. This case study draws on the Wilson papers in the Congregational Library in London administered by Dr Williams's Library. It also introduces the spectacular unpublished Bateman archive in the

Beinecke Library at Yale University. When used together, we see that letters of the sisters in one archive are often replies to those in the other. They give a picture of three generations of a Congregational family at the end of the eighteenth century. Records in the Manchester City Library and Derbyshire Record Office further describe their lives.

The Batemans and Wilsons used letters to create personal relationships and identities, but for very different ends than those of the Tuckers. In long runs of correspondence, we see ties being created between husbands and wives, parents and children, sisters and cousins. Letters also reveal bonds between writers and their churches, and, most importantly, to God. In fact, they offered a crucial space for defining and professing religious beliefs. Along with prayer and sermon, they became a place to focus on Christ and an instrument for achieving grace. Yet this was a serious and demanding task. Letters offered a breathing space where writers could cope with tensions between God, chapel, family, and the commercial world. In happier moments they were sites for the expression of joy and the creation of supportive networks.

We see both happiness and tension in the letters of Rebekah Bateman, which continued to her early death in 1797. She lived at a time when Congregational chapels were rapidly increasing in number. Independents grew significantly before 1800, from about 200 congregations in the early eighteenth century to over 900 by its end. Thereafter the total increased by a stunning quarter or third each decade.[163] The records of Moseley Street Chapel confirm it was being re-energized by gifted itinerant preachers, charitable donations, and increased membership.[164] In a world marked by industrial expansion and worker insecurity, Congregational Dissent offered men and women important lay roles.[165] In contrast to the central authority of the Church of England, each congregation enjoyed freedom. Like the Tuckers, Congregationalists longed for independence. They achieved it, however, in a different way—through separation from the established Church. On his deathbed, Rebekah's brother-in-law pleaded that his family would 'be preserved from conformaty to the world'.[166] Rebekah's sect has been called 'the most middle class of all the noncon-formist groups . . . Everything about them—preaching, buildings, ministers, manners, notions and practices—all ha[d] on them the air and impress of English middle class life.'[167] An active membership encouraged women's education, travel, and literacy.[168] They also selected ministers and applicants for membership.[169]

The Batemans and Wilsons were influenced by Whitefield and other evangelicals. They believed that 'the way to salvation [was] . . . reached only through suffering and renunciation of the world'.[170] Worshippers focused on man's relation to God's grace and conversion through a covenant with 'blessed Jesus'.[171] Emotional public worship was encouraged, in order to discover if one was saved.[172] Sermons were used to induce a crisis as worshippers struggled for salvation. Hence, Rebekah's brother-in-law told new ministers: 'Urge what you deliver as a man would plead for his own life . . . Go out into the highways and hedges, and *compel* them to come in.'[173]

Rebekah was thus part of a tightly knit chapel world that was 'fervent with a sense of new spirituality'.[174] Yet constant discipline and self-examination produced a life filled with worries about personal salvation. Unlike the Tuckers, failed efforts to repeal the Corporation and Test Acts for Dissenters meant families could not engage fully in politics. This created 'legal and social disabilities, which made them a people apart in the national life'.[175] Clyde Binfield notes the tensions this created for economically independent families in an industrializing society.[176] The American and French Revolutions and the radicalism of the 1790s pitted many Dissenters against the government.[177] Again like the Tuckers, but for different reasons, epistolary literacy was used to cope with anxiety about family, business, and politics. Gender was also a source of concern for Congregational women.

In Rebekah's city of Manchester, Nonconformity had a history of splintered churches. There had been an Independent Chapel in Cross Street, Manchester as early as 1693.[178] In 1761, when it became too Unitarian for some members, a minority founded a Congregational meeting house in Canon Street.[179] After disputes with its minister, a majority of elders, including Rebekah's father, again withdrew to found a new chapel. His warehouse was used for worship until Moseley Street Chapel was opened in 1788.[180] Yet Elizabeth feared its first minister, Thomas Kennedy, was 'not possessed of popular gifts'[181] and she grew 'anxious for the cause of Religion at Manchester'.[182] After Kennedy left, itinerant ministers preached each Sabbath.

At last, after endless ballots by male and female seat holders,[183] Joseph Smith of Coventry was elected in 1798. A former businessman with no collegiate training, Smith revived the congregation.[184] On the day of his ordination, 'there was a small scaffold erected in the middle Isle' for him 'to stand on while he gave in his confession of Faith'. One minister was 'so much afected that he could scarce be heard in... his prayer', whilst another had to 'recover himself' before speaking. 'The sencible presence of God was amongst us', wrote Rebekah's mother, Sarah Clegg. She thought there were '3,000 within & some Hundreds out of doors'. 'Mr S[mith] was very alarming... & so animated he could scarce go over.' Sarah later 'felt my heart so knit to him' that she went 'into the vestry to shake hands with him'.[185] Membership lists and minutes track the Clegg family as they made donations[186] and handed in numbered tickets that monitored attendance.[187] Membership grew under the leadership of Smith, and then Samuel Bradley, as a long series of letters show.[188]

This revival of religious activity took place when Manchester was itself expanding. City maps and directories record leaps in population, trade, and transport in the last quarter of the century. In 1760, it took three days to reach London by stagecoach; by 1788 the post coach took only one. The population almost doubled from 23,000 in 1774 to over 43,000 in 1788, whilst the Bridgewater Canal lowered the price of coals and linked Manchester to international markets.[189] The cotton trade became the economic lifeblood of Manchester. Yet it lacked political clout and was still 'a Dull, Smoky, Dirty Town in a Flat, from whence the Black Soot rises in clouds'. In 1788, a visitor to Rebekah's street noted: 'We got to Lever's Row... where our lodgings are small and Indifferent, but the best Manchester affords.'[190] In 1777 Samuel Curwen found manners 'inhospitable and boorish... The dissenters', he remarked, 'are some of the most wealthy merchants and manufacturers here, but mostly abhorred by the Jacobites.'[191] His comments provide a backdrop for the economic depression and political riots of the 1790s. They included an attack on the Unitarian Chapel in Mosley Street near Rebekah's own church.[192] The Lord 'restrained the mob', she noted, 'so that very little carnage was done'.[193]

Comments about current events are found in hundreds of letters of the Batemans and Wilsons. The first letters received by the sisters were sent by their mother Sarah Clegg, who begged them to 'be submissive & Teachable'.[194] Her expressions of feeling 'high' or 'low', 'thankful', or 'blessed by God' were used later by both daughters. Sarah was happy they were progressing in writing at school, 'but should be much more so to hear that you are improving in Spiritual Knowledge... of your Original depravity & ... by your getting an intrest in the Merrits and Righteousness of A Pretious Redeemer'.[195] Their father, Arthur soon moved out of the city to a 'new upcoming place near Shude Hill'.[196] A friend called Arthur 'for plainness...a Jacob, for sincerity a Nathaniel',[197] but he was 'not fond of writing'. He refused to correspond with Elizabeth's father-in-law 'because he thought he was a bad speller'. Happily, his daughter recopied his letters.[198]

Both sisters were educated in well-disciplined boarding schools and were more skilled in writing than their mother. They wrote in straight lines in small flowing hands and inserted biblical references from sermons. (See Plate 27.) Both girls used proverbs, literary metaphors, and quotation marks to show dialogue. They played music and read religious works by Bunyan, Hervey, and Newton. Yet unlike the Tuckers, their cultural life was centred upon endless sermons.[199]

Young Rebekah was known for her funny verses,[200] and her love of life kept bubbling up in sombre religious letters about the 'vanity of ye world'.[201] She tried hard to contemplate her death, but 'no sooner get my thoughts there but...some worldy thoughts or something intervenes & I am again immersed as deep as ever'. It was hard for merchant families, caught up in busy lives, to remain focused on God. Letters provided a place to renew that focus and conduct self-examination. In letters, Rebekah admitted things she was ashamed of and vowed to return to a better path.[202] 'My wicked heart ensnares & draws me aside too often', she wrote. 'I am distressed for ye lord is gone from me...May ye Lord never suffer me to wonder any more.'[203] Letters became a place to work out her basic dilemma—she had no proof that she was saved. 'Be this my ambition', she prayed, to 'make my calling & election sure.'[204] During her life she continued to use letter-writing as an instrument for attaining grace.

In a long series of letters to and from Rebekah, we see her struggle as a young woman, then grow more serious after marriage. She adored her children and wrote regularly to other women. Though she ran a busy household, she visited them when they needed her. She tried to reject the world, but still embraced its creatures too fully. Once after a rousing sermon, she had 'a Day I hope never to forget. I could say from my very heart: what I have long wish't for yt the Lord Jesus was & is more to me than anything here below.'[205] Four years later she was admitted into the church,[206] yet her fears remained. At her death aged 33 in 1797, she finally found peace in a deathbed letter that was saved, copied, and used to help later generations.[207] In letters, Rebekah worked out the most precious thing in life—her salvation.

Letters also helped her to deal with an unhappy marriage to cotton dealer, Thomas Bateman. Though fewer of his letters survive, those by others describe a gruff distant man, who was immersed in business. The couple lived near the Exchange in Lever's Row in the town centre,[208] until a move to the village of Gatley in 1795. They had three children spaced at three and four year intervals: William (1787–1835),[209] Thomas (1791–1810),[210] and Rebekah (1794–1838).[211] After his wife's death, Thomas resided in Gatley with an office in town.[212] By 1810, however, he was in business with his sons in Liverpool.[213] He trained them to fill letters with 'all the details you can about the cotton market', but they both died before their father.[214]

Thomas wrote hurriedly in a cold, competent manner.[215] Rebekah warned him not to think about business, 'so as to make you ill, which I know you art apt to do'.[216] He was often away from home 'upon cotton expeditions'[217] and he worried about debts. '*Disgrace* is coming', wrote Rebekah in 1788, 'I hope you can bear it.'[218] God must be relied on, she insisted. 'It's easy to be trusting with shops & warehouses full...but to be submissive under such strokes as these requires divine assistance.'[219] In contrast to his wife, Thomas seems not to have used letters as emotional outlets. At Rebekah's death, her sister begged him to vent his feelings by writing to her. If not, she warned, 'you will lose the relief which opening our minds gives to the spirits'. Unlike other male writers, who wrote in a language of sensibility, Thomas appeared to be resistant to opening up himself in letters.

The couple's major difference, however, was centred on their attitudes to religion. Thomas lacked Rebekah's evangelic zeal and refused to help her pass her beliefs on to their children. 'These are important things', she pleaded, and begged they might 'come to the Table of the Lord together'.[220] Thomas's long absences from home, his reluctance to answer her letters, and his refusal to let her make lengthy visits made things worse.[221] Pregnant almost immediately, Rebekah prepared an inventory of her sombre clothes and linens (just a lone pair of ruffles), in case she died.[222] Thomas continued to travel when her first child was due, though she begged him not to do so. We feel her fright and loneliness in her letters at this time.[223]

Because of her marital situation, Rebekah at first seems to be a weak, apologetic letter-writer. When she wrote to Thomas, she was forced to repress her epistolary zeal and could only lecture him about religion in small doses. Yet we learn to recognize and decode her subtle hints, complaints, and masked anger. Soon we understand that she was using her epistolary literacy to 'manage' a difficult husband. Constrained by spouse and religion, however, Rebekah remained unbowed in her desire for independence. With rhetoric, irony, and feminine excuses, she fought for family visits and found ways to avoid returning home. Her many letters to Thomas expose a primary function of correspondence—the construction of a personal relationship.

We also observe that Rebekah wrote letters in a markedly gendered way. Her apparently deferential style was, in part, a product of her patriarchal relationship with a neglectful husband. But it also stemmed from expected epistolary norms that she was determined to resist. Instead she created distinct standards for her own writing by apologizing for, but still stating, her religious beliefs. Thus she hoped she 'need not beg pardon . . . for the transgression I sincerely wish for myself, to taste the sweetness of religion'. In fact when it came to speaking God's words she could not help herself. 'I seem'd imperceptibly drawn to speak so largely on a favourite subject', she admitted, 'that before I was aware I was at ye bottom of my paper.'[224] Another long letter about religion, she conceded, was 'so uninteresting' it was 'enough to make you wish for the conclusion'.[225] Yet she had a duty to try to encourage his faith and refused to bow to custom.

The problem was that she was supposed to write entertaining letters. ''Tis generally expected', she noted, 'that a letter from a women should contain a good deal of news, but . . . I am afraid I shall not be able to fill the sheet.'[226] She had 'little to say in the entertaining way to a man of Business'.[227] Even worse, she begged him to write about his work, knowing others might object. 'Mr Holland', she admitted, 'wonders what ye Deuce his sister has to do with anything belonging to ye compting house. He should hate a wife yt was anxious as I am.'

Her final comment revealed frustration regarding her gender and her lack of freedom to write letters as she pleased. Indeed, the inequality in her marriage clashed with Dissenting ideas about the equality of every soul. 'My letter', she confessed, 'is quite out of your way', but 'you could expect nothing of any consequence from a woman. I wonder what *we* are fit for according to my master Mr Hollands idea.'[228] This pointed remark showed suppressed anger, but did not give way. It was in part strategically apologetic, but also partly defiant. Rebekah had mastered the feminine technique of protesting while apologizing. She might employ sarcasm, but her letters gave the appearance of staying within gendered norms. As the couple wrote letters, they were constructing a relationship, in which Rebekah's right to express zealous religious beliefs was always contested. Neither partner liked the letters of the other, and neither would change their ways. This epistolary difference caused problems in their marriage and underpinned much of their discord.

Marriage had its thorns, Rebekah noted pointedly: 'Mr Roscoe talked foolishly about his coming marriage. Had you been here you might probably have said something from our own experience of the troubles of the state to have damped him a little.'[229] Rebekah used letters as instruments to vent angry feelings and bring cathartic relief. Yet after Thomas's 'cross letter' in 1792, Rebekah paused strategically: 'Had I thought a letter from me wou'd have been acceptable there had been one at your service. But it struck me that a night's reflection might make things appear more in my favor. I therefore concluded to let it alone till today.'[230] The gendered aspects of letter-writing, are visible in Rebekah's tactics. Not willing to be docile, she tried to use letters to convince her husband to become more outwardly religious. As she wrote them their tense relationship was constantly being transformed.

Rebekah's letters urging Thomas to be more religious apparently fell on deaf ears. After she was admitted as a full member of the church, Elizabeth was disappointed. She 'had hoped to have heard Mr Bateman's name had been mentioned also'.[231] At Rebekah's death, a deacon suggested that Thomas 'take public possession of the name of Christ'.[232] Thomas eventually returned to his family home in Derbyshire and became High Sheriff. In 1823, a newspaper described his attendance at the assizes 'with a large party of Gentlemen'. On Sunday, it reported, all the judges and gentleman 'attended divine service at All Saints Church'. These events would have been part of the duties of his office, which was not an optional one. But it is telling that Thomas attended this Anglican sermon.[233]

It appears that during their marriage, Thomas was a less enthusiastic type of Independent than Rebekah. Later in life, however, he erected at least three Congregational chapels, including Middleton near Youlgreave, where he was an active member.[234] Rebekah would have preferred him to be more zealously outward in his faith. Indeed, this fact underpinned their epistolary quarrels. Sceptical, but in command of her domestic situation, she accepted the limitations of marriage and found joy in family and friends. She had been fearful about God—but not about life.

* * * *

The opposite might be said of her sister Elizabeth Wilson,[235] who was more confident about religion but more fearful of living. Fortunately, her forceful, optimistic husband offered a strong arm to lean upon. 'We ought not to give way to gloomy forebodings', he insisted. 'Difficulties ... can only be conquered by daring to attempt them.'[236] In 1798, Thomas Wilson abandoned his London silk business after inheriting an uncle's wealth. He had been 'aiming after diligence in business, and fervency in spirit, serving the Lord',[237] but he found it impossible to attain both simultaneously. 'I thought it was a duty to relinquish Trade', he wrote. 'This step I have had great reason to be thankful for.'[238]

As treasurer of Hoxton Academy, later Highbury College, he instead devoted his life to educating Congregational ministers, building chapels, and spreading the gospel in foreign lands.[239] His hurried handwriting betrayed his commercial education and active life, whilst his reading showed an intellectual curiosity outside the bounds of religion.[240] Wilson's life was filled with Christian zeal and accomplishment. Ever engaged in public disputes, he was accused of running Hoxton Academy 'like it belonged to me'.[241] Yet his unwavering confidence led him to cooperate with other groups. 'Undenominational evangelical religion at its most stately', wrote Binfield, 'is characterized by Thomas Wilson of Highbury.'[242] John Creasey called him 'that colossus of English Congregationalism'.[243] Robert Halley thought him 'the most prominent layman for many years in his denomination', who built more chapels than one could count.[244] A founder of London's Congregational Library, in this chapter he emerges as a family man.

He was lucky in his marriage partner, for he prayed to God to 'find a companion who ... had real piety'. In contrast to Rebekah, Elizabeth had a loving marriage and resisted taking off her wedding ring when it became too large.[245] After she married this forthright evangelical, she was plunged into the capital's political and intellectual life. Fresh from her honeymoon Elizabeth reported: 'In this place there are variety of ministers and great opportunities of hearing faithful zealous men ... I think I have heard 12 or 14 since I came.'[246] The couple had a son Joshua and two daughters, both of whom married ministers.[247] Thomas once compared his wife's 'tender affection' to that of Lady Rachel Russell, who took notes for her husband at his trial for treason. 'Who would live without love?', Wilson asked, as he copied a passage from Lady Russell's letter.[248] 'I think the more we love home, the happier we shall be.'[249]

Yet his courtship letters dwelled on a sinful world with transient pleasures: 'Let us always remember not to expect too much from each other, nor of anything below the sky.'[250] This gloomy message in a love letter struck a chord in Elizabeth. Fearful of death, childbirth, and her husband's politics, she was frequently depressed. 'I am apt to look forward towards trouble', she admitted, 'more than does me any service.'[251] She was afraid Rebekah hid bad news about her parents,[252] and talked to their portraits in her lonely room.[253] Letters gave Elizabeth comfort, when she had time to write them. 'I am rocking the cradle while I am writing', she remarked.[254]

Elizabeth was also afraid of her husband's outspoken public views. He believed 'the whole business of religion is a matter of conscience . . . not to be regulated in any degree by civil legislation'.[255] 'The Church of England, he insisted, does 'deceive the people, and cause too many of them to "trust in a lie"'.[256] In the 1790s, Elizabeth used letters to express her anxiety about his statements: 'I hear of so many being taken up that I give my Husband a charge to keep his sentiments to himself . . . Mr Edinger got into trouble with only cursing the Empress of Russia . . . Much more was made of what little Politics there were in it . . . I wish all Ministers would entirely leave them out of the pulpit.' Yet her husband would not be silenced. 'War is contrary to Christianity', he noted in 1805, when asked to donate funds for Nelson's victory. 'The American War & all the wars since with France have been neither just or necessary.' He would 'never give anything voluntarily to support a system of murder abroad and corruption at home'.[257] Letter-writing helped Elizabeth to deal with Thomas's outspokenness.

In fact, the couple used letters in ways that were often gendered. Thomas wrote his confidently to accomplish great works and strengthen the resolve of friends. Elizabeth employed hers to cope with the problems of all women—the marital relationship, fear of death in pregnancy, and the loss of children. Letters between Elizabeth and other females helped them to define their roles as daughters, wives, and mothers. They also show the value of epistolary networks for young women, who were frightened about sin. Pregnancy was a frequent topic and Elizabeth was determined 'to

take [her] good time'.[258] 'You may think well that you have not had 4 in
4 years', she told Rebekah, 'as Mrs Greaves has... This is the second time
she has been confined since I was.'[259] When pregnant, Elizabeth felt 'low'
and wished 'I could leave myself in his hands who can do all things'.[260]
She hoped not to be pregnant in the summer, for it would keep her from
family visits.[261]

Elizabeth was obsessed by deaths in childbirth and took each one as a
'warning'.[262] Marriage was another problem.[263] At the age of 16, Rebekah
described a schoolmate who had 'begun the world soon & may perhaps
repent it... If she has got a serious good man t'will... make her troubles
seem lighter.'[264] Elizabeth had a 'serious' spouse and thought their husbands
were 'not so bad'.[265] Be thankful, she wrote Rebekah, 'we have both got
good partners. It is seldom all in one family are comfortably married.'[266]
Both sisters assumed they might only wed 'one of my sort' or 'church
folks'.[267]

Loving children more than the Lord was another problem for women.
After Rebekah's first child was born, Elizabeth prayed: 'I heartily wish you
may be enabl'd to love him subserviently to the love of God.'[268] Yet after
the birth of her own daughter, she found this hard to do. The baby had
'found out those corners of our hearts, which we did not know ourselves',
wrote Mary Wilson of Elizabeth's child. 'This little creature is a great
tempter.'[269] When Elizabeth lost a boy in childbirth, she struggled not to
'murmur'.[270] 'O may we sit loose to the creatures', she implored, '& enjoy
them as fading things.'[271] Just as men might love money and business too
much, women might too deeply adore children. 'I do love Domestick
Happiness', summed up Elizabeth, 'notwithstanding the care & anxiety.'[272]
Letters brought cathartic relief in these gendered situations and were used
differently by husband and wife. 'My pervers nature is my burden', she
added later. 'I... long to be entirely changed.' Women welcomed the time
to sit down with a pen and think about their lives. When Rebekah feared
her sister was angry, Elizabeth responded quickly: 'I am quite the reverse
to angry with you. It won't do to be so at so great a distance. A loving
letter is all the comfort one has when absent from each other.'[273]

These loving letters show how epistolary experience was gendered.
They also depict active women who led disciplined lives, but were
not slavishly dependent. Lenore Davidoff and Catherine Hall's idea of
separate spheres does not work for all women, especially Congregational
Dissenters who played important lay roles in their churches.[274] Thus

Elizabeth engaged in evangelical work and was consulted by ministers, whilst Rebekah was deeply involved in Moseley Street meetings.[275] The sisters add complexity to general theories about the place of late eighteenth-century women.

Their husbands also complicate Weber's model of the Protestant work ethic by choosing different ways to reconcile religion with the commercial world.[276] Bateman may have allowed business to override religious concerns. Yet he was glad when his wife's Chapel defended his credit and reputation. 'Whenever any member might fail in business', noted Charles Leach, 'enquiry was made, if owing to misfortune or . . . criminality, the object being . . . to vindicate their character.'[277]

In contrast, Wilson rejected trade due to an unusual inheritance. Yet even he could not give up the world of masculine accomplishments. He threw himself into building Highbury College even more obsessively than he conducted his silk trade. 'If, by the constant pressure of affairs', worried Reverend Samuel Bradley, 'you . . . acquire ye habit of continually pushing on business as far as you can . . . the days may come when you find that you have lost ground in the divine life, for which nothing can be a counterbalance.'[278] Pride in his academy threatened Wilson's focus on God. In a different way from the Tuckers, he also voiced feelings of superiority over those in polite society. 'I really pity the genteel part of the world that are slaves to fortune', he wrote.[279] Like Leeds clothier, Joseph Ryder, he valorized 'his middling social place' by seeing those richer than himself 'mired in sin'.[280] For Dissenters, the 'primacy of inner spirit' stood in contrast to the fleeting pleasures of the aristocracy.[281] Politics offered another problem for Wilson. Nonetheless, he was able to gain real influence within Congregationalism by training its ministers. This was a different type of power than that of the Tuckers, but it was accompanied by more independence.

The Bateman and Wilson letters were firmly centred on the search for salvation. Writers tried hard to focus on the doctrine of grace, but this was not always possible. This led to a particular kind of anxiety, which was different from that of the Tuckers, about whether or not one would become a member of the elect. The fact that Rebekah's and Elizabeth's correspondents were all co-religionists leant a hothouse effect to their letters and little disagreement. Writers seemed to keep a social distance from the wider world. 'Indulge me with a line', a friend wrote to Rebekah. 'The friends of *Jesus* need to keep close to one another.'[282] Born into marginality,

Dissenters clung together. Letters played a crucial role in linking and protecting them from a corrupting world.

Congregational writers employed a distinctive religious language, again far different from that of the Tuckers, which grew out of their minority position. Fearful dichotomies were used—light and darkness, heights and depths, life and death. The metaphor of warfare was also often employed. 'How inclined are we to seek rest in the field of Battle', wrote Elizabeth, 'but how inconsistant! May the Lord make us good soldiers of Jesus Christ that we may war a good warfare against the World of the Flesh ... I wish I could feel disposed to *endure hardship* as a foot soldier but alas—I am ready to shrink when any severe attack comes on.'[283] Rebekah and Elizabeth found this language in the biblical texts and fiery sermons that they copied into correspondence. Then they imitated this language in the body of their letters. Over time it became embedded in consistent ways.

'I am glad to see in your letter the Language of one in the School of Christ', a friend wrote Rebekah.[284] This meant that Rebekah had written in a manner with which a co-religionist could identify. Another friend thanked Rebekah for her 'kind & Christian letter' and sent 'Christian respects'.[285] A 'Christian letter' contained language used regularly by chapel members. Its subject matter was dominated by themes of conversion and election. A Christian letter was also filled with hope and thankfulness for the privilege of faith. This meant that some letters possessed a heightened sanctity. Despite her husband's disdain, Rebekah thought that people who wrote religious letters were 'serious'. A truly Christian letter might thus become a means of grace.

The Bateman and Wilson letters reveal how religion, family, gender, and business competed for a place in a person's self-identity. Rebekah and Elizabeth wanted to put God first, but their human interests kept bursting through. Still religion was the driving force behind everything they did. The Batemans and Wilsons used letter-writing to construct their faith as they strove to achieve grace in a commercial world.

The Follows family of Castle Donington, Leicestershire and Woodbridge, Suffolk

Although we may be outwardly separated, yet we are as epistles written in one another's minds.[286]

In 1782, a grocer's apprentice, Samuel Follows (b. 1755) wrote testily to his mother Ruth Follows (1718–1808), who had declined to send him money. He did not 'perceive that flow of affection nor tender readiness to administer a little help'.[287] Yet Ruth, a Quaker minister, had tried all of her life to bring harmony to her family through a series of loving letters. In 1782, however, aged 65, Ruth had other problems. Storms had forced her to leave her long boat on a visit to Irish Quakers, and she found herself stranded amongst people 'little better than cannables'. Yet once she safely carried out her mission, she had feelings of elation. 'O that peace of soul may be continued', she prayed. 'We shall have a gloryous inheritance.'[288]

This case study examines the role of letter-writing in the lives of the Follows family. It asks how Quaker letters compared with those found in other collections. The Follows letters span four generations and contain both sides of Ruth's correspondence from the 1730s to her death in 1808, aged 91.[289] Ruth's love of God and family came shining through, as she wrote each letter. Not surprisingly, her mother had 'trained her up in a religious life and conversation'.[290] Yet Ruth had 'trod her testimony under my feet and took a large swing in vanity frequenting such as had like to be my ruin'. The Lord 'took off my chariot wheels', Ruth happily admitted, 'so that I could not overthrow'.[291] In 1740, she married George Follows (1717–1803), a basket maker in Castle Donnington, Leicestershire.[292] They farmed a little and scraped to make a living. 'I was thy fathers partner', Ruth once told her children, 'at sharing last harvest and was scarce able some nights to turn my self in bed.'[293] In 1747 Ruth recalled that 'my mouth was first opened in a public manner'.[294] At a meeting in a simple barn, she was called by God to the ministry.[295] In contrast to Moseley Street's noisy emotional sermons, Ruth's calling evolved out of Quaker silence. For sixty years she visited Quaker meetings in England, Scotland, and Ireland,[296] while her supportive husband cared for their children: George (1742–66),[297] Richard (b. 1745),[298] Joseph (1751–1809),[299] and Samuel (1755–1811?).[300] Revered by other Quakers, she was called 'that faithful solider in the Lamb's Warfare',[301] 'a true living gospel minister',[302] and 'one of the most musical preachers . . . ever heard'.[303] At times Ruth admitted she was 'prity much stript of . . . temporal goods',[304] but George proudly refused poor 'releife'.[305]

Though Ruth and George were lower class in terms of wealth, their faith encouraged epistolary literacy, and their family lived as part of a middling-sort religious community. One of their sons and their grandchildren earned money as retail clerks. Reading and writing thus pervaded their business and religious lives.[306] Even more than Congregationalists, Quakers stressed female equality and allowed women to become ministers. Ruth had a position of respect and power in her career and marriage. Her gender issues arose from the fact that she had to cede her maternal duties to George.[307] This caused her pain and guilt.

Though she may have had little or no formal schooling, Ruth read worldly literature in her youth. Rebekah Bateman, in contrast, limited herself to works of devotion. But though Ruth's skills were not polished like Rebekah's, she did not write letters phonetically.[308] Her hurried hand crammed eager thoughts onto every page, without regard for presentation.[309] Each letter discussed others that were sent, received, lost, or unwritten, for letters were integral parts of life. 'We . . . received thy letter as we sat at dinner', Ruth told her son, 'Brought by A Boy of Cosen Sam.'[310] Another son's letter arrived during one of Ruth's journeys: 'We were both of us on horseback when thy acceptable Letter came . . . which I read over as I sat.'[311] At the age of 86 she was still 'willing to salute my dear grandchildren' in a letter of advice,[312] and in 1794, while travelling in the Peaks, she 'ordered pen ink and paper to be brought . . . so you will . . . be informed that I am yet alive'.[313] Networks of Quakers acted as private postmasters bringing mail to and from far-flung ministries.

Ruth had deep maternal feelings and was anxious when she left her children. Nor was her sacred calling assured. After thirty-five years of service she confessed, 'I am still sorely beset and oft in great fear least I should become prey to the enemy.'[314] Like the Tuckers and Batemans, she had to live with uncertainty—in her case as to when she would be 'called' to travel. Yet she struggled to be present when her family was in need. On her journeys, Ruth turned to letters and filled them with loving salutations: 'Dear and Loveing Husband in unfeigned Love to thee and my Dear and Tender Children do I now write and although it is so ordered that wee are separated one from another . . . yet I am near to you in spirit . . . I hope my Dear Ones do not forget me.'[315] (See Plate 28.) In 1773 she was 'in great distress, not having heard of my dear husband for many weeks, so that I sank exceedingly low and had great conflict of soul'.[316] Without the comfort of letters, the maternal part of Ruth's identity would have been lost. She and her family suffered from anxiety, albeit for other reasons than the Tuckers and Batemans.[317]

Different sides of the correspondence offer different points of view of the same situation. 'Mary Lever . . . is gone of a religious visit into America', wrote her most troublesome son, Joseph. This 'is a great trial', he added, 'to her husband and dear children'. He was indirectly criticizing Ruth without rudely naming her, but his own feelings were evident.[318] Yet Rebecca Larson explains that 'careful nurturance of a child's religious growth, instilling obedience, self-discipline, and humility, was congruent with an exemplary mother's absences from the household "in the service of Truth"'. Periods of absence represented not 'lack of emotional attachment but rather the denial of the self'.[319]

Ruth discussed this problem in chains of letters to female friends, who understood the pressures of family and religion. 'When a child is in trouble', one remarked, 'a parent is ready to cry out, "My son, my son!"'.' Yet it was perilous 'to shew too much countenance . . . to transgressing children . . . & so supersede . . . the Testimony of the Truth'.[320] Ruth's greatest fear was that her children would not remain Quakers. 'Ah that my children were fellow labourers with me', she wote.[321] But a long series of letters show that this hope was not wholly fulfilled. Family correspondence, however, was as crucial to her sons as it was to their mother.[322]

The changing relationships between Ruth and her sons, Ruth and her husband, and those between siblings are clear in their letters. This is also true of the Follows's relationships with members of the Quaker community, and, most importantly, to God. An interesting example of relations between parent and child concerned Ruth and her most promising son, Samuel. In 1769 she used Quaker networks to arrange an apprenticeship as a grocer's clerk for Samuel. Ruth hoped he would be socialized into a separate Quaker community. Only then would he be safe from the corruption of the wider world. The Wilsons who lived in London were less cut off in this respect, whilst the fully integrated Tuckers differed from them both. Ruth also hoped a position in an urban mercantile trade would teach Samuel hard work and thrift.[323] He was joining a growing mass of middling-sort clerks, who were trying to make a living using writing skills. In his case, employment took place in a Quaker context, but it was part of a larger middling-sort trend.

Aged 14, young enough to complain about his pimples,[324] Samuel was sent to work for a Quaker grocer, Haggitt Peckover in Yarmouth, Norfolk.[325] Long a place of Dissent because of its maritime relations with the Low Countries,[326] Yarmouth's Quaker meeting house, bought in 1694, contained a writing school in 1728.[327] Samuel's fine presentation letters in a round 'copperplate' hand bear marks of instruction by a writing master.

(See Plate 29.) Perhaps he acquired his penmanship at a school funded by Quakers.[328] Because he could 'write well', unlike his brothers, Samuel was urged to 'say more' in letters. Ruth sent a 'Recept' on 'How to make Ink' to help him in his work.[329] Samuel was defensively proud about his writing skills: 'It was a mistake of Mother thinking that my Master Indited my Letters', he wrote. 'They are all my own works.'[330] A 'deformity' in one letter arose when he was 'obliged to write in the seller in order to [keep it] secret from my Master'.[331] After rising at six, Samuel had 'full imploy' until his nightly dinner at eight. Then he shut the shop at nine. Peckover kept him 'so ingaged' that he could 'well write only of a 1st day [Sunday]'.[332] He was 'distracted by customers' as he penned his letters, but remembered to append his usual P.S.: 'Answer me as soon as opportunity permit, I long so to hear of thee.'[333]

Like other middling-sort youths, Samuel was trying to rise in business by using his epistolary literacy.[334] Through constant writing, he developed a literary style marked by vivid narrative. 'I'll indeavour to be as descriptive as I can', he wrote, when he moved to Woodbridge, Suffolk in 1775[335] to work for grocer Simon Maw.[336] He drew a picture of a lively market town—'its trade by sea', its markets 'filled with buyers and sellers of grain'.[337] 'With the Advantages of a Turnpike Road, and the Post, and Stage-Coaches passing to and from London every Day', Woodbridge offered excitement.[338] Samuel's description of the character of his master, Simon Maw[339]—'unstable & snaffling'—and his Mistress Mary—'steady and thoughtful with laborious religious exercises'—dovetail nicely with comments found in Woodbridge Quarterly Meeting minutes and memoirs of another of Maw's apprentices.[340]

In 1768, there were '26 [Quaker] families, so that the Meeting-house was well-filled three times each first day,[341] and eight Friends sat in the Ministers Gallery,' including Mary Maw.[342] 'Agreable friends invite me to their houses', noted Samuel, 'so that my first Days (Sundays) are completely engaged.'[343] A list of tradesmen in 1782 includes most of them, along with several merchants, who sold wine, brandy, and hops. Yet Quaker numbers were shrinking nationally, in contrast to an expanding Congregationalism.[344] Despite its community of Friends, established in 1678, the town was filled with moral temptations. Ruth wrote that she was 'fearful of thee Least thou should be hurt by Reading Bad Books'.[345] In 1775, two apprentices quickly came and left Maw's shop, before Samuel arrived. The last, Benjamin Candler, was sent away when he was found 'guilty of the Act of Whoredom' after only five months of employment.[346] Like Congregationalists, Quakers believed that salvation would come only after worldly concerns were renounced. But the discipline of Quaker life flowed from strong central authority, in contrast to Moseley Street's independence.

Samuel found this control difficult to bear. He grew to hate the heavily monitored life of 'getting up the orders for Country-shops', making out 'bills of parcels', and functioning as a menial servant.[347] He warned his brother to stay away from shopkeeping, and his own position seemed dead-ended. Worse yet, it put him in contact with non-Quakers—the very situation that Ruth dreaded. In letters of 1777, written deftly to persuade his parents, Samuel begged to leave the 'fickle situation of commerce' for farming.[348] His potential partner, with whom he had 'contracted an intimacy', was a farmer named Waspe. He had been 'educated in the Church of England', Samuel reported, 'in which capacity he yet remains figuratively, tho' he has espoused the True Principal of Christianity. I found that among his Books his favourite authors were Robt Barkley, Wm Penn etc.'[349] Monthly meeting minutes reveal a Quaker family of Waspes, one of whom 'was 'Married contrary to the Rules of our society' in 1777.[350] In 1779, another Waspe admitted to entering the Militia and taking its oath of service.[351] Samuel was saved from this alliance by the local middling-sort Quaker network. Thus he 'listened to the sound reasoning' of John Gurney, a member of the well-known Norfolk family, and gave up his plan.[352]

By the 1780s, Ruth's letters show Samuel was ill, in debt, and looking for work. It is significant that when he lacked stable employment, he functioned as a scribe and was paid for his writing. Thus in 1783 he went daily to the house of a friend and 'I do his writing business for him'.[353] On a trip to Norfolk in 1784, Samuel remarked: 'As I was able to do a little writing for my friend Peckover, he was so generous to pay me for it.'[354] In his later letters to Ruth, he confirmed 'that affection that I . . . feel towards you, that tho' absent in Body we might be sensible in our spirits that we are one family in deed'.[355] It was only through letters, that their spirits could be united.

Samuel disappears from view until 1799, when Norwich Monthly Meeting minutes declared their 'disunity' with a Samuel Follows, who 'has lately married contrary to the rules of our Society to a person not in profession with us'.[356] Though we have no proof that this was Ruth's son, the will of a Samuel Follows of Castle Donnington in 1811 gives a possible ending to our story. He had left his estate to 'my natural son William Follows Taylor who now resides with me'.[357] If this was Ruth's son, Samuel, her letters of advice had failed to make him a 'fellow labourer'. They had, however, kept the family close in spirit.

Ruth's efforts were more successful with her libertine son Joseph, who admitted: 'I am not at all ready with my Pen.'[358] His cramped scrawled letters filled with blots and crossed out words reflected his disorderly life. After years of drinking, and possibly prison, his letters from Newfoundland and Nova Scotia were colourful travel accounts of a prodigal son.[359] 'Oh what satisfaction did it give us to hear of they safe arrival', wrote his worried parents.[360] Before Joseph emigrated, Ruth insisted he write to Samuel, who was 'thankful . . . we have had the satisfaction . . . to converse together before we are so far separated'.[361] Despite war and postal difficulties,[362] family letters sustained Joseph.[363] Eventually he returned, reformed, married a sober Quaker woman, and accompanied Ruth on her last missions.[364] Joseph's children grew up to be avid readers and their correspondence remains in the archive.[365] At the age of 14, his eldest son George wrote to his mother of going into book selling or drapery. (See Plate 30.) He had early success as a Liverpool grocer. Then his 'tea house' failed in 1834, and he tried his luck in America. Returning to England, George found work 'in the [Birmingham and Gloucester] Railway Office . . . as Chief Clerk under the Engineer in Chief'. He had hopes for 'a good or better situation' when 'the line is finished'. Like Joseph Morton in Kendal, his large ornamental handwriting helped him to gain employment in industry.[366]

All of the Follows letters reveal distinctive Quaker epistolary patterns. They evolved from the sect's early persecution and its stress on keeping written records. Like the Muggletonians, the seventeenth-century Quakers built their revolutionary movement on a network of epistles and testimonies. These were passed, read, discussed, and distributed from London to provincial meetings.[367] Though the fiery language of the founders had cooled, eighteenth-century letters still had distinctive Quaker elements in their language, content, and rhythm.[368] Those written by Quaker leaders like Ruth, as well as Thomas Story, and Elizabeth Payne,[369] opened with statements about letter-writing, then moved quickly to inward matters of religion and the soul. Gradually topics widened outward to parents, kin, and friends, then to trivial items.[370] Spiritual matters returned in intense closing statements accompanied by deeply affectionate sentiments. We can thus observe a rhythmic flow from inward to outward content, and then back again to spiritual matters.

As we move from letters of the Tuckers to those of the Batemans and Follows, epistolary practice becomes more distinctive. Quakers took common epistolary language and conventions, and adapted them radically to religious purposes. As in the world at large, letters were called 'salutations'[371] or 'acceptable favours'.[372] But Quaker postscripts sent spiritual love instead of 'humble services'.[373] In contrast to the Bateman letters, language was more often joyful.[374] For example, writers opened letters with 'I am bravely'.[375] Letters overflowed with biblical verses and proverbs, but this was a common trait.[376] Yet we also find a different Quaker language. References to the purity of the inward light offered contrasts to corruption in the outward secular world. Ruth's 'new Jerusalem' was a foil for cities like Bristol, where lost souls had 'built up towers like to Babel'.[377] More uniquely, the names of pagan months and days were never used. A special dating system replaced them with numbers: for example, 1st 1 month meant 1 January and 1st day was Sunday.[378] The use of 'thee' and 'thy', instead of more deferential pronouns, is well known.

But Ruth went a step further regarding forms of address. In her view, equal respect was due to all; only God had special honour.[379] 'I had rather thou did not say Hon'd etc', Ruth wrote Samuel, when he addressed them as 'Honored Parents'.[380] (See Plate 29.) 'As to saying Hon'd etc. before I wrote', he replied, 'I took it under consideration and I thought I had an Hon'd and Dutiful regard for you ... but as you rather I did not write so I will not.'[381] His next letter opened with 'Dear Father and Mother'. This equality would have been appreciated by Rebekah Batman, whose gender subjected her to a domineering husband.[382] Unique Quaker language patterns were not just repetitious window dressing; they were rituals impressed into the minds of the writer. As distinctive terms were chosen, writers were reminded that they were different from others. The banning of 'Hon'd' thus became a statement of faith.

As with language, motives and uses of Quaker letters could be conventional or distinctive. Samuel's motive for using letter-writing to help him earn a living was common to a vast number of middling-sort youths. The same could be said of his employment of letter-writing to develop narrative techniques. 'Now my paper being almost spent', he noted, 'I must draw to a conclusion.' He was conscious that his letter told a story with a beginning and an end.[383] But though all families told stories as they wrote letters, Quakers also wrote testimonies. These provided narrative models and recorded calls from God in an ennobling manner. In practice, public testimonies and letters had overlapping language and boundaries. At Ruth's death, some Friends praised her in personal letters, though she was already deceased: 'Thou art gathered as a Shock of Corn fully ripe into the heavenly garner', wrote an admirer. He signed it 'thy real friend, John Abbott'.[384]

Because groups of Quakers were so tightly linked together, personal letters were used to create community conversations, thus emulating epistles sent to local meetings.[385] As they were passed to others and quoted at length, letters bound people together. This was apparent before and after meetings, as Joseph's wife reported: 'Thy very acceptable Letter we Rec'd a week since today & as it was in time, several at our Quarterly meetings was glad to hear of thy . . . welfare . . . Thy near connections was much rejoiced.'[386] Quakers were not the only group to write letters to the community, but their epistles were more integrated into institutions, like the Monthly Meeting.

The constant separation that begot letter-writing was universal. Yet because Ruth's absence was ordered by God, there was a spiritual dimension to her correspondence, in which writers attempted to realize a communion of souls. 'Oh! our son,' wrote Ruth to Joseph, 'didst thou but feel our affectionate regard, and the many visits that our spirits pay thee, frequently flying as over the ocean to see what thou art about!'[387] Unlike other missives, Ruth's letters attempted to spiritually bridge distance and create actual presence as two souls joined together. One letter was particularly revealing of this distinct bonding. 'Although we may be outwardly separated', Ruth remarked, 'yet we are as epistles written in one another's minds.'[388] In this sense, letters became the embodiments of the two correspondents and instruments for impressing thoughts onto another person's consciousness. Margaret Routh repeated this idea as she sent Ruth a friend's writing: 'I, believing it will be satisfactory . . . to hear the language of her mind, shall give thee the following account out of her letters.'[389] Entering into the language of another's mind was an intense epistolary experience, especially when writers believed they possessed religious truths. Though Quaker and Congregational families used letters for religious purposes, there was a possibility of perfection in Ruth Follows's letters—more anxiety in those of Rebekah Bateman and Elizabeth Wilson.

As in the case of our Congregational sisters, the spiritual role of Ruth's letters was gendered in female correspondence. Ruth mentored and had deep friendships with women, not only on her travels, but in the pages of her letters. Her experience with two wayward sons helped her relate to problems faced by other wives and mothers. In addition, her position as a travelling female minister, unheard of in the outside world, gave her words unusual authority for a woman.[390] The ordinary advice letter became a spiritual document when written by her hand. 'Thy letter seemed to Revive me', Hanna Evans told Ruth: 'The feeling of each other in that nearness in which we...Salute Each other [was]...better than all the Eloquency of fine words.'[391] Sarah Taylor also analysed how words were used in a letter to Ruth: 'My spirit is replenished in feeling a spring of love flow towards you as I write...Without Gods divine presence...what are words but like sounding brass or a tinkling cymbal.'[392] Like Elizabeth Strutt in Derbyshire, Quaker women were self-conscious about how they used language, but here they were concerned about whether it was touched with divinity. In their hands, letter-writing became a transformative experience.

These comments about the power of God's words reveal a final distinctive role for Quaker letters. Though silence was extolled by Ruth,[393] so were words that came from God. Everyone had access to the Inward Light, if they made themselves open to it.[394] Twice Ruth prayed that her sons might 'all overcome the wicked one, so I may salute you as young men, who are strong, having the word of God abiding in you'.[395] But how did one know if God's word was present? Years of self- and group-examination in Quaker meetings were normally required. Yet letters gave separated Friends, as well as Rebekah Bateman, another space for an account of the state of their souls.

'I with gladness received thy letter', wrote Ruth, 'but in the reading of it, was seized with a jealousy that thou art not yet emptied enough of self.'[396] Quakers were supposed to weigh their words and speak Godly language, yet the writer of this letter merely gave an outward account of her life. In Ruth's terms, she was not yet 'fluent'. In 1774, Ruth praised Samuel for a letter of advice he had written to his brother, Joseph. 'Thou wast Aiming at fluency', she wrote in compliment, and 'did not say too much...I desire thee', she added, 'not to Abridg nor keep Back what Comes right.'[397] Letter-writing was a place to practice and attain 'fluency'—that easy cathartic outpouring of God's divine words that came after silence. It was part of a cluster of many types of Quaker writing that helped to shape one's inward state and prepare the soul for salvation.

Conclusion

Epistolary literacy was a unifying attribute and powerful weapon in the business, family, and spiritual lives of our four families. As in previous chapters, the motives, uses, and impacts of epistolary literacy were analysed. But the quantity and quality of middling-sort letter collections allowed us to observe epistolary patterns that were hidden in smaller collections. We saw how letters were used to transform aspects of personal identity regarding gender, family, business, religion, and class. Changing relationships were also observed between husbands and wives, parents and children, and clients and patrons. All of our families used letter-writing to cope with anxiety. Some of their worries, I suggested, arose from their ambiguous 'station' in the middle of the social structure. At the same time, the case studies provided ample evidence of epistolary differences. As the chapter progressed, the families under discussion were shown to be less integrated into mainstream society. Political and social participation grew more marginal, as did economic and social status.

The most important differences emerged from the conscious division of this chapter into families of different religions. It is rare that we have the opportunity to compare writings by people of different faiths. Hopefully, this foray into religious letter-writing will stimulate future work. The findings of this chapter indicate that Dissenters may have had a greater impact on letters than their numbers indicated. Most important, the study confirms that the epistolary experience of Dissenting families was distinctive in many ways. Unlike the Tuckers, they were self-conscious about religion. Their natural enthusiasm extended itself to letters, which they turned to with zeal and sometimes filled with divinity.

Dissenters' obsessive use of letter-writing evolved out of earlier historical periods when the written word was used to deal with persecution. Yet even in the eighteenth century, their minority position heightened the need for members to stick together. Letters both strengthened and connected

Nonconformists, who had fewer avenues of self-expression than Anglicans. Letter-writing was one way to compensate for this disadvantage.

The most significant difference between Dissenters and other letter-writers lay in their distinctive writing styles and linguistic patterns. As the case studies progressed in this chapter, these distinctions became more pronounced. Though Rebekah and Elizabeth wrote 'Christian letters', the language, style, and rhythm of the Follows's correspondence remained unique. Quakers put their own stamp on epistolary conventions by radically changing forms of address, dating systems, and names of days and months. Their letters moved from inward to outward content, then back again to inward matters. A spiritual dimension tried to dissolve physical space and achieve a communion of souls. Hence a 'fluent' letter became a spiritual document that released the word of God from inside the writer. Quaker epistolary patterns were not just peripheral, they were declarations of faith.

For both Quakers and Independents, letters were a place to focus on God. But the Batemans and the Wilsons suffered higher levels of anxiety. They yearned to be saved, rather than to become genteel. Evangelicals, I suspect, may have had similar problems. Anxiety about business and politics clearly differed from fears for one's salvation. As a result, our Congregationalists, unlike the Tuckers, used epistolary literacy in obsessive ways. It is telling that the way Rebekah and Thomas wrote letters to each other had terrible consequences for their marriage. Each partner was dissatisfied with the letters they received from the other, yet neither would change the way they wrote. This was another sign of the importance of epistolary literacy.

Rebekah Bateman gendered her letters by her resistance to epistolary norms. No matter how much Thomas disliked them, she refused to stop writing religious letters. By pretending to be apologetic, she was able to conform outwardly to conventions and preserve her right to religious self-expression. In contrast, Ruth Follows's problems regarding gender came from too much freedom, not too little. Her travels as a minister forced her to give up her domestic duties. Only letters ensured the survival of the maternal part of her psyche. Gender and religion were always entwined in the lives of these two women. Congregational and Quaker women also shared and resolved domestic problems through epistolary networks. For women frightened about sin, this was especially important. By the end of the century, wives and daughters wrote as easily as men. Both sexes contributed to a rise in the general level of epistolary expertise. This dexterity may have influenced the rise of the novel, as we shall see in the next chapter.

The Tuckers did not preserve series of women's letters, though there are interesting individual examples. They were also not self-conscious about religion in their letters. Of course, this fact cannot be generalized to all Anglicans. It can be suggested, however, that Anglicans did not use letter-writing as a group to the same extent as eighteenth-century Dissenters. Anglicans appear to have had fewer shared understandings and looked upon their church primarily as an institution. Because their faith was not in jeopardy, they had less need than Dissenters to use letters in defensive ways.

Instead, the Tuckers wrote letters for social, economic, and political ends. Issues of class and power dominated their correspondence. In addition, languages of interest and resentment were used to construct personal identities. The Tuckers showed little taste for gentility and concentrated on acquiring middling-sort virtues of honesty, productivity, reputation, and independence. Dissenters could not engage in politics, and the riots and repression of the 1790s were an added source of anxiety.

It has been argued that epistolary literacy was a hallmark of middling-sort culture. We may therefore think of middling-sort families as heralds of the democratization of written culture—whether the impetus came from religion or commerce. Because merchants, clerks, and Dissenters wrote large numbers of letters on a regular basis, they developed skills and raised epistolary standards over the generations. We should not be surprised then to find the graceful 'copperplate' hands of their letters in the journals and account books of eighteenth-century businesses. This concurrence stemmed, in part, from the role of merchant letters as bridges between work and home. Writing was treated as a precious skill in both of these worlds.

In Chapter 1 it was suggested that during the eighteenth century, the merchant's hand handwriting dominated personal and commercial correspondence. The development of trade, noted Stanley Morrison, led to a 'speedy, cursive, and eminently legible English hand'. The 'Lettre Anglaise', he added, ousted 'the Lettre Bâtarde' in France, and equivalents imposed themselves in other countries. It is revealing that the ceremonial 'ronde' hand was used in the text of a French passport, but the receipt for it was written in 'Anglaise'. 'In this way', concluded Morrison, 'the English writing-masters changed the tradition of European hand-writing and their neat, dull, "copper-plate" became the accepted mode.'[398] In contrast, elite papers often contained hastily dashed-off letters, or those written by a secretary, with just a signature by the aristocrat. The 'neat' middling-sort hand, not the writing of the nobility, would set the standard for commercial correspondence by the end of the eighteenth century.

1. *A Booke Containing Divers Sortes of hands* by John de Beauchesne, 1602 edition.

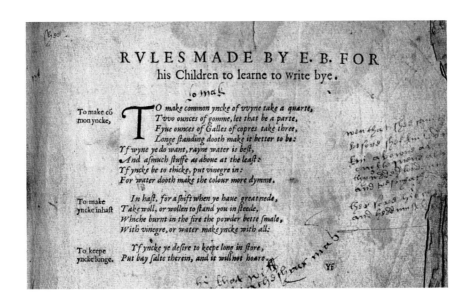

2. 'Rules Made by E. B. For his Children to learne to write bye' in de Beauchesne, 1571 edition with hand-written notes.

3. Self Portrait, *c.*1771–5 by James Jefferys.

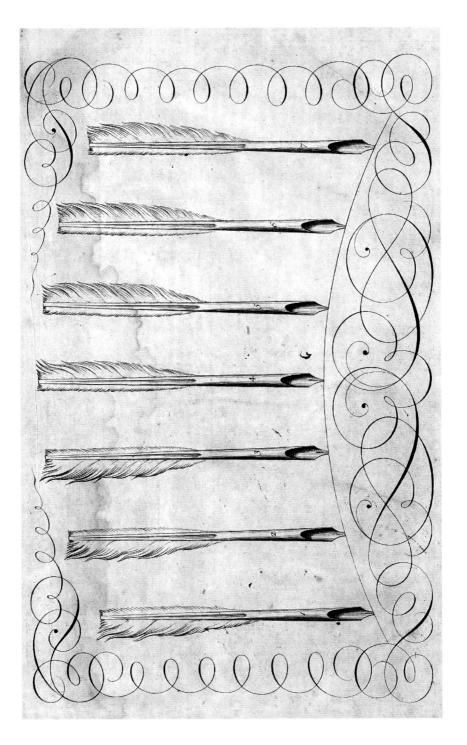

4. Pen Angles cut for different hands in George Shelley, *The Second Part of Natural Writing*, 1714.

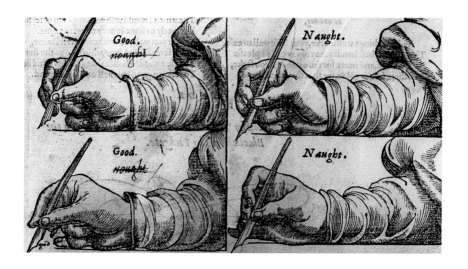

5. 'Howe you ought to hold your penne' in *A Newe Booke of Copies*, 1574.

6. 'Fine Writeing Inke' in Marcellus Laroon, *The Cryes of the City of London*, 1711 with ink barrel, funnel, measure, and quills.

7. A Girl Reading a Letter, with an Old Man Reading over her Shoulder, *c.*1767–70 by Joseph Wright of Derby.

Birmingham 27. 6mo 178[

Dear Charles

    I was glad to receive thy
Letter, and to hear that thou lovest
read thy lefson; for I wo[
have thee learn to read, [
as Pappa, and would not
be clever?
    I thank Grandma and mama
for their kind letters; and
desire my very dear love to
them; pleafe to tell them, that
Pappa, and Jemmy, and Robert,
and Thomas, are well: I love
thee dearly.   Charles Lloyd

Te/lP nss 4o3/4/5/1/1

8. Letter from the banker, Charles Lloyd Sr to Charles Lloyd Jr, 27. 6mo 178[?] written as a model to copy.

Youngsbury 2nd of 7th mo 1788.

Dear Grandmamma

I wish to shew my attention by writing to thee as I suppose that thou will be glad to hear from me. I am very much pleas'd with being at Youngsbury it is a very pleasant place. I have written several copies with John Hodgkin and I hope that I shall be rather improv'd in my writing when I return.

Cousin Robert and Rachel Barclay came here last night. We were much pleased with Roberts letter. Pappa and Mamma Aunt Barclay and Charles send their dear love.

We are all well. our respects to master (please turn over) I am thy dutiful Grandson James Lloyde

9. Letter from James Lloyd to his grandmother, Priscilla Farmer, 2nd of 7th mo. 1788 written at age 12.

10. Robert Pease of Amsterdam, a merchant, *c.*1670 drawn by T. Windall Wildridge in *Old and New Hull*, 1874, plate LIX with inkwell and letter.

11. Joseph Pease of Hull, a merchant, *c.*1754 drawn by T. Windall Wildridge in *Old and New Hull*, 1874, Plate LX with inkwell and letter.

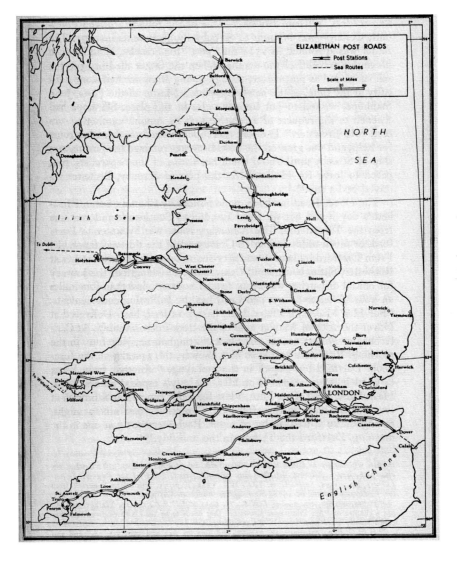

12. Elizabethan post roads in Howard Robinson, *The British Post Office* © 1948, 17.

13. The great roads and principal cross roads in 1756, in Howard Robinson, *The British Post Office* © 1948, 104. Note the increased density of post roads.

14. 17th–Century Post Boy.

15. John Palmer's original Bath mail coach, 1784.

A a b c d e f g h h i j k l m n o p q r s t u v
A a b c d e f g h h i j k l m n o p q r s t u v w x
A a b c d e f g h h i j k l m n o p q r s t u v w x y
A a b c d e f g h h i j k l m n o p q r s t u v w x y
A a b c d e f g h h i j k l m n o p q r s t u v w x y
A a b c d e f g h h i j k l m n o p q r s t u v w x y x
A a b c d e f g h h i j k l m n o p q r s t u v w x y
A a b c d e f g h h i j k l m n o p q r s t u v w x y
A a b c d e f g h h i j k l m n o p q r s t u v w x y

An hour in a day may much profit a man
in his study. Titus Wheatcroft.

If a man will endeavour he may in time
increase his learning, but no man can think
to be perfect all on a sudden. Titus.
Amendment belongs to every man.
Titus Wheatcroft. 1744.

16. Titus Wheatcroft's Commonplace Book, writing exercises, 1744.

Will nuacks your bones to Rock
And Harwith might will giva shout
Unto fare ashborn town

To Disprais of ashborn boys
And prase of our town

Charls Soosby
His book god giue
grace him on to Looxk
But not to Looxk but understand
for Learning is bolter than Mony hous
or Land
Anno Dom
1678

17. 'Charls Soosby, His book', 1678.

18. Letter from Dorothy Sorsby to her 'cosen Roger', 19 May 1677.

Most Honoured Sir after my humble service presented
To you & to the rest of yr familly let these Comunicate
you with my desires which are these followeng first
I hore that you are for parting with Samuell Ullin
Which is your man at present I beleeve And if your
worship be not provoyded I would be very glad to
Supply his place & if your worship pllase to honcur
to mean A man who am betwixt foure & five & twenty
years of age I hope in a litle time I shall gain your
Favour for Haveing gott some learning but
Especially Accounts hopeing that it will answer in very
good Buisness And would willingly increase it and every
Thing else Amongst my Betters so that I might be in
serviceable to my Master & for yr Credit of both his
And me which is from yr Use of an humble hea
And so haveing an unexpressable besire to serve yor
Worships I with yt some body may give you a further
Account of my breeding & behaviour Not Doubting
That it would Recomend me to your service so wishing
That my late words may take effect & for yr want of such
wishing that you would recomend me to some other
Hopeing that you will never here no worse a Carrector
then is here present
                        so I beg leave to subscribe
            my self Sir yr Humble & obliged
            servant Gilb Sorsbie

19. Draft letter from a famer, Gilbert Sorsbie Sr seeking employment, n.d.

20. Gilbert Soresby Jr's copybook with the text: 'An ingenious Person is an Ornament to the Nation', 23 Nov 1677.

My Friend   Derby March the 3: 1748

I reced your Letter of friendship

January ~~~~~ ye 16th but what shall I say to it, Surprise & p
taken place by turns ever since. you cou'd not pay me a greater
then by ranking mee amongst ye number of your friends, which
I hope I shall allways endeavour to deserve, and as such sha
look upon my self as a sharer in your misery. But shall I be
~~be~~ you to be, in jest, or are you sincear, I cant but say it apears to r
little romantick, (tho there's not a duke, a portius, a [ ], yt
ye passions in a more elagant manner.) When I compare your Letters
& are some what inconsistant: in ye first you say you are a utters
to writeing, in your next that y [ ] [ ] [ ]
she is at ye distance of near forty miles, is verry young, and yet your
Tenderr, But I will judg favourably and imagine it be ye efect of a m
disorderd, but I hope this fit of Frenzy will soone abate, yo
much oblige me if you'l tell me who this cruel Charmer
incensable fair, who lets you sigh, and languish, mourn and
away your pressious moments, which mights be rendred by her s
so easy in ye insoyment of, em, Unfeeling soul, to y [ ]
you can say tis impossiable, it can never be, no.
Complaints and approves your passion. at least for you
she does, since your Happyness nag your life depends u
But if nothing you can say, nothing you can dow wil
stubbourn he banish her your thoughts, give awa

21. Letter from a domestic servant, Elizabeth Woollat to her future husband, Jedediah Strutt, 3 March 1748 with phonetic spelling and crossed-out words.

22. Letter from a wheelwright, Jedediah Strutt to Elizabeth Woollat, 28 June [1755] in a well-trained hand.

23. Mr. Crank, a City merchant, *c.*1765 by Mason Chamberlin with writing equipment.

Round Text Copies;

By Willington Clark,

of Christ-Church Southwark.

Aaabbccddeefffgghhijkkllmm

nnooppqqrrsfstttuvvnvwxxyyzzz

A B C D E F G H I K L M

N O P Q R S T U V W X Y Z

Authority. Barbarity. Centurions.

Demands. Encomium. Fraternity.

24. Round text copies by Willington Clark in George Bickham, *The Universal Penman; Or, the Art of Writing Made Useful*, 1741.

Various Forms of Shopkeepers and Trades mens Bills.

Bills given to Persons on Book Debrs.

A Mercers Bill. Dr

Mr Samuel Newman

1711.
Apr 4. To 17½ Yards of Silk .... at 16:9 ... £ 14 13 1
7. To 12. Yards of Genoa velvet at 25:8 .... 15 8 —
May 16. To 12 Ells of Sattin mesca ... at 9 — ... 5 8 —
July 2. To 10 Yards of Lutestrong at 6:6 ... 3 5 —
                                                    38 14 1

A Linen Drapers Bill. Dr

The Honourable the Lady Gay

1711.
Sept 2. To 16 Ells of Dowlas .... at 1:9 ... £ 1 8 —
11. To 25 Ells of Holland .... at 4:7 ... 5 14 7
Oct. 9 To 32 Ells of Muslin .... at 6:11 ... 11 1 4
16. To 18 Ells of Damask .... at 4:8 ... 4 4 —
                                                    22 7 11

But if part of the mony is Paid write as follows

Received November 16 1712 of the Hon[ble] Lady Gay the sume of Seven Pounds ten Shillings in part of this Bill for the use of my Master James Turner &c

Palmar

Bills made on Buying of Wares.

A Woollen Drapers Bill.

Bought of Samuel Summers Janu[ar] 7, 1712. Dr
9. Yards of fine mixt Cloth ...... at 19: = ... 8 11 —
7. Yards of superfine Spanish at 22:6 ... 7 17 6
13. Yards of Silver Gray Cloth. at 15:6 ... 10 1 6
8. Yards of Scarlet in Grain ... at 32:8 ... 13 1 4
                                                    39 11 4

A Milleners Bill.

Bought of Thomas Dummer March 16 1712
22 Yards of Flowred Ribband 4:7 .... at 5 10
10 Yards of Sarsnet Hoods white ... at 5:6 ... 2 15 —
14 Pair of Roman Gloves ... at 10:6 ... 7 7 —
2 Laced suits for the Head. at 36:3 ... 3 13 4
                                                    18 16 2

If all the mony is imediately Paid write viz:

Received Mar 16 1712 of Mr Samuel Kennway y[e] Sume of eighteen pounds, Sixteen Shillings in full for the use of my Master Thomas Dummer &c

Bryman

Dr. Sir

The Commrs. of Customs will by this Post send to Weymouth to enquire into the Character of Saml. Martin & whether he is fit to be presented to the Treasy and on the Report of Mr Colr. & Comptr. in the affirmative he will be presented to the Treasy for a surveyor to Wt Young — The Difficult Commt. goes out of Town monday next so that we shall then I hope have Weston fixed without a negative I am sorry you have been disappointed in yr. Journey to Childhey & thank you for the prudent method you propose in the communicating my donation to the Freemer I know nothing of the inclination of Penny to buy or Exchange with me, the former would be very agreeable the latter attended possibly with as much trouble as what I now have and full as little profit, but in any shape I should gladly get rid of it — You have never once told me what the Island Chaps offer to sell their Mahogany at so that I can form no judgment if tis worth while to Venture. I am going to dinner to Sydenham so bid you adieu most affectly. yours

27 Augt. 1748   J Tucker

26. Draft letter from John Tucker, a stone merchant, to his brother Richard, 27 Aug. 1748 written hurriedly with abbreviations and without margins.

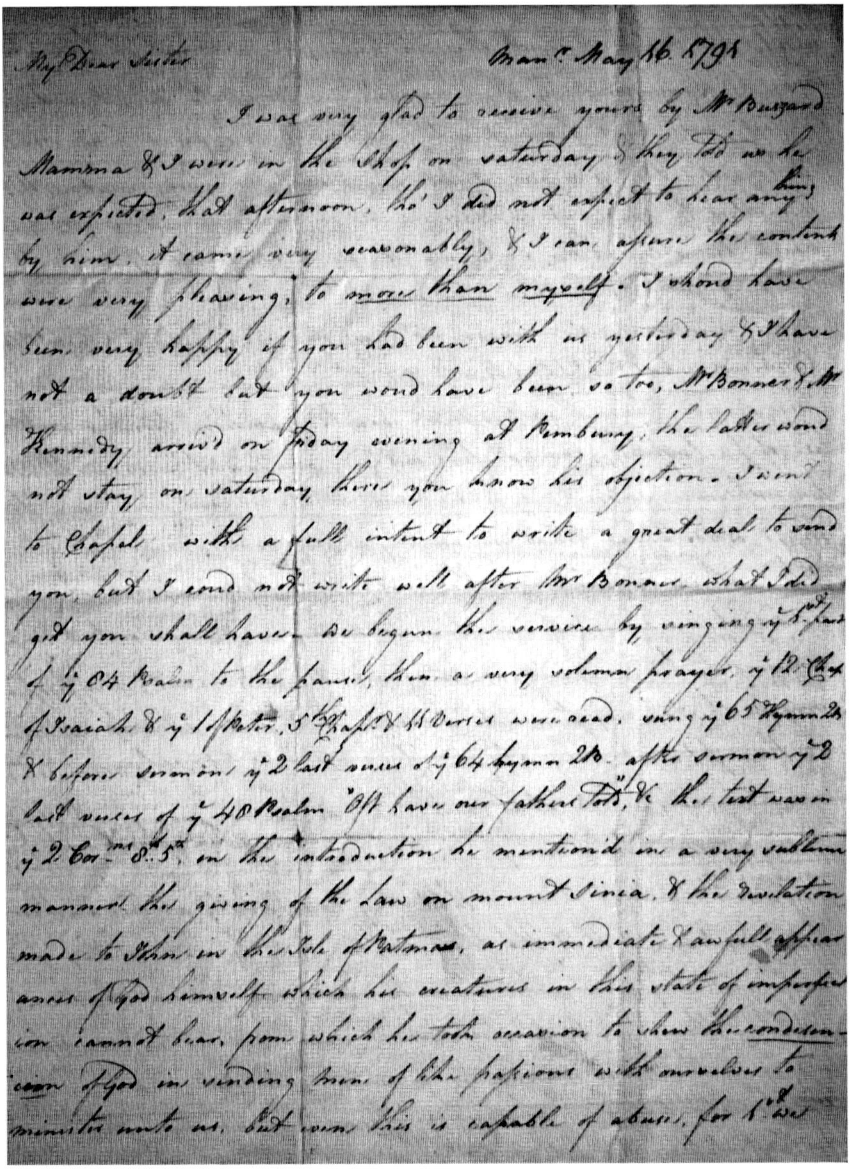

My Dear Sister Man.r May 16. 1791

I was very glad to receive yours by Mr Buzzard
Mamma & I were in the Shop on saturday & they told us he
was expected that afternoon, tho' I did not expect to hear any thing
by him, it came very seasonably, & I can assure the contents
were very pleasing, to more than myself. I should have
been very happy if you had been with us yesterday & I have
not a doubt but you would have been so too, Mr Bonner & Mr
Kennedy arrived on friday evening at Kimbury, the latter would
not stay on saturday there you know his objection. I went
to Chapel with a full intent to write a great deal to send
you, but I could not write well after Mr Bonner, what I did
get you shall have. we begun the service by singing ye 5th part
of ye 64 Psalm to the [illegible], then a very solemn prayer, ye 12 Chap
of Isaiah & ye 1 of Peter, 5th Chap & 11 verses were read. sung ye 65 Hymn 2d
& before sermon ye 2 last verses of ye 64 hymn 2d. after sermon ye 2
last verses of ye 48 Psalm "Oft have our fathers told," &c the text was in
ye 2 Cor.ns 8th 5th. in the introduction he mention'd in a very sublime
manner the giving of the Law on mount Sinia. & the revelation
made to John in the Isle of Patmos, as immediate & awfull appear
ances of God himself which his creatures in this state of imperfect
ion cannot bear, from which he took occasion to shew the condesen-
cion of God in sending men of like passions with ourselves to
minister unto us. but even this is capable of abuse, for 1st we

27. Letter from Rebekah Bateman, daughter of a Congregational merchant to her sister, Elizabeth Wilson, 16 May 1791.

28. Letter from a Quaker minister, Ruth Follows to her husband George Follows, ye 11[th mo] & 22nd 1761 in an untrained hand without careful presentation.

Hon.d Parents   Yarmouth 1 m.o 29th. 17[6]

                              Having heard from you several times
since I wrote
by Bro. Rich.d, think it my Duty to write a few lines to you this
Evening, the reason that I did not write sooner was because I expected a
Letter from you first, so now I take this opportunity, letting you know
I am in a good state of Health, through divine favour, hoping these
may find you enjoyers of the same Blessing.
Your intent in placing me hear I know was for my good, and so I hope it
will prove, I like the Bussiness very well, and will endeavour to press
forward therein, I do not yet forget yours & my friends good advice
which I hope thereby to obtain service; Yarm.t Air agrees with one
bravely, having had good Health since I came except d Cold which I
think but trifling.
     Bro. Rich.d was bravley when I heard from him, but it is some time
since, how he goes on with his Affairs I don't know, I suppose you know
more than I, so not having much more to mention but my Master and
Mistress kind love presented to you with Bro. Rich.d and my
Duty and dear love to you all I still remain
                              Your Dutyfull loving
     P.S   and affectionate Son
I understand that K Oxley
is gone to Hitching and   Samuel Follows
I am affraid you can't send the Books

     Please to give my Duty to Grand Mother & Aunt
     and love to all enquiring Friends
                                   Don't fail writing
                                   to me soon

29. Letter from a grocer's apprentice, Samuel Follows to his parents, Ruth and George
Follows, 1 m°. 29th 1769 in a well-trained hand with polite conventions.

Ackworth School, 25th. of 3rd. Month 1814.

Beloved Mother;

I received thy truly acceptable letter, and was gratified to learn that thou wast well, as this leaves me. I likewise received the parcel which thou sentest me, and for which I am much obliged to thee. As thou requestedst in thy last letter to know what business I should like to be, I may inform thee that I should prefer a Bookseller, or a Linen and Woollen Draper, if thou canst find a proper situation for me in either of these Branches. I was very sorry to learn that Ann and Hannah Hawley were not getting any better, but as Spring has now set in, I should hope it will be a means of furthering their recovery. I have been very much surprised at not receiving a letter from Brother since the 12. Mo. 1812; but I hope I shall receive one before long. It was very gratifying to me to understand that he was well when thou wrotest, and hope that he continues so still. Two of our Teachers,

30. Letter from a Quaker grocer, George Follows to his mother, Rebecca Follows, 25th. of 3rd. Month 1814.

My dear George.

for being so vastly fond of you.
Pray don't trouble your self
to write to me.   May 9. 1750.

Having an opportunity of
writing to you again, am willing
to make use of it, to thank
you for your very pretty Letter,
which pleas'd us all vastly, but
I don't doubt your improving
in every thing at such a charming

Master Crony, Master Nicoll, S. Master
Johnson coming from Rugby=School

31. Letter from Jane Johnson to her son, George Johnson, 9 May 1750 written as a model with a drawing.

Dear Mrs Brompton.

I think it a vast deal of pity that any thing you write shou'd be lost, am therefore very sorry that you did not enclose the Letter you mention along with that I receiv'd, nor can I see any reason why you did not, had the case been my own am sure I shou'd, & if ever the like happens beg you will do the same; otherwise the unhappiness must center in your Humble Servant.

You express so many fine things in praise of my Cousin Knollys that I can't help wishing I was acquainted with her, & must acknowledge that I esteem it a happiness to stand in any degree of affinity to a person of so much merit, who I cou'd not help having a particular regard for, even if she was no Relation, & as nearness of Blood ought to strengthen the affection, can't forbea presenting my Compliments tho' unknown, & begging you will make them acceptable when you see her; I think she is a Widow, & has one Son, I hope he is a comfort to her, & will marry wisely, & make her a happy Grandmother of many of both sexes. I am very glad my Cousin Garth is in the way you mention, for I don't know any body so fit to people the world as she, who always does it upon such easy terms, & then sure it must be esteem'd a Bless -ness to be the immediate instrument in the hands of God to give Life to Immortal Spirits! to Beings that can never die! To meet our own Sons & Daughters in Heaven, must add great joy to the Happiness of that glorious place, when we reflect that had it not been for us, such had never been there, to enjoy a Blessed immortality, & glorify God, to Eternal ages. I heartil wish she may have as good luck as usual, better it wou'd be unreasonable t wish her. I am at a loss to find words to express my sense of the Favour, prett obliging Miss Evelin designs me. Her having an inclination to oblige me, is the obligation, which she cannot heighten by any thing she gives, for the intention is all. I therefore beg she will accept of my most grateful thanks, & not give her self the trouble to put her design in execution, for upon my word I had rather she wou'd not, & this for more reasons than one. What thes reasons are I don't know how to acquaint you with, & yet cou'd wish to do so, but greatly fear offending in the attempt, where I wou'd wish for nothing more than an opportunity to oblige. What can I say? I want Rhetorick & Eloquence to put my sentiments in a proper light. Have you & Miss Evelin goodness enough to pardon the Liberty I am going to take in return for her intended Favour? I believe you have, will therefore without further apology will begin my story which I assure you has its foundation in truth.

The History of Miss Clarissa of Buckinghamshire

There is a Lady in this neighbourhood (& because I take pleasure in the name shall be call'd Clarissa) who when she was about twenty years of age began to take much pride & pleasure in obliging her friends with the works of her hands, & being proud for her ingenuity, to obtain this intoxicating pleasur she spent all the time she cou'd spare from visits, & other such like Business in making Purses, Flowers, Stomachers, needle Books, cutting watch papers, &

32. Letter from Jane Johnson to Mrs Brompton [1749] with 'The History of Miss Clarissa of Buckinghamshire' inserted near the bottom (see arrow).

33. Crawford's Circulating Library in *A Description of Brighthelmstone* (1788). Note the words 'Post Office', 'Bookseller', 'Stationer', 'Book Binder', 'Post Office' below the sign.

34. Robert Johnson's Notebook, list of letters 'to' and 'from', 1777.

PART
III

From letters
to literature

5

Letter-writing and the rise
of the novel

The epistolary literacy of Jane Johnson and Samuel Richardson

M erchants, clerks, and Dissenters were busy people—but not too busy to read books, periodicals, and pamphlets. This was also true for working families in Chapter 3. One of the patterns found in the case studies is how common it was for all ranks of people to mention books and printed material in letters. This fact reflects a central theme of this book—that letters and literature were unusually connected during the eighteenth century.

Chapters 5 and 6 show how letters enabled people, who were eager to become more cultured, to participate in a tempting literary world filled with newspapers, periodicals, bookshops, and libraries. It is evident that provincial letter-writers imitated epistolary models that they encountered in printed literature. What is less obvious is how letters, themselves, had a significant impact on the literary world. Once people in the next two case studies felt comfortable writing letters, they used their epistolary literacy to fulfil cultural aspirations like writing their own stories and evaluating the work of others. This leap from letter-writing to composing literature was a more sophisticated process than has been encountered in this book.

But why did this extraordinary shift take place? How did new readers and writers develop literary expertise? Did they affect or just respond to the mainstream world of letters? Can we identify patterns and strategies that helped them to create a literary culture based on reading novels and other secular material? These questions are difficult to answer. Fortunately, the

Bodleian Library's recently acquired Johnson family archive offers some answers.[1]

The Johnson collection tells the 200-year story of six generations of family members as they roamed through Buckinghamshire, Lincolnshire, the Midlands, London, and Bath. The family was chosen as a major case study for this book, because their papers not only include letters, but also masses of genealogical material, wills, settlements, and other papers. Most important, the collection contains rare reading and writing records of several generations, whose lives spanned the eighteenth century. Part 3 uses this material to reveal continuities and changes in both letter-writing and literature. They also help us to understand how they affected each other.

This chapter analyses the epistolary practices of Jane Johnson (1706–59),[2] wife of Woolsey Johnson (1696–1756),[3] vicar of Olney, Buckinghamshire in relation to the epistolary writings of the novelist, Samuel Richardson (1689–1761).[4] We will see how a provincial woman without formal education, read, wrote, and interacted with eighteenth-century texts. Once functional needs were met, Jane Johnson learnt to write imaginative letters, poetry, and short stories in a literary manner. Critics accustomed to examining works of high culture may question the 'literariness' of Johnson's work, for it was as mundane, in some respects, as the epistolary literacy that underpinned it. Yet her writings reveal the practices of untrained readers that are usually hidden from view. Johnson was able to construct a distinctive literary world that lay midway between popular and elite culture because she possessed epistolary literacy. This was a skill that Samuel Richardson would also manipulate to his advantage.

The Johnson papers also reveal links between London's booming print marketplace and provincial readers—a group who rarely occupies centre stage.[5] In his widely known study of the novel in 1957, Ian Watt linked its rise to the emergence of a middling-sort reading public. This new audience lacked formal education but had both time and money to devote to literary activities. Women played a prominent role as consumers of printed texts, especially in urban settings.[6] Though Watt's book has been criticized by literary scholars, his 'then defiant act of attributing creative power to readers' has been called 'his most important and...enduring contribution'.[7] Jane neatly fits Watt's description of one of Richardson's readers, though she lived deep in the country. Nonetheless, literature from London filled her library.[8] She was living at a time of major literary developments: the expansion of publishing, libraries, readers, and leisure;

the emergence of women as authors; alterations in copyright and marketing of printed material; and shifts in the relationship between popular and elite culture. This chapter shows how Jane engaged with all of these changes.

In contrast to the letter-writers in earlier chapters, Johnson was representative of upper middling-sort women, below the level of gentry, who were either self-taught or educated in provincial homes. These women were united by their possession of reading and writing skills, access to printed materials, and enjoyment of poetry and prose. As they learnt new skills and adapted to intellectual stimuli, their literary aspirations grew. Johnson's case, I believe, is a telling one that sheds light on cultural practices and values. In addition, a substantial body of recent work on women writers confirms many of the patterns and strategies found in this study.[9]

The joy reaped from the possession of epistolary literacy is evident in Jane's letters. Like Elizabeth Strutt, Elizabeth Wilson, and Ruth Follows, she and her correspondents longed for more time to indulge in epistolary pursuits. 'I could write forever', noted Ann Ingram, 'on the subject of my friendship for you.'[10] Because letter-writing was so important, some writers kept monthly records of letters sent and received.[11] (See Plate 34.) Little epistolary events were noted with pleasure. Anne Smythe, for example, created original poetry as she fell asleep, and tried to reconstruct it in the morning so that she could send it to Johnson in a letter. Jane and her friends could hardly wait to discuss the reading and writing that had become thrillingly central to their lives.[12] They gleaned models from novels, travel writings, periodicals, and printed collections, as well as letters that were sent and received. Sad events also shaped epistolary discourse. A close friend wrote a farewell sonnet in a letter at the time of his death. Of course the Johnsons learnt about both the death and the sonnet in yet another letter.

The ordinary act of letter-writing underpinned Johnson's literary pursuits. In fact her epistolary way of thinking shaped all of her poetry and prose. She used her writing to examine the meaning of her life and to confront its problems. But letter-writing was also a crucial training ground for entering the mainstream world of letters—a world in which Samuel Richardson was a central figure. Richardson, meanwhile, was aware of his readers' epistolary literacy and shared Johnson's belief in its importance. In his novels he described people like her, busily exchanging letters. His stories were written 'to the moment' in an epistolary format, a technique with a long history used in a wide range of genres.[13] Epistolary writing had already flooded the market in periodicals, newspapers, pamphlets, and especially romances, often from France.[14] Richardson's adoption of the epistolary format was hardly exceptional, but we must look closely at exactly how he used it and why he chose it at this specific historical moment.

Richardson's middle-class background and early life offer some clues. The son of a joiner, he became a printer. As a tradesman, he was therefore an outsider on the fringe of the polite society he described.[15] Like Johnson, he was largely self-taught, with little formal education—merely a smattering of classics in translation and scant time for reading.[16] Yet he had unique advantages. He was an insider and an expert on the London print marketplace, where writers, booksellers, and his fellow printers were striving to make a profit. He observed what people were writing, reading, and, most importantly, buying. He noticed that the letter was increasingly becoming the most common vehicle for expressing everyday thoughts. All around him, people were telling little stories about their lives by writing letters. Unsurprisingly, one of his early publishing ventures was a collection of letters by Sir Thomas Roe.[17]

After achieving fame, he was keen to stress that his childhood was marked by epistolary activities. He claimed to have written love letters for illiterate school friends and sent letters of advice.[18] An early work, *The Apprentice's Vade Mecum* (1734) was an expansion of a letter to his nephew.[19] In 1739, two astute commercial booksellers, John Osborn Sr and Charles Rivington, commissioned him to write an epistolary manual. He sensed that people were interested in letter-writing—a commonplace yet exciting activity for those newly literate. He also knew from his own experience that many middle-class readers needed to know how to write properly. His goal, however, would be broader than mere instruction: 'Will it be any Harm,' he asked his publishers, 'in a Piece you want to be written so low, if we should instruct them how they should think and act in common cases, as well as indite?'[20] He was positioning himself as an author with an eye to the market—one who was intensely aware of moral debates about the dangers of non-elite reading.

Drawing on John Hill's *The Young Secretary's Guide* (1734), Richardson composed model letters for his *Letters Written to and for Particular Friends, on the Most Important Occasions* (1741). They were written in the form of mini-narratives about ordinary events. One was from a young servant girl in danger of amorous advances from her master. This letter gave Richardson an idea for a book, and he unexpectedly created *Pamela* in two months, writing at a furious pace.[21] Richardson, I argue, observed the central place of letter-writing in the way people communicated at that moment. To meet the needs of a widespread and expanding audience, he used the familiar methodology of epistolary writing. His earnest moralizing, however, distanced his work from dangerous romances. This would, he believed, reduce anxiety about the deleterious effects of reading for pious women like Jane Johnson.[22]

As is well known, Richardson's novels centred about the experience of letter-writing. His heroines in *Pamela* (1741) and *Clarissa* (1748) told epistolary tales of female virtue in distress.[23] Pamela, a household servant, staunchly defended her chastity and was rewarded by marrying her master. Clarissa, on the other hand, was raped by her lover and abandoned by her family. Rather than sacrifice her virtue, she chose death, a conclusion that caused heartbreak to some readers. *Pamela* created a media sensation. '[A]t Ranelagh', noted the editor of Richardson's correspondence, 'it was usual for ladies to hold up the volumes of *Pamela* to one another, to shew they had got the book that every one was talking of.'[24] The storm of response to *Clarissa* was even greater and spread to the continent and the American colonies.

One explanation for this extraordinary furor, I suggest, lay in Richardson's awareness, encouragement, and manipulation of his readers' epistolary literacy. Unlike previous writers of epistolary fiction, Richardson consciously encouraged readers to engage with him in a dialogue about his work. This invitation was in keeping with the way he structured his texts. His epistolary method offered multiple points of view and latitude for varied interpretations, with little sense of closure. Moreover, the serial format and his use of 'cliffhangers' gave Richardson time to respond to his readers. As his novels rolled off the press in edition after edition, he asked readers for comments, material for prefaces, alternate versions of plots, and original letters appropriate to his fictional characters. Many willingly complied, especially women,[25] yet only readers with epistolary literacy could participate in this dialogue. Though he said that he depended on readers for inspiration, few of their suggestions were incorporated. In fact, he constantly invited, though rarely responded to, their suggested revisions.[26] This technique drew his audience into networks of interpretation. At the same time Richardson maintained strict control over his texts. He hoped he could convince readers to read in ways that he chose—ways that would lead to moral regeneration.

The desire to reform reading was accompanied by an energetic struggle to sell books in a competitive market. Richardson was self-conscious about both motives, and they existed in tandem. Techniques that resemble modern-day marketing strategies were employed—for example, *Pamela* was available for purchase along with fans and other memorabilia. Rival authors quickly leapt into the fray with anti-Richardson fiction, as well as plays, an opera, and public endorsements or criticisms. Richardson responded with sequels, dedications, letters of advertisement, and postscripts.[27] The media blitz was even more intense with the publication of *Clarissa* and its many editions, separate spin-offs, and commentary, both pro and con. Into his ever-changing texts he integrated extra-textual material such as tables, indexes, and abstracts of letters, revisions, restored passages marked by tiny dots, and indexed collections of moral sentiments and meditations.[28] His intention, he noted, was to avoid misreadings and to assure every reader's '[u]nderstanding of it, in the Way I chose to have it understood'.[29]

Richardson required an audience with epistolary literacy, cultural aspirations, and literary skills, both to interpret his texts and to buy each sequel. Yet his motives were not just commercial; they also embraced a moral project. While he borrowed and profited from earlier romance narratives, he carefully distinguished his own work from this tradition. In fact, his goal was not only to reform reading practices, but to reform lives as well.

In doing so, Richardson appealed to the creative power of the reader and, as we shall see, Jane Johnson took the bait. Her archive shows that he achieved both goals: she read his books, created her own Clarissa story, and questioned her society's morality as she did so. As we shall see, the relationship between reader and novelist was a two-way street. Johnson, and others like her, did not just absorb novels; they had their own important impact on a literary culture that extended deep into the provincial world. As we analyse Johnson's epistolary literacy, we will observe the ties that bound Johnson to the novelist in both directions—Richardson's influences on her work and her influence on his.

Jane Johnson of Olney, Buckinghamshire and the Johnson family archive

Before analysing Johnson's epistolary practices, we must look at the sources that allow us to do so. In addition to written records, some of Johnson's material artefacts survived. In the 1740s, she created a homemade nursery library, which she used to teach her children how to read. It may be found in its original box in the Lilly Library at the University of Indiana. Historians of education have analysed her teaching kit, which contains 438 pieces: 78 word chips; 2 hand-lettered books, some with published illustrations; and various card series that teach the alphabet, syllable combinations, and the construction of sentences. The cards draw on everyday experience and traditional genres such as fables, street cries, and nursery rhymes.[30]

In addition, delicate paper cutouts of flowers, the sun, and snowflakes tumble out of the archive. Two of the nicest of these cutouts are folded up in a note marked, 'For My son George William Johnson When I am Dead, Jane Johnson'.[31] Birth records in pen and ink are carefully shaped into intertwined four-leaf clovers, whilst a handmade family pedigree graces two wooden boards.[32] The Bodleian Library has published a recently discovered work by Johnson, which she called: *A very pretty story to tell Children when they are about five or six years of age* (1744). It is now considered the first fairy tale written in English for children.[33] Since she wrote it in the aftermath of the publication of *Pamela*, we are not surprised to find similarities between it and Pamela's 'Specimen of Nursery Tales and Stories'.[34]

The reading kit, artefacts, and fairy tale offer evidence of the creative role played by mothers, who were teaching reading and writing informally in the home. Morag Styles, who was instrumental in bringing the archive to light and Evelyn Arizpe have shown how Jane educated her children. Their research suggests that other mothers were absorbed in practices of domestic literacy outside institutional walls.[35] I focus here on Johnson's adult reading and writing and her epistolary literacy, which has not received attention. Her manuscript notebook contained fair copies of what she considered to be her best work, including original prose, poetry, excerpts from books, and inspirational prayers. Another book filled with meditations, gave Johnson room to express her religious views.

The most exciting find, however, was Jane's commonplace book. When the reading records it contains are combined with online full-text searchable databases, we can see how Jane read, copied, and then incorporated extracts from her reading into her writing.[36] Analysing these records and referring to these databases, I show how Johnson interacted with a wide range of literature, especially the works of Richardson. Jane made this task easier for us to see by inserting her own comments between the extracts in her commonplace book. One comment tells us how to distinguish her copied abstracts from her original thoughts: 'All the Paragraphs marked thus + are my own.'[37] The fact that Johnson dated and signed her name to every piece of work is important, since her female contemporaries were just starting to sign and publish their writings. In private papers, Johnson was able to assert authorship over a body of literary work.[38]

Unfortunately, we know little about Johnson's early education.[39] She and her sister Lucy (d. 1731) were daughters of Richard Russell of Warwick (d. 1720) and Lucy Rainsford (d. 1752). Her mother came from a respectable London family, but she is not mentioned in surviving letters. Russell had started life as a 'menial estate servant', but he managed to buy land in Warwickshire, which the sisters eventually sold. The Russells probably lived in London, where Jane's future husband, Woolsey Johnson (1696–1756), a graduate of Clare College, Cambridge, served as curate of St Andrew's Holborn in the 1720s. Woolsey and Jane married in 1735. In the same year he was presented as vicar at Olney, where his father, William Johnson (1665–1736) owned the rectory, tithes, and advowson, but not the manor.[40]

In this market town, Jane and Woolsey raised four children: Barbara (1738–1825), George William (1740–1814), Robert Augustus (1745–99), and Charles Woolsey (1748–1828).[41] Olney lay in the northern corner of Buckinghamshire, fifty miles from the capital and close to the London Road.[42] It is surprising that there are few references to Jane's town or to her husband's work in Olney. But by combining a broad range of historical sources with the Johnson papers, we can reconstruct fragments of what their life must have been like. We can also speculate as to why some groups of their letters did not survive. As the Soresbie papers in Chapter 3 confirm, family archives were often purposely shaped by self-appointed 'guardians'.

Jane's house in Olney was set 'over the churchyard wall', with a view of the River Ouse and its bridge.[43] Her children ran up and down a great oak staircase that linked the two wings of the house.[44] Jane could walk directly across a field to the river and mill, where her son George once fell into the water. She 'jump'd in after him at the extreme hazard of her own life . . . being very big with child' and saved him from the mill wheel.[45] Her children likely watched sheep and packhorses approach a toll bar at the bridge. After they were counted, the toll was paid.[46]

Turning right on to Bridge Street,[47] Jane would approach the marketplace with its Shiel Hall, roundhouse gaol, and two cattle fairs each year.[48] Under an elm tree in the square, cows and chickens gathered, whilst boys played at 'tops and marbles'.[49] The High Street was just a widening of the road to Newport Pagnell, over a half-mile long.[50] A 'raised pitched causeway to prevent floods' ran down its middle from the Swan Inn and Post Office.[51] 'The ancient whipping distance' run by town offenders ended near the Independent meeting house, where John Drake preached. A Baptist church lay nearby in Bear Lane.[52] Samuel Teedon taught in Shiel Hall in the curate, John Newton's time. Yet Betsy Catlett was sent to a Northampton boarding school, 'because there was no suitable day school in Olney'.[53]

Though William Legge, second Earl of Dartmouth (1731–1801) owned much of the land, most houses in town were freehold properties of artisans and small tradesmen.[54] Olney was noted for its bone lace and impoverished workers. The poet William Cowper called it 'a . . . place inhabited chiefly by the half-starved and ragged of the earth'.[55] Johnson could see the lace dealers coming in and out of the slums of Olney, 'deep in the abyss of Silver End', behind a corner of the marketplace. There in closely packed thatched cottages, poverty-stricken women and children worked ten to twelve hours a day producing lace.[56] Most of them, noted Newton, from the 'lowness of diet, the confinement of lace-making, and the want of exercise and fresh air, were nervous in different degrees, which gave a melancholy cast to their whole religious experience'.[57]

Jane might have peered into their cottages and found three women sitting with pillows on their laps, whilst a fourth turned the bobbin wheel and filled it with thread. In between them was a three-legged stool, topped by one precious candle. Its light was reflected through three adjacent glass balls filled with water. To keep their feet warm, the women put pots with hot ashes under their gowns, as they marshalled 'regiments of pins'.[58] At the age of 6 or 7, children were 'put to the pillow'.[59] To help them count numbers of pins stuck in an hour, women and children sang little poems of the same class as nursery rhymes [like] 'hush-a-bye baby on the tree top'. Jane must have heard them 'chant . . . the amount of work to be got over', like '20 miles have I to go; 19 miles have I to go, etc'. These songs called 'Lace Tellings'[60] were repeated to keep workers in step and were a source of popular culture. Some were similar to the poems Jane used in her homemade reading books and those in the Soresbies' notebooks. The songs also inspired John Newton to write his Olney Hymns that were sung in workers' cottages.[61] Jane never directly referred to Olney's poverty. We will find it, however, hidden between the lines of her letters. Jane also failed to mention that Olney was home to 'the first characteristically eighteenth-century workhouse' in England. Founded in

1714 by Matthew Marryott, the Olney workhouse was a new prerequisite for poor relief.[62] Thirty paupers working sixteen hours a day brought in 15s. a week. By 1724, Olney's poor rate of 3s. 9d. dropped to 1s. 9d. due to new workhouse policies.[63] Naturally, Woolsey's name appeared regularly in workhouse account books.[64]

The Johnson archive is also silent about the presence of Nonconformists, but, as Chapter 4 demonstrated, it is crucial to discern their strength. In truth, the town had been one of the largest centres of Calvinist Dissent since Huguenots arrived in the sixteenth century.[65] By the seventeenth century, one could find John Bunyan in Bedford, John Gibbs in Newport Pagnell, and Anabaptists and Quakers in Olney. In 1709, only 100 of 2,000 people took Easter communion. By 1715, there was a third Independent meeting house. Estimates of Dissent ranged from 25–40 per cent of the population.[66]

By the time Woolsey became vicar, Philip Doddridge in Northampton and John Drake in nearby Yardley Hastings had already inspired Olney's independent congregations.[67] Jane must have been shocked when 500 people, 'including a great number of churchmen', turned out to hear Drake and other Dissenters.[68] Drake's wife, Elizabeth, was a presence to be reckoned with, and helped her husband in his long career at Olney.[69] At the same time, there were early stirrings of Evangelicalism and Methodism in and around the town. In 1739, Woolsey denied the pulpit to George Whitefield (1714–70), who preached in a nearby field to about two thousand people. That night, Whitefield noted in his journal: 'Great numbers were assembled together...All, I really believe, felt, as well as heard, the Word, and one was so pricked to the heart, and convinced of sin, that I scarce saw the like instance.'[70]

In 1753, Woolsey resigned his living in Olney. He planned to move to a small estate he had inherited at Witham-on-the-Hill in Lincolnshire.[71] This change of residence may have been prompted, in part, by intense competition from other ministers.[72] Church of England 'incumbents were aware of, and regretted, the strength of Dissent in the town', noted D. Bruce Hindmarsh. 'Johnson himself opposed local evangelical and Dissenting activity vigorously.'[73] Woolsey certainly was not leaving on the winds of success.

Prior to moving, however, he suddenly died. The Earl of Dartmouth, a friend of Lady Huntingdon, supported an evangelical, Moses Browne (1704–87), to succeed Johnson.[74] In 1753, Browne was inducted as vicar at a salary of £60.[75] A former pen-cutter, he became 'one of the leading preachers of the Evangelical Party'.[76] His successor, John Newton, remembered, with apparent bias, the rancor that greeted Browne: 'The gentleman [Johnson] who gave Mr Browne the living resided in the parish and soon became his open enemy...Mr Browne went through a great deal—was often abused to his face—put in the spiritual court.'[77] Jane had 'great disputes and squabbles' with Browne,[78] who tried to stop her sale of house and land to the Countess of Dartmouth.[79] As Woolsey's wife, and then widow, she was in an untenable position.

A comment in her commonplace book alluded to her unhappiness as she departed from Olney: 'I made a strong proof of my Courage, made a Bold Stand against Vice, but my forces were weak & the Enemy soon got the better & drove me out of the Field. May Virtue for the future have a more powerful, & more successful Advocate+.'[80] It was not surprising that she expressed these thoughts in writing. Like Richardson's heroines and the real women around her, Johnson found comfort by revealing her interior world on paper.

What is surprising is the fact that in the vast Johnson archive, there are few references to Olney, its poverty, or its Dissenters. Nor do Woolsey's letters of this period survive. In fact, there are fewer letters from Jane's generation, than that of her children. These silences are important. Letters that still exist must have been considered precious, for the Johnsons consciously kept some papers and threw out others. After her husband died, Jane reread family records and decided which ones to save. 'Turn over before you destroy this paper', she wrote, or 'I would have this paper kept'. Her criteria for preservation included love for kin,[81] family pride,[82] and future legal and financial needs.[83] Each of Jane's surviving records was a guide to how she wished to be remembered. Her letters must thus be read critically with an ear for omissions. We must ask which aspects of life were present, which were not, and why?[84] Many letters, I suspect, were intentionally destroyed due to prudish attitudes of later men and women, who were socialized to be modest. Because women often assumed the task of preserving personal papers, they may have eliminated those that reflected negatively or too intimately on their families. This fact has surely affected perceived rates of female literacy.

Jane Johnson and her reading

In keeping with Johnson's modesty, she says little about her own qualities. But her letters reveal an artistic, imaginative woman with a lively sense of humour who delighted in working with her hands. Three intense passions filled her life with joy. The first was her love of family and her delight in motherhood. She offered her children a domestic world filled with storytelling, poetry, and affection. Second was her deep commitment to her Anglican faith, which was confirmed in acts of letter-writing. Jane's prominent position as the vicar's wife heightened her need to be considered exemplary. She tried to lead a virtuous life on earth and was concerned about her salvation. In contrast to some sterner Calvinist tenets, her religious views as expressed in her letters were cheerful and rational.[85]

Johnson's third passion was her enjoyment of reading and writing. Her letters reveal a developing ability, to use everyday language in constructed and allusive ways. Unlike sombre seventeenth-century diary writers, Johnson employed an animated conversational mode. But genteel letter-writing was not a spontaneous art; it was achieved only by dedicated practice. As Johnson told personal stories, she developed narrative skills, far greater than that of writers in preceding chapters. Then she transferred the narrative mode of letters into more difficult forms of writing.

Johnson used letter-writing for two fundamental purposes. First, it was an entry point into a larger world of print culture that was spreading in the countryside. Though Johnson had access to a clergyman's library, she lacked academic training. Through letter-writing she developed techniques needed for more complex forms of expression, such as the short story and poetry that relied on more sophisticated sources and conventions. Johnson's second motive for writing letters was to work out problems that she faced as a parent, wife, friend, and servant of God—that is, problems of hierarchy, authority, and obedience. The evidence for this claim lies in a group of themes that continually surfaced in her writing. In all of her work, Johnson asked the same questions, which were also at the centre of Richardson's novels: how could a woman attain goodness in this world and salvation in the next? How could a woman work out her religious beliefs, encircled by Nonconformists in a world riddled with inequality? How could a woman best express her values to family and friends? As she wrote, Johnson constructed a moral perspective that she passed on in letters, initially to her children, then to other women, who provided a sympathetic network of listeners.

In order to understand the themes in Johnson's letters, however, we must also consider her reading. Innovative studies have provided a theoretical framework for investigating the history of reading. Case studies, however, have generally been concerned with elite rather than ordinary readers. In addition, the search for one overarching model has produced narratives of shifts from script to print, intensive to extensive reading, or state control to personal freedom.[86] Steven Zwicker has recently proposed another eighteenth-century model: a shift from the polemical humanist reader expressing himself actively in the margins of texts to the lonely, passive, eighteenth-century reader. Yet this model does not reflect a time of active practices, when people read aloud in family circles. Nor does it describe a period when access to newspapers, periodicals, bookshops, and circulating libraries enhanced the social dimension of literary life.[87]

In fact, Johnson's writing was informed by constant reading, through which she found both literary models and ideas for moral guidance. First she copied out passages and paraphrased them in her own words. Later she integrated them into poetry and prose.[88] A great deal of what Johnson read was in the form of letters, including those found in her favorite thriller, the *Turkish Spy* in eight volumes. Other collections she read included Alexander Pope's *Letters*, *Letters on the English Nation by a Jesuit*, *Persian Letters*, and of course, the fictional letters in Samuel Richardson's *Clarissa*, which I discuss in detail below.[89] Like the novelist, Johnson was not well-versed in classical languages. We see her taking short cuts into history and literature by gleaning information from translations and more popular books, including facts and maxims that she copied from the *Turkish Spy*. Because of the book's popularity, William Warburton suggested that Richardson make Pamela 'a plebian Turkish Spy', or Indian, who satirized all the 'follies and extravagances of high life'.[90]

The *Turkish Spy* was supposedly based on 'real' letters, a device that Richardson also used. Its readers enjoyed the adventures of its Muslim hero, whilst examining the hypocrisy of European states and their religions.[91] Johnson used it to comment on her own world as she copied a quotation that began: 'This Western World lies drown'd in Wickedness.' Then she noted in the margin: 'This is the exact picture of Great Britain at this present time Anno Domi 1755. Pray God Grant my sons may escape the contagion, & live Virtuous in a nation flowing with...wicked practices. Amen.'[92] This is one of many examples of Johnson's use of secular non-fiction to address moral problems.

Yet the primary purpose of her reading was to know God. 'When I read, O Lord,' she prayed, 'strengthen my memory, that I may allways retain those Things that may well contribute to my increase in the Knowledge and Love of Thee.'[93] The Psalms comforted her and apochryphal books provided stories. She consulted *The Psalm-Singer's Pocket Companion* and made copies of her favorite hymns.[94] Nevertheless, the most remarkable characteristic of Johnson's reading was the diversity and breadth of secular material. Though the extracts were heavily didactic, there was also room for bawdy jokes.[95] Still her favorite authors that she helpfully listed, were entirely respectable:

> The Books that are to be Read by All that would be Eloquent, Polite, Genteel & agreeable; Wise in this world, & Happy in the next; are the Bible, Homer, Milton, the Guardians, Spectators & Tatlers. These should be Read over & over again, & short Extracts Learn'd by Heart . . . these are the only Books necessary to be read for improvement, all others only for Diversion. Whoever follows this rule will think justly, & write & talk eloquently +.[96]

Johnson's comment shows that she read for entertainment as well as moral instruction.[97] It also indicates that her desire for genteel learning shaped her choice of reading. The marketplace provided her with abridged translations of the classics, which she used in her writing. Thus she knew Homer through the words of Pope. 'Can any man of sense be tired with reading Homer?' she asked, on two different occasions. Then she used the quotation that started with this sentence in an original poem, but altered the fourth line.[98] Like the *Spectator* numbers she read, Johnson also quoted lengthy extracts from Milton,[99] Horace,[100] and Juvenal's satires,[101] which she then paraphrased in her own words.[102] Classical texts provided maxims about the battle between virtue and corruption.[103] Johnson's extract from Plutarch's *Lives* cited Aristotle, Plato, Demosthenes, and Theophrastus.[104] Like Richardson, Johnson probably had not read their works in the original languages, but she knew their place in literature, through works that 'modernized' ancient authors.[105] Still, she also relished more popular fare such as editions of *Arabian Nights Entertainments* and Aesop's *Fables*. Richardson would have approved of the latter, for he had published his own edition of the *Fables* early in his career.[106]

After *The Turkish Spy*, Johnson's most frequently consulted sources were the London periodicals—the *Spectator*, *Guardian*, and *Tatler*. By providing models of letters to and by the editors, they acknowledged and encouraged their readers' epistolary literacy. Letters, which comprised over half of the *Spectator*'s 555 numbers, were an integral element—one that invited reader participation.[107] This practice, of course, dated back to the 1690s in the pages of John Dunton's *Athenian Mercury*. His call for readers' questions to be answered by a club of 'Athenians' cleverly sold issues, whilst satisfying readers' aspirations to appear in print.[108]

Yet the *Spectator* took this marketing tool to a higher plane. As it published readers' letters, it also discussed the process of letter-writing, the distinctions and quality of submissions, and whether they were authentic or fictitious editorial creations. By this means, the *Spectator* created an ongoing epistolary style manual. It also provided a venue for the publication of letters. These epistles had commercial value, for some that were submitted, but never printed, were published later.[109] Early periodicals thus encouraged epistolary literacy, a technique that Richardson would adopt later. Johnson's extracts from these periodicals and other commercial sources sat jumbled together on the pages of her notebook. They were likewise intermixed in her mind. As she composed her letters she was able to draw upon a rich store of ideas. We are observing a literary development that connected popular and elite culture to epistolary literacy.

Jane Johnson and the practice of letter-writing

Turning to Johnson's correspondence, we find lengthy epistles, some continued for as much as six leaves.[110] A few were written in an easily legible hand, with the individual letters detached. Others, breathlessly dashed off in a careless manner, covered every bit of paper. Johnson's letters to her school-age children were creatively constructed to delight a child of a particular age and literacy. (See Plate 31.) They demonstrated a threefold epistolary strategy: to teach letter-writing skills, to entertain, and to give moral and religious guidance—a strategy also addressed to adults in Richardson's novels.

Sometimes Johnson concentrated on writing techniques; other times she told stories or included original poems. To aid the moral development of her son Robert,[111] she told the tale of King Solomon, who listened to his mother's advice and was made wise and rich.[112] Then she added an original poem about happiness. Its last two lines also appeared in a poem by Phineas Fletcher (1582–1650). Simple verses that could be remembered became an integral part of her letter. 'Learn this by heart before you come home', she admonished, and added, 'Oh! Robert Live for Ever.' The latter exclamation is paraphrased from *Spectator* 537.[113] Her letters might appear to be spontaneous, but they were carefully constructed literary texts based on models found in her reading.

Johnson's epistolary literacy developed further when she wrote to her female friends. Like Ruth Follows and Elizabeth Wilson, she composed these letters not just to keep in touch, but also to solve problems that women faced in common. Johnson's correspondence, like that of Dissenters, was propelled by questions about virtue and morality—questions that also absorbed Richardson's heroines. As she worked out answers, she sent them to friends in letters of advice.[114] They offered a gendered view of life, woman to woman. 'Female Virtues are of a Domestick turn', she wrote. 'The Family is the proper province for private women to shine in.'[115] This idea was also prominent in *Clarissa* and *Pamela*.

There is good reason for making connections between Johnson's letters to women and those that Richardson exchanged with intimate female friends. Though both Richardson and Johnson requested spontaneous epistolary outpourings from their correspondents, their own letters were constructed works marked by careful artifice.[116] Like Johnson, many of Richardson's correspondents came from clerical families. Some of them, like Sarah Westcomb, Frances Grainger, and Margaret Dutton, were relatively untutored and without pretence to intellectual accomplishment. Others, such as Sarah Fielding, Jane Collier, Elizabeth Carter, and Hester Chapone, were themselves authors. Many of them were motivated by a deep piety.[117] Their real letters give insights into the epistolary literacy of women that Richardson described in his novels.

Once he became famous, his epistolary circle expanded to include more prominent women from the upper levels of the middling sort, such as Mary Delany, her sister Anne Dewes, and their friends. With their aristocratic connections, they served as cultural bridges between middling and elite circles.[118] Two sisters, Lady Dorothy Bradshaigh and Lady Elizabeth Echlin, corrected Richardson's social blunders and suggested alternative endings to *Clarissa*.[119] These women were not just consumers of literature but also suppliers of information about manners. Mrs Delany was aware of what Richardson needed to hear from someone of her class. His 'genteel characters', she remarked, are 'not so really polished as he thinks them to be'. Delany and her group had their own 'pretensions to being part of "Society"', though a society perhaps more intellectual than fashionable'.[120] Like Johnson, they were anxious to participate in the grand project of interpreting novels. Their epistolary literacy made this reciprocal interaction possible.

In different ways, Richardson, Johnson, and Dissenting women, depended on a circle of women correspondents. These exchanges offered the opportunity to work out common problems. Yet Johnson, like Richardson, was experimenting with the epistolary mode not just to give moral advice, but also to tell stories. This format allowed Johnson to develop characters, experiment with descriptive language, and invoke pastoral and satirical modes of writing—in short, to develop literary expertise.

The style and content of three epistolary examples show Johnson confronting problems that she faced in Olney. They also reveal how she turned her letters into literary texts. In each composition, Jane was writing her life story, through real characters as well as imaginary ones, like those she found in Richardson's epistolary novels. As she identified with his heroines she engaged with his texts in a way that Richardson had encouraged. At the start of this literary journey lay the ordinary letter. At the end, we see Johnson's presentation of her ideal self.

Thus a letter to Mrs Brompton of 1756 contained a satire about the court and its immoral attitudes to marriage. Johnson described the process of letter-writing by likening herself to a spider at the centre of an epistolary network. 'I Dreamed last night (Arachne like),' that 'I was metamorphosed into a spider as big as the full moon, & sat upon a Throne in the Center of a Web of my own spinning, as Large as Lincolns-Inn-Fields.' Johnson knew that in Greek myth, Arachne's pride in weaving led to her fall. Through imagery, she wittily inflated the size of the spider and its throne. The reader was left with a mental picture of a huge royal arthropod reigning over central London. This dream was a portent, she explained, that 'I must this day spin out of my own Brains a Long Letter . . . w'ch w'n wrote & Read will be no more worth than a monstrous Spider's Web.' A dream of a silkworm would have been 'a far more fortunate prognostick' that I would make 'this sheet of paper the better instead of the worse'.[121] Johnson used classical imagery in an imaginative way by juxtaposing the mean country spider with the elite silkworm.

In the second part of the letter, Johnson again employed this imagery, but in a different context. God's world was full of natural beauty, though, she insisted modestly, she lacked the skill to describe it.

> The very Frost & snow, have their distinguish'd pleasures & Beauties to me. What can be more Beautiful than a Hoar frost! that shows every Fibre & String in a Spiders Web . . . What makes the Ice so hard? The snow so soft &

white & Light as Air? The Winds so strong & yet Invisible to Mortal Eye? The Snow-drop, bowing down its Drooping Head as if it mourn'd being produced in such an inclement season.[122]

The spider now graced a winter world, but it was the moon that most concerned Johnson here. 'Nothing pleases me so much as the moon, & all the Gems of Heaven Glitt'ring round her', she wrote. 'This is to me a far more delightful sight, than Mrs Spencer encircled with jewels, when she was presented to his Majesty.'[123] A satire followed about the secret marriage of John, first Earl Spencer (1734–83)[124] that contrasted the values of court and country. Johnson described the wholesome garden spiders and the corrupt elite silkworms that existed in each of these worlds. But her real topic was the sanctity of marriage ordained by God, a subject that also absorbed Richardson. 'Promoting matrimony', she insisted, 'is . . . obeying the will of God whose First injunction . . . was increase & multiply.'[125] The Spencers' covert nuptials stood in contrast to a church wedding blessed by the Lord. Johnson's letter was not a simple piece of writing; it integrated language and ideas from Scripture, myth, pastoral odes, and classical satire.

For a second example, we turn to a group of letters to a friend, Mrs Garth.[126] They were actually religious essays, in which Johnson drew upon Newton, reason, and the Bible to explain her beliefs. She noted that 'religion' was her 'subject'[127] and set out rhetorical arguments as if writing a sermon. Johnson chose biblical passages that reflected her own positive experience with family life and connected them to her moral argument. In a similar manner, Richardson published a collection, *Meditations*, and linked the material in the volume to the events in Clarissa's life.[128]

'What I propose then,' Johnson told Mrs Garth, 'is to consider God as set forth in scripture to be *our Father.*'[129] This approach, she was sure, would make sense to any woman who had nurtured a family. If God loved, pitied, and forgave his children like 'an Earthly parent', she reasoned, this must 'disperse all gloomy, & melancholy thoughts, all uneasy fears & apprehensions of incurring his displeasure'. Johnson's cheerful argument and her belief in reason aligned her with doctrines associated with latitudinarianism.[130] Like Rebekah Bateman, Johnson worked out her relation to God in letters, and advised friends with similar concerns. Richardson and his female characters employed similar networks of epistolary advice.

Johnson also confronted the question of how to conduct herself while surrounded by rival sects—a fact of importance that she never mentioned openly. Indeed, her case for rational faith was built up by discrediting evangelical approaches. We 'loose the innocent injoyments of life', she insisted, 'by spending too much time in Praying Reading, Fasting, and Self Examination'. In Johnson's view, obsession with these practices was not supported by the Bible. 'A good Man or Woman is as easily known by their works', Johnson maintained, 'as when I gather a Bunch of Grapes, I know that that tree that bore them is a vine, & not a Bramble Bush.' In this passage, then, she showed a concern with how good deeds were viewed by the community. She also mixed biblical ideas with domestic symbols and common sense in a way that Locke would have appreciated. 'Open your Eyes,' she instructed Mrs Garth, '& . . . be guided by that Share of Reason & Good Sense with which God has Bless'd you.'[131]

Yet Johnson's confident tone changed when she turned to the nagging question of marriage. She knew it was a wife's 'Principal Duty, to do as her Husband commands her, according to St. Paul'. Yet there were limits to this rule. 'You can't think that I mean any more than St. Paul did', she insisted, 'that we are to obey them, if they command us, to do a wicked action . . . In that case, we ought rather to obey God, than man.'[132] She was especially concerned about a man's control over his wife's good deeds. 'I think a married Woman has but little to do with them', she wrote, 'for as she is really possess'd of nothing that is her own, she can have nothing to give, except by her Husband's orders or permission. So that in alms, deeds, as well as in MOST other things', a woman had to bow to her husband's authority.[133] This statement makes us wonder if Johnson's charitable acts in a town filled with poverty had been restrained by her husband. As we shall see, Johnson had become dissatisfied with her church's ability to relieve the poor. Through letters, she defined right conduct and fulfilled the Christian duty to spread the word to friends. Both Johnson and Richardson addressed the problems that a patriarchal society imposed on married women.

Jane Johnson's History of Miss Clarissa of Buckinghamshire

The duty to help her friends was most clearly manifested in a letter to Mrs Brompton of 1749. The letter opened with advice about the role of women. Yet Johnson searched for a new medium as she struggled to express her thoughts. She hoped that her reader would have 'goodness enough to pardon the Liberty I am going to take. Without further apology [I] begin with a story which . . . has its foundations in truth', a phrase used by Richardson on *Pamela*'s title page.[134] In a stunning shift in genre, the reader suddenly sees an indented title to a narrative called 'The History of Miss Clarissa of Buckinghamshire'.[135] (See Plate 32.) Her use of the term 'history' suggested fact, not fiction, and the same term was used by Richardson in *Clarissa*'s title.[136] A close reading of Johnson's 'history' shows that she read and employed *Clarissa* in a way that Richardson had encouraged.

Johnson's Clarissa story was crammed onto both sides of three large sheets. Like Richardson's novel, it examined the life of a woman who was at odds with conventional norms.[137] Though she never admitted it, her narrative also told a story about the problems she faced as a vicar's wife. Johnson constructed a character with virtues and flaws who provided answers to her larger question: how could a woman live a moral life in an unjust world? What was striking, however, was the way that Johnson's 'novel' was slipped into a letter to a friend. She began: 'There is a Lady in this neighbourhood (& because I take pleasure in the name [she] shall be call'd Clarissa,) who began to take much pride & pleasure in obliging her friends with the works of her hands . . . She spent all the time she could spare . . . in making Purses, Flowers . . . & many other pretty things.' Artistic Jane was recognizable in the character of Clarissa, and there were also parallels to the story of proud Arachne, described above.

Like Johnson, her Clarissa married 'a Gentleman of . . . easy fortune', but she suddenly fell ill and was expected to die. 'Death & Judgment appear'd to her with all their terrors . . . She cou'd not help being doubtful whether at the day of judgment she shou'd be set on the right hand or the left.' She wished that 'instead of obliging her friends with unnecessary Triffles . . . she had imploy'd every moment . . . in performing such works that she cou'd with pleasure have reflected upon to all Eternity'. Clarissa pleaded with God to 'prolong her life for fifteen years, as he once had done for good King Hezekiah'. Here Johnson had recalled a letter from Mrs Norton in Richardson's *Clarissa*. With prayer, wrote Mrs Norton, ' "Altho' your days may seem to have been numbered, who knows, but that, with the good King Hezekiah, you may have them prolonged." '[138] Like Richardson, Johnson privileged this story in her own Clarissa narrative. The story that Johnson told was her own, but it had greater literary depth because of its relationship to Richardson's work.

After a conversion, Johnson's Clarissa underwent a reformation. Unlike Richardson, however, Johnson spared her converted Clarissa, who now lived a life of good works—an ending preferred by Richardson's friend, Lady Bradshaigh.[139] 'Whenever she [Clarissa] hears of any poor body sick in the Parish she goes to them . . . At first, visiting the . . . poor was to her a most . . . disgreeable task . . . She was afraid of being call'd a Methodist, asham'd to enter their Houses, at a loss to know what to say.' But resolution and duty overcame these problems. Now she 'goes chearfully in, sits down, or stands according as the house is clean or dirty', and asks questions about 'how they come to be so very poor, Ragged & dirty'.[140] From their answers she 'makes a judgment of their merits' and gives them linen, not money, for they are not wise enough to use it properly.

This conventional conversion story, stimulated by reading *Clarissa*, was derived from Johnson's Olney, with its poverty-stricken lace makers and evangelical clergy. Though not a word was said about the parish in which she lived, Johnson's picture of the poor was too real to have been invented. Johnson's Clarissa sometimes found 'a man & his wife & five or six small children in a house little better than a Hogsty, with a small room above & a couple of beds in it, four of which family lye in each of them, eaten up with vermin, for want of change of Linnen'. Again, Johnson came close to Richardson's language and ideas. His Clarissa bewailed the fact that she could no longer visit 'the cots of my poor neighbours, to leave lessons to the boys, and cautions to the elder girls'.[141] Richardson's heroine also restricted her charity to 'the lame, the blind, the sick, and the industrious poor'.[142] Johnson's Clarissa story, however, ended with virtue rewarded, as in Richardson's *Pamela*.

Johnson's position as a cleric's wife had evidently created feelings of remorse. In her writing she confronted her guilt about the difference between her own life and the poverty she found in Olney's Silver End. The reference to being 'call'd a Methodist', for example, revealed a breach between Anglicans like Woolsey and evangelicals, who preached to the poor. Because some Methodists permitted women to lead Bible study, testify to the Gospel, and engage in pastoral activity, this reference suggests that Johnson was examining the question of women's charity. John Wesley's early ideas gave women a prominent role, especially concerning good works. 'You, as well as men,' he insisted, 'are rational creatures . . . Whenever you have opportunity, do all the good you can, particularly to your sick neighbour.'[143] At the time of Woolsey's death, furthermore, local evangelicals led by John Thornton were trying to reinvigorate the Church of England. To accomplish this end, Woolsey's successors Moses Browne and John Newton were active in ministering to Olney's poor.[144]

When these facts are considered, Johnson's concerns about women's charity take on new meaning, and her Clarissa story must be viewed in light of a contemporary debate about the value of good works. In Johnson's view, morality had to include charitable actions. This was made clear in her notebook entry: 'Knowledge of good without a suitable Practice (or Faith without Works) is like a Bell without a Clapper+.'[145] On another page she noted: 'Read the 459 *Spectator* about Faith & Works & 465, & *Tatler* 257. EXCELLENT!'[146] These articles supported Johnson's personal views about the importance of good deeds.

Johnson's Clarissa story both drew upon her reading and helped her develop answers to the moral problems of her day. Her story captured the plight of a pious Anglican, who was fearful of rival groups, yet acknowledged and regretted her church's inability to improve economic conditions. It would have been unseemly for her to question the church publicly, but in private letters, Johnson could hide behind a story, albeit one with 'a foundation in truth'.[147] Letters gave her an opportunity to reflect on the causes of inequality and to develop a reasoned argument aimed at improving the lot of the poor. To better present her views, Johnson switched to an analytical mode. Though she pleaded ignorance, she was actually well informed about economic conditions, poor relief, and social welfare policy. Her Clarissa now discussed poverty and its causes:

> On seeing the miserys of others, she often laments that there shou'd be any such objects in such a nation as this...There must certainly be some great fault somewhere, either in the Laws, or in the actions of Individuals...since God does every year send vastly more Corn, Meat, Wool, Flax, & Hemp than it is possible for all the Inhabitants of the Land to consume...Therefore the fault is not in Providence, but in men...She thinks that cloathing the naked...might be so order'd as to promote Trade, encourage the English manufactory, make all our people Happy at home & the nation Great & Terrible to Her Enemys abroad...She allows that many good Laws have been made for the Relief of the Poor, but she thinks many better might be made, were the Hearts of Both Houses of Parliament as good as their Heads.[148]

Johnson's Clarissa blamed men who had 'Power, or Riches' and offered them a warning: 'At the Day of Final Distribution of rewards & punishments, all the Rich and Polite World may . . . be sent amongst the Goats on the Left [hand of God] for having withheld the Wool of the sheep from the Backs of their fellow creatures, & sufferd them . . . to shake with cold.' In her Clarissa story, Johnson showed how a provincial woman without formal education could use a story to develop ideas about power, class, gender, and political economy. Her tale was shaped by the rise of local Dissent, a desire for personal and social reform, and a longing for a place on the right side of God. Yet she returned to her letter format as abruptly as she had departed from it. Now she scorned the 'fine taste' of a Miss Hackshaw, who did 'not approve of Miss Clarissa Harlow' or the novel. 'I believe she is the only person of fine Taste & judgment upon Earth that does not approve of it', wrote Johnson. 'For my part I think it will do great things towards reforming the World.'[149]

Johnson's story and Richardson's *Clarissa* both revealed the wish to improve the world. Both of their Clarissas struggled to become virtuous women in an imperfect society. Both wrestled with issues of authority and obedience. Both wrote about an ideal woman in the context of constraints of gender and class. Each writer tried to construct a model of 'how to think and act' in the light of reason and religion.[150] Though there were many ways to disseminate these ideas, both writers embraced the domestic letter as the most effective means at hand.

Richardson understood the importance of epistolary literacy of readers like Jane. Indeed, she used it to engage with his work in the way that he had encouraged. As she wrote her letters, Johnson looked both outward and inward. She observed her husband, family, church, and life in Olney, and wrote her Clarissa story, abruptly, in the middle of a letter. Johnson's surge of creativity was a response to reading Richardson's *Clarissa*. She distinguished it from scandalous romance, identified with its heroine, and used it to examine her own moral values. Yet Jane's letter takes on new meaning when placed in Olney's historical context. Her tale reveals the religious tensions and strained relationships that existed in Olney, but which were omitted from the Johnson archive. Modesty, pride, remorse, and conscience may have led the Johnsons to destroy incriminating letters about Olney.

Of course, Johnson was only one of many readers, who responded to *Clarissa*. Letters written by individuals of both sexes were filled with references to Richardson's work and reflected responses to it.[151] Catherine Talbot recorded reading *Clarissa* 'en famille, at set hours, and all the rest of the day we talked of it'.[152] Sarah Chapone's daughter Sally was 'accustomed to meeting any unusual situation by asking what Clarissa would do'. Sally's father, we are told, was even 'helped to die by the example of *Clarissa*'.[153] Because the Johnson archive contains dense and continuous sources, it is possible to place Johnson in both her historical and literary contexts and to uncover the complexities of her hidden story. We can analyse what she read, what she wrote, and how Richardson inspired her to write her own Clarissa story. We may also observe how Johnson used *Clarissa* to think about her methods of writing. She saw how Richardson inserted letters into the structure of his story and realized that she too could combine a letter with a moral tale. Proceeding in reverse order, she put a story into a letter, instead of a letter into a story, as Richardson chose to do. Mixing genres seemed natural to Johnson, because the boundaries between fact and fiction were blurred in her world.[154]

Clearly, Johnson and Richardson were experimenting with the epistolary mode to tell stories and develop narratives. With different degrees of skill, each transformed letters into literary texts, creating literature out of letters. This was not a new activity for Johnson, but an easy, comfortable habit, formed long before she encountered Clarissa. When she read Richardson, she recognized her own world with particular vividness, a world in which writing was at the centre of human pleasure. In *Clarissa*, Richardson's characters were forever 'at writing-desks, struggling to fix their experiences adequately in prose and so define and assert their own conflicting senses, psychologically, epistemologically, and above all morally, of what is happening in their world'.[155] This was very much like Johnson's world, where epistolary literacy was prized.

Of course people saw themselves reflected in novels, and in Johnson's case this was emphatically true. But I also want to argue that Richardson imagined his novel by observing real women like Johnson writing letters. The juxtaposition of epistolary fiction and letter-writers in real life reveals influence and feedback in both directions. Johnson's shadow falls gently upon the pages of Richardson's novels in regard to both content and method. The letters that he received from women similar to Johnson strengthen this link. Jane's epistolary literacy was therefore a primary theme of *Clarissa* and *Pamela*. Because she and women like her regularly asserted their identity in epistolary prose, Richardson could imagine his own Clarissa doing the same thing. In his novels, he immortalized what Johnson did every day—the act of writing a life through letters. That is why we found her own 'novel' tucked into intimate correspondence. Johnson could find no better home for her 'Clarissa' than in the sheltered space of a letter to a female friend.

Jane Johnson's poetry and literary culture

This section suggests how Johnson combined the moral themes found in Richardson's novels with scientific inquiry and reason in a more complex genre—poetry. It also shows how her varied readings elevated the literary quality of her writing. 'A conversation between Stella & her guardian Angel, One Star Light Night, in the Garden at——' is a six-page poem about another ideal woman. Like Johnson's Clarissa, her Stella learns how to think and act in the light of rational religion. But Johnson now used a wider range of sources to create a higher form of literature. Johnson, we have seen, had easy access to translations of Latin verse.[156] As Hunter noted, 'All those who could do more than just read a few words under necessity or duress regularly read at least some poetry as a matter of course.'[157] Johnson read modern and classical poems, copied out extracts, and then composed her verses.[158]

Johnson's poem 'Stella' exists in two formats: an early draft and a fair copy. The second version imitated the format of a published book in minute detail, with an indented title, introductory quotation, decorative lined borders, numbered pages, and even a footnote. As in Leonard Wheatcroft's case in seventeenth-century Derbyshire, this format indicated that she thought of herself as an author.[159] Changes in the fair copy showed efforts to make the text more poetic. Words were substituted and contracted to create a sensuous mood, and lines were moved to produce a more logical structure. Johnson was familiar with poetic conventions. She used couplets, employed antiquated words such as 'yon', and reversed the order of verbs and nouns to create rhymes. Her vocabulary was simple but evocative of a luminous nightscape: orbs dazzled, stars shone, and angels shimmered.

The poem was preceded by a quotation from Psalms: 'The Heavens declare the Glory of God, & the Firmament showeth his handy work.' Here Johnson was clearly imitating number 465 of the *Spectator*, a periodical whose pages were filled with readers' original poetry as well as letters.[160] In number 465, Addison used the same quotation before his own ode about

God's universe.[161] Johnson's poem, however, was not just an imitation. It arose from her experience and depicted her ideal self. The poem opened in a garden as Stella contemplated the skies. She contrasted the heavens with ephemeral man-made pleasures and yearned for answers to eternal truths.

> How Happy says she shall I be when I Die!
> By Angels conducted to Tread yon Blue Sky!
> To visit each Star! & see all that's done there!
> What pleasures on Earth with these can compare?
> To View the Expanse! the Vast Universe scan!
> And be certain what Distance each star is from man!
> To know if those worlds that now Dazzle my eyes
> Are Peopl'd like This, or with others more wise!
> How far the *great Newton with Truth does agree,
> And be in an instant much Wiser than He![162]

Johnson's references to Newton and the planets recalled those in John Hughes *Ode to Ecstasy* (1720). In this ode, Hughes called out to the ghost of Newton, who suddenly appeared:

> 'Tis he—as I approach more near
> The great Columbus of the skies I know.
> Tis Newton's soul! That daily travels here.
> O stay, thou happy Spirit! Stay
> And lead me throu' all the unbeaten wilds of day
> Here let me, they companion, stray,
> From orb to orb, and now behold
> Unnumber'd suns, all seas of molten gold,
> And trace each comet's wand'ring way.[163]

In Johnson's poem a stranger also appeared suddenly and led Stella from orb to orb. He was the angel Raphael, who travelled with Tobias in the apocryphal Book of Tobit. Hughes admitted in his preface that both he and the poet Cowley had imitated a Latin ode by Casimire.[164] Yet Hughes insisted that his passage about Newton was 'entirely original'. We find similar language in William Stevenson's poem *Stella*. His Stella also yearned 'to soar with Newton to the Skies'. Like Johnson's angelic heroine, this Stella spurned social pleasures. Her only looking glass was a telescope with which she surveyed 'planets, stars, and comets'.[165] We recognize a combination of references found elsewhere in Johnson's writing: Newton, telescopes, God's universe, and criticism of man-made works. Casimire,

Hughes, Cowley, Stevenson, Addison, and Johnson were all linked together in their focus upon the figure of 'Stella' and their wish to probe the heavens.

Moses Browne, the new vicar of Olney, also wrote verses to Stella and *An Essay on the Universe*.[166] Despite her quarrels with Browne, Johnson copied extracts from his works,[167] as well as those of his mentor, the evangelist James Hervey, who composed *Contemplations on the Starry Heavens*.[168] Though both Browne and Hervey were evangelicals, Johnson picked and chose what she wanted from their work. Johnson's 'Stella' was truly a hybrid work nourished by a variety of texts. The chain of authorial emulation cited above shows the many way-stations in a complex journey that started with a Latin ode and ended with Johnson's poem.

After Johnson's introduction, the mood of her poem changed with the arrival of the angel Raphael.[169] As he shone in glory, Stella trembled in fear. Then, without warning, Johnson inserted a new literary format—the dialogue—into the poem. She put the words 'Stella' and 'Angel' in boldface to indicate that they were speakers and used quotation marks to show their dialogue. Stella glorified God in the poem, but she also questioned the nature of the universe. Johnson's search for truth, or what we might call scientific inquiry, was evident in her poetry. She was acknowledging the impact of Newton and Locke and their concept of an ordered universe. But though God had made the cosmos, humans had to find their way. As Stella noted: 'All for man He has done that their maker could Do, Only left their Will Free, which way to Pursue.' Challenging strict predestination, Johnson called for a more rational religion than that of her Dissenting neighbours.[170]

Johnson's writings show how an untrained provincial reader attempted to resolve tensions between religious, scientific, and humanist ideas. As she did so, she incorporated language and thoughts from the works of others. The varied texts that informed her 'Stella' show that a common store of literature from London's marketplace was now available to provincial readers. Libraries and commonplace books of Johnson's contemporaries show a similar wide-ranging pattern of reading that relied on secular as well as biblical sources.[171] Poetry claimed an important place in reading that extended far beyond the novel. Provincial readers were constructing a middling-sort literary culture that was derived from and fit into the wider world of literature.

From letters to literature: Jane Johnson, Samuel Richardson, and epistolary literacy

To understand this literary culture, we must return to the concept of epistolary literacy. Letter-writing offered Johnson a training ground for composing other types of literature. In letters, she developed writing skills and accomplished personal goals. She examined her role as a clergyman's wife, taught her children, advised her friends, defined her religious beliefs, and considered how to be virtuous in this world and the next. She also expressed and fulfilled intellectual aspirations. This study cautions us to look for women's education in makeshift methods and informal places and to recognize the importance of domestic literacy. Unfortunately, home education by one's mother usually left few records.

The practice Johnson gained by writing letters and the information that she absorbed by copying extracts were strategies used by other women to enter the world of literature. The letters of Elizabeth Strutt, for example, may be recalled in this regard. But when Johnson combined epistolary literacy with a range of improving reading, she moved along the spectrum and became more 'educated' in the broad sense of the word. This road from letters to literature was a self-generated, cumulative process. It altered intellectual expectations and produced pride in writing. Thus Johnson signed and dated each poem and story. Thus she kept a journal of her reading, but distinguished her own thoughts by adding a plus sign (+).

Johnson's extracts provide a map of her reading, whose guiding principles were freedom of choice and active engagement. She read both print and manuscript materials for both instruction and entertainment. Sources were not limited to those advocated by the established church. In fact, most of her sources were secular in nature. Ironically, she strove for salvation and right conduct by reading and copying extracts from worldly texts. Though there was a strong didactic dimension to Johnson's texts and comments, neither heavy religious matter nor novels dominated.[172] There was no trace of Zwicker's passive reader. The social aspect of reading would become even more intense in the last half of the century, as novels of Richardson and Rousseau were read aloud to weeping friends. An analysis of the reading of Johnson's children in Chapter 6 confirms that in a later age more engaged with sensibility, they interacted with books even more passionately than she did.[173]

The book wheel of the humanist scholar was no longer present, but its ghost still presided over fragments in Johnson's commonplace book. She read extensively like a magpie plucking whatever she needed to cope with everyday problems. Yet the maxims she copied were united by the broad moral themes that marked both Richardson's novels and every genre of her own writing. The literary marketplace in which she revelled was decidedly commercial, designed for a wide range of middling-sort consumers. It was the same one in which Richardson was thoroughly immersed.

Richardson knew that epistolary literacy was crucial to the audience for which his novels were created. We think of him as an innovative author with literary skills, but he was also an astute observer of historical trends: the rise of literacy; the growing wealth of the middling-sort; the uses of print culture; and the cultural aspirations of women like Johnson. His epistolary format was based on knowledge of the market, and of many a 'plain writer' like himself.[174] He saw the symbiotic relationship between real and fictional letters and flourished on the porous boundaries between them. Of course epistolary fiction and romantic stories long predated the 1740s, both in England and on the continent. But by the second half of the century, there was an epistolary moment when real letters and fiction were most closely intertwined. Their relationship was clearly a two-way street.[175] If readers imitated epistolary models, they also affected the epistolary novel.

Their influence was, in part, a result of Richardson's desire for dialogue and his respect for his readers' needs and judgements. Though he rarely adopted their specific suggestions, his audience still shaped the way he composed and sold his works. He needed to know how readers were reacting to his work, while it was still in progress. Some of them merely provided insights into manners, yet their more subtle fears about his view of the human condition prodded him to make endless revisions. This reciprocal interchange was important to Richardson, because he believed that writing could change people's attitudes.[176]

Buoyed by notoriety and commercial success, he assumed he could control his readers. Yet this was not possible. Once he had authorized his readers to write their own stories, they were free to express their own gendered views in spaces outside of his influence.[177] Johnson's case uncovers the way this worked for a previously untapped reservoir of non-elite women writing at home. Her Clarissa story allowed her to think independently and write critically about the social, economic, and religious inequalities of her patriarchal world. As she wrote, Johnson provided Richardson with a perfect subject. Though they never actually met, his novels acknowledged their literary interaction. At the moment when their writings intersected, the letter was moving 'from the periphery to the centre of the literary system'.[178] At the same time, Jane was becoming a woman writer. It was not until the advent of a broad-based epistolary literacy that *Pamela* and *Clarissa* could achieve the wide audience that Richardson had anticipated. His readers identified with his characters in many ways. But, surely, the epistolary literacy of Pamela and Clarissa would have struck them as closest to their own lives.

Richardson knew all of this by heart, for he had witnessed a shift in the way people communicated with each other. In the light of this historical framework, his innovations take on new colours. They may appear more muted for their portrayal of such an ordinary activity, but to acknowledge the importance of such a mundane act was breathtakingly audacious. When we connect Richardson's historical insights to Johnson's epistolary literacy, the study of the novel is enriched.

6

Letter-writing, reading, and literary culture

The Johnson family and Anna Miller

'You have seen advertised Letters from Italy by an English Woman', wrote Jane Johnson's son Robert to his sister Barbara in 1776. 'They were written from Mrs [Anna] Miller to her mother, and I am told contain many capital strokes of character [such] as the history of the Pope's being in love with her.'[1] *Letters from Italy, Describing the Manners, Customs, Antiquities, Paintings, &c. to a Friend Residing in France*[2] was the talk of the Bath community that included Jane Johnson's children, Barbara (1738–1825)[3] and Robert (1745–99).[4] Their friend, Anna Riggs Miller (1741–81),[5] began her literary journey by writing letters—the only genre she knew well. As in Jane Johnson's day, letter-writing was still the training ground for entering the literary world. But Jane would have been shocked at the blatant commercialization of Anna's letters, in contrast to her own modest ways of writing. Miller had discarded the old epistolary model of a woman writing virtuously in private. Of course, exceptional women had published letter collections in Britain and on the continent. By the 1770s, however, public authorship had become openly accepted for women of lesser abilities. After the book's second edition, Anna created a poetry salon in Bath with her husband's newly acquired money.

This chapter analyses and compares the motives, uses, and impacts of Mrs Miller's public letters with the private correspondence of Jane Johnson and her children. We will see how middling-sort individuals, possessing different levels of epistolary literacy, used letters to construct a vibrant literary culture in the last quarter of the eighteenth century. As in Jane Johnson's case, letter-writing underpinned our trio's reading and writing activities. Their letters also influenced mainstream literature in the last quarter of the century. Yet the epistolary playing field and literary landscape had changed dramatically. In contrast to Jane's quiet provincial world, her children were engulfed in a fast-paced literary culture. No longer hidden in a country vicarage, they led much of their lives in public, where they could be seen to have good taste. Unlike modest Jane, Robert, Barbara, and Anna Miller had social and literary ambitions. Fortunately, they had more resources to devote to a range of new cultural activities.

Of our three letter-writers, Jane's second son, the Reverend Robert Augustus Johnson (1745–99) had the highest status and wrote the largest number of surviving letters. Yet though he was the son of a vicar, there is no evidence of his attending university or engaging in clerical life.[6] After a stint in the army, he married upward socially. Happily, his brother-in-law presented him with a Shropshire living that was maintained by a curate. As an absentee cleric, Robert lived in Kenilworth near Coventry, but spent much of the year in fashionable Bath. His letters reveal the insatiable reading and writing habits of middling-sort individuals with a bit of money and a lot of leisure. Eventually he became a member of the Birmingham Bean Club and the Lunar Society,[7] where he met entrepreneurs and scientists of his day.

Jane's eldest child, and only daughter, Barbara inherited her mother's poetic talent. In 1776, her verses won a prize at Anna Miller's poetry salon.[8] Though she never married, she had intimate epistolary relationships with a wide group of friends and family. Barbara spent much of the year away from her own modest home in Northampton visiting Catherine Wodhull (c.1744–1808)[9] of Thenford (near Brackley) and Berkeley Square, London. Catherine's husband Michael (1740–1816) was a book collector, a translator of Latin verses, and owner of a large library. Barbara's access to books and stimulating conversation is revealed in her spirited letters.[10]

Anna Miller started life with the least exposure of the three to literary society. In an eighteenth-century novel, she and modest, home-loving Jane Johnson might have served as perfect foils. Anna was an ambitious, entrepreneurial, self-publicizing woman, who was mentioned in the dedication of Sheridan's *The School for Scandal,* and has been suggested as an inspiration for a character in Dickens's *The Pickwick Papers.*[11] Anna's father was a London customs official and her mother, noted Horace Walpole, was 'an old rough humourist who passed for a wit'.[12] In 1780, Fanny

Burney described Anna as 'a round, plump, coarse-looking dame of about forty ... While all her aim is to appear an elegant woman of fashion, all her success is to seem an ordinary woman in a very common life, with fine clothes on. Her movements are bustling, her air is mock-important, and her manners inelegant ... However [she] seems extremely good-natured, and ... is, I am sure, extremely civil.'[13] All three of our letter-writers were essentially middling-sort individuals. Yet inherited money, wealthy friends, and powerful in-laws enabled them to borrow cultural capital as well as books. Other middling-sort families, with at least one well-connected member, may have followed a similar pattern.

The letters of Anna Miller and literary culture in Bath

Mrs Miller's *Letters*, which received glowing reviews, takes us a step further into the development of provincial culture at the end of the eighteenth century. Unfortunately, Anna's epistolary literacy has been neglected and overshadowed by negative views of her poetry salon. Yet she could have used her money for a variety of purposes. The fact that she wished to become a published author is significant. She was typical of an expanding group of individuals, who enjoyed reading and writing, but lacked a university education or residence in London—the two requirements of groups, who often dominate literary studies. People like Anna were attracted to the tempting, new world of leisure filled with newspapers, periodicals, bookshops, and libraries. They wished to enter this world, but were uncertain how to do so. Letters were often the only literary genre with which they had long experience. Like Jane Johnson, Mrs Miller used letters to construct a literary culture, but for very different ends.

In 1765, Anna married Captain John Miller (*c.*1744–98) of an undistinguished Irish family.[14] After dabbling at university, John rose to captain in the Seven Years War. By 1778, when he became an Irish baronet, his wife was known as Lady Miller, though solely out of courtesy.[15] Following his marriage, the captain assumed his wife's surname, and inherited a fortune. 'The captain's fingers are loaded with cameos', remarked Horace Walpole, 'and his tongue runs over with *virtú*.'[16] He is 'a dilletanti man, [who] keeps a weekly day for the Litterati, and is himself literate'.[17] Though Miller eventually dined with Walpole and Dr Johnson, he appears never to have been accepted in London society.[18] In Bath, however, the couple had a fighting chance to establish themselves as literary figures.

Whilst its Georgian upper town was developing, the Millers built a 'villa' in Batheaston, two miles from the town centre. It commanded 'a most pleasing prospect of a rich vale, washed by the river Avon, and bounded by romantick towering hills'.[19] The Millers' huge construction costs, however, forced them briefly into continental exile. This gave Lady Miller an excuse to wander freely abroad, where she wrote her three volumes of *Letters*.

Lady Miller's success was predicated on two simple assets: she knew how to write a letter; and she understood the commercial marketplace. Anna's private letters show that she became an experienced letter-writer. 'Excuse the hurry I write in', she pleaded in 1780, 'for this is the fifteenth letter I have written this day.'[20] She also used letters to indulge in intimate conversation that flattered her recipient and invited flattery in return. Thus she wrote to Dr Thomas Whalley in a language of sensibility. At the thought of answering his letter, she confessed, 'I tremble all over, and have actually a nervous complaint...conscious of my own deficiency.' Whalley's own letters, she swore, warranted publishing 'for the elegance of the style, the purity of the language, [and] the heavenly benevolence which beams throughout'. They should, she concluded, receive 'applause and imitation of all those who attempt letter-writing'.[21] Yet she dropped this deferential pose in public letters, when it was useful for her to do so.

In private letters, Anna could assume intimacy with mere acquaintances, without having to obtain entry into their homes. Indeed, Anna claimed close personal ties with all of her correspondents, no matter how slightly she knew them. 'I cannot resist...asking you a very familiar question', she wrote an attendee of her soirées. 'If you think me impertinent burn this scrawl instantly.'[22] Anna also used letters to increase membership in her salon by soliciting verses for her poetry competitions from people at home and abroad. In 1780, letters from Rome, Basle, and Geneva came from a rising young architect, John Soane, who was designing a Roman temple for her grounds. 'If you have poetical talent yourself', she begged, 'or if you have a friend that has, I shall be happy to hear from you on the Subject for the 8th of March, vis. CONTENT.'[23] As she searched for odes, Mrs Miller was trying to establish a miniature republic of letters.

For her first appearance in print, Anna wisely chose travel letters to a friend. Letters written on a journey demanded less formal literary standards and were easily adapted for publication. What is more important, they were fashionably in vogue. Epistolary travel fiction of Laurence Sterne and Tobias Smollett had become popular, along with tales of real journeys.[24] As touring became easier with the peace of 1763, travel narratives became 'predominantly a middle class form'. It also influenced working-class people, like the gardener, Joseph Morton in Chapter 3.[25]

One of the ways in which travelogues developed was in private letters and journals. In 1776, Barbara Johnson observed the normalcy of this practice as she wrote to her brothers on tour: 'If either of you kept a little journal of your route . . . please send it . . . I dare say you could not go so far and see so many places without making Memorandums and observations.'[26] In 1779, Robert Johnson noted that he was writing letters en route 'in a kind of journal-like manner'.[27] The heightened sensibility of the genre was in keeping with its origin in the pages of intimate letters.

In fact, a debate had arisen over how far travel accounts should indulge in sentimental language. Thus in 1774, Henry Wyndham lashed out at 'what the fashionable writers and readers call Sentiment . . . the criterion of merit by which every modern publication is judged'. His *A Gentleman's Tour through Monmouthshire and Wales*[28] delighted Robert, who had just returned from a similar tour.[29] Anna understood that this was a literary moment, when female travelogues might be appreciated. Before the 1770s, few women had published travel accounts. Yet twenty appeared to favourable reviews from 1770–1800. 'Letters of female travellers', wrote the *Critical Review* in 1777, 'are now become not unusual productions.'[30]

With these trends in mind, Mrs Miller, a born publicist, devised a daring plan. First she would publish her *Letters* anonymously, knowing she would be discovered as their author. Then she would use her fame to become patroness of a poetry circle. Only a vain, self-centred woman would have had the audacity to embark on this project. But Miller was thick-skinned and confident. To insulate her from attack, her publisher, Charles Dilly,[31] appealed to readers in the preface to forgive Anna's mistakes. He praised her 'spirit of tenderness and benevolence, that animated warmth so honestly avowed, and so feelingly exerted . . . in the interests of humanity'.[32] Dilly thus made a virtue out of Anna's emotional way of writing, which was likely to appeal to a middle-class market, uninterested in pedantic texts.[33] The book's second edition proved that Miller's *Letters* had found their intended niche.

Miller's book offered an art-appreciation course on Italian masterpieces to readers who had little background. People 'unacquainted with . . . the merits of painting' were advised to 'turn over a few pages', when they came to material they did not understand.[34] This statement reveals a stratified audience with elite and middling-sort readers at different levels. They were treated to Anna's personal views of paintings, which, she insisted, surpassed those of Mr Addison. Though Anna's comments show she misinterpreted Addison's views, she confidently claimed superior knowledge.[35]

Miller wrote as if she was talking spontaneously, using italics, dashes, and exclamation points to add intensity to her prose. On page two, she told her audience: 'My journey must have a fiery end, Mount Vesuvius.—I tremble at the thought—though perhaps I may be...reconciled to a burning mountain, when I shall fancy myself...petrified to crystal, amidst the eternal snows and iced mountains.'[36] Anna aroused excitement through novelistic accounts of perilous adventures in which she was the intrepid heroine. Her confident letters rejected the private modest epistles so often linked to women. When Miller's letters are compared with those of Jane Johnson, we can see how epistolary norms had expanded.

Samuel Richardson's friend, Mrs Delany thought Miller's *Letters* 'very conceited...and not worth buying', and at 18s. she had a point.[37] But Anna's publisher understood the market for which the book was intended. In a review of over eight pages, *The Monthly Review* praised Miller for using 'her own judgment in a manner which casts an agreeable air of originality over the work'.[38] The rival *Critical Review* praised her 'vivacity of disposition...though care should be taken that this quality does not deviate into an ostentatious display of frivolous pleasantry or superior acuteness'.[39] Though Miller was enthusiastic, her feminine qualities had to be 'held firmly in check lest they intrude on male territory'.[40] She therefore resisted indulging in excessive sensibility and used letters to present herself as an informative, tasteful writer.

Unlike Jane, Anna employed letter-writing to become a published author and to rise socially. There was also a psychological component to Anna's epistolary pursuits. Her constant need for flattery revealed the fragility of a woman who had recently entered the arena of public authorship. Thus *before*, not after, she wrote her *Letters*, Miller shrewdly moved to Bath, the home of women writers such as Sarah Scott, Sarah Fielding, Catharine Macaulay, Sophia Lee, Ann Thicknesse, Anna Seward, and Jane and Harriet Bowdler.[41] Elizabeth Child has shown how women were able to appropriate a cultural authority in Bath unavailable to them in London.[42] Once in Bath, Miller encouraged women poets, who attended her salon.

Norma Clarke has cited provincial circles 'full of men and women of "taste", who took seriously their duty to form and monitor the nation's culture'. 'Letters', she added, were 'key to this project'.[43]

The wisdom of Anna's move to Bath was confirmed by her success in shaping its literary culture. Indeed, the accomplishments that flowed from her *Letters* were impressive. The salon that she created was elegantly classical in tone.[44] Poems on selected themes were placed in an Italian marble vase, allegedly 'found' near Cicero's villa. Topics included 'the history of dreams',[45] 'the tyranny of custom',[46] and a debate about 'Genius' won by Barbara Johnson.[47] After verses were read aloud, a committee dominated by Anna chose the winning authors. She decked their brows with myrtle wreaths amidst great flattery. Then the guests supped on 'jellies, sweetmeats [and] ice creams'.[48] Even critical Fanny Burney admitted: 'Notwithstanding Bath Easton is so much laughed at in London, nothing here is more tonish than to visit Lady Miller, who is extremely curious [i.e. select, particular] in her company, admitting few people who are not of rank and fame.'[49] Though the list of prominent visitors included the actor, David Garrick, the writer, Catherine Macaulay, the poet, Christopher Anstey, and a sprinkling of titled nobility, most of the guests were middling-sort people, like the Johnsons.[50]

If Lady Miller's aim was to be noticed, she was a smashing success. Yet the sneers of London's literary elite, as well as provincial writers, alert us to the Millers' impact on the culture of this period. Public debates over Batheaston's merit appeared regularly in London newspapers. The *St James Chronicle*, for example, ridiculed the 'Proud Knights, silly Squires, and bald-pated Seers [who] beat their Brains once a Week, and weave with Penelope's Maids their Taffety Trappings'. In response, poets like Christopher Anstey defended Anna with *Envy, a Poem addressed to Mrs Miller, in which is introduced a panegyrick on the respective merits of the Batheaston Poet*.[51] Robert Johnson recorded Anna's notoriety in his journal. Yet despite his scorn, he rarely missed a meeting. 'I at Bath Easton', he reported, 'Read some excellent verses in ridicule of the Vase—the subject The Amusements and Beauties of Bath.'[52]

Yet Mrs Miller's achievements can not be denied. She made poetry writing fashionable by offering a literary alternative to balls and gossip. Unhampered by constraints of class and gender, she opened the floodgates of the commercial marketplace for her middling-sort disciples, such as Anna Seward, Jane Bowdler, and Mary Alcock. To obtain a wider audience for poems that still fill our libraries, she published seven annual collections of prize-winning verse.[53] After selling-out in days, their proceeds went to the Bath Hospital, where Captain Miller was a Governor. Funds also were sent to Bath's pauper charity whose president was, again, Miller.[54] In one fell swoop, the couple dominated and entwined Bath's literary and charitable arenas.[55] Anna's public use of epistolary literacy thus had a political dimension that gave her power in her chosen areas. Consequently when Mr Miller came to call, Robert contributed to his fund for paupers.[56]

At Anna's death in 1781, Anna Seward published verses in her honour, and a monument was erected in Bath Abbey.[57] Not to be outdone, Dr Harrington of Bath composed 'An ELEGY to the Memory of LADY Millar, set to music for three voices'.[58] At very different times and in very different ways, Anna Miller and Jane Johnson used letters as a springboard into the literary world. At the bottom of their literary activities lay the comfortable act of letter-writing.

To make sense of the success of Mrs Miller's letters and compare them with those of Jane's children, we must place our trio in the context of Bath's 'urban renaissance'.[59] The Millers and Johnsons settled there, after a period of great rebuilding. In 1774 Robert reported: 'The town...is very neat and the regularity of the new part...has a most pleasing effect. The crescent is now completed and is really one of the most striking things I ever saw in my life.'[60] The population would grow fourfold from 1766–1821, and it hosted over 40,000 annual visitors.[61] As early as 1760, Bath had four newspapers, and by 1800, there were at least ten bookstores with circulating libraries.[62] One sign of Bath's expanding literary culture was the success of Mrs Miller's inclusive competitions that mixed elite and middling-sort poets.

Because of Anna's fame, Hester Thrale introduced her to Fanny Burney in a private home on the Crescent.[63] The three women had very different backgrounds, but they mixed socially in Bath, where the range of society was wide and interactions relatively free. Still a hierarchy of levels marked Bath society, and Anna, it appears, was not accepted in Burney's world. After they met, Fanny joked about Miller to friends. It was understood that she was to be called on, but never imitated.[64] Yet Bath embraced them all in a cultural alternative to London. It was in some ways characteristic of spas and cathedral towns, and often at odds with the capital.[65] Though Bath society drew on London, Rome, and Paris for inspiration, it extended lower into the social structure than its French counterpart.[66] As Marilyn

Butler has suggested, 'the provinces in this period were more go-ahead in the arts' and 'in the vanguard of the cult of sensibility'.[67]

Bath offered a new type of cultural model for a growing residential community. Its visitors, meanwhile, returned to their homes inspired by novel ideas.[68] This fact makes Bath an ideal place in which to observe cultural formation. In 1779, Mrs Montagu noted: 'In point of society and amusement, it [Bath] comes next (but after a long interval) to London. There are many people established at Bath who were once of the polite and busy world... They retain a... politeness of manner and vivacity of mind which one cannot find in many county towns.'[69] It is in this cultural context that we will examine the epistolary literacy of Robert and Barbara Johnson. They fit neatly into the category of 'polite and busy' people that Montagu described above.

The 'vivacity of mind' that characterized Jane's children may be seen in their surviving writing and reading records. It is crucial to analyse both of these practices together, for this generation integrated them in new ways. Letter-writing still underpinned the world of letters, but the content of the correspondence of Jane's children was quite different from that of their mother. Though Robert was an absentee clergyman, there was little mention of God or religious matters. The deep moral concerns of the letters of Jane Johnson and Samuel Richardson had vanished. Instead, we find the witty satire and sensibility that graced epistolary works by Smollett and Sterne.[70] Jane's children had resolved the anxious questions about the soul that had plagued their pious mother.

Yet as the language of sensibility intruded into letter-writing, it raised new problems about acceptable self-expression. The empathy and emotions of letter-writers, I suggest, became new yardsticks for assessing epistolary literacy. There were also marked differences in the way that Jane and Robert incorporated their reading into letters. With the exception of one outburst about Richardson's *Clarissa*, Jane copied short abstracts into a commonplace book, with little or no comment. In contrast, a major pleasure of letter-writing for her children lay in the robust exchange of views about reading. As we shall see, this exchange played an overlooked role in the development of literary criticism.

Since Jane's children were constantly on the move and often separated, letter-writing was more important than ever. Fortunately, Bath's improved postal service kept the family in touch. Captain Miller's colleague on Bath's Hospital Board was Ralph Allen,[71] whose work had revived the post office.[72] In 1773, the mail was carried to London five days a week, whilst 'machines, waggons, and carriers' linked Bath in every direction'.[73] For £1 8s. Robert could ride the Flying Post to the capital. It left at 11 p.m. and arrived in town the next evening.[74] When post boys were replaced with coaches, Robert's newspaper arrived sooner than before.[75] Letter-writing could more easily assume new functions, when the postal service was quick and reliable.

The Letter-writing and reading of Barbara Johnson

This ease in communication is seen in hundreds of letters between Jane's children: George (1740–1814) of Witham-on-the Hill, Lincolnshire; Charles (1748–1828), a fellow of Clare College, Cambridge; and especially Robert and Barbara.[76] Barbara inherited Jane's sense of female propriety as well as her talent for poetry. Mother and daughter had much in common with Jane's imaginary Clarissa, who found 'intoxicating pleasures' in making beautiful things. Barbara's album in the Victoria and Albert Museum is stuffed with materials snipped from her dresses. A bill for £8 15s. 7d. from a 'Habit maker to . . . [the] Princess of Wales' reveals her passion for clothes.[77] Barbara clearly revelled in society, unlike her retiring mother. In 1776, she received 'surprising accounts of the present Fashions, and of the Ladies Heads, which are quite enormous'.[78] She also enjoyed balls, assemblies, and theatre in Northampton. Ironically, she was partial to Sheridan's *The School for Scandal*, the play that contained a parody of Anna.[79]

Barbara's pleasant way of life was financed by small family legacies that made her self-sufficient.[80] 'I have always kept myself independent,' she stated proudly, 'and have . . . learn'd to be content with a slender income.' 'I have gone very well thro' the world to an advanc'd age and have . . . met with . . . real friendship, affection, and esteem (the true blessing of life).'[81] The many gifts that she left to women[82] showed her high regard for female friendships. These attachments underpinned Barbara's very wide epistolary networks, in which she assumed a central place. She was the only family member to have so many correspondents that they had to be catalogued in alphabetical order.[83] Barbara's own letters in a hand that resembled Jane's, often came from Thenford, where she lived like a member of the family with Catherine and Michael Wodhull. Their stylish literary epistles became models for her own letters and displayed the easy wit she found in their company.[84]

As she aged, Barbara held the family together through letter-writing.[85] Requests from the next generation about family history were immediately sent to her. Moreover, she selected and trained a nephew to become her successor as 'guardian' of the family papers.[86] Though letters *to* Barbara are copious, we have fewer letters *from* her. Yet she assiduously collected those written by others and preserved, reread, and annotated four generations of family papers.

I suspect it is no accident that some of Barbara's letters were lost. A clue to their absence lies in the appearance of those that Barbara sorted and kept. She edited them prudishly by obliterating references to her own person. Whenever anything unpleasant or personal was brought up, heavy black inkblots concealed the text.[87] This pattern is, in itself, interesting. It also explains Barbara's open admission that she feared the effects of mislaid correspondence. Because she had 'known great mischief ensue in families by keeping letters', she suggested burning those that might hurt others.[88] Barbara's selective editing shows the constraints imposed by gender and class. By the end of the century, her prim sense of propriety replaced Jane's fond desire to save every scrap of writing. This anxiety was understandable at a time when women like Anna Miller were immodestly publishing personal letters.

In fact, the best way to describe Barbara's motives for writing letters is to compare them with those of Mrs Miller. Barbara's were written for private purposes; Anna's were public and commercial. Barbara mainly wished to unite far-flung friends and kin. The thought of being a public celebrity would have been abhorrent to her. But though her verses won several of Mrs Millers' prizes, she still needed Robert to confirm their worth.[89] 'Your verses have real merit', he wrote encouragingly, 'though your modesty and diffidence won't permit you to discern the whole of it, which is really the case with every thing you write.'[90] Barbara was, however, recognized by members of Fanny Burney's circle, unlike Anna Miller. The author Harriet Bowdler admired Barbara's 'genius for poetry' and begged her for a poem.[91] Barbara's modesty and Mrs Miller's lack of it reveal dissimilar attitudes to writing. Yet both women's lives depended upon epistolary literacy.

Barbara showed more independence in her choice of reading. Though she handled 'first editions of the classics and rare specimens of early printing' in Wodhull's library,[92] she also read the latest books. When in

Northamptonshire, she easily obtained volumes from her local Brackley reading club.[93] We can contrast her situation with that of the 1740s, when Catherine Talbot and Elizabeth Carter were 'exercised by . . . whether or not to subscribe to Mr Fancourt's innovation, a circulating library'. Indeed, Carter called it a 'wild scheme'.[94]

Barbara was not alone in her passion for reading. After the Seven Years' War, peace and prosperity led to a popular interest in British literature.[95] In 1774 when perpetual copyright was altered, some books became available at lower prices.[96] By the 1790s, 988 firms engaged in book trade activities in 316 towns.[97] By 1800, libraries and reading clubs had spread throughout England.[98] Yet there was more than just an increase in numbers. Throughout English towns, there was an intrusive combination of maturing transport, postal services, and printed matter, especially newspapers. The latter had their own agents, who supplied booksellers, stationers, and libraries. This cluster of integrated services was mutually reinforcing, as a picture of Crawford's Circulating Library in Brighton shows. (See Plate 33.) The building not only housed a Post Office, its proprietor functioned as a bookseller, stationer, and bookbinder. A visitor would have found these related services, a natural and ubiquitous aspect of provincial life.[99] Though these cultural facilities had originated earlier, they were more stable and well-developed by 1800.

All of these enhancements affected the reading patterns of Jane's children. Letters describe their regular use of libraries, bookshops, book clubs, and book catalogues.[100] Robert subscribed to Bull's circulating library the moment he arrived in Bath.[101] Like Jane Austen's female characters, Barbara's ability to borrow books at will, must have given her a sense of personal freedom.[102] Indeed, letter-writers of every rank confirm that people constantly read books that they did not own. Sharing printed matter became a universal obligation, for no one had all they wished to read in one place. As H. L. Jackson discovered, 'reading was part of the texture of everyday life, seemingly for everyone, as it had not been a generation before'.[103]

Not surprisingly, Barbara absorbed huge quantities of books, newspapers, and magazines, some of which come from her local book club. In February 1776, she reported: 'We were amus'd with no less than NINE different magazines last month and two reviews.'[104] Her mention of reviews was an acknowledgement of the growth of literary criticism that was sweeping the country. Barbara's favourite printed format, however, was the newspaper, and she was known for being well informed. When an election loomed, her political views were widely sought after. 'My father often wishes for you', wrote a cousin, 'and says "what would Mrs Jonson say?" '[105] When Lord North threatened to raise the newspaper tax, Barbara wittily voiced displeasure in a mock letter to the editor. The ministry, she claimed, was 'robbing us of one of our principal comforts, may I say necessarys, for what is Life without a Newspaper?...I look upon it as one of the glories of the present reign that...upwards of 12 million of newspapers are annually printed...I have...seen your entertaining paper three times a week', she concluded, 'and custom has made it as necessary to me as Light or Air...I had rather live upon water-gruel and go in rags, still bless'd with the sight of your paper, than without it to be cloathed in purple and fine linnen.'[106]

Barbara also exchanged reading recommendations with a circle of female correspondents, who read the latest periodicals and reviews. 'If you look into the *Gentleman's Magazine* of last month', wrote a friend, 'you will read a criticism upon Lewesdon Wiles.'[107] 'I have never read the life of Marmantel', admitted another, 'but the extracts...in the reviews give me reason to believe it must be very entertaining.'[108] In 1776, Barbara alerted Robert to criticism of Lady Luxborough's letters in the *St James Chronicle* of 20 January. She implied that either she or someone she knew was the anonymous author.[109] The fact that Barbara might have written an anonymous review is in keeping with her love of reading and her aversion to publicity.

Many of the books read by Barbara were written in the language of sentiment that was prevalent in provincial circles. In 1776, for example, Barbara wrote excitedly: 'I am now reading Goldsmiths Animated Nature which entertains me extremely. I have not met with a Book to please me so much in a great while.'[110] We know that Goldsmith wanted to write 'a popular as opposed to a scholarly book, a book...that mankind would actually read'. He therefore wrote about animals with 'authorial sensibility, and human sympathy'.[111] Barbara's epistolary comments show how well Goldsmith understood the needs of readers. Avoiding novels for meatier fare, she and her brother enjoyed history, politics, travel, and, of course, letters by Lord Chesterfield, Lord Lyttleton, Lady Luxborough, Lady Rachel Russell, and Hester Chapone.[112]

By the end of the century, comments about romantic poetry and prose filled Barbara's thoughts. 'You do not...mention...Southey's Madoc', wrote one correspondent, 'which I am at this time in the middle of...

Miss Seward . . . thinks it is the brightest poetic luminary of the British Hemisphere, since the Miltonic sun arose. It is really a fine poem', she added, 'but whether it deserves to be placed above Young, Thompson, Akenside, Mason, Cowper and all the other blank verse writers, since the time of Milton, I am by no means a sufficient judge.' Sir Walter Scott's work, in contrast, won her instant approval. 'The Lays of the Last Minstrel', a friend noted, is 'a work most deservedly entitled to praise'.[113]

The most adored author of members of Barbara's circle was Jean Jacques Rousseau. When her brother George was in Switzerland, she assumed he had 'visited the . . . Mansion of the great Rousseau, late Citizen of Geneva. I . . . wish he was alive now that you might see and converse with him . . . Was I a Man', she continued, '[I] would certainly set out directly. But you know women are helpless animals and not calculated to launch out so far as their inclinations would carry them.' Whilst her brothers travelled throughout Britain and the continent, Barbara remained at home. 'I have no descriptions to give you of beautiful places and new scenes', she wrote in 1778, 'but must content myself with relating what passes amongst your acquaintance in poor old England.'[114] To George's reports of Wales, she responded wistfully: 'I am delighted with your account of those Romantic scenes and often wish myself with you on those cloud-capt mountains.'[115] Barbara's restricted horizons stemmed from her gender, unmarried status, and limited income. Mrs Miller, on the other hand, travelled abroad and published her letters. Barbara collected the correspondence of others and used letters for private ends. Thankfully, reading offered the adventures that men experienced through travel.

Yet Barbara used epistolary literacy in a way that differed from her mother by filling her letters with shrewd recommendations for reading. Her access to books gave her a stake in the wider culture and the authority of an informed reader, on which others could rely. Gender issues kept her from publishing her writing, but not from reading. Elizabeth Strutt merely incorporated literary extracts in letters. Barbara went a step further by becoming a sought-after literary critic.

The letter-writing and reading of Robert Johnson

Barbara's brother, Robert was well aware of her consummate taste. 'I assure you I read with partiality every Book you recommend', he wrote, 'and have rarely found you mistaken in what you thought I should like.' Lucky in life, in 1773 Robert married a wealthy widow, Anna Rebecca Craven (1745–1816), sister of William, Lord Craven (d. 1791).[116] After leaving the army, Robert expected 'to have a part of her fortune unsettled... to clear off old scores and set us out in the world'. Lord Craven, however, opposed the union, for 'Johnson was a younger brother and had nothing but a lieutenant's pay to live on'.[117] Even so, Robert and Anna, whom he called 'my little Madam Ann'[118] married and had six children.[119] 'Mr Johnson was a mild and good man', wrote Lady Craven, 'but entirely governed by his wife... She was... very entertaining, but generally engrossed all the conversation to herself.'[120] Little details in Robert's letters confirm the accuracy of this view. 'Matrimony, though it has many roses, has some few thorns', he admitted. 'One must be content to make home comfortable and agreeable.'[121]

Despite these 'few thorns', Robert remained cheerful. In fact, a poem by Michael Wodhull, which he dedicated to Robert, was entitled *The Optimist*.[122] After Robert's marriage, he wrote of being 'perfectly happy; easy in my present circumstances with a certainty of my family being comfortably provided for'.[123] In 1791, Robert became the abstentee vicar of Wistanstow, Shropshire, where the Cravens owned the living.[124] His days were spent commuting between Kenilworth, Bath, and the Cravens' homes in Combe Abbey, Benham, and London. In 1774, he settled his family in Bath's fashionable Brock Street, which linked the Circus to the Crescent. His friends, the Liddiards and the Digbys, lived on the same road. Brock Street was one of the best locations in town, as Robert's poor rate of over 11s. 3d. shows.[125] Yet at death he left his family in financial straits. Apparently, he failed to save money from legacies for a rainy day.[126]

In his prime, Robert was intellectually curious about the science and technology that was energizing industrial towns. In 1772, he visited Matthew Boulton's plant in Soho, where he saw 'seven hundred men, women and children employed as one may say under one roof'.[127] He admired the 'genius' of men whose canals 'reduced the price of coals'.[128] In December, 1788 and April, 1793, he purchased chemical equipment—a lamp, glass tubing, and a hygrometer—with Matthew Boulton's help. It is not surprising, then, to find that in the 1790s, he attended meetings of the Lunar Society, a group of men centred about the scientist, Joseph Priestley.[129] In his will, Robert left his 'chemical apparatus' to his son, Robert Henry.[130] Robert's interest in science had been piqued earlier in Bath, where he attended scientific lectures on electricity and globes.[131] His political allegiance was noted only once in 1779, during the trial of Admiral Keppel: 'We Whigg people', he wrote, 'are sure he will be most honourably acquitted.'[132] He was clearly less interested in politics than he was in literary pursuits.

In fact, Robert's chief forms of leisure were reading and writing letters in a language of sensibility that we have not seen before. His list of regular correspondents confirms that letter-writing was an integral part of his everyday routine. Columns headed 'to' and 'from', in the flyleaf of a journal for 1777 listed 121 letters written and 94 received to an inner circle of correspondents. They included family members, the Wodhulls, friends of both sexes, and a Mr Webb of Wistanstow, who might have handled Robert's clerical duties.[133] (See Plate 34.)

Robert's letters, written in a bold cursive hand, displayed ink blots and crossed-out phrases. Words were scrawled across the page with few margins, as if there was much to say quickly.[134] Once he sent Barbara franks in hopes of 'larger portions of letters', for he was 'so much entertain'd with every thing you say'.[135] Barbara asked her brother to write her, 'whenever you have a quarter of an hour's leisure', implying that this was the time allotted to write one letter.[136] On another occasion, Robert told her he spent 'a half-hour in scribbling a few lines to you'.[137]

Over time, we can see Robert's progress in using letter-writing to develop literary techniques. In contrast to Jane's letters, his narrative mode was highly developed. Instead of using just a sentence to delineate an event or character, Robert wrote copiously, as if savouring epistolary description.[138] He was able, for example, to create an imaginary picture of Barbara and her friends on a snowy day:

> I see you all surrounding a cheerfully blazing Fire, Kitty with some sound Divine in her hand, by turns attentive and distrait . . . deeply commiserating the miseries many of her fellow creatures suffer from the inclemency of the weather. Good Mrs Smyth in the chimney corner complaining 'tis bitter cold', but by her lively sallies convincing you it is only a temporary inconvenience she suffers from it. Mary at her harpsichord, Mrs Ann writing a satire on the Beaux for suffering the snow to prevent their joining so agreeable a party, and you with a look of curiousity walking backwards and forwards, stopping each time at the window . . . Well I wonder Osborne don't come, what can possibly detain him?[139]

Character development and dialogue give this report a novelistic tone and show intimacy with the reader. Robert wrote with empathy and sensitivity.

His use of the imagination may have been stimulated by reading Wollaston's *Religion of Nature* from which he copied the following passage: 'That you may take a truer prospect of any act, place yourself in your imagination beyond it; suppose it already done, and then see how it looks.'[140] Robert developed a literary self-consciousness by incorporating techniques found in reading into letters.

Robert's interest in language had been, in part, stimulated by writing epigrams and participating in word games at Anna's Batheaston competitions. Though he spoke of them scornfully, they gave him experience in manipulating words. Thus, in 1777, he was 'taxed to death with charades from morning to night'. People who 'look into the dictionary' to find rhymes, he sighed, 'mangle the first compound word they meet with, with far fetch'd allusions and unheard of similes'.[141] Robert's contempt stemmed from his love of beautiful phrases, like those he found in the Psalms.[142] Letters gave him space to play with language that was growing increasingly sentimental.

Because Robert recorded extracts from his reading in a series of thumb-worn journals, we can reconstruct at least part of his library. He also tells us *how* he read in a long series of letters. Thus in 1755 he noted: 'I have not so much time for reading as I could wish, various avocations break in upon any regular plan, and a work of any length is not to be read to advantage by bites and scraps. I therefore during my winter's sojourn at Bath deal principally in little Brochures or any light reading that I meet with.'[143] When he had more leisure in April 1776, his reading differed. 'I am at present for grave reading', he wrote, 'deeply engaged in Paley's moral philosophy one of the most instructive bookes I ever met with, and for afternoons & leisure quarters of hours, Boswell's life of Johnson furnishes abundance of amusement...I have not been so completely at leisure a long time, and therefore get on with both these books pretty rapidly.' Robert read 'grave' matter intensively and a range of 'light' reading extensively at different places, months, and times of day. Moreover, he thought about the best way to match his reading with his busy schedule. As in Jane Johnson's case, his reading patterns were more nuanced and varied than historians usually imagine. They spanned a range of different theories of reading, rather than one overall model. As Roger Chartier has suggested, diversity of reading modes may have been the defining characteristic of reading at this time.[144]

The content of his reading also differed from that of Jane. Whereas she emphasized classical literature, Robert preferred modern authors and books on painting, architecture, geography, history,[145] and the customs of different peoples, which he sometimes read in French.[146] In 1772, he purchased Johnson's *Dictionary*, Smollett's 'continuations', Baskerville's *Congreve* and a complete set of Voltaire's work.[147] Robert's favourite books, however, were written by Scottish enlightenment writers, Ferguson, Hume, and Smith, from which he copied long passages.[148]

Robert and Barbara are good examples of active, not passive, readers.[149] Like Jane, they read freely for both instruction and entertainment, but their scope was wider. We find no communal standards of gendered or 'right reading', but, instead, intellectual exploration, unfettered by outside authorities. This practice, I suspect, generated a heady feeling. Glimpses of this exhilaration are found in letters about books, which they begged, borrowed, and passed on to each other. 'Is Johnson in the Brackley book club?', asked Robert.[150] 'Pray how many volumes of Ogdens sermons are there?', demanded Barbara. 'I am oblig'd to Charles for sending Lord George Gordon's Trial.'[151] 'Do read Payne's answer to Burke', Robert instructed in 1778: 'It is excellent.'[152] The regularity and breadth of these recommendations and opinions show letters were being used differently than in Jane's day.

As numbers of available texts rose dramatically, letters gave space for critical comments that gradually shaped taste and judgement. Writing them contributed to the development of literary criticism by ordinary people. The commercial success of helpful new review journals confirms this trend. Yet there has been little recognition of the effects of letter-writing on the growing field of critical writing. Of course, reviewing scholarly books was common in the late seventeenth century. Yet it was not until the 1750s that review journals covered a wide range of publications on a regular basis. The *Monthly Review* (1749) and its rival the *Critical Review* (1756) spawned a host of imitators. Their initial mission was the 'Giving an Account with proper Abstracts' of a few titles. This goal later expanded to reviewing 'all the new Things in general, without exception to any, on account of their lowness, rank, or price'.[153]

Though review journals were commercial ventures with a price tag of a shilling, myths about their incompetence have been recently challenged. Surely, these attacks and defences were also indications of the impact of reviews on readers. 'There are many Readers who seldom venture to judge for themselves', noted a letter to the *Critical*, 'or, even, to peruse a Work until they are informed of its character.'[154] When Mrs Miller published her

Letters, review journals were the rage.[155] She therefore did well in receiving a nine-page review of her book.[156] The Ely pamphlet club subscribed to both the *Monthly* and the *Critical*. This indicates they helped customers to choose new material.[157] One critic has suggested that 'as much as one-sixth of the reading public had access to one or more review journals on a regular basis'.[158] As Marilyn Butler has noted, 'reading reviews was itself a sign of cultivation, a ticket of entry to polite society'.[159]

As we read the letters of Barbara and Robert, we observe them developing a critical approach to literature. We can therefore grasp how reading and letter-writing became more directly linked to each other. Since Robert's correspondence is both copious and consecutive, we may use it to view how one writer used epistolary literacy to evaluate literature. Robert's first attempts at criticism were crudely done. Abbe Raynal's history of the Indies, he noted, 'is very clever, but there is a mixture of true and false in it I don't much admire'.[160] His view of William Hay's *Religio Philosophi* was more skilful: 'Some few of his notions seem built on no firmer ground than an hypothesis of his own raising, but the general tenets are very instructive, shew a thorough good heart, and a most liberal way of thinking.'[161]

Over time we see patterns in Robert's literary criticism. He read books, copied extracts, consulted reviews, quoted views of others, and eventually presented his own opinions in letters. Like other middle-class readers, he gained confidence with practice. It was vital to first consult respected authors, for taste and reputation had become important public matters. 'You remember', he wrote Barbara, 'what Lord Huntingdon said of Chesterfields's letters. "His . . . letters to his son are very just . . . Had there been more benevolence and philanthropy throu' out the whole of them . . . they would have held up the most useful lesson for the instruction of young men." '[162] Another comment on a letter collection showed readers were aware of the close relation between real letters and fiction: 'I think I read it when first published; and ventured to declare my scepticism at a Time, when it was the fashion to assert it to have been a real correspondence.'[163] Robert summed up the difficulty of doing literary criticism without help from others: 'In books people are so apt to embellish their descriptions that one hardly knows what to rely on.'[164]

Robert's critical skills also helped him to appraise the literary quality of Anna's salon. Her blunders provided a perfect topic for writing about Bath in the satiric tradition of Smollett's novel, *The Expedition of Humphry Clinker* (1771). Despite regular attendance, at least once with his wife,[165] he had 'tiffs' with Mrs Miller and could not bear her love of praise. Madam Miller he insisted, selects poems 'in which she is most highly complimented, [rather] than those that have the most merit'.[166] He oscillated between scorn for the Millers' enterprise, and enjoyment of its fashionable status. Once Anna had 'swallowed a *very literal* paraphrase of Pope's epistle of Abelard to Eloisa', supposing it to be 'from the late Pope . . . to herself. It was ludicrous', he insisted, 'beyond exception.'[167] On another occasion, Robert wickedly read a poem in Lady Miller's presence that was critical of her salon. Though Anna burned it publicly, two hundred prints of the hated verses were distributed the next day.[168] Robert participated in Anna's literary soirées, but used them selectively to shape his own middling-sort culture.

He was particularly scornful of an epistolary poem by Anna's protégé, Christopher Anstey, author of *The New Bath Guide*:[169] 'I have been told that Dictionary Johnston said on first seeing the Bath guide: "This poem has great merit, but it has exhausted the whole genius of the author, he will write nothing more worth reading" . . . I own it gave one the highest opinion of Dr Johnston's penetration.'[170] In another letter, Robert paraphrased Johnson's quotation and presented the words as his own opinion: 'Ainstree's Poem has great merit, but too great a resemblance to the Bath Guide shews us we have little more to expect from his genius.' Again we see a pattern. In letters, Robert criticized the salon. Then he appropriated Samuel Johnson's views to support his own opinions.[171] Robert's negative views served as first steps in his development of literary criticism. As he ridiculed others, he gained confidence in his own judgement, always looking a level below him to find comfort in his superior taste. This reminds us of the Tucker's 'language of resentments', but here, literary matters replaced those of politics. The end result of Robert's epistolary practices was the development of his capacity to make critical judgements.

Letter-writing and the language of sensibility

A literary culture based on private writing, unsupervised reading, and independent opinions had political implications. So did the heightened language of sensibility in letters written by Robert and his friends from the 1770s–90s. This section shows how people expressed themselves when the language of sensibility was at its height, a fact illustrated by the popularity of the sentimental epistolary novel. During the eighteenth century, I believe, sensibility found its natural home in personal letters—a genre based on sympathetic feelings. Robert's huge cache of letters depicts an epistolary milieu that encouraged writers to express their deepest emotions. Of course, sentimental writing had always existed. But now untrained people with epistolary literacy divulged their feelings in unregulated corners of daily life.

Literary scholars have seen the eighteenth century as a transition period, when the Augustan Age, dominated by Pope, gave way to an emotional aesthetic that encouraged sentimental feelings.[172] Various ranges of dates have been proposed for the onset and demise of sensibility.[173] By the 1760s, however, large numbers of authors were indulging themselves sentimentally in every literary format. A preference for this way of writing was expressed in letters in 1748 by the critic, Thomas Edwards. After examining Richardson's novels, he praised that author's sensibility, 'which I think it is as bad to be without, as . . . to have no ear for music'.[174]

In practice, letters gave Robert a space to actively experiment with how feelings should be articulated. As he wrote them, he was joining an epistolary debate about how far sensibility could be extended without causing a backlash? In a journal entry of 1771, Robert summed up his desire to liberate his emotions: 'The disposition that leads us to speak our sentiments without constraint seldom fails to please.'[175] Robert's revelation of his sentiments differed from the self-discipline found in his mother's commonplace book, which was filled with maxims about restraining one's passions. This shift in expression was attended by a growing anxiety after the French Revolution about letting emotions run free. A man of feeling, Robert used letters to work out a proper balance between linguistic freedom and strict control. Since letters were themselves a form of self-expression, their construction became a moral issue about authority and liberty in the harsh political climate of the 1790s.[176] How much restraint, Robert wondered, should one have over one's passions? As he read Scottish enlightenment writers he found some answers.

Philip Carter has argued that a culture of sensibility emerged out of an earlier tradition of politeness, whereby 'polite artifice' was replaced by 'genuine emotion'. Sometimes called the key term of the period,[177] sensibility was a complex concept related to histories of philosophy, religion, linguistics, aesthetics, medicine, and psychology.[178] In a journal entry, Robert incorporated Locke's idea that impressions were received by the senses:[179] 'I enjoy afresh the thousand pleasing sensations that . . . society . . . never fails to afford to a feeling mind.'[180] Like Hume, Smith, and Ferguson, Robert believed that human nature was good. He shared their interest in how people formed social relationships and found comfort in their concept of sympathy, through which sentiments were communicated. In the *Theory of Moral Sentiments* (1759), Smith explained how people imagined the pain felt by other human beings. Empathy, he claimed, was among the highest human virtues. Robert emulated this ideal each time he wrote each letter—itself a relationship that created sympathetic bonds.[181]

Robert's filled his letters and journals with extracts from his reading that reflected notions of sensibility. One of the most prominent was a concern for the happiness of others. Word searches reveal his favourite adjectives: agreeable, amiable, cheerful, benevolent, and sensible—the latter meaning capable of feeling.[182] Sentimental effusions about his family piled up joyfully as he wrote. During courtship, for instance, he found his future wife, Nan, was 'sweetly sensible, amiable in every sense of the word'.[183] At the birth of his first child, he was so emotional that he could not describe his feelings. 'Your own good heart will conceive what I feel much better than I can describe it', he wrote his brother George. 'I will say I never felt so many pleasing sensations before.'[184] He mooned over Nan's supply of milk for nursing and enthused about his children's looks, first steps, and words.[185] He and Nan had liberal ideas about raising children, no doubt influenced by their reading of Rousseau.[186] Consequently, they found their cousins' children 'dull and heavy'. 'Mine . . . are riotous and troublesome', Robert wrote happily. 'I own I like children as children much better than formal premature men and women.'[187] These remarks show a man of feeling, who was proud of his sentimental views.

Outside the family, Robert longed to get along with others. 'Nothing is more graceful than habitual chearfulness', he noted.[188] 'Happy is the man that is possess'd of an affectionate turn of mind.'[189] Exasperated by a grumpy dinner partner, he declared: 'It must be a bad mind that loves to be employ'd in discovering the faults and follies of others in order to expose them.' To be amiable was thus a moral quality as well as a social asset.[190] An extract from Adam Smith encapsulated his views: 'To feel much for others and little for ourselves, to restrain our selfishness, to indulge our benevolent affections, constitutes the perfection of human nature.'[191]

Achieving this ideal state was a moral duty, but it also took a great deal of work. 'Only resolute people can be truly good-natured', Robert remarked, copying a text by Rouchefoucault.[192] Robert followed Hume in stressing the central place of the passions, but he also felt the importance of human responsibility. Thus his New Year's resolution for 1772 stated: 'How very difficult it is at all times to command our temper, even on trifling occasions. But though it may not be in our power to prevent feeling disagreeable sensations, we may at all times be able to keep them to ourselves.' Yet in a later journal entry, he despaired of resolving this problem: 'Lively sensations of grief are not in the power of reason to control.'[193]

In Robert's correspondence, we observe his struggle over how to achieve a balance between reason and passion, or, as the Johnsons called it, 'head' and 'heart'.[194] Thus he envied Mrs Napier, who achieved a perfect equilibrium. 'I never know', he commented, 'whether one ought most to admire, her heart or her head.'[195] His cousin Hugh discovered the same balance in the conduct of the Bishop of Gloucester: He 'pays equal attention to his Heart as to his Head, both of which . . . are good'.[196] Robert's own recipe for success was to 'act constantly with tenderness and attention . . . Exert spirit and resolution where necessary and you will rarely have occasion to acknowledge yourself in the wrong.'[197] Letters and journals gave him time for reflection. They also offered space to incorporate extracts from reading, which enabled him to work out his views.

Finally, Robert's letters from others revealed the downside of having too much sensibility. They showed that people became more upset than usual, when they indulged their feelings too deeply. Long extracts copied from Ferguson's *Essay on the History of Civil Society* helped him to ponder this predicament. 'Fancying we feel more than we do instead of resisting what we really do suffer', noted Robert, 'is the cause of a great deal of uneasiness in the world. Many people make themselves unhappy about trifles, till they meet with real misfortunes. They then . . . think themselves fools for not being happy when they might.'[198] At times, we see Robert drawing back from expressing himself too passionately. 'I am afraid I have been effusing great nonsense', he once confessed, but then asked for freedom to write without constraint. 'I shall hope for this privilege', he continued, 'as a studied Letter is generally wrote more for travelling round a Table than for the party to whom it is addressed.'[199] Robert preferred to write naturally with a good deal of intimacy, yet he sensed the dangers of indulging himself too intensely.

There was good reason for Robert's hesitation in the 1790s, when the effects of the French Revolution were being felt in England, and all kinds of liberties were being questioned. A group of letters from Robert's male correspondents displayed the extreme forms of sentimentality that worried him. Some of his friends, for example, wrote of suffering agonizing emotional experiences. Hence his cousin, Charles Smythe, could not bear to leave university friends. 'At parting with such men', he confided, 'with whom I have ... lived in the strictest intimacy ... I must ... feel the most painful sensations—sensations that cannot be conceived ... unless they were described with the same warmth ... and ... energy as they were impressed upon my soul.'[200] Charles's agonies even extended to what should have been pleasurable theatrical experiences. He dreaded 'the grief & horror which always attends' performances of 'the divine Mrs Siddons'. When she failed to appear on stage one night, he experienced relief.[201]

Similar pain was eagerly incurred by reading melancholy poetry enclosed in letters. Thomas Pitt's verse, for example, was passed from one friend to another with exquisite pleasure. One poem described Pitt's boyhood emotions on looking at his dead mother's picture. Pitt was left 'struggling', 'trembling', and crying aloud: 'Is she then gone?' These verses were recommended to Michael Wodhull, who had 'an head and heart to make him feel them with all the sensibility and taste with which they were written'.[202] Wodhull appears in letters as a true man of feeling. Before starting a continental journey, he stood on the cliffs of Dover, pretending he was King Lear whilst the rough winds roared. This dramatic reaction to nature was also evident in Wodhull's poetry and letters.[203]

Robert avoided Wodhull's excess of sentiment in his own letters. Instead, he defined his ideal man of feeling in a eulogy for his brother George: 'He had so much respect for the feelings of others, that he never utter'd a harsh expression that could give pain to any one, and was always hurt when anybody else did ... Now spring returns without my feeling its chearful influence,' Robert added, 'all nature seems a blank.'[204] This last sentence was similar to one found in a letter in Rousseau's novel, *Julie, or the New Heloise*.[205]

This was not surprising, for Robert was writing at a time when real letters and sentimental fiction were influencing each other. But as the language of sensibility penetrated all types of literature, a backlash occurred in the harsh political climate of the 1790s.[206] This negative reaction was reflected in hostile attitudes to the sentimental novel in epistolary form. It is not surprising that this fiction soon reached its peak, and declined by the end of the century. The real letters, which underpinned novels, flourished as usual, adapting resiliently to cultural change as they had always done before.

Conclusion

The letters of Anna Miller and Robert and Barbara Johnson help us to see the close connections between real letters and epistolary literature. A language of sensibility connected them both. James Raven and Thomas Beebe have recently documented the rise and fall of the epistolary novel. It comprised only 10 per cent of all fiction at mid century. But by 1776 when Anna published her letters, epistolary novels totalled 70.6 per cent. In the 1770s and 1780s, they consistently averaged over 40 per cent of all fiction. The turning point seems to have occurred in 1791, when only 20 per cent of published novels used an epistolary format, with a further decline to 10 per cent in 1799. At the dawn of the new century, many authors had forsaken the epistolary format.[207]

Literary scholars have suggested causes for this decline, including the shift of the narrative voice to the third person. Others point to the diversity and scale of historical epics and Gothic narratives, which made them ill suited to the epistolary format. Since the cult of sensibility was bound up with the sentimental novel, it too declined in the same period. By the end of the century, argued Christopher Jones, 'the concept [of sensibility] and its associated vocabulary were virtually unusable except for purposes of satire'.[208]

Yet the ties between real and fictional letters remained unusually close. In the second half of the eighteenth century, new types of connections based on literary criticism and sentimental writing had arisen between them. The first practice represented the 'head' of the letter-writer; the second represented the 'heart'. Just as Jane Johnson's epistolary literacy had an impact on Richardson's novels, so the epistolary literacy of her children and Anna Miller influenced the travel account, the critical review, and the sentimental novel. Letter-writing offered practise in describing journeys, evaluating literature, and writing in a language of empathy. Satire and sentiment pervaded letters of this generation of Johnsons, replacing the religious concerns of their mother. But the impact of letter-writing on literary forms was, perhaps, even stronger.

This chapter has witnessed the rise of epistolary sensibility from the gushing letters of Anna Miller to the higher-pitched sentiments in those of Charles Smythe. Each letter-writer had to decide how to respond to shifts in epistolary conventions. At the same time, each writer operated at a different level of epistolary literacy. Anna Miller turned her private letters into public stories by mixing sentiment and cool composure. She showed that women were not, by nature, tied to a specific type of letter. Like men, they wrote in many styles for a rich array of purposes. Anna published her letters at a time when women writers were converging on a field previously dominated by men. Thus, she had to be careful about the way she presented herself in public. She shrewdly calibrated her epistolary style and avoided excessive sentimentality. Anna proved that letters of middling-sort women could become best sellers. For a time, she succeeded in presiding over Bath's salon culture. Yet her background and personality prevented her from being truly accepted in Fanny Burney's world. Anna's motives for letter-writing were social, economic, and psychological. On the other hand, she genuinely longed to improve her literary skills and bring culture to others.

In contrast, Barbara was constrained by traditional roles of gender and class. Though her epistolary literacy far outshone that of Anna, she modestly avoided the limelight. We saw this in her attitude to her private writings and in the censoring, and possible destruction, of her own correspondence. Anna's public letters and Barbara's private ones were thus differently motivated. Yet both Barbara and her mother proclaimed their independence and developed their talents through adventurous reading and creative writing. Inside her private circle, Barbara was respected as a perceptive critic, who could recommend books and evaluate literature. People wanted to know her political views. We therefore can claim that both mother and daughter achieved literary agency at different times and in different ways.

Robert's character, letters, and reading patterns fit comfortably into the image of a man of feeling. He loved to write letters and keep journals, and they are still a pleasure to read. He also prized reading, but was, in some ways, subservient to Barbara's choices. Instead of indulging his emotions, he spent pleasant hours copying extracts from Scottish authors. They urged him to enjoy sociable company, but also to maintain self-control. Unlike Jane, who longed to be righteous, Robert wished to be happy. Though he wrote his own letters empathetically, he worried about the effects of a language of sensibility that intruded into writings of others.[209] In contrast, the letters of Michael Wodhull and Charles Smythe reveal the language of sensibility at the height of its influence.

During the lives of Anna, Robert, and Barbara, the links between letters, sensibility, and epistolary novels were visible. Their common political agenda in the 1790s was equally apparent to contemporaries. Some critics attribute attacks on the sentimental novel to the way it addressed disenfranchised people in a language that encouraged free self-expression.[210] I want to claim a similar subversive role for the letters showcased in this book. Though they may have lacked openly radical content, epistolary literacy as a process had political consequences. It created a mass of new writers engaged in private writing, unsupervised reading, and independent judgements.

Once a comfortable level of epistolary literacy was acquired, writers had all the tools they needed to criticize their society. When they combined writing skills with reading and the use of personally chosen extracts, writers could form opinions and deploy them critically. This was a simple process that took place on a daily basis. The danger lay in its setting inside private closets, where state institutions lacked presence and rights of supervision. This technique was clearly transferable from the confines of domestic writing to the political realm. Epistolary literacy thus provided a base for a free and active electorate at a time when political participation was still limited. In the nineteenth century, its revolutionary dimension would become publicly understood.

Conclusion: Letter-writing and eighteenth-century culture

Findings, patterns, and impacts

This book has suggested that a popular culture of letters developed in England by 1800. It initially acquired its purpose, format, and conventions from an older classical tradition. During the eighteenth century, it shed many of its formalities and adopted aspects of middling sort culture. A national letter form that employed the merchant's round hand gradually became the norm. It embodied plain-spoken English virtues, instead of the flamboyant mannerisms of French letters. People who mastered it possessed a valuable skill—epistolary literacy. Yet letter-writing was not just important to individuals. Its democratization had a deep, but hidden, impact on eighteenth-century culture.

Chapter 1 asked a simple question: how did people learn to read and write letters? This query was, in part, answered by observing the step-by-step process of composing a typical letter. Clearly, writing a letter was not a simple task. Nonetheless, a determined youngster who attended school or had home instruction could master materials and conventions. The ubiquitous letters of children, saved by proud parents, offer further evidence of how epistolary skills were acquired. These early compositions created epistolary patterns that were passed on to the next generation. Both elite families like the Evelyns and merchant families like the Peases, Cotesworths, and Langtons believed that letter-writing would help their children to function in the adult world.

Yet merchants never took epistolary literacy for granted, since economic survival depended on regular written communication. Instead of classical models and Latin epistles, their offspring imitated letters found in bibles, business correspondence, account books, and real letters. Copybooks were especially important, and by the 1680s, they were linked to business and trade. Moreover, writing masters in town and country ensured that the material aspects of eighteenth-century letters were shaped by merchant culture. Multiple hands gave way to the English round hand, whose clear, all-purpose, flowing cursive could be written with speed. The use of one accessible hand for all writers stood in contrast to the earlier tradition, in which complex hands defined writers by gender, class, and occupation. This, I believe, had a levelling effect and was important in establishing a popular epistolary tradition.

Chapter 4 showed more fully how letters, influenced by merchant correspondence, were generally embraced by the middling sort. The ideal letter was written in an easy natural style that was clear, direct, and simple to understand. This more succinct approach differed intentionally from extravagantly written letters associated with continental letter manuals. Chapter 4 suggested that this ideal letter form, became a symbol of English pride for writers without a university education.

The democratization of letter-writing could never have taken place without the Royal Mail. Though the British Post Office was established later than on the continent, after the Restoration it developed with surprising speed. This book maintains that letter-writing is best viewed historically in the context of contemporary postal practices. Archival evidence shows that the Royal Mail was originally created to control and censor mail. Yet its interaction with the newspaper, as well as public demands for service, had unintended liberating consequences. Chapter 2 described how ordinary people regarded the post, how they used its services, and how it affected people's lives. Obviously, the Royal Mail was far from perfect and it caused numerous problems for its users. Yet complaints, which are usually cited as evidence of inefficiencies, were also expressions of the post's importance. Hopefully, this book will serve as a counterweight to more negative perceptions and illuminate strengths, as well as weaknesses, of the Post Office.

According to Royal Mail records and comments of letter-writers, basic routines were in place by the eighteenth century. By the 1760s, the structure of the post had been nationally reconfigured, whilst coaches replaced post boys in the 1780s. As we have seen, letters were routinely received in rural northern villages, where many of our letter-writers lived. Yet though the poor found ways to avoid postage, the middling sort gained most from postal improvements. Overburdened postmasters worked amazingly well on low salaries, but inertia, corruption, and obsolete practices hindered needed reforms. They were later enacted in the 1840s, when economic, social, and political pressures led to universal postage and higher levels of efficiency and growth.

The letters of individuals, who commented on the Post Office, were analysed in Chapters 2–6. These correspondences were, of course, 'self-selected' to show skills of people who were already literate. Appendix I contains a discussion about selection criteria and decisions that were made about how to use the collections. The unexpected discovery of long runs of correspondence offered a rare opportunity, along with a responsibility, to address the topic of popular literacy. Quantitative methods that establish basic indicators of illiteracy have been essential to researchers. They offer useful comparative measures of factors that affected learning, such as age, gender, occupation, and geographical location.

This book has presented a complementary qualitative method by employing the concept of 'epistolary literacy' to evaluate writing skills. In every chapter, the same factors found in all types of letters were examined. They included visible elements of the material letter like layout, spelling, and punctuation. Intellectual aspects were also evaluated such as content, originality, strategic use of language, and literary techniques. Numerous extracts were used to show different levels of literacy. They revealed compositional skills as well as abstract thinking. As a result, a range of competencies was established in each chapter.

The findings of the case studies in Chapter 3 suggest that epistolary literacy might be found lower down the social structure than we have imagined. Letter-writing encouraged literacy by offering constant practice in writing, routine copying, and continuous repetition of a single format. These well-known modes of learning were already firmly in place. Fortunately, the regularity of epistolary conventions made it easy for untrained writers to adopt the genre. Though more case studies are needed to generalize these findings, the unexpected skills of some workers warn us not to underestimate the human spirit or, indeed, the body. Recent interdisciplinary work in cognitive science has stressed the growth and adaptability of the brain's functions in response to usage. Thus singing birds' cells multiply in the spring, and areas of the brain controlling hand spans may be more highly developed for concert pianists. In the same manner, artisans' hands may have become adept at manipulating small parts and instruments, like the pen. This fact might have given craftsmen an epistolary advantage.[1]

The basic literacy of our writers, which preceded their epistolary literacy, was acquired in makeshift ways. It required determination and support from kin and the community. The presence of intermittent, informal schooling that complemented working lives may have been more widespread than our cases can show. They do, however, give us actual glimpses of how reading and writing could be learnt outside the walls of licensed schools. Letters suggest that popular literacy arose from a combination of forces: the motivation and life experience of determined individuals; the passing on of skills by supportive families; the shared resources and brokers provided by the community; and, especially, self-learning and informal schooling.

Yet this rosy view of epistolary literacy did not affect the majority of the population. The grinding poverty that marked the lives of the poor reminds us that effects of epistolary literacy were still limited at this time. Literacy appears to have spread in a patchy and uneven manner according to local demands. One factor that might have led Morton to send his children to school was the growing awareness by all ranks that literacy had become necessary to cope with life. In 1745, Bishop Joseph Butler admitted that unlike earlier times, the poor felt a sense of stigma, if they could not read and write: 'The ordinary affairs of the world are now put in a way', he noted, 'which requires they should have some knowledge of letters', which was not the case then.[2] Letter-writers in Chapter 3 were exemplary precursors for the larger numbers of literate people that would mark the nineteenth century.

The patterns of eighteenth-century letters

Epistolary patterns may be discerned by looking collectively at answers to the three questions addressed to all collections: *why* were letters written, how were they *used*, and what were their *impacts*? Paradoxically, a diversity of answers is one epistolary pattern. Letter-writers penned their messages from Cumbria's lakes to the chalky cliffs of Dorset; from seafronts in East Anglia to flax wharfs in Lancashire. As intended, their religions, occupations, and economic prospects varied. Perhaps, the most valuable distinctions were the clearly observable differences in their levels of epistolary literacy. That is why the order of case studies started with writers with the least training and ended with more highly skilled individuals.

This book has told a story about the diversity and flexibility of family letters. During the eighteenth century, they adapted to social and economic change, as well as to the needs of new users. At the same time, this book has highlighted the decline of differences in the visible aspects of the material letter. Printers, lexicographers, and linguists began to regiment a genre that was, and still is, known for its extreme individualism. Standardization of spelling, grammar, and punctuation brought an ordered 'look' to letters, especially when this was combined with the use of the round 'copperplate' hand. The rise of boarding schools, Dissenting academies, and all types of female education led to more equal skills amongst the sexes.[3] During the second half of the eighteenth century, the gap in epistolary expertise between males and females declined noticeably. By the end of century, there was little trace of the former awkward constructions and phonetic spellings that had marked women's writing. The homogenization of the letters of the Strutt children illustrated this trend. Standardization, however, merely applied to *material* aspects of their letters. Despite early epistolary problems, Jedediah and Elizabeth Strutt's children inherited their parents' literary skills. Their letters, therefore, displayed both the flexibility of the genre and the unique personalities of each son and daughter.

The inherent tension between the rigid conventions of the letter form and the impulse to write naturally was never wholly resolved. The struggle for dominance between these two epistolary dimensions is evident in eighteenth-century letters. New writers wished to observe accepted norms and write correctly. They, therefore, eagerly adopted the epistolary frame-work that had endured for centuries. At the same time, lower- and middling-sort letter-writers had less training and discipline. Consequently, the general style of writing became more relaxed. Moreover, formulaic aspects of structure and content declined. Age, gender, rank, and kinship still affected the degree of epistolary artifice, flattery, and deference. But older rules regarding titles, forms of address, letter parts, and spacing had little appeal for new letter-writers. 'Humble and obedient services' gave way to closings from 'affectionate' sons and daughters. The balance between discipline and self-expression had tilted towards more liberty in writing. By 1800, parents and children, as well as husbands and wives, wrote more directly to each other in less obsequious ways. This was especially true of letters between middling-sort individuals. Perhaps that is one reason why letters based on continental letter manuals rarely appear in their family collections. Non-elite letters were far more influenced by learning in the home, domestic copying, and the experience of reading real letters.

Every chapter in this book considered how basic patterns of letter-writing were inflected for age, class, gender, and religion. In Chapter 4, however, these factors were more fully examined in regard to middling-sort writers. Case studies included three overlapping groups who were dependent on letters: writing clerks, merchants, and Dissenters. This book has argued that the possession of reading and writing skills was a unifying feature of middling-sort families. In fact, they constantly wrote letters in real life and in fiction. Consequently, letter-writing became a powerful asset in their business, family and spiritual lives. Studies in every geographic region confirm high rates of middling-sort literacy. Not only was it needed for success in business; reading and writing were incorporated into a middling-sort ethos that encouraged education, self-discipline, independence, and moral virtue. Because middling-sort letters usually bridged family and business lives, they were markedly multifunctional. They were also characterized by high levels of anxiety, which may have been linked to their writers' ill-defined status in the middle of the social hierarchy.

The intentional division of Chapter 4 into families of three different faiths offered an opportunity to observe religious patterns of letter-writing. This book claims that religious affiliation *did* indeed cause disparities in the way people constructed letters. The most important differences concerned writing styles and the use of language—a language of political 'interests' and 'resentments' for the Anglican Tuckers, and a distinct 'Christian' way of writing for the Quaker Follows and the Congregational Bateman and Wilson families. Nonconformists were more self-conscious about religion than Anglicans, and they used letter-writing as a group more compulsively. Dissenters' anxieties were centred on doubts about personal salvation and one's relationship to God. These worries were expressed quite differently in letters from those concerned with business. Quaker letters had their own unique language, style, rhythms, and dating system that turned their letters into declarations of faith. The high level of Dissenters' literacy suggests that they had a greater impact on letter-writing than their numbers warranted.

Letters of female Dissenters were particularly plentiful and leant themselves easily to the analysis of gender. Because of current interest in this issue, the relationship between women and letter-writing requires special comment. Changes in letters of females over the century are instantly visible. Dorothy Soresbie's phonetic scrawl penned in 1677, for example, required a gigantic effort, even for a determined woman. (See Plate 18.) By 1800, Elizabeth Wilson wrote with consummate ease. (See Plate 27.) As Chapter 1 noted, before the eighteenth century both elite and non-elite girls had less formal education than their brothers. This was as true for the aristocrat, Catherine Fairfax as it was for Mary Bowrey, wife of a London sea captain.[4] During the seventeenth century, gender overrode class as an epistolary factor.

In contrast, middling-sort case studies indicate that both sons and daughters were routinely given epistolary training. Early in the eighteenth century, daughters of the merchant Pease family wrote letters home from school. In cases where their education is unknown, their letters imply a writing master had been consulted. The middling-sort parents in our case studies thought epistolary literacy was crucial for both sexes. As education became available for middling-sort daughters, their letters brimmed with confidence.

Of course, apologies were still present in young girls' correspondence. But as Mary Pease and Rebekah Bateman demonstrated, regrets were now a sign of strategy, instead of weakness. It is telling that Rebekah's resistance to female epistolary norms had a terrible effect on her marriage. By alternating periods of compliance and rebellion, she was able to preserve her right to self-expression, when writing to her husband. As a Quaker minister, Ruth Follows's gender problems came from too much freedom from domestic duties. When travels forced her to leave her family, her letters kept alive the maternal part of her psyche.

Intellectual ideas about the relationship of women to both real and fictional letters also were transformed over time. Letter-writing has been seen by some as a particularly feminine form of self-expression. In this view, letters became a lifeline for cloistered women, who were isolated from public life. This idea had a long history throughout Europe, and was especially apparent in romantic literature of the sixteenth and seventeenth centuries.[5] In these fictions, which were often written in an epistolary format, women were portrayed as victims, eternally writing love letters. Samuel Richardson and writers of later sentimental novels inherited, but then transformed, this tradition.

Naturally, real letters of eighteenth-century women present a broader, more complicated picture. Elizabeth Strutt's letters early in the century, like later ones of Barbara Johnson and Anna Miller, exhibited a similar love of literature. Yet their abilities, techniques, and contexts could not have been more diverse. Moreover, women who wrote in the same period, such as Johnson, Miller, Bateman, and Fawdington engaged in different types of correspondences for different reasons. Bateman's were driven by religion, whilst Miller published hers to obtain social and cultural status. Barbara Johnson's letters, though as modest as Elizabeth Strutt's, were daringly intertwined with Bath's public literary culture. Yet all of these letters existed in the same accepted framework of epistolary conventions and norms. Even Miller had to follow them, if she wanted to become a published author.

This book has considered a number of ideas about why fewer female letters survive, even in families where letter-writing was routinely practised. First, home education of daughters by mothers left few recorded traces. Fortunately for us, Jane Johnson's writings were preserved. They give us unique information about how *her* children learnt to read and write, but we have no idea how *she*, herself, was educated. Nor do we know what happened to some of Barbara Johnson's letters. The odds are high that she destroyed them herself, out of principles of class-based modesty. Another spinster, Esther Masham, reread all her letters and burned those that did not reflect highly on her family. Later she admitted on the title page of her letter book that she deeply regretted her actions.[6] Other women destroyed letters to ensure the safety of loved ones. Naturally, we have fewer examples of letters of lower-sort women due to lower rates of female literacy. Those described in this book are intriguing examples of others that presumably lie hidden from view.

The influence of age on letter-writing was also noted in this book. It was most easily observed in childish letters on ruled paper. As youngsters matured, their writing became smaller, cursive was adopted, and nicknames replaced 'your humble and obedient servant' over the eighteenth century. One never lost one's basic hand, however, and its features persisted in letters of the next generation. More poignantly noticeable was the frail, shaking hand of old age. A letter written by a scribe for an older person was often the first sign of illness, or impending death. It was typical of the strong personality of Ruth Follows that she used her own hand to write her last letter to her grandchildren.

Patterns were also discovered regarding the uses of letter-writing by different groups of people. The roles of correspondence varied from being merely functional to ministering to psychological needs. Letters were also employed to fulfil cultural aspirations. Naturally, all of these categories overlapped with each other. Thus the letters of the Soresbies were at first related mainly to farming. Later they were written to woo lovers, advise children, and search for employment. As a group, the letters of workers in Chapter 3 were motivated by a wide range of goals. In addition to using them to keep records, do work, earn money, and teach children, they provided legal evidence, preserved dynastic and individual memories, created social networks, satisfied literary desires, and were read and written for pleasure and entertainment.

Though the role of correspondence varied with different families, the most important needs were common to all of them. Comfort in times of separation, illness, and death knew no regional, temporal, or class boundaries. Likewise, support from social and kinship networks was welcomed by all correspondents. Letters were naturally written at the time of major events in the life cycle. Births and deaths were announced, courtship letters were written, and marriages were recorded. Education was discussed, careers were planned, and businesses were managed. Nor was one's soul neglected in correspondence. Family letters thus take the reader into every corner of life. The use of letters to 'talk' about everyday minutiae may have been a particularly satisfying reason for writing them.

Importantly, all classes of writers used letters to describe reading activities, even early in the century. Some, like Edward Tucker Jr deftly inserted quotations, which had been copied and preserved. This was a complex cognitive act that required many sequential actions. Chapter 6 showed that discussing books in letters became a cherished practice. Jane Johnson used a letter as the site for her History of Miss Clarissa of Buckinghamshire. Barbara Johnson inserted poetry in letters, whilst her brother discussed book reviews.

Writers in all case studies used their epistolary literacy to contemplate abstract ideas in a reflective manner. Because writing was slower than speech, it gave people time to think about what they are doing.[7] An eighteenth-century woman, Anne Capper, expressed this idea in a letter: 'The transcribing a few of our thoughts on paper has a tendency to calm our spirits and relieve our minds. We think, and we answer our thoughts, and become insensibly relieved.'[8] Anne understood that an idea is often clarified during the process of writing. In fact, we often do not know what we want to say until we write it down. This was apparent to a young

Manchester grocer, George Heywood. 'A circumstance once wrote over', he noted, 'leaves more impression upon the mind than five times read or heard.'[9] For untutored writers, a letter might offer the first leisured opportunity to slowly construct written meaning.[10]

The impact of letter-writing on eighteenth-century culture

Letter-writing had powerful impacts on the lives of individuals described in this book. In practice, epistolary literacy offered people three important benefits: they were given ample practice in constructing narratives, they were able to record their life stories, and they could communicate those stories over distances to people outside their own neighbourhoods.

All of our writers developed narrative skills as they told their epistolary stories. In an unguarded comment, John Evelyn's grandson showed he understood this process. 'I have run through each of the things I saw in some order', he wrote, 'and have offered to your eyes events of daily life . . . as if putting together a story.'[11] Some scholars have insisted that all human experiences possess an intrinsic narrative structure. As David Carr noted: 'Life can be regarded as a constant effort . . . to maintain . . . narrative coherence in the face of an ever-threatening, impending chaos.'[12] The conventions of a letter were geared to control this chaos, offering dates, locations, addresses, and a system of serial ordering. This was, perhaps, a hidden reason why letter-writing was so satisfying to people described in this book.

Once letter-writing helped them to compose narratives, they might engage in epistolary forms of life-writing about themselves and their families. As Thomas Jefferson's editor, Julian Bond, was keenly aware: 'The letters of a person . . . form the only full and genuine journal of his life.'[13] Life-writing was an apt pursuit for this period, for autobiography and biography were developing into literary genres. What is more, epistolary accounts of a person's life could be circulated by post throughout Britain and the larger world. In an age of empire, this was important.

After all three benefits had become routine, persons were known to have acquired epistolary literacy. This gave them a certain standing in their communities. On a practical level, they could write coherent prose, and engage in accepted conventions. Moreover, they were competent to conduct business and construct personal relationships. In short, they 'fit' into their commercial society and had mastered its basic means of communication. Because of these advantages, epistolary literacy became a defining attribute of the middling sort and those who rose into its ranks. It became a basic requirement for employment, office holding, and, with luck, success in business. Thus Joseph Morton and Samuel Follows, though careworn workers, found good jobs because they wrote well.

Epistolary literacy also implied that its owner had some learning, along with interests and social relationships outside one's immediate locality. This gave them a wider outlook than that of local inhabitants with more limited experience. Every family described in this book had kin and connections in London, the continent, or the colonies. The fast pace of urbanization and imperial expansion made people personally aware that the globe was shrinking.

We usually think of the cohesive role of letters as applying to individuals and families. Yet this was also true for the nation. In an age of empire, war, and expanding trade, governments, as well as citizens, needed to stay connected. Fortunately, letter-writing functioned as a thick, spreading 'glue' that drew elements of society together. This role grew more important as mobility and migration affected more people. Consequently, a growing number of individuals both needed and wished to join the literate part of the nation. As this book has shown, that sector included more than gentlemen and scholars. People from all ranks were able to share in an epistolary moment, which is still called the golden age of letters.

This book claims that when the pen and the people became connected, the wider culture was affected. The economic impact of this linkage may be seen in the expansion of the Royal Mail and its use by the trading classes. It is helpful to think about how commerce might have been affected, if England had lacked a national post at this time. The fact that a popular letter form grew out of the commercial world, shows it was an integral part of the nation's economic system. This system surely benefited from the expansion of literacy, if not to man its mines then to provide the innovative entrepreneurship that made England an industrial leader.

The social impact of letter-writing on eighteenth-century culture is easier to see. It taught people how to interact with those above and below them in rank—the very people with whom one might expect to have little regular contact. In practice, letters forced writers to decide how to address and send 'services' to people of different ranks. As they did so, they had to consider their own identities and relationships with the addressee. Negotiations about social status, therefore, were constantly taking place. This two-way dialogue, I suggest, provided the preconditions for what E. P. Thompson called 'the making of class'.[14] The Tucker's 'language of resentments', for example, was a part of this dialogue. The acquisition of epistolary literacy might be an early sign of a later shift in a person's social status. On the other hand, when letters proved to be substandard or not sufficiently genteel, they singled out the writer in a negative way. For William Cotesworth and Jedediah Strutt, this was a painful experience.

Epistolary literacy's most visible impact was seen in the way it affected the literary world. Clearly, this was a time when letters and literature were closely intertwined. For Jane Johnson, letter-writing underpinned all of her efforts to compose original poetry and prose. In contrast, her children used their epistolary literacy to enter a public world of letters. Literary studies stress the influence of literature upon individuals. Yet they often fail to notice the reverse effects that people with epistolary literacy had on literary forms. This book has claimed that letter-writers influenced travel literature, the cult of sensibility, methods of literary criticism, and the rise of the novel.

This was true, not only for celebrated London figures, but for unknown provincial writers like the Johnsons. Yet none of our amateurs wrote great literature. Instead, their literary culture was a solid middling-sort development. Located on a spectrum between elite and popular culture, it is perhaps the point at which 'literariness' becomes easiest to track, through analysis of reading and writing records. Part III described common elements of this middling-sort literary culture and observed its shifts over the century. It is important to note that Miller's salon has been widely satirized, whilst her letters, and those of the Johnsons, have been overlooked. Yet they show how unknown manuscripts can offer a new historical interpretation of a literary subject.

Finally, this book suggests that epistolary literacy had a political impact on eighteenth-century culture. This argument has its foundation in larger claims about the power of writing and the basic right of all writers to have their 'say'. As the chapter on the Post Office demonstrated, the government was well aware of the power of the written word from its long experience with censorship. Benstock has claimed that letters are 'a vehicle for the expression of that which is, for whatever reasons, denied, repressed, and silenced by the culture'.[15] With their many points of view and open-ended conversations, letters have always been associated with opposition movements from Commonwealth men and Jacobites to salon members and pamphleteers.[16] Thus whenever the state wished to restrict free communication of ideas, letters were routinely opened.

During the eighteenth century, a new epistolary tradition, built on older foundations, welcomed people eager to use the power of the pen. Letters of workers offer glimpses of the thoughts of untrained people, when they first obtained the right to commit independent ideas to paper. This privilege was not given to everyone in society. As Sheridan notes: 'The invisibility of the writing of ordinary people in their everyday lives is not just a technical matter . . . It is also a power issue.' According to this view, writing has agency, and who is allowed to write has political implications. When groups with this privilege expanded without state supervision, old lines of authority were being subtly challenged.[17] Surely, letters could be subversive without proclaiming militant views. This became evident, as we witnessed the power felt by Joseph Morton when he found his epistolary voice.

By the end of the century, epistolary voices had become integral parts of daily discourse. Anna Miller forthrightly published her letters in 1776. The Johnsons used theirs to discuss political ideas shaped by private writing and unsupervised reading, including the work of Thomas Paine.[18] After reading William Godwin's *Enquiry*, Elizabeth Strutt warned her brother Joseph about his culpability as a manufacturer, if he did not aid the poor.[19] In the harsh political climate of the 1790s, letter-writing once again appeared ominous to the authorities. Yet if epistolary literacy empowered individuals, it also subtly indoctrinated writers, by forcing them to accept the norms and values that underpinned each letter. Writing letters was, therefore, a two-edged sword with both liberating and restrictive effects. Hence the Dissenter, Elizabeth Wilson self-censored her letters in the 1790s. Alas, she could not repress the fiery epistles of her eloquent husband, Thomas.

This book has focused on letter-writers whose voices have hitherto been unheard. Because they possessed epistolary literacy, they were able to take pen in hand—stop and reflect a bit—then commit their thoughts to paper. The letter offered them an accessible technology, easily imitated conventions, and the great asset of 'practice'. In the non-threatening arena of private correspondence, farmers and workers, as well as women and children, could make mistakes, cross them out, and start again. For each of them, letters were foundational instruments for developing independent opinions. For twentieth-century readers, they offer a pathway into eighteenth-century culture. On crisp white paper in bold dark ink, the thoughts of a nation were quietly taking shape.

Research plan and selection criteria

Designing the project

The goal of the research plan was to find substantial family letter collections written by unknown men and women that spanned the entire long eighteenth century. Ideally, these collections would include a representative sample of writers from different classes, occupations, religions, and geographical areas. Family letters that extended over more than one generation would be used to show continuity and change over time. It was expected that most correspondences would be written by the upper classes, with a sprinkling of middling-sort and mercantile correspondences. This proved to be a false assumption.

Catalogues of the British Library, the Bodleian Library, the Beinecke Library, Yale University, and a wide range of local archives were sampled to see if there was enough new material for the book. Discussions about sources and methodology were held with the Public Record Office and the Historical Manuscripts Commission, which have since become part of The National Archives. The Internet was searched for new databases, along with traditional bibliographies.

Despite initial assumptions, it appeared that extensive letter collections written by people below the rank of gentry might indeed exist. To test this supposition, the Access to Archives Database (A2A) was searched in detail. Now part of the larger UK Archives Network, A2A contains catalogues describing archives held locally in England and Wales, many of which were previously inaccessible to online users. A list of correspondence that appeared suitable was then compiled for each archive. Next a questionnaire was sent to all local record offices requesting data about letter collections of non-elites, especially items that had already been found in a broad range of sources. Positive responses were received from archives in the north of England. Since Scottish literacy was high and northern boundaries were porous, numerous visits were made to that area. The combination of electronic and archival searches was useful in targeting possible sources. It soon became evident there was more material than one book could encompass. A rigorous selection process would, therefore, have to be developed.

Data collection

In order to examine each archive in a consistent manner a checklist of required data was constructed. Information would be collected on three levels: (1) for the collections of family papers, (2) for the persons who wrote the letters, and (3) for the letters themselves. Appendix II provides information about selected family archives that were used in this book. It includes the location of the archive, catalogue references, types and dates of documents, and principal locations of writers. Appendix III presents data about persons who wrote the letters including their dates, occupations over time, religion, and geographical location. Much of this information was gleaned from other supporting documents. Appendix IV describes the letters, themselves, including types, principal subjects, social relationships and uses. It is important to note that archives contain many types of letter forms: drafts, copies, those in albums, letter books, diaries, and journals, those post marked, hand delivered, and those never sent. All of these letter forms, which give insights into the writing process, were used in this study.

To obtain the data, notes pertaining to individual letters were indexed by standardized subject headings. The basic literacy of writers was evaluated in a separate data field. Strengths of collections were also recorded, for example if they answered questions about gender, region, or religion. A final summary of the motives, uses, and impact of letters was completed for each collection. These last three summaries of skills, strengths, and uses were crucial in supplying candidates for case studies.

Selecting the case studies

Rules were established at the outset for deciding whether to read letters in a particular collection. The basic requirement was a substantial unbroken series of letters that spanned at least two consecutive generations. Collections that included replies were highly rated, for this permitted the reconstruction of actual dialogues. To be considered as a case study, however, additional materials that provided background about writers were also necessary. These might include family trees, wills, birth records, marriage settlements, genealogical research, extracts from reading, writing exercises, and annotated instructions about how to maintain the collection. With these references in hand, it was possible to begin to reconstruct the lives of specific letter-writers. Without these sources, it would be difficult to interpret and place in context the overwhelming minutiae of letters.

The discovery of only a few 'exceptional' letter-writers would have made the task of choosing case studies easy. Instead, disciplined cutting was necessary. One alternative was to use brief quotations from all or most of the collections. Because this would have produced a kaleidoscope of fragments, the decision was made to create fewer, but fuller, case studies that were as in-depth as space would permit. Finally, a chart of sixty-three collections that had been located was compiled.

Because of the large number of possible collections, it was decided to eliminate titled and gentry archives and focus on those written by people lower down the social scale. The Evelyn papers were used, but only to present a contrast with those of merchant families. Likewise, a few elite archives contributed to overall themes in general chapters. For example, thirty-four letter collections, numerous local histories, and a wide range of secondary literature were drawn on to describe uses and attitudes to the post office in Chapter 2. Eventually fifteen core collections were chosen as case studies. I believe they present a representative sample of the collections consulted. Together, they comprise a diverse group of letter-writers and different types of letters penned at various times and locations.

As the project developed into one that examined levels of literacy, it was clear that manuscript letters should be used whenever possible. Only then would there be a comparable base of texts that showed original spelling, punctuation, and grammar. Editors of printed letters often deleted information that revealed literacy skills, especially those of women, children, and the lower sorts. Manuscripts also showed how language was reworked: words crossed out or added between lines or in margins; dates forgotten or inserted; annotations and endorsements added by others. Most important, editors of printed collections often omitted references to letter-writing and the post office that occurred at the beginning and end of letters. A large database of these references was constructed and used to write this book.

As more case studies were chosen, common patterns emerged. These shared ways of thinking suggest that they are representative collections. Of course, letters of literate writers were 'self-selected' and also biased towards northern areas. Yet without counting all letters, no group of them could ever make the claim to be wholly representative. Those that are included here have the advantage of being carefully selected from a sample of unused collections. The common questions that were addressed to all collections and the use of 'epistolary literacy' to measure universal traits of letters (see Chapter 3) have helped to control the random nature of all correspondence. Finally, because this book has dealt with letter-writing on a popular level, the universe of possible writers is smaller than that of elite individuals. This increases the probability that the letters are representative of their kind.

Obviously, bias in the selection and interpretation of correspondence is inescapable. Yet current awareness of the constructed nature of letters has acted as a safeguard against overly transparent readings. Studies of this kind are rarely possible for periods before the eighteenth century. Indeed works about earlier eras assume that letters were exceptional, written by a tiny portion of the population. The discovery of so numerous and wide a range of eighteenth-century letters indicate that this stereotype had ceased to be relevant long before 1800.

Selected family archives

Family	Archive	Documents	Dates of Documents	Location of Writers
Arkwright	Derbyshire Record Office, Matlock (DRO) D5991/1–4	Family/Latin and schoolboy letters	c.1770s–1843	Cromford, Derby.; Eton, Berks.
Baker	Guildhall Library, London (GH) MS 16927–8	Letter book, pedigree, will	1771–82	New Street, Shoe Lane, London
Bateman (see also Wilson)	Beinecke Library, Yale University, New Haven CT (BLY) OSB MSS 32; Bodleian Library, University of Oxford (Bodl) MS Top Derbyshire D1; DRO D258/23/8/16, D258/54/3, 6, D2323/11/2; F511, D6755; Manchester Central Library (MCL) M162	Family letters, inventory, will, poem, prayers, school exercise, accounts, children's letters; chapel minutes, membership rolls, deeds, newspapers	1760s–19th cent.	Manchester, Liverpool, Lancs.; Gatley, Cheshire; Middleton, Derby.; London
Bower	East Riding of Yorkshire Archives and Local Studies Service, Beverley (EY) DDBR 11–13	Family letters, wills, pedigree, inventories, legal/financial accounts, settlements, travel	1714–19th cent.	Bridlington, Scorton, York, Yorks.; London

Name	Reference	Description	Dates	Places
Bowrey	GH MS 03041, MS 24176–8	Letter books, business papers, diaries, charts, maps, wills, settlements, prayers, poem, travel, ledger, household accounts	1650–1714	Cornhill, Marine Square, Wapping, London; India; Malaya; Persian Gulf; Ceylon; Batavia; Sumatra
Braithwaite papers with Quaker families	Library of the Society of Friends, London (LSF) Temp MSS 403 (especially 403/1/1/1–5; 403/1/2/1–3; 403/4/8/1–2)	Family/children's letters, papers, index	1700–19th cent.	London
Conyers	EY DDX 152/9/1–3	Family letters	1766–73	Helmsley, Yorks.; London
Cotesworth	Tyne and Wear Archives Service, Newcastle upon Tyne: DF. COT; DF. HUG	Letter books, wills, settlements, legal, business, trade, household, estate papers. E. Hughes, *North Country Life* (1952), vol. i.	1715–80s	Gateshead, Newcastle on Tyne, Northumb.
Dawson	Sheffield Archives, Sheffield (SA) TC 515–22	Letters, legal records, accounts, business	1715–75	Sheffield, Bawtry, Yorks.; Amsterdam, Holland
Edwards	Bodl MS Eng. Lett. e. 92; MSS 1007–10012	Private letters, letter books	1720–56	Bucks.
Fawdington	North Yorkshire County Record Office, Northallerton (NY) Ref Z. 640 [Microfilm 1958, 1976]	Family letters, copybook, arithmetic book, apprenticeship indenture, poem, births, wills, parish records	1698–1825	Asenby, Yorks.; Kendal, Milnthorpe, Westmorland; Carlisle, Cockermouth; Penrith, Whitehaven, Cumberland; Lancaster, Lancs; W. Indies
Follows	LSF Temp MSS 127	Family letters, wills, settlements, journal, travel accounts, birth records, memoirs, indexes	1738–19th cent.	Castle Donington, Leics.; Norwich, Great Yarmouth, Norfolk; Woodbridge, Suffolk; Newfoundland

Continued

Family	Archive	Documents	Dates of Documents	Location of Writers
Frank	SA BFM 58–9, 61, 1290, 1300–4, 1319–38	Over 1,300 letters and extensive papers, index	1657–1805	Campsall, Pontefract, Yorks.; Cambridge
Grimston	EY DDGR 41–43; zDDX 894	Family letters and papers	1727–19th cent.	Grimston Garth, Yorks.; London
Hubbertsy	Cumbria Record Office (CRO), Kendal WDX 744	Family letters	1748–58	Kendal, Westmorland; Liverpool, Lancs.; Birmingham, Warwicks.
Johnson	Bodl Don. b. 39–40, c. 190–6, d. 202, e. 193–200 (see also Bucks., Lincs., and Staffs. Record Offices)	Family letters, fairy tale, poetry, reading records, Clarissa story, writing books; cut paper toys, genealogical material	17th cent.–19th cent.	Olney, Bucks.; Witham-on-the-Hill, Lincs.: Bath, Somerset; Coventry, Warwicks.; London; Northampton, Northants.
Langton	Lancashire Record Office, Preston DDX/190/1–119	Family letters, diary, probate, pedigree, travel, passport, J. Wilkinson, Letters (Chetham Soc., 1994)	1771–88	Kirkham, Lancaster, Liverpool, Lancs.; Bristol, Glos.; London; Oxford, Oxon.; Ambleside, Askham, Westmorland
Lee	NY ZJL	Family letters, wills, settlements, accounts, 16th cent. book list, accounts	1720–43	Pinchinthorpe, Yorks.; London
Le Neve	British Library (BL) Add. MS 71573	Family Letters	1662–1711	Great Witchingham, Harling, Norfolk; London

Levett	BLY MS Osborn Shelves c207	Private letters, bound transcripts	1720–7	Oxford, Oxon.; Blithfield, Staffs.
Lucas	GH MS 25597	Private letters	1724–31	London; Eton, Berks.; Pendarves, Cornwall
Maister	Hull City Archives, Hull (HCA) DMI, especially 3/30; 4; DFP 1371–5, 1376–9	Family letters, index play/opera inventory	1743–1807	Hull, Yorks.; Gothenburg, Sweden
Masham	Bodl MS Facs e. 54, MS Locke c. 16, fos. 3–5; The Newberry Library, Chicago, IL Case MS E5.M3827	Letter book in French and English	1686–1708	Oates, High Laver, Essex; London; France
Metcalfe	NY ZOA	Family, letter books settlements, wills, mining papers, index	1742–56	York, Yorks.; London
Morton	National Library of Scotland, Edinburgh MS 10789; CRO WDY 75	Family letters	1765–1805	Kendal, Applethwaite, Levens, Westmorland; Kelso, Scotland
Muggletonians	BL Add MS 60168	Religious letters	Late 17th cent.–18th cent.	London
Newton	SA TR 292/3, 446/1–14	Family letters, memoir, journals	1761–1825	Sheffield, Yorks.
Nicholls	BLY OSB MSS c467	Private/children's letters	1750–1811	Blundeston, Suffolk; Cambridge
Palmer	Bodl MS Eng Lett. c. 438	Letter book	1690–1735	Little Chelsea, London; Oxford, Oxon.
Paupers	GH MS 11280, 11948, 18982–3, 19233	Letters concerning poor relief	1723–71	All Hallows Lombard St, St Dionis Backchurch, London

Continued

Family	Archive	Documents	Dates of Documents	Location of Writers
Payne	SA MS MD 5856/1–50	Family letters, farming notebook	1756–1800	Newhill, Doncaster, Mansfield, Yorks.; Nottingham, Notts.; Wisbech, Cambs.
Pease	HCA DFP/1–3370	Family letters, index, journal, pamphlets, family history, press cuttings, literary papers	1688–1778	Hull, Yorks.; London; Amsterdam; Ireland
Smith	Cambridge University Library, Cambridge Add. MS 7621	Family/children's letters	1760s–70s	Daventry, Northants.; London; Ware, Herts.
Soresbie	DRO D5202, D331	Family letters, copybooks, writing exercises, accounts births, wills, settlements	1670s–19th cent.	Brailsford, Derbys.
Spencer	SA SpSt 60502–53, especially 60548–53	Family letters, travel/shipping accounts,	1729–55 especially 1750s	Cannon Hall, Yorks.; Liverpool, Lancs.; London
Story	LSF Temp MSS 388	Courtship/family letters	1702–9	Carlisle, Cumberland; New York, Philadelphia; W. Indies
Strutt	DRO D5303, D2943/F9/1–2, D2043/F1/1, D3772	Family letters, memoir, journal, pedigrees, accounts	1748–19th cent.	Belper, Blackwell, Findern, Derby, Derbys.; London
Tucker	Bodl MSS Don b. 16–28, c. 101–34.	Family letters, wills, settlements, inventories, accounts, catalogue	1662–19th cent.	Weymouth and Melcombe Regis, Dorset; London

| Wheatcroft | DRO D5433/1–2, D2079/1, D5433/2, D5458/11/2, D5775/1–3, D6127 | Commonplace books, poems, autobiography, courtship letters, library catalogue | 17th cent. –1750 | Ashover, Derbys.; London |
| Wilson (See also Bateman) | Dr Williams's Library, Congregational Library, London: MSS II c. 34–5, MSS II c. 36, MSS II c. 88, MS II d. 5, Hd 4/9, Surman Index | Family letters, wills, settlements, memoir, letter books | 1760s–19th cent. | London; Manchester |

Selected family letter-writers

Family	Principal Letter-Writers	Occupation[1]	Religion[2]	Location[3]
Arkwright	Richard Sr (1732–92), Richard Jr (1755–1843) and Susanna Arkwright (b. 1761)	Wigmaker, textile entrepreneur	NA	Cromford, Derbys.; Eton, Berks.
Baker	Edward Sr (1705–79), Edward Jr (1730–97), Edward III (b. 1757) and Mary (b. 1758) Baker; Benjamin Cole, John Newton, Polly Dix	Mathematical instrument maker	ANG	New Street, Shoe Lane, London
Bateman (see also Wilson)	Rebekah (c.1764–97), Thomas Sr (1760–1847), William (1787–1835), Thomas (1791–1810) and Rebekah (1794–1838) Bateman; Arthur (1732–1818) and Sarah (1733–1811) Clegg; Margery Smithson; Mary Jane Hodson	Cotton merchant, timber merchant, apothecary, postmaster	CG	Manchester; Liverpool, Lancs.; Gatley, Cheshire; Middleton, Derbys.; London
Bower	Leonard, Henry, Robert, Richard, John and Henry Bower; William Scorborough	Merchant, farmer	NA	Bridlington, Scorton, York, Yorks.; London

Bowrey	Thomas (1650–1713) and Mary Bowrey; Frances Gardiner (d. 1720); Robert Callant; Jacob Larwood; Martha and James Davis	Ship captain, merchant, shop owner, seaman	NA	Cornhill, Marine Square, Wapping, London; India; Malaya; Persian Gulf; Ceylon; Batavia; Sumatra
Braithwaite papers with Quaker families	Joseph (1704–66) and John Freame; James and Mary Plumstead Farmer; Charles (1748–1828) and Mary Farmer Lloyd (d. 1821)	Businessman, banker, industry	Quaker	London
Conyers	John, Richard, and Jane Conyers; R. Bentley	Printer, linen draper	NA	Helmsley, Yorks.; London
Cotesworth	William Sr (1688–1725), William Jr (d. 1721?) and Robert (d. 1729?) Cotesworth; Henry and George Liddell; Carr family; Ellison Family	Tallow chandler, coal mine owner, trader	NA	Gateshead, Newcastle on Tyne, Northumb.
Dawson	Samuel Sr and Samuel Dawson Jr (18th cent.)	Attorney, merchant	NA	Sheffield, Bawtry, Yorks.; Amsterdam, Holland
Edwards	Thomas Edwards (1699–1757); Samuel Richardson (1689–1761)	Literary critic	NA	Bucks.
Fawdington	John Fawdington (fl.1757–1817) and Jenny Jefferson Fawdington	Saddler/bridlemaker, grocer, ironmonger	NA	Asenby, Yorks.; Kendal Milnthorpe, Westmorland; Carlisle, Cockermouth, Penrith, Whitehaven, Cumberland; Lancaster, Lancs.; W. Indies

Continued

Family	Principal Letter-Writers	Occupation[1]	Religion[2]	Location[3]
Follows	Ruth (1718–1808), George Sr (1717–1803), George Jr (1742–66), Richard (b. 1745), Joseph (1751–1809) and Samuel (1755–1811?) Follows	Basket maker, grocer's clerk, writing clerk	Quaker	Castle Donington, Leics.; Norwich, Great Yarmouth, Norfolk; Woodbridge, Suffolk; Newfoundland
Frank	Richard, Robert, Anne, Matthew, and Bacon (c.1740–1812) Frank	Hamburg merchant, attorney, recorder, Esq.	NA	Campsall, Pontefract, Yorks.; Cambridge
Grimston	Thomas (1702–51), John (1725–80), Thomas (1753–1821) and John (19th cent.) Grimston	Esq.	ANG	Grimston Garth, Yorks.; London
Hubbertsy	Zachary, John, and Robert Hubbertsy (fl.1740s–60)	Writing clerk, curate, student	ANG	Kendal, Westmorland; Liverpool; Birmingham
Johnson	Jane (1706–59), Barbara (1738–1825), and Robert Augustus (1745–99) Johnson; Craven family; Katherine (1744–1808) and Michael (1740–1816) Wodhull	Clergyman's wife, army, spinster	ANG	Olney, Bucks.; Witham-on-the-Hill, Lincs.; Bath, Somerset; Coventry, Warwicks.; London; Northampton, Northants.

Langton	Cornelius (1691–1762), Thomas (1724–94), John (1756–1807), and William (1758–1814) Langton	Flax merchant	NA	Kirkham, Lancaster, Liverpool, Lancs.; Bristol, Glos.; London; Oxford, Oxon.; Ambleside, Askham, Westmorland
Lee	Roger Sr (*fl.*1660s–70s), Roger Jr (b. 1674), Roger III (18th cent.), Dorothy, Anne, Eleanor, and James Lee	Attorney, physician, Esq.	ANG	Pinchinthorpe, Yorks.; London
Le Neve	Oliver (1662–1711) and Peter (1661–1729) Le Neve; John Millicent	Herald and antiquary, Esq.	ANG	Great Witchingham, Harling, Norfolk; London
Levett	Richard Sr (1675–40), Richard Jr (b. 1696), and Richard III (1731–1805) Levett	Clergyman, merchant	ANG	Oxford, Oxon.; Blithfield, Staffs.
Lucas	James Lucas (*fl.*1720s); Henry Godolphin (d. 1733); Pen Pendarves	Clerk of the Works, St Paul's Cathedral	ANG	London; Eton, Berks.; Pendarves, Cornwall
Maister	Philip Samuel (*c.*1759–1814), John (1790s), Nathaniel, and Henry (1748–12) Maister	Merchant	NA	Hull, Yorks.; Gothenburg, Sweden
Masham	Sir Francis (d. 1723), Damaris (1658–1708), Esther (b. 1675), and Francis Cudworth Masham (1686–1731); John Locke (1632–1704); Pierre Coste (1668–1747)	Spinster, Huguenot exiles, army, authors	ANG	Oates, High Laver, Essex; London; France
Metcalfe	Thomas Metcalfe (*c.*1687–1756), Henry Wilmot; Thomas Weddell	Esq., professions	NA	York, Yorks.; London

Continued

Family	Principal Letter-Writers	Occupation[1]	Religion[2]	Location[3]
Morton	Joseph (fl.1765–99), Augness, James Sr, James Jr, and Thomas Morton; Jacob Morland	Itinerant gardener, weaver	ANG	Kendal, Applethwaite, Levens, Westmorland; Kelso, Scotland
Muggletonians	Lodowicke Muggleton (1609–98)	Tailor	Muggle-tonianism	London
Newton	George (1761–1825), Sally Marshall (1765–1829), and Thomas (1796–1868) Newton	Ironmaster	Methodist	Sheffield, Yorks.
Nicholls	Norton Sr, Jane Floyer, and Norton Jr (1741?–1809) Nicholls; Thomas Gray (1716–71)	Merchant, clergyman	ANG	Blundeston, Suffolk; Cambridge
Palmer	Ralph Palmer (d. 1746)	Lawyer	ANG	Little Chelsea, London; Oxford, Oxon.
Paupers	Catherine Jones (fl.1758); Abraham Robinson; Mary Norwood; Patrick Kearney; Merey Williams	Paupers, poor law officials	NA	All Hallows Lombard St, St Dionis Backchurch, London
Payne	Elizabeth Ecroyd and William Payne; Susanna Peckover	NA	Quaker	Newhill, Doncaster, Mansfield, Yorks.; Nottingham, Notts.; Wisbech, Cambs.
Pease	Robert (1643–1720), Joseph (1688–1778), Esther (1720–97), Robert (1717–70), Mary (1727–57), and Joseph R. (1752–1807) Pease	Linseed oil dealer and manufacturing, merchant, banker	Unitarian	Hull, Yorks.; London; Amsterdam; Ireland

Smith	William Smith Sr and William Smith Jr	Trade, politician	Unitarian	Daventry, Northants.; London; Ware, Herts.
Soresbie	Dorothy (fl.1670s–80s), Charles (fl.1670s), Jane Moseley, Roger (d. 1693), Edward (1665–1729), Roger (1699–1762), Charles (1700–63), Gilbert Sr (d. 1775), and Gilbert Jr (1750–c.1836) Soresbie	Husbandman, yeoman	NA	Brailsford, Derbys.
Spencer	John (d. 1729), William (d. 1756), Benjamin (d. 1759), and John (1718–75) Spencer	Apprentice, Liverpool/London merchant, Esq.	NA	Cannon Hall, Yorks.; Liverpool, Lancs.; London
Story	Thomas Sr (1630?–1721?), Thomas Jr (1662–1742), and Anne Shippen Story	Minister	ANG to Quaker	Carlisle, Cumberland; New York; Philadelphia; W. Indies
Strutt	Jedediah (1726–97), Elizabeth Woollat (1729–74), William (1756–1830), Eliza (1758–1836), Martha (1760–1793), George Benson (1761–1841), and Joseph (1765–1844) Strutt	Servant, apprentice wheelwright, textile mill owner	Unitarian	Belper, Blackwell, Findern, Derby, Derbys.; London
Tucker	Edward (d. 1707), Edward (d. 1737), John (1701–79), and Richard (1704–77) Tucker; Rebecca, Martha, and Sarah Gollop; Steward family	Stone merchant	Man of Love, ANG	Weymouth and Melcombe Regis, Dorset; London

Continued

Family	Principal Letter-Writers	Occupation[1]	Religion[2]	Location[3]
Wheatcroft	Leonard (1627–1706), Elizabeth, and Titus (1679–1762) Wheatcroft	Tailor, farmer, teacher, gardener, parish clerk virginal tuner, carpenter, soldier, water works,	NA	Ashover, Derbys.; London
Wilson	Elizabeth (1762–1847), Ann, Thomas Sr, (b. 1731), Thomas Jr (1764–1843), Joshua (1795–1874), Rebekah Stratten (d. 1870), and Elizabeth Coombs (d. 1878) Wilson; Revd Samuel Bradley	Silk merchant, philanthropist	CG	London; Manchester

Notes: [1] Occupations of principal writers are listed as they changed over time; [2] Ang=Anglican; CG=Congregation; NA=not available; [3] Locations are listed in order of importance.

Selected family letters

Family	Letter Types	Principal Subjects	Social Relationships in Letters	Uses of Letters
Arkwright	Family, child, school	Education, social status, marriage, children, business, sociability	Father/son, parent/child	Social networks, family relations
Baker	Family, letter book, courtship, patronage	London, careers, religion, popery, friendship, middling sort, masculinity, social status	Father/son, sister/brother, lovers	Individual identity, courtship, social networks, employment, entertainment
Bateman	Family, religious, condolence, advice	Religion, sermons, education, gender, individual/community identity, marriage, children	Husband/wife, sisters, parent/child, minister/congregation, cousins	Religious networks, advice, condolence, comfort, identity
Bower	Family, business, legal, courtship	Religion, education, reading, advice, printing, business, courtship, marriage	Extended family relations	Legal/financial evidence, advice, courtship, networks
Bowrey	Family, begging, patronage, business	London, trade, ships, coffeehouses, shopkeeping, women, merchants, travel, Asia	Husband/wife, ship captains' network, merchants' network	Comfort, social/kinship and business networks

Continued

Family	Letter Types	Principal Subjects	Social Relationships in Letters	Uses of Letters
Braithwaite papers with Quaker families	Family, children, advice	Reading, education, children, gender, business, Quakers	Mother/daughter, parent/child, grandparents	Remembrance, kinship networks, education
Conyers	Religious, advice	Family, religion, London, community, business	Extended family relationships, uncle/nephew	Religious/business advice, comfort, family separation
Cotesworth	Child, schoolboy, advice	Politics, Jacobites, elections, education, social mobility, trade	Father/son, brothers	Kinship/social networks, politics
Dawson	Family business	Lawyers, London, business, trade	Attorney/merchant networks	Family and business networks
Edwards	Literary, friendship	Reading, Richardson, language, literary criticism, Post Office,	Literary friendships	Literary and social networks, comfort, entertainment
Fawdington	Family, courtship, poetry	Post Office, courtship, poetry, language, travel, mobility, trade	Husband/wife, extended family	Courtship, comfort, identity
Follows	Religious, advice, condolence	Post Office, Quakers, education, community, language, forms of address, travel, masculinity	Husband/wife, mother/son, parent/child, friends	Religion, identity, family and Quaker networks, comfort, salvation, advice
Frank	Family, legal business	Education, London, coffeehouses, business, family	husband/wife, mother/son,	Family/social networks, advice

Name				
Grimston	Family, children, begging, courtship, literary, patronage	Reading, French/American Revolutions, Post Office, politics, provincial culture, courtship, friendship, education, marriage	Father/son, client/patron, lovers	Family and social networks, entertainment, information, literary goals, language
Hubbertsy	Family, begging, patronage	Writing, careers, merchant life, trade, education, money, curacy, books, gentility	Father/son, brothers	Employment, business/social networks, comfort, patronage
Johnson	Family, literary, poetry, short stories	Literature, poetry, reading, writing, provincial culture, children, religion	Mother/son, mother/daughter, friends, extended family	Literary goals, salvation, advice, kinship/friendship networks, comfort
Langton	Family, school, travel, advice	Letter-writing, Post Office, business, merchant life, leisure, education, writing, business	Father/son, brothers	Family/business networks, information, comfort, travel
Lee	Family, begging, legal	Dreams, legal affairs, money	Father/son, friends	Family/social networks, legal
Le Neve	Family, patronage	Post Office, inheritance, house, city/country, language, patronage, status	Brothers, neighbours	Family/social networks, patronage
Levett	Patronage, friendship, literary	Social status, friendship, literature, provincial culture	Patron/client, friends	Patronage, literary goals, friendship
Lucas	Family, begging, courtesy	Post Office, letter-writing, St Paul's Cathedral, transport, social status	Master/servant	Employment, patronage
Maister	Business, travel	Merchant life, Gothenburg, Hull, trade, plays, opera	Family/business networks	Family/business networks
Masham	Family, friendship	French Huguenot refugees, politics, philosophy, Locke, family, gender, education, authorship, step-families	Parent/child, French/English family, step-parents/step-children, intellectual networks, lovers	Family networks, national/family and individual identity, self-expression

Continued

Family	Letter Types	Principal Subjects	Social Relationships in Letters	Uses of Letters
Metcalfe	Friendship, courtesy, advice	Ill health, friendship, old age, finances, legal, marriage, books	Friends, family networks	Literary goals, information, comfort, social networks
Morton	Family, begging	Education, mobility, family, Post Office, marriage, employment	Father/son, brothers, master/servant	Comfort, identity, family networks, self-expression
Muggleton	Religious	Muggletonianism, persecution, family	Religious networks	Religious networks
Newton	Family, courtship, religious	Conversion, courtship, business, education, reading, religion	Family, husband/wife	Courtship, religious/business and family networks
Nicholls	Children, family, literary, friendship	Literature, education, children, family, clerical life	Father/son, friends, patron/client	Literary goals, friendship, patronage
Palmer	Literary, friendship	Literature, London, classical learning, reading, rhetoric, education, Latin	Lawyer networks	Literary/friendship networks
Paupers	Poor relief	Poor relief, Post Office, money, sickness, friendship, literacy	Poor relief officials/paupers, scribes/paupers	Poor relief, identity, social networks, self-expression
Payne	Family, friendship, condolence	Quaker meetings, farm experiments, religion, family, language	Sisters, friends	Remembrance, information, news, comfort
Pease	Advice, children, family, business	Education, gender, family conflict, money, trade, Holland, family, career, travel	Parent/child, husband/wife, siblings, grandfather/grandchildren	Family/individual identity, advice, kinship/trade and international networks, comfort, information

Smith	School, advice	Education, career, family	Father/son	Family, advice
Soresbie	Advice, patronage, family	Education, literacy, reading, gender, popular culture, copybooks	Father/daughter, husband/wife, siblings, cousins, friends	Family networks, identity, self-expression, storytelling, literary goals, employment, information
Spencer	Family, business	Family, career, travel, ships merchants, business, London, Liverpool	Parent/child, brothers	Family/business and trade networks, comfort
Story	Courtship, travel	Religion, Quakers, language, travel, North America	Quaker minister, journal writer	Courtship, religious networks, comfort
Strutt	Family, courtship, advice	Literature, reading, literacy, writing, language, social status, gentility, gender	Husband/wife, parent/children, father/son, master/servant	Literary goals, advice, comfort, self-expression, family/social networks; identity
Tucker	Family, patronage, election, advice, travel, condolence, courtship	Politics, elections, stone trade, travel, merchant community, literature, courtship	Grandfather/father/son, brothers, patron/client, politician/elector	Individual/family identity, political/social networks, comfort, patronage
Wheatcroft	Courtship, family	Literacy, writing, reading, scribe, courtship, poetry, popular culture, education, school	Father/son, teacher/students, scribes	Courtship, literary goals
Wilson	Family, religious, condolence, advice	Religion, sermons, marriage, childbirth, London, children, chapels, pregnancy	Husband/wife, parent/child, sisters, cousins, minister/congregation	Religious networks, advice, salvation, comfort, identity

Notes

Place of publication is London, unless otherwise noted. Years start on 1 January. Names of archives are given in full in the first reference, followed by a standard abbreviation used in further references.

INTRODUCTION

1. The Morton letters are in the National Library of Scotland, MS 10789, fos. 1–33. Copies in the Cumbria Record Office (CRO), Kendal have been used and cited throughout this book. CRO WDY 75, fo. 1, Joseph Morton/James Morton Sr, 18 Feb. 1765.
2. British Library (BL) Add. MS 62019, Thomas Gardiner, 'A Generall Survey of the Post Office' (*c*.1682).
3. William Dockwra, *The Practical Method of the Penny Post* (1981).
4. Royal Mail Archive (RMA) Post 68, fo. 1, Ralph Allen's Instruction Book, 1729–40.
5. Alan Robertson, *Great Britain Post Roads, Post Towns, and Postal Rates* (1974), 13.
6. Bodleian Library (Bodl), University of Oxford, MS Don. c. 193, fos. 13–14, Barbara Johnson/George Johnson, 2 Mar. [1776?].
7. Jane Austen, *Emma*, ii (1816), 313–14.
8. Thomas Beebe, *Epistolary Fiction in Europe 1500–1850* (Cambridge, 1999), 6.
9. Chauncey Tinker, *The Salon and English Letters* (NY, 1915), 252; J. C. Bailey, *Studies in Some Famous Letters* (1899); Dena Goodman, *The Republic of Letters* (Ithaca, NY, 1994), 137. Elizabeth MacArthur, *Extravagant Narratives* (Princeton, NJ, 1990), 24, notes: 'The eighteenth-century writer chose, more often than writers of any century before or since, the epistolary form.'
10. Library of the Religious Society of Friends (LSF), Temp MS 127/3/3, Samuel Follows/Ruth and George Follows, 12 Mar. 1769.
11. Derbyshire Record Office (DRO) D331/26/1, John de Beauchesne, *A Booke Containing Divers Sortes of hands* (1571). The illustration is the title page of the 1602 edition in the Bodleian Library.
12. DRO MS D331/10/15, Dorothy Soresbie/Roger Soresbie, 18 Aug. 1689.
13. Hull City Archives (HCA) DFP/111, Esther Pease/Joseph Pease, 8 Feb. 1731.

14. HCA DFP/276, Joseph Robinson [Pease]/Joseph Pease, 7 Jan. 1760.

15. Guildhall Library (GH) MS 19233, no. 5, Merey Williams for Catherine Jones/Peter Pop'll, 17 Oct. 1758. I thank Tim Hitchcock for references.

16. Samuel Stansfield, 'Memoirs of Ruth Follows', *The Friends' Library*, iv (1840), 59.

17. David Vincent, *The Rise of Mass Literacy* (Cambridge, 2000); R. A. Houston, *Literacy in Early Modern Europe*, 2nd edn (Harlow, 2002).

18. For ancient and classical letters see Stanley Stowers, *Letter-writing in Greco-Roman Antiquity* (Philadelphia, PA, 1986); J. White, *Light from Ancient Writers* (Philadelphia, PA, 1986). For medieval letters see Giles Constable, *Letters and Letter-Collections* (Turnhout, 1976); H. J. Chaytor, *From Script to Print* (1945). For Renaissance and early-modern letters see Claudio Guillén, 'Notes toward the study of the Renaissance letter' in Barbara Lewalski (ed.), *Renaissance Genres* (Cambridge, MA, 1986), 70–101; Jonathan Goldberg, *Writing Matter* (Stanford, CA, 1990); Heather Wolfe and Alan Stewart (eds.), *Letterwriting in Renaissance England* (Washington DC, 2004); Gary Schneider, *The Culture of Epistolarity* (Newark, DE, 2005).

19. Jonathan Gibson, 'Letters' in Michael Hattaway (ed.), *A Companion to English Renaissance Literature and Culture* (Oxford, 2001), 609–14; J. R. Henderson, 'Erasmus on the art of letter-writing' in J. J. Murphy (ed.), *Renaissance Eloquence* (Berkeley, CA, 1983), 331–3; David Randall, 'Epistolary rhetoric, the newspaper, and the public sphere', *Past and Present*, 198 (2008), 3–32. I thank Gibson for suggestions.

20. D. Erasmus, 'De Conscribendis Epistolis' in J. K. Sowards (ed.), *Collected Works of Erasmus*, xxv (Toronto, repr. 1985), 1–254 (20); A. S. Osley, trans., *Erasmus on Handwriting* (Wormley, 1970).

21. T. Baldwin, *William Shakspere's Small Latine & Lesse Greeke*, ii (Urbana, IL, 1944), 239–52; Harris Fletcher, *The Intellectual Development of John Milton*, i (Urbana, IL, 1956), 204–6.

22. [William Kempe], *The Education of Children in Learning* (1588), fo. G1r; Edward Corbett and Robert Connors, *Classical Rhetoric for the Modern Student*, 4th edn (NY, 1999), 500; Baldwin, *William Shakspere's Small Latine & Lesse Greeke*, i, 287, 297–301; ii, 252–4.

23. [John Brinsley], *Ludus Literarius* (1612), 166.

24. Ibid., 167–71.

25. Roger Ascham, *The Scholemaster* (1570); Richard Mulcaster, *The First Part of the Elementarie* (1582); Kempe, *The Education of Children in Learning*; Fletcher, *The Intellectual Development of John Milton*, i, 182.

26. William Fulwood, *The Enimie of Idlenesse* (1568); Jean Robertson, *The Art of Letter-writing* (1942) and K. Hornbeak, 'The complete letter-writer in England 1586–1800', *Smith College Studies in Modern Languages*, 15 (1934), 1–150.

27. Thomas Sprat, *The History of the Royal-Society of London*, 2nd edn (1702).

28. CRO WDY 75, fo. 18, Joseph Morton/Thomas Morton, 12 Feb. 1780.

29. Bodl MS Don. c. 191, fo. 3, Robert Johnson/Barbara Johnson, 1 Aug. 1776.

30. Martin Daunton, *Progress and Poverty* (Oxford, 1995), 285−318 (314).

31. Duncan S. Bell, 'Dissolving distance', *Journal of Modern History*, 77 (2005), 523−62; William Dekker, *Epistolary Practices* (Chapel Hill, NC, 1999).

32. CRO WDY 75, fo. 4, Joseph Morton/Thomas Morton, 4 Jan. 1770.

33. Bodl MS Don. e. 195, fo. 5, 17 Feb. 1772. Working by the 'great' meant being paid by the piece. I thank Joanna Innis for this point.

34. Bodl MS Don. e. 195, fo. 7, 12 Mar. 1772.

35. I thank Jane Humphries for this point.

36. CRO WDY 75, fo. 16, Joseph Morton/Thomas Morton, 5 Oct. 1779; fo. 1, Ebeneezer Bell/James Morton, 2 Oct. 1805.

37. William St Clair, *The Reading Nation* (Cambridge, 2004), 10−11; James Raven, *The Business of Books* (New Haven, CT, 2007).

38. Alexander Pope, *Mr Pope's Literary Correspondence for Thirty Years* (1735); James Winn, Anderson, *A Window in the Bosom* (Hampden, CT, 1977); Paul Baines and Pat Rogers, *Edmund Curll* (Oxford, 2007).

39. R. Day, *Told in Letters* (Ann Arbor, MI, 1966), 77, 237−70.

40. Ian Watt, *The Rise of the Novel* (Berkeley, CA, 1957).

41. See Appendix I. A few elite collections act as foils or illustrate general points.

42. James Daybell, *Women Letter-writers in Tudor England* (Oxford, 2006); Lynne Magnusson, *Shakespeare and Social Dialogue* (Cambridge, 1999); Alan Stewart, *Shakespeare's Letters* (Oxford, 2008).

43. Rebecca Earle, *Epistolary Selves* (Aldershot, 1999); James Daybell, *Early Modern Women's Letter-writing, 1450−1700* (Basingstoke, 2001); Jane Couchman and Ann Crabb, *Women's Letters Across Europe* (Aldershot, 2005).

44. *Huntington Library Quarterly* 66: 3−4 (2003); A. Gilroy and W. Verhoeven (eds.), 'Correspondences: A special issue on letters', *Prose Studies*, 19: 2 (1996).

45. Mary Favret's *Romantic Correspondence* (Cambridge, 1993); Linda Kauffman, *Discourses of Desire* (Ithaca, NY, 1986); Elizabeth MacArthur, *Extravagant Narratives* (Princeton, NJ, 1990); Ruth Perry, *Women, Letters, and the Novel* (NY, 1980).

46. Janet Altman, 'Political ideology in the letter manual', *Studies in Eighteenth-Century Culture*, 18 (1988), 105, 114; Goodman, *The Republic of Letters*.

47. D. F. Mc Kenzie, *Bibliography and the Sociology of Texts* (NY, 1999); Adrian Johns, *The Nature of the Book* (Chicago, IL, 1998); Armando Petrucci, *Public Lettering* (Chicago, IL, 1993).

48. Susan Whyman, 'Paper visits' in Rebecca Earle (ed.), *Epistolary Selves* (Aldershot, 1999), 15−36; 'Gentle companions' in James Daybell (ed.), *Women's Letter-writing in England* (Houndmills, 2001), 177−93; 'Advice to letter-writers', in Frances Harris and Michael Hunter (eds.), *John Evelyn and his Milieu* (2003), 255−66; 'The correspondence of Esther Masham and John Locke', *Huntington Library Quarterly*, 66 (2003), 275−305; 'Letter-writing and the rise of the novel', *Huntington Library Quarterly*, 70 (2007), 577−606.

49. Clare Brant, *Eighteenth-Century Letters and British Culture* (Houndmills, 2006); Susan Fitzmaurice, *The Familiar Letter in Early Modern English* (Amsterdam, 2002). See also Eve Bannet, *Empire of Letters* (Cambridge, 2005); Sarah Pearsall, *Atlantic Families* (Oxford, 2008).

50. Howard Anderson et al. (eds.), *The Familiar Letter in the Eighteenth Century* (Lawrence, KS, 1966); Alan McKenzie (ed.), *Sent as a Gift* (Athens, GA, 1993); Bruce Redford, *The Converse of the Pen* (Chicago, IL, 1986); Claudia Thomas, *Alexander Pope and his Eighteenth-Century Women Readers* (Carbondale, IL, 1994).

51. For example, Bodl MS Eng. Lett. e. 92, The Letter Book of Thomas Edwards 1727–35; Bodl MS Eng. Lett. c. 438, Letters of Ralph Palmer.

52. CRO WY 75, fo. 7, Joseph Morton/Thomas Morton, 9 Jul. 1770.

CHAPTER I

1. Karen Lipsedge, 'Enter into thy closet' in John Styles and Amanda Vickery (eds.), *Gender, Taste, and Material Culture in Britain and North America 1700–1832* (New Haven, CT, 2006), 107–22 (111); J. P. Hunter, *Before Novels* (1990), 157; Alan Stewart, 'The early modern closet discovered', *Representations*, 50 (1995), 76–100.

2. Anthony Petti, *English Literary Hands from Chaucer to Dryden* (1977), 7.

3. Peter Bales, *The Writing Schoolemaster* (1590), R1r.

4. Jonathan Goldberg, *Writing Matter* (Stanford, 1990), 94–7.

5. John Clark, *Writing Improv'd or Penmanship Made Easy* (1714), 2.

6. James Hodder, *The Pen-mans Recreation* (1667), [2].

7. Francis Clement, *The Petie Schole* (1587, repr. 1967), 52; [John Brinsley] *Ludus Literarius or, The Grammar Schoole* (1612), 29.

8. Petti, *English Literary Hands from Chaucer to Dryden*, 7; Clement, *The Petie Schole*, 53.

9. Michael Finlay, *Western Writing Implements in the Age of the Quill Pen* (Carlisle, 1990), 8–12; Bales, *The Writing Schoolemaster*, Q2r–3r.

10. Clement, *The Petie Schole*, 53–5, Brinsley, *Ludus Literarius*, 29; George Shelley, *The Second Part of Natural Writing* (1714).

11. Brinsley, *Ludus Literarius*, 30.

12. *A Newe Booke of Copies* (1574), fo. A3v; Clement, *The Petie Schole*, 55.

13. Clement, *The Petie Schole*, 52. In BL Add. MS 71573, fo. 87, Oliver Le Neve complained he could not 'gett any [good ink] here either in powder or Liquor... wt I Have in Liquor clods in ye jack and grows thick'.

14. Finlay, *Western Writing Implements in the Age of the Quill Pen*, 32–4, 38–9.

15. Ibid., 36, 40–5.

16. Ibid., 36–7, 40–5.

17. Ibid., 29–30.

18. Petti, *English Literary Hands from Chaucer to Dryden*, 5.

19. Eva Simmons (ed.), *Augustan Literature* (1994), 7.

20. Martin Nystrand, *The Structure of Written Communication* (Orlando, FL, 1986), 156.

21. Dave Postles, 'The politics of address in early-modern England', *Journal of Historical Sociology*, 18 (2005), 99–121; Jonathan Gibson, 'Significant space in manuscript letters', *Seventeenth Century*, 12 (1997), 1–9; Peter Beal, *In Praise of Scribes* (Oxford, 1998).

22. Terttu Nevalainen, 'Continental conventions in early English correspondence' in Hans-Jürgen Diller and Manfred Gorlach (eds.), *A History of English as a History of Genres* (Heidelberg, 2001), 203–24; Minna Nevala, 'Inside and out', *Journal of Historical Pragmatics*, 5 (2004), 271–96; Pattison Collection, Jacob Pattison Jr/Jacob Pattison, 1 Sept. 1781, quoted in Penelope Corfield, *Youth and Revolution in the 1790s* (Stroud, 1996), 19, n. 57. I thank Corfield for this reference.

23. Finlay, *Western Writing Implements in the Age of the Quill Pen*, 32.

24. Ibid., 59–60. Black indicated mourning.

25. Nystrand, *The Structure of Written Communication*, 47.

26. Kenneth Charlton, *Women, Religion and Education in Early Modern England* (1999), 143; V. E. Neuburg, *Popular Education in Eighteenth-century England* (1971), 22.

27. David Cressy, *Literacy and the Social Order* (Cambridge, 1980), 37.

28. Ibid., 19, 48.

29. Charlton, *Women, Religion and Education in Early Modern England*, ch. 7.

30. Ibid., 143.

31. Harris Fletcher, *The Intellectual Development of John Milton*, i (Urbana, IL,1956), 95.

32. Ibid., 96; [William Kempe], *The Education of Children* (1588). Coote's *English School Master* had forty-eight editions by 1696.

33. Cressy, *Literacy and the Social Order*, 23, 26; Fletcher, *The Intellectual Development of John Milton*, i, 96.

34. Margaret Spufford, *Small Books and Pleasant Histories* (Athens, GA, 1982), 23–4.

35. Kempe, *The Education of Children*, f3v.

36. Cressy, *Literacy and the Social Order*, 27; W. A. Vincent, *The State and School Education* (1950).

37. *G. D.'s Directions for Writing Set Forth for the Benefit of Poore Schollars* (1656, repr. 1933), 8.

38. Brinsley, *Ludus Literarius*, 32; Kempe, *The Education of Children*, f3v.

39. Spufford, *Small Books and Pleasant Histories*, 23–4, 26–7.

40. Neuburg, *Popular Education in Eighteenth-century England*, 57, 96.

41. Andrew Tuer, *History of the Horn-Book* (1987), 2; Charlton, *Women, Religion and Education in Early Modern England*, 78; Fletcher, *The Intellectual Development of John Milton*, i, 94.

42. Tuer, *History of the Horn-Book*, 2; Keith Thomas, 'The meaning of literacy in early-modern England' in Gerald Baumann (ed.), *The Written Word* (Oxford, 1986), 99.

43. Fletcher, *The Intellectual Development of John Milton*, i, 96–102.

44. Bruce Smith *The Acoustic World of Early Modern England* (Chicago, IL, 1999), 119.

45. Thomas, 'The meaning of literacy in early-modern England', 97–133.

46. Kempe, *The Education of Children*, f3v.

47. A. S. Osley (ed.), *The Value of Handwriting* (Wormley, 1980), 5, 10.

48. Osley, *Scribes and Sources* (1980), 21–2, 26.

49. Rosemary O'Day, *Education and Society 1500–1800* (1982), 60; Brinsley, *Ludus Literarius*, 37.

50. Osley, *The Value of Handwriting*, 12.

51. O' Day, *Education*, 59.

52. Brinsley, *Ludus Literarius*, 39.

53. Ambrose Heal, *The English Writing-masters and their Copy-books 1570–1800* (Cambridge, 1931). Heal's references were examined chronologically by the author. See also W[illiam] Massey, *The Origin and Progress of Letters* (1763), 136; Richard Christen, 'Boundaries between liberal and technical learning', *History of Education Quarterly*, 39 (1999), 31–50.

54. John de Beauchesne, *A Booke Containing Divers Sortes of hands* (1571); Heal, *The English Writing-masters and their Copy-books*, 127.

55. John Davies, *The Writing Schoolemaster* (1659); Thomas Watson, *A Copy Book Enriched with . . . the most Usefull & Modish Hands* [1683]; Richard Gethinge, *Calligraphotechnica* (1619); J. Johnson, *A Copy Book*, (1669); Nathaniel Strong, *England's Perfect School-Master* (1676); John Matlock, *Fax Nova Artis Scribendi* (1685); Charles Snell, *The Pen-man's Treasury Open'd* (1694).

56. Henry Nass, 'The lost art of penmanship', *New York Times*, 21 Aug. 2002.

57. Heal, *The English Writing-masters and their Copy-books*.

58. *A Nevv Booke of Spelling with Syllables . . . Devised Chiefly for Children . . . Also this Book is very necessary for the ignorant, to teach them to write Orthographie in a short time* (1621).

59. Edward Coote, *School Master* (1687), a2r, a3r.

60. *G. D.'s Directions for Writing Set Forth for the Benefit of Poore Schollars*, 8,10.

61. Brinsley, *Ludus Literarius*, 'To the Loving Reader', 2; Coote, *School Master*, 5v.

62. Coote, *School Master*, title page, 17, 78.

63. Cambridge University Library, MS Dd.5.49/2, fos. 65r, 72v.

64. Stanley Morison, 'The development of hand-writing' in Heal, *The English Writing-masters and their Copy-books*, xxiii–xl (xvi–ii); Hans Nicholas, *New Trends in Education in the Eighteenth Century* (1966), 186; Edward Cocker, *England's Pen-Man* (1703); Robert More, *Of the First Invention of Writing* (1716); Abraham Nicholas, *The Young Penman's Copy Book* (1715).

65. John Ayres, *Tutor to Penmanship* (1698), 'To the Reader'.

66. Clark, *Writing Improv'd or Penmanship Made Easy*, Dedication.

67. Aileen Douglas, 'Making their mark', *British Journal for Eighteenth-century Studies*, 24 (2001), 145−60 (146).

68. Morison, 'The development of hand-writing', xxiii−xxx.

69. Osley, *Scribes and Sources*, 228−9.

70. Morison, 'The development of hand-writing', xxix−xxxix. To compare secretary and italic see *A Newe Booke of Copies 1574* (New York, repr. 1962), plates 3−4.

71. Charles Snell, *The Penman's Treasury*, quoted in Heal, *The English Writing-masters and their Copy-books*, 102; Richard Daniel, *A Compendium of the most Usuall Hands of England, Netherland, France* (1664).

72. Martin Billingsley, *The Pen's Excellencie* (1618), c4r.

73. For examples see Clark, *Writing Improv'd or Penmanship Made Easy*, 3; and George Bickham, *The Universal Penman: or, the Art of Writing* (1741).

74. Douglas, 'Making their mark', 148.

75. L. C. Hector, *The Handwriting of English Documents* (1996), 65; Joyce Whalley, *The Pen's Excellencie* (Tunbridge Wells, 1980), 243−6.

76. Morison, 'The development of hand-writing', xxxviii−ix. The admirer was the Abate Domingo Maria Servidori.

77. Bickham, *The Universal Penman: or, the Art of Writing* and *The British Youth's Instructor* (1754), Preface; Heal, *The English Writing-masters and their Copy-books*, xxxiii.

78. Morison, 'The development of hand-writing', xxxiii.

79. John Ayres, *A Tutor to Penmanship* (1698), quoted in Douglas, 'Making their mark', 150−1.

80. Eve Bannet, *Empire of Letters* (Cambridge, 2005), x, 54; Katherine Hornbeak, 'The complete letter-writer in English 1568−1800', *Smith College Studies in Modern Languages*, 15 (1934); Jean Robertson, *The Art of Letter-writing* (1942).

81. Roger Chartier 'Secretaires for the people' in Roger Chartier et al. (eds.), *Correspondence* (Princeton, NJ, 1991), 59−101.

82. John D. Baird, 'Model rules', *Times Literary Supplement* (2006).

83. Chartier, *Correspondence*, 78−84.

84. Ibid., 95−100.

85. *ODNB* Searches. I thank Allison Wall for suggestions.

86. Cary McIntosh, *The Evolution of English Prose* (Cambridge, 1998); Terttu Nevalainen and Helena Raumolin-Brunberg (eds.), *Sociolinguistics and Language History* (Amsterdam, 1996); David Graddol et al. (eds.), *English* (1996).

87. Bodl MS Eng. lett. e. 92, fo. 79, Thomas Edwards/[J. Clerke], 15 Dec. 1733.

88. Bodl MS 1011, fo. 94, Thomas Edwards/J. Wilkes, 13 Jan. 1748.

89. James Hogg/[Adam Bryden], 1 July [1800] in Gillian Hughes (ed.), *The Collected Letters of James Hogg* (Edinburgh, 2004), 5.

90. Whyman, 'Advice to letter-writers' in Frances Harris and Michael Hunter (eds.), *John Evelyn and his Milieu* (2003), 255−66.

91. John Evelyn, *Diary*, Guy de la Bedoyere (ed.) (Woodbridge, 1995), 24, 16 July 1635.

92. BL Add. MS 78442, John Evelyn/John Evelyn Jr, 1673–93.

93. BL Add. MS 78462, John Evelyn/Sir John Evelyn, 1698–1701; John Evelyn *Memoires for My Grand-son*, Geoffrey Keynes (ed.) (Oxford, 1926).

94. BL Add. MS 78301, fo. 622, John Evelyn Jr/John Evelyn, 13 Dec. 1665.

95. Ibid., fo. 623, John Evelyn Jr/John Evelyn, 30 Jan. 1667; fo. 624, 1667.

96. Ibid., fo. 626, John Evelyn Jr/John Evelyn, 10 Dec. 1675; fo. 635, 10 Dec. 1675.

97. BL Add. MS 78359, Susan Evelyn/Dr Ralph Bohun, May 4 n.d.

98. BL Add. MS 78442, Mary Evelyn/John Evelyn Jr, 1 Mar. 1676.

99. Ibid., Mary Evelyn/John Evelyn Jr, 24 Nov. 1682; 8 July 1684.

100. BL Add. MS 78439, Mary Evelyn's letters 1657–70 in the hand of Mary Evelyn, daughter of Sir John Evelyn.

101. See the British Library's Hatton, Wenthworth, Blenheim, Portland, Coke, and Trumbull collections.

102. BL Add. MS 78432, Martha Evelyn/Mary Evelyn, 13 Aug. 1692, 6 Nov. 1695. Martha was the daughter of Richard Spencer, Turkey merchant (d. 1667).

103. BL Add. MS 78462, John Evelyn/Sir John Evelyn, 8 Apr. 1699.

104. Ibid., John Evelyn/Sir John Evelyn, fo. 19, 26 Oct. 1700.

105. BL Add. MS 78462, fo. 694, Sir John Evelyn/John Evelyn, 23 May 1699.

106. Ibid., fo.2, John Evelyn/Sir John Evelyn, 26 Mar. 1698; fo. 3, 18 Apr. 1698.

107. Ibid., fo. 13, John Evelyn/Sir John Evelyn, 12 June 1699.

108. Ibid., fo. 15, 5 Aug. 1699; fo. 27, 19 Apr. 1701; fo. 29, 6 June 1701; fo. 33, 9 Nov. 1701; fo. 37, 2 Dec. 1701.

109. Ibid., fo. 13, John Evelyn/Sir John Evelyn, 12 June 1699.

110. BL Add. MS 78471, Sir John Evelyn Jr/Sir John Evelyn, 22 Sept. 1717.

111. BL Add. MS 78469, Francis, 2nd Earl Godolphin/Charles Evelyn, 25 Apr. 1726.

112. BL Add. MS 78472, Charles Evelyn/Sir John Evelyn, 6 Nov. 1731.

113. BL Add. MS 78442, Sir John Evelyn/John Evelyn Jr, 18 Aug. 1695.

114. HCA DFP/1–3356 Papers of the Pease Family of Hull, East Riding of Yorkshire with personal name index and descriptive catalogue notes; 3223–78 family history; 3313–56 published and literary material; 3325 pamphlet collection; 3326–46 press cuttings, 3346–56 misc.; T. T. Wildridge, *Old and New Hull* (Hull, 1884), 154–8.

115. Hugh Calvert, *A History of Kingston upon Hull* (1978), 201, 220. The Pease family business was based on a process to extract oil from linseeds. HCA DFP/2, Patent to Robert Pease, 27 Aug. 1708.

116. HCA DFP/3–329, Letters of Joseph Pease; DFP/421, Draft Will, 14 Mar. 1752; DFP/422, Will, 27 June 1755; DFP/439–81, Letters of Robert Pease; DFP/293–6, 482, Letters of Mary Robinson; DFP/111–21, Letters of Esther Pease.

117. HCA DFP/182, Robert Pease/Joseph Pease, 17 Mar. 1731; DFP/186, Robert Pease/Joseph Pease, 16 Oct. 1731.

118. HCA DFP/470−1, Robert Pease/William Pease, draft, 4 Aug. 1738; *The Kirkstead Story* (1968); Gordon Jackson, *Hull in the Eighteenth Century* (Oxford, 1972), 275. Kirkstead is near Horncastle.

119. HCA DFP/198, Robert Pease/Joseph Pease, 7/18 Aug. 1747, from Amsterdam, hence 2 dates.

120. HCA DFP/111, Esther Pease/Joseph Pease, 8 Feb. 1731.

121. HCA DFP/121, Esther Pease/Joseph Pease, 7 Sept. 1733.

122. HCA DFP/293−5, 436, 643−5.

123. Robert Robinson was in the cotton business in Manchester. HCA DFP/483−549.

124. HCA DFP/543, Mary Robinson/Robert Robinson, 26 June 1752.

125. HCA DFP/47−8, Petition from Joseph Pease and Joseph Robinson to allow the latter to add Pease to his name, granted 29 Apr. 1773. For the writings of his son, Joseph Robinson Pease II (1789−1866) see J. D. Hicks (ed.), *The Journal of Joseph Robinson Pease 1822−65* (Hull, 2000); BL MS Lansdowne 891; BL MS Egerton 2479; C. Caine (ed.) *Strothers Journal* (Hull, 1912).

126. To see changes in a boy's letters as they mature over time compare DFP/276, with envelope, Joseph Robinson Pease (JRP)/Joseph Pease, 7 Jan. 1760, aged 8; DFP/277, 11 Jan. 1762, aged 10; DFP/288, 9 Sept. 1769, with answer, aged 17.

127. HCA DFP/276, JRP/Joseph Pease, 7 Jan. 1760.

128. HCA DFP/277, JRP/Joseph Pease, 11 Jan. 1762; DFP/278, 28 Sept. 1762.

129. HCA DFP/466, JRP/Robert Pease, 26 Dec. 1764.

130. HCA DFP/466; H. McLachlan, *Warrington Academy*, Chetham Society, 107, new series (1943), 36−50.

131. *A Report on the State of the Warrington Academy, by the Trustees at their Annual Meeting, June 28th MDCCLXIV* (1764), 4, notes their 'Writing and Drawing-Master, of very considerable ability . . . well acquainted with Book-keeping and the forms of business in merchants counting-houses', who attends classes two hours a day. P. O'Brien, *Warrington Academy 1757−86* (Wigan, 1989); McLachlan, *Warrington Academy*, 40, mentions writing master, Jacob Bright, who gave lessons for a guinea a session; HCA DPT/466, JRP/Robert Pease, 26 Dec. 1764.

132. HCA DPT/468, JRP/Robert Pease, 24 May 1766.

133. HCA DPT/282, JRP/Joseph Pease, 20 Sept. 1766.

134. HCA DPT/283, JRP/Joseph Pease, 25 Feb. 1769.

135. See the Braithwaite papers with the Farmer and Lloyd families (Appendix II).

136. K. J. Allison, *Hull gent. seeks country residence, 1750−1850* (Beverley, 1981), 3−5, 22; Hicks, *The Journal of Joseph Robinson Pease 1822−65*, ii; Calvert, *A History of Kingston upon Hull*, 220. The Peases moved from 18 High Street over the bank to 12 Charlotte Street and leased the Hesslewood estate in 1778. Its chalk was used in the paint and whiting business.

137. Hicks, *The Journal of Joseph Robinson Pease 1822−65*, ii; James Sheahan, *General and Concise History and Description of the Town and Port of Kingston-Upon-Hull* (1864), 576−7, notes JRP's social activities. His son was educated at Little Shelford and Queens College, Cambridge.

138. Edward Hughes, *North Country Life in the Eighteenth Century*, i (1952); J. M. Ellis (ed.), *The Letters of Henry Liddell to William Cotesworth*, Surtees Society, cxcvii (1987); H. T. Dickinson (ed.), *The Correspondence of Sir James Clavering*, Surtees Society, clxxviii (1967); J. M. Ellis, *A Study of the Business Fortunes of William Cotesworth, c.1668−1726* (NY, 1981, hereafter *BF*), 3−4. The Cotesworth MSS are in the Tyne and Wear Archives, Newcastle, DF. COT, DF. HUG.

139. **Hughes, *North Country Life in the Eighteenth Century*, i, 6−8; Ellis, *BF*, 7; Ellison MSS A 36/15; Cotesworth MSS CM/2/824; [John Baillie], *An Impartial History of the Town and County of Newcastle upon Tyne and Its Vicinity* (Newcastle, 1801), 542.**

140. Ellis, *BF*, 214; F. Manderes, *A History of Gateshead* (1973), 323; Hughes, *North Country Life in the Eighteenth Century*, i, 9.

141. J. M. Ellis, 'The poisoning of William Cotesworth, 1725', *History Today* (Nov. 1978), 752−7 and *BF*, 214−15.

142. Ellis, *The Letters of Henry Liddell to William Cotesworth*; Hughes, *North Country Life in the Eighteenth Century*, i: Appendix A, 409−18.

143. Hughes, *North Country Life in the Eighteenth Century*, i, 363; Ellis, *BF*, 203. Hannah married Henry Ellison. Elizabeth married Henry Thomas Carr.

144. Ellis, *BF*, 197, 213.

145. Brian Mains and Anthony Tuck, *Royal Grammar School, Newcastle Upon Tyne* (Stocksfield, 1986); Hughes, *North Country Life in the Eighteenth Century*, i, 342−3; Ellis, *The Letters of Henry Liddell to William Cotesworth*, no. 120, 6 Mar. 1714.

146. Henry Clarke and W. N. Weech, *History of Sedbergh School 1525−1925* (Sedbergh, 1925), 61−4; Hughes, *North Country Life in the Eighteenth Century*, i, 346, William Cotesworth Jr/William Cotesworth, 21 Apr. 1716.

147. Hughes, *North Country Life in the Eighteenth Century*, i, 345, William Cotesworth Jr/William Cotesworth, 15 Apr. 1716; ibid., 354, William Cotesworth Jr/William Cotesworth, 6 July 1716.

148. Ibid., 353, William Cotesworth/William Cotesworth Jr, n.d. Henry Liddell (*c.*1673−1717) became involved in the coal trade.

149. Ibid., 358, William Cotesworth Jr/William Cotesworth, 21 Oct. 1716.

150. Ibid., 349−50, William Cotesworth Jr/William Cotesworth, 19 May 1716.

151. Ibid., 378, William Cotesworth Jr/Robert Cotesworth, n.d.

152. Ibid., 358, William Cotesworth/Robert Cotesworth, 17 Oct. 1716.

153. Ellis, *BF*, 198.

154. Hughes, *North Country Life in the Eighteenth Century*, i, 360.

155. Ibid., 358−60, William Cotesworth Jr/William Cotesworth, 3 Nov. 1716; Venn (ed.), *Alumni Cantab*, i, 401, May 1717.

156. Hughes, *North Country Life in the Eighteenth* Century, i, 375–6, William Cotesworth Jr/Robert Cotesworth, n.d.

157. Ibid., 377, n. 1; H. A. C. Sturges (ed.), *Registers of Admissions to the . . . Middle Temple* (1949), July 1717.

158. Ellis, *BF*, 201–6.

159. Hughes, *North Country Life in the Eighteenth Century*, i, 104–12. Robert Ellison became a banker.

160. Joan Wilkinson (ed.), *The Letters of Thomas Langton, Flax Merchant of Kirkham 1771–88*, Chetham Society, 28 (1994), 3, 9. The originals are in the Lancashire Record Office: DDX/190/1–119.

161. F. J. Singleton, 'The flax merchants of Kirkham', *Transactions of the Historical Society of Lancashire and Cheshire*, cxxvi (1977), 73–108 (73–4, 78, map, 80–6, pedigree); W. Farrer and J. Brownhill (eds.), *Victoria County History . . . Lancaster* (1912), vii, 143–53 (143 map); Henry Fishwick, *The History of the Parish of Kirkham in the County of Lancaster*, Chetham Society, 92 (1874), 17.

162. Wilkinson, *The Letters of Thomas Langton*, 7; John Aiken, *A Description of the Country from Thirty to Forty Miles round Manchester* (1795), 288.

163. Singleton, 'The flax merchants of Kirkham', 74; Wilkinson, *The Letters of Thomas Langton*, 15–18; Edmund Dixon, *Flax and Hemp* (1854), 50 ff.

164. Wilkinson, *The Letters of Thomas Langton*, 11, 130, n. 1.

165. Ibid., 18–19.

166. R. C. Shaw, *Kirkham in Amounderness*, 2nd edn (Preston, 1949), 693; Fishwick, *The History of the Parish of Kirkham*, 89.

167. Notebook of Shepherd Birley, quoted in Wilkinson, *The Letters of Thomas Langton*, 79: 'An awkward man-servant who was most probably oftener employed in the garden or the stables than as a waiter indoors' broke some china 'when the company were all assembled'.

168. Singleton, 'The flax merchants of Kirkham', 85, 96; Wilkinson, *The Letters of Thomas Langton Letters*, 19–20; NTA, ADM 106/3634.

169. Wilkinson, *The Letters of Thomas Langton*, 47–8; N. Carlisle, *A Concise Description of the Endowed Grammar Schools in England and Wales*, i (1810), 651.

170. Wilkinson, *The Letters of Thomas Langton*, 19.

171. Ibid., 25.

172. Ibid., 148–52, Thomas Langton/William Langton, 19 June 1775; 180–4, Thomas Langton/William Langton, 22 Oct. 1780; 294–5, Thomas Langton/Dear Sirs, 10 June 1787.

173. Ibid., 19.

174. Lancashire Record Office, DDX/190/1–119.

175. Wilkinson, *The Letters of Thomas Langton*, 161, Thomas Langton/William Langton, 1 Mar. 1777.

176. Ibid., 92.

177. Ibid., 109–10, Thomas Langton/William and John Langton, 2 Sept. 1771.

178. Wilkinson, 111, Thomas Langton/William and John Langton, 16 Nov. 1771.

179. Ibid., 114, Thomas Langton/William Langton, 20 Dec. 1771.

180. Ibid., 113–14, Thomas Langton/William Langton, 20 Dec. 1771.

181. John Lally and Janet Gnosspelius, *History of Much Woolton* (Woolton, 1975); Wilkinson, *The Letters of Thomas Langton*, 51.

182. *Williamson's Advertiser*, 7 Jan. 1765 quoted in Wilkinson, *The Letters of Thomas Langton*, 51.

183. Wilkinson, *The Letters of Thomas Langton*, 116, Thomas Langton/William Langton, 11 Jan. 1771.

184. Ibid., 119–21, Thomas Langton/William Langton, 11 Mar. and 17 Apr. 1772.

185. Ibid., 110, Thomas Langton/William Langton, 25 Oct. 1771.

186. Ibid., 57, 157, Thomas Langton/John Langton, 15 June 1776.

187. Ibid., 139–40, Thomas Langton/William Langton, 28 Jan. 1773.

188. Ibid., 119–20, Thomas Langton/William Langton, 11 Mar. 1772.

189. Ibid., 126–7, Thomas Langton/William and John Langton, 9 Aug. 1772.

190. Ibid., 117, Thomas Langton/William and John Langton, 7 Feb. 1712.

191. Ibid., 128, Thomas Langton/John Langton, 7 Sept. 1772.

192. Ibid., 89.

193. Ibid., 87, 101.

194. Ibid., 14, 57.

195. Anne Langton, *The Story of Our Family* (Manchester, 1881), 4–7.

196. Wilkinson, *The Letters of Thomas Langton*, 14, 58, 82.

197. Ibid., 57, 157–8, Thomas Langton/John Langton, 15 June 1776.

198. Ibid., 87, 158, n. 2.

199. Ibid., 58, 87. Tom was president of the Liverpool Royal Institution; his eldest son became Vice-Chancellor of Toronto University.

200. Library of the Society of Friends (LSF), Temp MS, 403/1/2/2, Braithwaite Papers, Priscilla Farmer/Mary Farmer, 20th 1 month; 403/1/1/3, 3rd month, 1760.

201. R. S. Fitton and A. P. Wadsworth, *The Strutts and the Arkwrights 1758–1830* (Manchester, 1964), 138; Derbyshire Record Office (DRO) D5303/13/9, ElizabethStrutt/Jedediah Strutt, 9 July 1774.

202. Fitton, *The Strutts and the Arkwrights 1758–1830*, 156, Martha Strutt/William Strutt, July 1775.

203. Beinecke Library, Yale University, OSB MSS 32/5, Rebekah Bateman/William Bateman, 11 Jan. 1807.

204. Bodl MS Fairfax 35, fo. 65, Catherine Fairfax/Thomas Fairfax, 15 Dec. 1711; GH MS 3041/4, fo. 11, Mary Bowrey/Thomas Bowrey [3 Feb. 1697], is written to her 'der tomas' from 'you loven wif till death'.

205. Cambridge University Library, Add. MS 7621/100, fo. 105, Samuel Smith/William Smith, 13 Feb. 1768; fo. 106, Samuel Smith/William Smith, 7 Oct. 1769.

CHAPTER 2

1. Bodl MS Eng. lett. e. 92, Letter book of Thomas Edwards 1727–35, fo. iiii, Thomas Edwards/Mr Clarke, n.d. (My italics in notes 1 and 2).

2. Royal Mail Archive (RMA) Post 40/1, fo. 216, W. H. Miles/Anthony Todd, 6 July 1792.

3. RMA POST 1/1–16, Treasury Letter Books Relating to the Post Office, 1686–1793; Alan Marshall, *Intelligence and Espionage in the Reign of Charles II 1660–85* (Cambridge, 1994) 78–96; G. E. Aylmer, *The Crown's Servants* (Oxford, 2002) 38. The terms 'post' and 'mail' are used interchangeably, as in the eighteenth century. 'Mail' often refers to a service that arrived and departed at a specific time; 'Post' is a noun and adjective describing services, towns, routes, and offices.

4. Kenneth Ellis, *The Post Office in the Eighteenth Century*, (1958); Martin Daunton, *Royal Mail* (1985); Rowland Hill, *Post Office Reform* (1837). For example, Robert G. Albion, 'The Communication revolution', *American Historical Review*, 37 (1932), 718–20 (718) omits the Post Office. For an earlier period see Mark Brayshay et al. (eds.), 'Knowledge, nationhood, and governance', *Journal of Historical Geography*, 24 (1998), 265–88.

5. H. A. Innis, *Empire and Communications* (Toronto, 1950), *The Bias of Communication* (Toronto, 1951); Melody Salter and L. Heyer (eds.), *Culture, Communication, and Dependency* (Norwood, NJ, 1981); Richard Kielbowicz, *The Press, Post Office, and Public Information, 1700–1860* (New York, 1989), 5–6; Wolfgang Behringer, 'Communications revolutions', *German History*, 24 (2006), 333–74. I thank Uriel Heyd for discussions.

6. [Richard Verstegan], *The Post of the World* (1576); V. Wheeler-Holohan, *The History of the King's Messengers* (1935); Philip Beale, *History of the Post in England from the Romans to the Stuarts* (Aldershot, 1998), 12; J. W. Brooks, *To and Fro* (Maidenhead, 1981), 4. In France there were royal posts by 1464. The Von Taxis family ran continental posts.

7. J. Crofts, *Packhorse, Waggon, and Post* (1967), 1–21; BL Add. MS 27418, fo. 727, Calverley Papers.

8. *The Post Office: An Historical Summary* (1911, hereafter *Historical Summary*), 5; Beale, *History of the Post in England*, 113, 118.

9. RMA POST 71/35 and BL 8242. k. 12, House of Commons, *Report from the Secret Committee . . . On the Post Office: Together with the Appendix* (1844, hereafter *Secret Report*), 4; *Historical Summary*, 5; Howard Robinson, *The British Post Office: A History* (Princeton, NJ, 1948), 12.

10. BL Harleian MSS 5954, Collection of Tracts relating to ye Generall and Penney Post Office, fo. 8, An Abstract of the Case of the First Undertakers for Reducing Letters to Half the Former Rate, Dec. 1642; fo. 21, Complaint to Parliament, Aug. 1642; RMA POST 94/12, Roger Whitley Notebooks, fos. 111, 19 Apr. 1673; fo. 411, 21 Apr. 1674; *Historical Summary*, 6–7.

11. RMA POST 1 FOW, Kenneth Fowler, 'The demand for and provision of postal services during the seventeenth century', 1982, unpublished typescript, 18−23.

12. Alastair Bellany, *The Politics of Court Scandal in Early Modern England* (Cambridge, 2002), 86−90, 121−34; Joad Raymond, *The Invention of the Newspaper* (Oxford, 1996), 5−10; David Zaret, *The Origins of Democratic Culture* (Princeton, NJ, 2000), 100−32.

13. RMA, Portfolio Collection, Acts file, Proclamation, 3 July 1635; The Settlement of the Farm, Grant of Patent, June 1637; RMA POST 114/140, *A Collection of Statutes Relating to the Post Office* (1793); W. Stitt Dibden (ed.), *The Post Office 1635−1720* (Bath, 1960), 2−15. The public would pay 2d. for carriage of a single-sheet letter, the same fee charged by carriers. *Secret Report*, 5; Michael Frearson, 'The distribution and readership of London corantos' in R. Myers and M. Harris (eds.), *Serials and Their Readers 1620−1914* (Winchester, 1993), 1−25.

14. *Historical Summary*, 7.

15. BL Harleian MSS 5954, fo. 20, John Hill, *A Penny Post: or a Vindication of the Liberty and Birthright of Every Englishman in Carrying Merchants & other men's Letters* (1659).

16. BL Add. MS 62019, Thomas Gardiner, *A Generall Survey of the Post Office* (*c.*1682), and Foster W. Bond, (ed.), *A General Survey of the Post Office, 1677−82* (1958), 2; Dibden (ed.), *The Post Office 1635−1720*, 2.

17. James Hyde, *The Post in Grant and Farm* (1894), 238; F. M. G. Evans (Mrs C. Higham), *The Principal Secretary of State* (Manchester, 1923), 108−21; BL MS 4166, Thurloe Papers, fo. 94; BL Add. 32471, fo. 1. A Breife Declaration of Moneys; C. H. Firth, 'Thurloe and the Post Office', *English Historical Review* 13 (1898), 527−33.

18. RMA, Portfolio Collection, Acts File, Extracts from *CSPD*, 1657, vol. clv, 9 June 1657; 'An Act for the settling of the postage of England', *Post Office Magazine*, June 1975.

19. RMA POST 1 FOW, 59.

20. Gardiner, *A Generall Survey of the Post Office*, 2; *The Book of Postal Dates 1635−1985* (n.d.), 2; *Historical Summary*, 134.

21. Evans, *The Principal Secretary of State*, 283−4. Charles I's plans to annex the Post Office to the Secretary's office in the late 1630s were thwarted by Civil War.

22. *ODNB*/29571; B. Henning, *The House of Commons 1660−90*, iii (1983), 736−40; Bodl MS Eng. lett. c. 5, d. 37; MS Firth b. 1, 2; Queens College, Oxford, Benefactor's Book; State Paper Office, *Thirtieth Annual Report* (1869), 244−52. Williamson's papers make up the bulk of *State Papers Domestic* for Charles II's reign. See TNA (The National Archives) SP/87, his notebook, 8 Sept.−17 Nov. 1663; SP29/366, fos. 1−260, notebook, 1674−9; SP 29/319A, fos. 2, 157, 183, 188, 190, 192; Peter Fraser, *The Intelligence of the*

Secretaries of State and their Monopoly of Licensed News 1660–88 (Cambridge, 1956).

23. BL MS Rawl A. 477, fos. 12v, 13r.

24. *Secret Report*; RMA POST 94/15, fo. 587, Roger Whitley Letter Book, Sept. 1673–Feb. 1675; 9 Anne c. 10; 35 George III c. 612; BL Add. MS 25125, fo. 31, Henry Coventry/Lord Arlington, 18 Sept. 1677; Evans, *The Principal Secretary of State*, 284. Coventry wrote: 'a Secretary of State may demand an account of any letters that come to the post house.'

25. BL Add. MS 32499, John Wallis Letter Book; D. E. Smith, 'John Wallis as cryptographer', *Bulletin of the American Mathematical Society*, 2nd series, xxiv (Nov. 1917), 82–96; Bodl MS Smith 31, fos. 38–50; C. Scribe, 'The autobiography of John Wallis', *Notes and Records of the Royal Society of London*, 25:1 (1970), 17–66.

26. *ODNB*/7833; Evans, *The Principal Secretary of State*, 15; BL Add. MS 25125, fo. 36v; BL MS Rawl A. 477, 10–14; TNA SP 29/209, fo. 118. Dorislaus was son of the Rump Parliament's Ambassador to Holland 1653–81.

27. H. W. Dickinson, *Sir Samuel Morland* (Cambridge, 1970); Foster W. Bond, 'Samuel Morland and the secret opening of letters', *Postal History Society Bulletin*, 79 (1955), 26–8; BL Add. MS 61689, fo. 51; Add. MS 61690, fo. 104; *ODNB*/19282.

28. Sonia Anderson (ed.), Historical Manuscripts Commission 71, *Report on the Manuscripts of . . . Allan George Finch*, v (2004), Introduction. This secret room was destroyed by the Great Fire, but its work was carried on in other places. Evans, *The Principal Secretary of State*, 111–16.

29. *Secret Report*. Secret operations were variously called 'the Private Foreign Office', 'the Foreign Secretary's Office', and 'the Secret Office'.

30. Dickinson, *Sir Samuel Morland*, 95; HMC Downshire I, 594–5, 609–10. I thank Sonia Anderson for advice.

31. BL MS Rawl A. 477, fos. 10–14; E. R. Turner, 'The secrecy of the post', *English Historical Review*, 33 (1918) 320–7.

32. Janet Todd, 'Fatal fluency', *Journal of Eighteenth Century Fiction—Special Edition: Reconsidering the Rise of the Novel*, 12(2–3) (2000), 417–34 (426).

33. Dickinson, *Sir Samuel Morland*, 96; Fraser, *The Intelligence of the Secretaries of State*, 25; Mark Thomas, *The Secretaries* (Oxford, 1932), 155.

34. Alan Marshall, 'Sir Joseph Williamson and the conduct of administration in Restoration England', *Bulletin of the Institute of Historical Research*, 69 (1996), 18–41; TNA SP 29/87, fo. 10r. Williamson's method was 'to read all my letters of all heads my selfe in my owne chambre and marke wt for ye print and what for ye mss'.

35. TNA SP 29/319A, fos. 58, 188–9; SP 29/87, fo. 68v. Williamson's journals list informers, letters received, and the speed of mail from abroad. SP 29/87, fos. 2–3, 41–8, 70, 72, 74; SP 29/271, fos. 228; SP 29/319A, fos. 22, 28; Fraser, *The Intelligence of the Secretaries of State*, 41, 43–5.

36. Thomas O' Malley, 'Religion and the newspaper press 1660–85' in M. Harris and A. Lee (eds.), *The Press in English Society* (Rutherford, NJ, 1986), P. M. Handover, *A History of the London Gazette* (1965), 14–17; Hazel Garcia, 'Letters tell the news (not "fit to print"?) about the Kentucky frontier', *Journalism History*, 7 (1980), 49–53, 67.

37. RMA POST 1 UNK, 'In the days of the Post Office man', typescript (*c*.1980); BL Add. MS 38863, 'Establishment of the Duke of York's Household' (1682). For Hickes's correspondence with Williamson see *CSPD, 1660–9*.

38. There were 23 postmasters in 1674. TNA SP29/319A, fos. 189, 190; W. D. Christie (ed.), *Letters Addressed from London to Sir Joseph Williamson*, Camden Society, new series 9 (1874), Appendix: Report of H. Ball, 'The State . . . of Your Honour's Paper Office, 24 Oct., 1674', 161–5; Fraser, *The Intelligence of the Secretaries of State*, 30–1, Appendix II, 140.

39. Christie (ed.), *Letters Addressed from London to Sir Joseph Williamson*, 165. Newsletters were written under Williamson's direction by Robert Francis, Henry Ball, and Robert Yard. In 1667 Hickes sent 30–40 newsletters per week. By 1676 he sent 100 per week. Jeremy Greenwood, *Newspapers and the Post Office 1635–1834*, special series publication no. 26, Postal History Society (1971), n.p.; Marshall, 'Sir Joseph Williamson and the conduct of administration', 45.

40. *CSPD* (1666–7), 570, quoted in Fraser, *The Intelligence of the Secretaries of State*, 31.

41. RMA, Portfolio Collection, Acts File; BL Harleian MSS 5954, fos. 27–8, 35; Dibden (ed.), *The Post Office 1635–1720*, 25–33.

42. Gardiner, *A Generall Survey of the Post Office*, 26.

43. Ibid., 3; RMA POST 1 UNK.

44. RMA POST 1 UNK. Letter carriers at first lived in at Lombard Street; then moved to lodgings.

45. Ibid.

46. Dibden (ed.), *The Post Office 1635–1720*, 26, 28.

47. Gardiner, *A Generall Survey of the Post Office*, 19–20, 22.

48. Dibden (ed.), *The Post Office 1635–1720*, 27; Gardiner, *A Generall Survey of the Post Office*, 20–7. Comptroller Thomas Gardiner, noted: 'The wholl produce of each Mayle is sum'd up, being reduced to 18 severall heads or charges' (20) including overcharged letters, dead letters, merchants letters, King's expresses, franked letters, etc.

49. Gardiner, *A Generall Survey of the Post Office*, 33.

50. Ibid., 16; RMA POST 1/6, fos. 57–61. In 1716, it was noted, 'we find by every days Experience that it occasions the people to endeavor to find out other conveyances for their letters'. 1/6, fos. 138–40 cites carriers, drivers of stage coaches, boat owners, and watermen taking letters illegally.

51. RMA POST Post 94/12, Roger Whitley's Notebooks, Letters to Mr Bellamy and Captain Lullman, 8 Mar., 13 Mar. 1673.

52. The Treasury Board admitted that postal employees 'lie under very great temptation of being prevailed upon to do things very prejudicial to the revenue...Though divers of them have been turned out for the same, yet it is no terror to their successors.' RMA POST 1/1, fo. 51; James Sutherland, *The Restoration Newspaper and Its Development* (Cambridge, 1986), 116.

53. RMA POST 94/17, Whitley Letter Book, fo. 43, 7 Mar. 1675; fo. 69, 30 Mar. 1675; Greenwood, *Newspapers and the Post Office 1635–1834*; BL Add. MS 62019, fo. 6. See also postmasters' letters from Malden, Margate, and Dorchester.

54. Greenwood, *Newspapers and the Post Office 1635–1834*; RMA, Portfolio Collection, Franking File.

55. RMA, Portfolio Collection, Clerks of the Road and Franking files; RMA Paper no. 16—Franks; RMA Post 1/2, fo. 207; 1/9, fos. 168–71, 239; 1/10, fos. 30, 34, 37; Francis Freeling, letter, June 1820; Post Office Correspondence, letter to Mr Haldane, 23 Nov. 1966; Letter to Dr C. B. Henry, 4 July 1973.

56. George Brumell, *A Short Account of the Franking System in the Post Office* (Bournemouth, 1936), 13; Robinson, *The British Post Office*, 114.

57. Mark Knights, *Politics and Opinion in Crisis, 1678–81* (Cambridge, 1994).

58. *True News or Mercurius Anglicus*, 14–17 Mar. 1680; *Mercurius Civicus*, 22, 24 Mar. 1680; BL MS Harleian 5954, no. 13, *The Case of William Dockwra, Mercht* [1689]; Frank Staff, *The Penny Post 1680–1918* (1964), 37–8.

59. F. Bagust, *Some Notes on the Small Post Offices of London in the Seventeenth and Eighteenth Centuries* (1937); T. Delaune, *The Present State of London* (1681), 353; BL Harleian MSS 5954, no. 4, *The Practical Method of the Penny Post* (1681); no. 1, *A Penny Well Bestowed* (Apr. 1680).

60. T. Todd, *William Dockwra and the Rest of the Undertakers* (Edinburgh, 1952), 31, 99–109.

61. Alan Mc Kenzie (ed.), *Sent as a Gift* (Athens, GA, 1993), 6; Staff, *Penny Post 1680–1918*, 56; Robinson, *The British Post Office*, 85–6.

62. *CSPD*, 1683–4, 52; *Politics and Opinion in Crisis, 1678–81*, 173, Richard Ashcraft, *Revolutionary Politics and Locke's Two Treatises of Government* (Princeton, 1986), 172–3; Todd, *William Dockwra and the Rest of the Undertakers*, 35–6.

63. RMA POST 1/1, fos. 82–3; Todd, *William Dockwra and the Rest of the Undertakers*, 45; BL MS Harl 5954, fo. 45; *London Gazette*, 23–7 Nov. 1682.

64. Todd, *William Dockwra and the Rest of the Undertakers*, quotation after title page; BL Harleian MSS 5954, fo. 20.

65. Robinson, *The British Post Office*, 80–1, 109; *Report of Committee on Palmer's Agreement* (1797), 151. Receipts were £90,000 in 1688, £100,000 in 1694, £116,000 in 1698, and almost £150,000 in 1700.

66. Robinson, *The British Post Office*, 85. By 1702 numbers were respectively 886,583 and 86,719 rising to 951,090 and 95,694 in 1703. Revenue grew from £3,623 in 1689 to £4,437 in 1704.

67. Guildhall (GH) MS 24176, Bundle 1, fo. 28, Letter to Captain Thomas Bowrey [1707?]; Edward Chamberlayne, *Angliae Notitia* (1690), 344.

68. Delaune, *Present State of London*, 341.

69. J. Taylor, *Carrier's Cosmographie* (1637); RMA, Road Book Collection; Robinson, *The British Post Office*, 58–63. In the 1660s, the average speed on the Plymouth Road was 3–4 mph; Gloucester and Yarmouth roads 3.5 mph; Bristol, Chester, and York, 4 mph. Four days were needed for sending and receiving a reply from London to Bristol; 5 days were needed for a reply from Manchester, just over 5 from Plymouth, and just under 5 from Chester.

70. RMA, Portfolio Collection, Acts File, 9 Queen Anne Chap. 10, 28 Sept. 1711.

71. RMA POST 1/3 fos. 79, 87, 97 reveal need for cross posts.

72. Robinson, *The British Post Office*, 96–8. A single sheet cost 6d. to Edinburgh, and Dublin, 10d. to France and Spanish Netherlands, 1s. 6d. to Spain and Portugal, 1s. 3d. to Italy or Turkey.

73. Ellis, *The Post Office in the Eighteenth Century*, viii.

74. For example, RMA POST 1/9, fo. 95; Duncan Bell, 'Dissolving distance', *Journal of Modern History*, 77 (2005), 523–62.

75. Bodl MS North c. 37, fos. 91–3, Alice Brownlow North/Lord Guildford [1714].

76. Bold MS North c. 37, fo. 96, Letter to Alice Brownlow North, Jan. [1715].

77. RMA POST 1/9.

78. Ellis, *The Post Office in the Eighteenth Century*, 10–19. Ten out of twenty-six had no ministerial experience. For lists of Postmasters General and other officials see RMA Portfolio Collection; Alan Robertson, *Great Britain Post Roads, Post Towns, and Postal Rates 1635–1839* (1974), 61–2; *Historical Summary*, 134–9.

79. Sir Thomas Frankland Papers, 1694–7 and letters of Sir John Evelyn 1708–15; BL Add. MS 78462, fo. 62, Mary Evelyn/Sir John Evelyn, 1 Sept. 1708; BL Add. MS 61601, correspondence of Postmasters General, 1706–10.

80. BL Add. MS 78477, fos. 5–6, Sir John Evelyn/Anne Evelyn, 2 Oct. 1708.

81. BL Add. MS 78477, fos. 25–6, Anne Evelyn/Sir John Evelyn, Sept. 1709.

82. BL Add. MS 78477, fos. 29–30, Sir John Evelyn/Anne Evelyn, 29 Sept. 1709; fo. 33, Sir John Evelyn/Anne Evelyn, 27 Oct. 1709.

83. Bodl MS DD Dashwood c. 2/1–47, Letters, 1766–81; c. 2/3, fos. 1a, 8b, accounts and computations concerning the postal service including expences of the Post Cart; b. 11, c. 5, Sir Francis Dashwood papers, 1708–81; Betty Kemp, 'Some letters of Sir Francis Dashwood, Baron Le Despencer, as Joint Post-master General 1766–81', *Bulletin of the John Rylands Library*, 37 (Sept. 1954), 204–48.

84. TNA PRO 30/8, Chatham Papers, 1st series, fos. 1–6, 7–10, William Pitt, 1st Earl of Chatham/Anthony Todd, 1761, especially fo. 2r. Letters were 'dipp'd in Vinegar and afterwards well smoaked with sulphur'.

85. RMA POST 40/1/264–9, 302–3, 'Specimens' of Mr Harbridge's and Mr Higham's writing 'found in Mr Feelings to Ld Walsingham', 16 Nov. 1792, 27 Dec. 1792; RMA POST 40/1/264, Sir Francis Freeling/Lord Walsingham, 16 Nov. 1792.

86. Bodl MS Don. c. 111, fo. 97, Richard Tucker/John Tucker, 30 May 1775.

87. W. H. Thomson, *History of Manchester to 1852* (Altrincham, 1967), 132.

88. 9 Anne c. 10, 1711, 63–4.

89. Ellis, *The Post Office in the Eighteenth Century*, 32–3.

90. Robinson, *The British Post Office*, 109–10; Ellis, *The Post Office in the Eighteenth Century*, 31–2; RMA POST 1/10/140–1, 3 June 1778; 1/10/136, 17 Mar. 1776.

91. TNA PRO 30/8/233, part I, fos. 1–2, Yearly net produce of Post Office revenue 1724–91; Robinson, *The British Post Office*, 109, 145–6. Ellis cites net revenue of pay letters, less cost of management rose from £59,637 in 1710 to £85,526 in 1711–12 after rate increases, then to £110,972 in 1721, followed by decline and fluctuations around £100,000 in the 1720s. For early calculations of gross and net income see RMA POST 1/6, fos. 61, 106–7, 129, 240.

92. *Report of Committee on Palmer's Agreement*, 60–1, 80, Appendix, 7; Ellis, *The Post Office in the Eighteenth Century*, 43–5; Robinson, *The British Post Office*, 109. For alternate figures see RMA POST 1/16, fo. 7, 1792–3.

93. *Report of Committee on Palmer's Agreement*, 60–1, 80; Robinson, *The British Post Office*, 109.

94. For Allen see RMA POST 68/1, Ralph Allen's Instruction Book, 1729–40; 1/9, fos.17–29, 122–40; 14/1, Ralph Allen, Copybook relating to Management of the Bye and Cross Road, 1757; Adrian Hopkins (ed.), *Ralph Allen's Own Narrative 1720–61* (1960).

95. J. Goodman, *The Experienced Secretary*, 4th edn (1707) and G. F. *The Secretary's Guide* (1720) included lists of post roads and stages.

96. RMA POST 21, Maps (1757–c.1990), vol. 1, includes postal circulation maps with postal routes and post towns. See also maps in Robertson, *Great Britain Post Roads*.

97. Hopkins (ed.), *Ralph Allen's Own Narrative 1720–61*, 12.

98. RMA POST 1/6, fos. 7–9, 138–40, 149–58.

99. Bath Central Library MSS AL 2355, a–z, letters from Ralph Allen and others; MS AL 169, 170, 224, Ralph Allen MSS accounts, receipts, inventory, letters, 1712–46; MS AL 1500–2, Letters from Ralph Allen to postmasters.

100. RMA POST 1/6, fo. 7.

101. RMA POST 68/1, fo. 6.

102. BCL MS AL 1500, Ralph Allen/Mr Lumley, 9 Jan. 1734; MS AL 1502, Ralph Allen/Mr Carter, 3 Sept. 1753.

103. Bodl MS Don. c. 110, fo. 134, John Tucker/Richard Tucker, 20 Dec. [1748].
104. RMA POST 1/9, fos. 17–29.
105. NTA PRO 30/8/232, fo. 48, Appendix 2.
106. For Yorkshire, see the Grimston, Metcalfe, Lees of Pinchinthrope, and Pease collections.
107. For Derbyshire, see Ch. 3.
108. RMA POST 14/1, fo. 1, A Memorial from Ralph Allen Esqr, 14 Sept. 1757; 1/9, fos. 127–8. By 1764 Allen claimed bye- and cross-letter revenue had improved £15–20,000 annually. For Bath's postal services see Richard Crutwell's, *New Bath Guides*.
109. NTA PRO 30/8 Chatham Papers, 1st series, fo. 19, Abstract of Mr Allens account for bye and cross posts, 1761.
110. Todd, *William Dockwra and the Rest of the Undertakers*, 53, quoted from M. Cesar de Saussure's letter, 29 Oct. 1726.
111. William Maitland, *Survey of London* (1756); Robertson, *Great Britain Post Roads*, 31–8; John Cary, *New Itinerary: An Accurate Delineation of the Great Roads* (1802); RMA POST 53/11, *A list of Post towns and principal places with the full postage of a single letter in Great Britain and Ireland . . . 1800*.
112. Jane Harrison, *Until Next Year* (Quebec, 1997); William Smith, *History of the Post Office in British North America 1639–1870* (1920); A. R. B. Haldane, *Three Centuries of Scottish Posts* (Edinburgh, 1971), 1–49; M. Reynolds, *A History of the Irish Post Office* (Dublin,1983).
113. RMA POST 1/8, fos. 217–21.
114. Anne Borsay, *Medicine and Charity in Georgian Bath* (Aldershot, 1999), 272–5.
115. BL Add. MS 61601, Mr Allen/Sir John Evelyn, 19 Mar. [1755].
116. North Yorkshire County Record Office (NY) Microfilms (Mic) 1976, John Fawdington/Jenny Jefferson, 30 Oct. 1787.
117. Geoffrey Wright, *Turnpike Roads* (Haverfordwest, 1992), 9, 24. One hundred and fifty-two trusts were added by 1800.
118. Robinson, *The British Post Office*, 130.
119. Frederick Wilkinson, *Royal Mail Coaches* (Stroud, 2007); RMA POST 10, Conveyance of Mails by Road, Inland Services 1786–90; 10/200, *Report of Committee on Palmer's Agreement*.
120. *Report of Committee on Palmer's Agreement*, Appendix, 33.
121. Robertson, *Great Britain Post Roads*, 13.
122. Robinson, *The British Post Office*, 139.
123. Alvin Harlow, *Old Post Bags* (NY, 1928), 162.
124. Bodl MS Don. c. 193, fos. 110–11, Robert Johnson/George Johnson, n.d; A. Emonet and Peter Hobbs, 'Ralph Allen's New Branch from Bath to Salisbury 1753', *Postal History*, 292 (1999), 117–19; *The Strangers Assistant and Guide to Bath* (Bath, 1773), 90–7.
125. RMA POST 10/200, Appendix III (A–C), 7–18.
126. Ellis, *The Post Office in the Eighteenth Century*, 120.

127. Ellis, *The Post Office in the Eighteenth Century*, 123. My italics.

128. Ibid., 113.

129. Peace and higher postage brought growth from 1765–74. Gross revenue rose from £262,000 to £313,000, though net remained stationary at a peak of £164,000. From 1775 to 1783, gross revenue grew from £322,000 to £398,000, while net decreased from £173,000 to £159,000. Reforms and postage hikes brought a surge from 1784 to 1793. Gross receipts rose from £420,000 to £627,000; net leaped from £196,000 to £391,000. Net produce had doubled and gross revenue increased 50%. Howard Robinson credits Palmer with £240,000 of the growth when postage increases are factored in. Alternate figures show net revenue at £97,834 in 1763, and £173,188 in 1775. It fell during the American war in 1775 to £117,325, then rose rapidly again with peace and higher rates to new levels of £331,180 in 1790, £409,497 in 1795. *Report of Committee on Palmer's Agreement*, Appendix 7, 61; Robinson, *The British Post Office*, 146; Ellis, *The Post Office in the Eighteenth Century*, 45; NTA 30/8/232, part 3, fos. 77–8, for gross and net produce 1763–83.

130. Harlow, *Old Post Bags*, 162.

131. Robertson, *Great Britain Post Roads*, 13; Robinson, *The British Post Office*, 222–3.

132. Kemp, 'Some letters of Sir Francis Dashwood', 204–48 (205).

133. BL Add. MS 71573, fo. 98, Oliver Le Neve/Peter Le Neve, 9 Sept. 1695.

134. H. T. Dickinson (ed.), *The Correspondence of Sir James Clavering*, Surtees Society, clxxviii (1967), 220.

135. Bl Add. MS 27518, fo. 2, Frances Cottrell/Sir William Trumbull, 27 Sept.

136. HCA DFP/543, Mary Robinson/Robert Robinson, 6 June 1762.

137. BL Add. MS 78471, Letter to Sir John Evelyn, 27 July 1727.

138. Bodl MS Don. c. 110, fo. 64, John Tucker/Richard Tucker, n.d.

139. Bodl MS Don. c. 105, fo. 103, John Tucker/Richard Tucker, 8 May [1742].

140. Verney Letters, BL microfilm (VL) 48/627 (reel/item), Cary Stewkeley/Ralph Verney, 29 Dec. 1695.

141. Bodl MS Don. b. 18, fo. 39, Richard Tucker/John Tucker, 13 Apr. 1728.

142. Beinecke Library, Yale University (BLY) MS OSB 32/6, Rebekah Bateman/Thomas Bateman, 7 July 1791.

143. BLY MS OSB 32/6, Rebekah Bateman/Thomas Bateman, 22 May 1788.

144. BL Add. MS 78477, fos. 1–2, Anne Evelyn/Sir John Evelyn, 22 Sept. 1708.

145. Library of the Religious Society of Friends in Britain (LSF), Temp MSS 127/3/1, Ruth and George Follows/Samuel Follows, 3 Feb. 1769. Dates in the Quaker style are converted to match the style of other letter-writers.

146. LSF Temp MS 127/3/13, Ruth Follows/Samuel Follows, 11 Nov. 1775.

147. NY MIC 1976, John Fawdington/Jenny Jefferson, n.d.

148. NY MIC 1976, John Fawdington/Jenny Jefferson, 12 July 1786.

149. GH MS 24178, fo. 118, John Starke/Thomas Bowrey, 12 Sept. 1708.

150. GH MS 3041/4, fo. 11, Mary Bowrey/Thomas Bowrey [1697?].

151. GH MS 3041/4, fo. 63, Francis Gardiner/Thomas Bowrey, 2 Aug. 1705.

152. Bodl MS 1011, fo. 76, Thomas Edwards/Samuel Richardson, 2 Dec. 1748.

153. David Hey, *Packmen, Carriers, and Packhorse Roads* (Leicester, 1980), 100–1.

154. Derbyshire Record Office (DRO) D239/M/E5025, George Fitzherbert to his wife, n.d.

155. Bodl MS Don. b. 18, fo. 62, Richard Tucker/John Tucker, 4 Oct. 1728.

156. East Riding of Yorkshire Archives and Local Studies Service, MS 42/19/4, Fra: Legard/Thomas Grimston, 18 Jan. 1769.

157. Robinson, *The British Post Office*, 130.

158. GH MS 3014/4, fo. 72, Thomas Bowrey/Captain Staples, 22 May 1706.

159. Bodl MS Don. b. 18, fos. 102–33, Edward Tucker/John Tucker, 20 Oct. 1729.

160. Bodl MS Don. c. 193, fos. 27–8, Barbara Johnson/George Johnson, 26 May [1779].

161. Bodl MS Don. c. 192, fos. 84–5, Michael Wodhull/Barbara Johnson, 9 May 1803.

162. RMA POST 107; VL 50–181, Nancy Nicholas/John Verney, 14 Oct. 1697; 50–182, Thomas Verney/John Verney, 16 Oct. 1697; 53–268, John Verney/John Deere, 10 Oct. 1706; 50–630, Thomas Verney/John Verney, 28 Apr. 1699; Bodl MS Don. c. 110, fo. 121, John Tucker/Richard Tucker, 3 Dec. 1748; R. S. Fitton and A. P. Wadsworth, *The Strutts and the Arkwrights 1758–1830* (Manchester, 1958), 331.

163. Bodl MS Don. c. 193, fos. 13–14, Barbara Johnson/George Johnson, 2 Mar. [1776?].

164. NY MIC 1976, John Fawdington/Jenny Fawdington, 30 Oct. 1787.

165. GH MS 3041/4, fo. 68, Martha Davis/Thomas Bowrey, n.d; MS 3041/4, Letter to Thomas Bowrey, fo. 79, 30 Dec. 1760.

166. Guildhall (GH) MS 25597, Pen Pendarves/James Lucas, 30 Oct. 1727; Gillian Clark and Jim Smart, 'Usage of the postal system in mid-eighteenth-century Berkshire', *The Local Historian*, 29:3 (Aug. 1999), 152–66 (156–7).

167. Tim Hitchcock, 'All besides the rail, rang'd beggars lie' in C. Brant and S. Whyman (eds.), *Walking the Streets of Eighteenth-Century London* (Oxford, 2007), 74–89.

168. GH MS 18982, no. 3, Abraham Robinson/'Gentlemen', 1750.

169. Thomas Sokoll (ed.), *Essex Pauper Letters* (Oxford, 2001), Anne Clark/Rev'd Dr Chambers, 9 Oct. 1768, 747; LSF Temp MS 127/3/13, Ruth Follows/Samuel Follows, 11 Nov. 1775.

170. LSF Temp MS 127/2/2, Ruth Follows/George Follows, 21 Mar. 1748.

171. LSF Temp MS 127/4, Ruth and George Follows/Joseph Follows, 12 June 1787.

172. BL Add. MS 78432. Letters of Mary Evelyn at Wotton were left at Mr Gabriel Collin's shop, the Post House next to the Middle Temple gate in Fleet

Street. Bodl MS Don. b. 18, fo. 29, Richard Tucker/John Tucker, 26 Dec. 1724 is addressed: For Mr John Tucker/On board ye Caesar/Capt Mabbot Commdr/to be left at ye Post Office/Deal/Kent/ . . . via London/If sailed return this letter/to Richard Tucker in Weymouth/Dorsett.

173. Joan Wilkinson (ed.), *The Letters of Thomas Langton, Flax Merchant of Kirkham 1771–88*, no. 38 in the 3rd series of *Remains, Historical and Literary, connected with . . . Lancaster and Chester* (Manchester: Chetham Society 1994), 155, Thomas Langton/William Langton, 24 July 1775.

174. Bodl MS Don. b. 18, fo. 130, Edward Tucker/John Tucker, 14 Feb. 1733.

175. Clark and Smart, 'Usage of the postal system in mid-eighteenth-century Berkshire', 159.

176. BLY MS OSB 32/39, fo. 39, Mary Wilson/Rebekah Bateman, 11 Feb. 1793.

177. Robertson, *Great Britain Post Roads*, 57–8.

178. VL 51/47, Nancy Nicholas/John Verney, 31 Aug. 1699; Huntington Library (HL) Ellesmere MS EL 8639, Bridgewater Accounts, week ending 29 Aug. 1690.

179. David Vincent, *Literacy and Popular Culture* (Cambridge, 1989), 35.

180. LSF Temp MS 127/4/9, Samuel Fellows/Joseph Follows, 5 Apr. 1775.

181. Bodl MS Don. c. 192, fo. 63, Harriet Dalyrmple/Barbara Johnson, n.d.

182. Bodl MS Don. c. 191, fos. 9–10, Robert Johnson/Barbara Johnson, 16 Jan. 1777.

183. RMA POST 1/8, fos. 202–7.

184. BLY MS OSB 32/13,Thomas Bateman/Thomas Bateman Jr, 18 Aug. 1809.

185. BLY MS OSB 32/23, Arthur Clegg/Elizabeth and Rebekah Clegg, 1778.

186. CRO WDY 75, fo. 4, Joseph Morton/Thomas Morton, 4 Jan. 1770. The bridle-maker, John Fawdington wrote similarly: NY MIC 1976, John Fawdington/Jenny Fawdington, 31 Oct. 1787.

187. CRO WDY 75, fo. 14, Joseph Morton/Thomas Morton, 8 Feb. 1779.

188. GH MS 19233, no. 5, Merey Williams for Catherine Jones/Peter Popll, 17 Oct. 1758.

189. Robinson, *The British Post Office*, 127–30; David Allam, *The Social and Economic Importance of Postal Reform in 1840* (1976), 3; *Report of Committee on Palmer's Agreement*, Appendix, 3–6.

190. Peter Miles, 'Humphry Clinker', *British Journal for Eighteenth-Century Studies*, 23 (2000), 167–82 (177–8).

191. VL 47–66, Ralph Verney/John Verney, 9 Sept. 1683; 48–513, Ralph Verney/John Verney, 15 Sept. 1695; 39–51, Ralph Verney/John Verney, Mar. 19 1685; HL Stowe MS STT 324, William Chapman/Sir Richard Temple, 13 July 1684.

192. BL Add. MS 78477, fo. 99, Anne Evelyn/Sir John Evelyn, 11 Sept. 1712.

193. GH MS 25597, Henry Godolphin/James Lucas, 19 Sept. 1725.

194. Bodl MS 1011, fo. 139, Thomas Edwards/Joseph Paice, 4 May 1749.

195. VL 47–66, Ralph Verney/John Verney, 19 Sept. 1683; 48–513, Ralph Verney/John Verney, 15 Sept. 1695; HL Stowe MS STT 324, William

Chapman/Sir Richard Temple, 13 July 1684; 39–51, Ralph Verney/John Verney, 19 Mar. 1685.

196. Michael Frearson, 'Communication and the continuity of Dissent' in Margaret Spufford (ed.), *The World of Rural Dissenters 1520–1725* (Cambridge, 1995), 283.

197. Bodl North MS D4. fo. 16, Francis Wise/Francis North, 9 Feb. 1728.

198. Bodl MS Don. c. 193, fo. 21, Barbara Johnson/George Johnson, 13 Feb. 1777.

199. A. M. Broadley and Lewis Melville (eds.), *The Beautiful Lady Craven*, i (1914), 47.

200. Bodl North MS c. 37, fo. 88, Alice Brownlow North, Francis North, 2nd Baron, 7 Dec. [1714].

201. CRO WDY 75, fo. 17, Joseph Morton Thomas Morton, 15 Nov. 1779.

202. CRO WDY 75, fo. 1, Joseph Morton/Joseph Morton Sr, 18 Feb. 1765.

203. LSF Temp MS 127/3/24, Ruth Follows/Samuel Follows, 19 Jan. 1779.

204. HCA DFP/33, Joseph Pease/Isaac Clifford, draft, 14 Feb. 1741; DFP/188, Robert Pease/Joseph Pease, 13 Dec. 1731.

205. Bodl MS Don. b. 23, fo. 58, Richard Tucker/Edward Tucker, 25 Sept. 1758.

206. Sheffield Archives MS 60528, fo. 5, Benjamin Spencer/William Spencer, 26 Dec. 1745.

207. DRO D5303/9/6, Jedediah Strutt/Elizabeth Strutt, 2 May 1764; Fitton and Wadsworth, *The Strutts and the Arkwrights 1758–1830*, 112, 331.

208. RMA, Portfolio Collection, Circulation of Letters, Letter to Dr C. Bowdler, 4 July 1973.

209. VL 50–626, Nancy Nicholas/John Verney, 20 Apr. 1699.

210. VL 50–441, Elizabeth Adams/John Verney, 12 July 1698.

211. BCL R69/12675 B920, pamphlet, Edmund Rack, 'A Desultory Journal of Events &c at Bath', Dec. 22 1779, typescript, 11 Jan. 1780, 12.

212. Bodl MS Don. c. 191, fos. 9–10, Robert Johnson/Barbara Johnson, 16 Jan. 1777; Fitton and Wadsworth, *The Strutts and the Arkwrights 1758–1830*, 112.

213. Kielbowicz, *The Press, Post Office, and Public Information*, 5–6.

214. John Feather, *The Provincial Book Trade in Eighteenth-century England* (Cambridge, 1985), 21–3, 38, 63, 68 (map, 20); Bob Harris, *Politics and the Rise of the Press* (1996); R. B. Walker, 'The newspaper press in the reign of William III', *Historical Journal*, xvii, 4 (1974) 691–709.

215. TNA SP 35/49/38, SP 36/6/220, SP 11/236; Michael Harris, *London Newspapers in the Age of Walpole* (1987), 46; Ellis, *The Post Office in the Eighteenth Century*, 48.

216. Laurence Hanson, *Government and the Press, 1695–1763* (1936), 110.

217. Feather, *The Provincial Book Trade in Eighteenth-century England*, 47; Michael Harris, *London Newspapers in the Age of Walpole*, 151–3.

218. Bodl MS Don. b. 18, fo. 57, Richard Tucker/John Tucker, 9 Sept. 1728.

219. Bodl MS Don. c. 111, fo. 6, Richard Tucker/John Tucker, fo. 6, n.d.

220. Feather, *The Provincial Book Trade in Eighteenth-century England*, 47.

221. Wallace Eberhard, 'Press and Post Office in eighteenth-century America' in D. H. Bond and W. R. McLeod (eds.), *Newsletters to Newspapers*, (Morgantown, WV, 1976), 145–54 (146–7).

222. RMA, Portfolio Collection, Clerks of the Road File. Letter to Dr Haldane, with extracts from J. C. Hendy's MS 'Newspaper privilege of the Clerks of the Roads', 23 Nov. 1966 states: 'The postage alone of the gazettes...would have been from 4–6d., whereas the clerks of the roads supplied them at 2d. or 3d. each.' Letter NDPS/OB/POR, Miss F. Coates/Mr Dowell, 1 Mar. 1968; RMA POST 24/6; Henry Snyder, 'The circulation of newspapers in the reign of Queen Anne', *Library*, Appendix C, 230–3; RMA POST 24/4, Papers concerning the circulation and franking privileges of the Clerks of the Roads with a history of their privilege by D. Stow and newspaper cuttings, 1811–33; 4 Geo III, c. 24; 23 & 24 Geo III, c. 17; 24 Geo III, c. 37.

223. Greenwood, *Newspapers and the Post Office 1635–1834*; Allam, *The Social and Economic Importance of Postal Reform in 1840*, 3, 17.

224. RMA POST 24, Newspapers; Greenwood, *Newspapers and the Post Office 1635–1834*.

225. Greenwood, *Newspapers and the Post Office 1635–1834*; Ellis, *The Post Office in the Eighteenth Century*, 53.

226. RMA POST 114/140, *A Collection of Statutes*, 85–97 (93–4); 4 Geo III c. 24 and 9 Geo III c. 35; RMA POST 24 Newspapers; *Tenth Report of the Commissioners on Fees* (1788), 29.

227. RMA POST 1/10, fos. 28–35 (30); 24/1, Plans to increase revenue and circulation of the newspaper post, 1791–[1797], last unfoliated page.

228. Estimates of London papers sent by the Clerks are: 1764, over a million copies (of 9.5 million stamps sold annually); 1782, over 3 million; and 1790, 4.65 million. RMA POST 24/1; RMA POST 24/2, 3 Apr. 1795; RMA POST 1/12, fo. 179; 10th Report on Fees, 29; Parliamentary Papers, ii (1807), 219; Feather, *The Provincial Book Trade in Eighteenth-century England*, 37.

229. RMA POST 24/4, Statements by the Clerks of the Road; letter from D. Stow to F. Freeling, 10 Mar. 1832; RMA, Portfolio Collection, Newspaper Cuttings, May 1811–July 1833.

230. RMA POST 24/4, Statement relative to the circulation of newspapers in England and Ireland; 24/2 Correspondence between the Postmaster General and the Clerks of the Road, 3 Apr. 1795–26 Mar. 1811.

231. Greenwood, *Newspapers and the Post Office 1635–1834*, table of newspaper prices by year.

232. The office cost £3,500 per year in 1742 and £5,000 by 1760. For postal censorship see *Further Report from the Committee on Secrecy* (1742); *Secret Report*, 8, Appendix, 111–12; Ellis, *The Post Office in the Eighteenth Century*, 127–31; BL Add. MSS 24321, 45518–23, Wiles Family Papers.

233. Karl De Leeuw, 'The Black Chamber in the Dutch Republic', *Historical Journal*, 42 (1999), 133–56; Ellis, *The Post Office in the Eighteenth Century*, 60–77.

234. For example TNA SP 36/25; BL Add. MS 38202, vol. 103, fo. 78, Anthony Todd, Secretary to the Post Office, 2 Feb. 1764; BL Add. 45518, fos. 46–52; BL Add. 24321, fo. 106.

235. *Secret Report*, 8; Ellis, *The Post Office in the Eighteenth Century*, 71; David Kahn, *The Codebreakers* (1967), 169.

236. C. F. Burgess (ed.), *The Letters of John Gay* (Oxford, 1966), 94.

237. *Secret Report*, 12; Michael Harris, *London Newspapers in the Age of Walpole*, 151; *Craftsman*, no. 28, 10 Feb. 1727.

238. DRO D5303/12/5, Elizabeth Strutt/Jedediah Strutt, 23 Feb. 1774.

239. LSF Temp MS 127/4/18, Joseph Follows/Ruth and George Follows, 20 Oct. 1776.

240. TNA PRO 30/8/232, Anthony Todd/Duke of Grafton, 12 July 1768; Ellis, *The Post Office in the Eighteenth Century*, 70–1, 139.

241. *Secret Report*; William Holdsworth, *English Law*, xiv (1964), 121–3. 9 Anne c. 11, provided that no letter was to be opened except by 'an express Warrant in Writing under the Hand of One of the Principal Secretaries of State'. This passage was reproduced in all later Post Office acts.

242. *Secret Report*, 9–14. Only one warrant was discovered 1660–1711. From 1712–98, 'it was not the practice to record such Warrants'. Only 101 were located for 87 years; only 22 in 20 years including the French Revolution.

243. *Secret Report*, 3; William Holdsworth, *English Law*, x, 491; David Vincent, *The Culture of Secrecy* (Oxford, 1998), 1–2. A picture of the secret office appeared in *The Illustrated London News*, 29 June 1844. See also M. V. D Champness, 'The end of the Secret Office', *The Philatelist* (Aug. 1981) 141–3; *The London Journal and Weekly Record of Literature, Science, and Art*, 1:3 (15 Mar. 1845), 33–4.

244. RMA POST 23/7, Newspaper Cuttings file 1, *The Sun*, 15 June 1844.

245. Hanson, *Government and the Press, 1695–1763*, 110.

246. Only 9 bills are indexed in the failed legislation database constructed by Joanna Innes and Julian Hoppit. They are 3:077, 3:090; 4:045; 8:036; 19:029; 20:025; 31:067; 133:057; 137:062. I thank Hoppit for these references.

247. See RMA POST 40/1, Resident Surveyor's Reports to the Joint Postmasters General, 1791–2, for internal correspondence at the highest level of the Post Office. 14/360 Middlewich Post Office letter copybook, 1798–30, Sir Francis Freeling/Mr Chatterton, 31 Dec. 1798; BLY OSB MS 36, Freeling Correspondence.

248. RMA, Local History Collection generally. For specific examples see D. Cornelius, *Devon and Cornwall* (Reigate, 1973); A. G. W. Hall, *The Post Office at Nottingham* (Nottingham, 1947).

249. RMA POST 40/1, fo. 144, T. Ga[nn]att/Sir Francis Freeling, 25 July 1792.

250. RMA POST 40/1, fo. 193, Petition, 15 May 1792; 40/1 fos. 190–3, Mr Robert Oliphant/Anthony Todd, 27 June 1792.

251. RMA POST 40/1, fos. 203–6, Letter forwarded first to Freeling, then to Walsingham, 30 July 1792.

252. RMA POST 40/1/216–18, W. H. Miles/Anthony Todd, 6 July 1792.

253. RMA POST 40/1, fos. 216–18.

254. RMA POST 1/10, fos. 90–100 (92), *Smith v Powditch*, copy of the Opinion of King's Bench, 21 Nov. 1774.

255. Holdsworth, *English Law*, x, 491. This decision made it necessary to appoint a large number of new letter carriers.

256. RMA POST 1/10, fo. 99.

257. Holdsworth, *English Law*, x, 491.

258. RMA POST 1/10, fo. 97.

259. RMA POST 1/10, fo. 100.

260. RMA POST 40/1, 203–5, Letter to Sir Francis Freeling, 30 July 1792.

261. RMA POST 1/10, fo. 232.

262. Jurgen Habermas, *The Structural Transformation of the Public Sphere* (Cambridge, MA, 1989) and *Moral Consciousness and Interactive Communication* (1990); Craig Calhoun (ed.), *Habermas and the Public Sphere* (Cambridge, MA, 1994); Steve Pincus,'Coffee politicians does create', *Journal of Modern History*, 67 (1995) 807–34.

CHAPTER 3

1. BL Add. MS 78476, Samuel Evelyn/Sir John Evelyn, 20 Sept. 1738. Samuel Evelyn of Nottingham noted: 'The people live here upon bread made of oates in large flat cakes as big as a dish, baked not in ovens but upon stone. It is very sad stuff.'

2. Mark Billinge, 'Divided by a common language' in Alan Baker and Mark Billinge (eds.), *Geographies of England* (Cambridge, 2004), 88–111 (89, 92); Neville Kirk, 'Constructing "the North" and "northernness"' in Neville Kirk (ed.), *Northern Identities* (Aldershot, 2000), ix–xiv; Stephen Caunce, 'Northern English industrial towns', *Urban History*, 30 (2003), 338–58.

3. Dave Russell, *Looking North* (Manchester, 2004), xii, 22; Kirk (ed.), *Northern Identities*, fig. 3.1; T. C. Smout, *Nature Contested* (Edinburgh, 2000), 8; Robert Cooper, *The Literary Guide and Companion to Northern England* (Athens, OH, 1995), Frontispiece.

4. Helen Jewell, *The North-South Divide* (Manchester, 1994), 23–4; Russell, *Looking North*, 15–37.

5. Melanie Tebbutt, 'In the Midlands but not of them' in Kirk, *Northern Identities* (Aldershot, 2000), 163–94 (164, 185); Mark Billinge, 'Divided by a common language', 99; Joy Childs, *History of Derbyshire* (Chichester, 1987), 13. Jewell, *The North-South Divide*, 23–4 notes Derbyshire was originally bound in with

northern counties in regional assize circuits and participated in northern revolts.

6. Wheatcroft documents in the Derbyshire Record Office (DRO) include D5433/1, MS volume compiled by Leonard Wheatcroft, 17th–18th cent., including letters, poetry, 'crosticks', 'love lessons', and items relating to his courtship; D5433/2, MS volume compiled by his son, Titus, 'Church and School or the Young Clarks Instructor', 1722, with notes on the parish, church, and school, including a catalogue of 384 books; D5458/11/2, Copy memoranda by Titus written in 1722, 19th cent., containing a history of the parish and school etc. with a copy of an epitaph written by Titus, 26 May 1739; D2079/1, 'A history of the life and pilgrimage of Leonard Wheatcroft of Ashover (clerk for 56 years), 1627–1749' with diary entries by Titus from Jan. 1706; D5775/1–3, Commonplace books: vol. 1, 'Wheatcroft's Divine and Profitable Mediations', c.1736; vol. 2, 'Wheatcroft's Collections', c.1728, fos. 33, 35, 37 show practice writing ornamental initials; fo. 269 is 'A Letter to a friend writen in Abraviations'; fo. 329 contains signatures of other members of the family—the last folio contains samples of ornaments in pen; vol. 3, Untitled, fo. 1, c.1744, alphabet and text extolling writing; inside cover of vol. 3, Instructions how to make a quart of good ink; D6127, A poem on hunting, 17th cent. Leonard's autobiography (D2079/1) has been edited by Dorothy Riden, 'The autobiography of Leonard Wheatcroft of Ashover 1627–1706' in *A Seventeenth-Century Scarsdale Miscellany*, Derbyshire Record Society, xx (1993), 73–117. His courtship narrative has been edited by George Parfitt and Ralph Houlbrooke, *The Courtship of Leonard Wheatcroft, Derbyshire Yeoman* (Reading, 1986). Maureen Bell, 'Reading in seventeenth-century Derbyshire' in Peter Isaac and Barry McKay (eds.), *The Moving Market* (New Castle, DE, 2001), 164.

7. Samul Bagshaw, *History, Gazetteer, and Directory of Derbyshire* (Sheffield, 1846), 577.

8. DRO D2079/1. This document is unpaginated, but roughly in chronological order. It is the source of my references, but see also Riden (ed.), 'The autobiography of Leonard Wheatcroft', 11, 90, Bell, 'Reading in seventeenth-century Derbyshire', 165.

9. DRO D2079/1; Riden (ed.), 'The autobiography of Leonard Wheatcroft', 81, 83.

10. DRO D2079/1; Riden (ed.), 'The autobiography of Leonard Wheatcroft', 92, 96.

11. DRO D2079/1; Riden (ed.), 'The autobiography of Leonard Wheatcroft', 92, 96.

12. DRO D5458/11/2.

13. DRO D5433/1, fo. 1. References are to this document but see also Parfitt and Houlbrooke (eds.), *Courtship*; Cedric Brown, 'The two pilgrimages of the Laureate of Ashover, Leonard Wheatcroft' in H. Dragsta et al. (eds.),

Betraying Our Selves (Houndmills, 2000), 120–35 (133) and 'The black poet of Ashover, Leonard Wheatcroft' in Peter Beal and Grace Ioppolo (eds.), *English Manuscript Studies 1100–1700*, xi (2002), 181–202.

14. DRO D5433/1, folio before page 1; Brown, 'The black poet of Ashover, Leonard Wheatcroft', 183.

15. Jean Robertson, *The Art of Letter-writing* (1942) includes similar miscellanies, for example, Cotgrave, *Recreation for Ingenious Head-peeces, Or a Pleasant Grove for their Wits to Walk in* (1683).

16. Parfitt and Houlbrooke (eds.), *Courtship*, 14–15; Brown, 'The black poet of Ashover, Leonard Wheatcroft'; Revd Charles Kerry, 'Leonard Wheatcroft of Ashover', *Journal of the Derbyshire Archaeological and Natural History Society*, xviii (1896), 29–80; S. O. Addy, 'Ashover and the Wheatcrofts', *Derbyshire Archaeological and Natural History Society*, xxxix (1917), 109–53; Parfitt and Houlbrooke (eds.), *Courtship*, 47; BL 9903. H20, Notes on the Flitcroft, Wheatcroft, and Woodcraft Families collected by J. R. Whitcraft, typescript, n.p.

17. DRO D5433/1, fo. 62; Parfitt and Houlbrooke (eds.), *Courtship*, 72.

18. DRO D5433/1, fo. 49; Parfitt and Houlbrooke (eds.), *Courtship*, 45.

19. DRO D5433/1, fo. 50; Parfitt and Houlbrooke (eds.), *Courtship*, 45.

20. DRO D5433/1, fo. 56; Parfitt and Houlbrooke (eds.), *Courtship*, 45.

21. Parfitt and Houlbrook (eds.), *Courtship*, 32, 73; Brown, 'The black poet of Ashover, Leonard Wheatcroft', 187.

22. DRO D2079/1; Riden (ed.), 'The autobiography of Leonard Wheatcroft', 97–8. Additional titles written by the Wheatcrofts are listed in Titus's book list.

23. DRO D2079/1; Riden (ed.), 'The autobiography of Leonard Wheatcroft', 96.

24. DRO D5433/2, 3, fo.1.

25. DRO D5458/11/2, unfoliated (9th page). For accounts of another Derbyshire school see Robert Thornhill (ed.), *About a Derbyshire Village 1770–1820, Accounts* (Duffield, 1958), 29–30.

26. DRO D2079/1; Riden (ed.), 'The autobiography of Leonard Wheatcroft', 102, 115.

27. DRO D2079/1; Riden (ed.), 'The autobiography of Leonard Wheatcroft', 99.

28. DRO D2079/1; Riden (ed.), 'The autobiography of Leonard Wheatcroft', 100. They were Richard Atkins and Joseph Wright.

29. The following description of the school is from DRO MS 5433/2, fos. 50–4.

30. DRO MS 5433/2, fos. 55–69, next folio numbered 90–3, 107–10. For Titus's work see fo. 66; for 'O come ye Gallants' see fo. 64. For possible aids to letter-writing see Titus's book numbers: 19, 'A Copy Book call'd ye pens gallantry'; 20–1, 'Cocker's Copy-Books' with cross reference to 74, 'A Copy book of all the Usual Hands by James Seamer'; 28, 'Practical rules for understand ye Grammar'; 30, two spelling books with cross reference

to 132; 31, 'Ye pens Dexterity for short hand' and 87, four other titles on shorthand; 44, 'A help to discourse written'; 95, 'The young clerks tutor'; 155, 'The paraphrase of Erasmus'; 381–3, three volumes of Marcus Tullius Cicero which were later 'Swapt'.

31. Bell, 'Reading in seventeenth-century Derbyshire', 161–8. I thank Dr Bell for allowing me to read her unpublished paper, 'Titus Wheatcroft: An eighteenth-century reader and his manuscripts'. Titus's library edited by Bell will be published by the Derbyshire Record Society. For another book list see *The Library of Mr Thomas Britton, Smallcoal-man, Deceased* (1715).

32. Addy, 'Ashover and the Wheatcrofts', 151.

33. Andy Wood, *The Politics of Social Conflict* (Oxford, 1999), 154, 157; Bell, 'Reading in seventeenth-century Derbyshire', 164; Rosemary Milward, 'Books and booksellers in late seventeenth-century Chesterfield', *Derbyshire Miscellany*, 10 (1985), 119–45.

34. T. Baldwin, *William Shakspere's Small Latine & Lesse Greeke*, ii (Urbana, IL, 1944), 425, 430.

35. Marion Johnson, *Derbyshire Village Schools in the Nineteenth Century* (NY, 1970), 16 (map), 27 (list).

36. For Yorkshire villages see W. P. Baker, *Parish Registers and Illiteracy in East Yorkshire* (Leeds, 1961), 9.

37. William Page (ed.), *The County of Derbyshire*, ii (1907), 274–81.

38. Margaret Spufford, 'The scribes of villagers' wills in the sixteenth and seventeenth centuries and their influence' in *Figures in the Landscape* (Aldershot, 2000), 28–43; *Contrasting Communities* (Stroud, 2000).

39. Wallace Notestein, *English Folk* (1938), 215–43.

40. Roger Lowe, *The Diary of Roger Lowe, of Ashton-in Makerfield, Lancashire, 1663–1674*, William Sachse (ed.) (New Haven, CT,1938), 4, 24, 28, 42–3, 46, 48, 51, 53, 62–3.

41. Notestein, *English Folk*, 221; Lowe, *The Diary of Roger Lowe*, 62.

42. Somerset Record Office DD/SAS C/1193/4; DD/SAS/C795/PA/181, John Cannon, Diary, Memoirs; Tim Hitchcock, 'Sociability and misogyny in the life of John Cannon' in Hitchcock and Michelle Cohen (eds.), *English Masculinities, 1660–1800* (1999), 25–43; Craig Muldrew, 'Class and credit' in Henry French and Jonathan Barry (eds.), *Identity and Agency in England, 1500–1800* (Houndmills, 2004), 147–77.

43. Thomas Turner, *The Diary of Thomas Turner 1754–65*, David Vaisey (ed.) (Oxford, 1984), 13, 19, 38–9, 47. References to keeping school are from Apr. 1755–May 1756.

44. DRO D331/13/8. This book adopts the spelling 'Soresbie', though correspondents spelt this surname in different ways over time.

45. The Soresbie collection is part of the Ogden of Stanley papers (1636–20th cent.). See D331 and D5202.

46. In 1846, Bagshaw, *History, Gazetteer, and Directory of Derbyshire*, 110, 125, 279, refers to Gilbert Soresbie, a farmer, James and William Soresbie, carriers,

and Edward Soresbie Cox, a lead merchant who had bought Brailsford Hall. Later at least two women married into an upper middling-sort family.

47. DRO D331/26/1, John de Beauchesne, *A Booke Containing Divers Sortes of hands* (1571); D5202 10/2, ix–x; Bundle of writing exercises and poems, some signed Gilbert Soresbie, others by Charles Soresbie; D5202/10/2/ix, Charles's copybook, 1678.

48. DRO D331/10/1–20. For a later Derbyshire farmer see Andrew Todd (ed.), *Two Years on a Derbyshire Farm* (Bury, 1994).

49. DRO D331/10/16, Dorothy Soresbie/Roger Soresbie, 19 May 1677.

50. DRO D331/10/15, Dorothy Soresbie/Roger Soresbie, 18 Aug. 1689; D5202/10/16.

51. DRO D331/11/1–36; Stephen Glover and Thomas Noble (eds.), *The History of the County of Derby*, ii (Derby, 1829), 138; Bagshaw, *History, Gazetteer, and Directory of Derbyshire*, 278. Brailsford had access to the Manchester to London road. It lay 6 miles south of Ashbourne and 7 miles north-west of Derby. In the early 19th cent. it had 724 inhabitants and 155 families.

52. Glover and Noble, *The History of the County of Derby*, ii, 138; DRO D331/11/1–3.

53. DRO D331/11/25–8, 31–5; D331/12/2–16.

54. DRO D331/19/17–18, William Chatterton/Jane Mosely, n.d. (late 17th cent.); DRO D331/11/25–8, 1699–1729.

55. DRO 331/19/23–4, copybook of Elizabeth Mosley with note by F. Ogden (17th cent.) shows repeated copies in a secretary hand and annotations throughout.

56. DRO D5202/10/1. See Henry Shirley's book, *c*.1705. He was living at the Manor House in Brailsford. The Soresbies had rented land from the Shirleys in the seventeenth century.

57. DRO D331/12/1–33; 12/30/1–4, Wills, 12 June 1763, 1772, 1774.

58. DRO D331/12/18/1–3, Account books of Gilbert Soresbie, 1732–89. Love poems are on the reverse of 18/3. On 2 Mar. 1740, he hired William Winson at £3 19s. 5d. On 25 Feb. 1751 another servant, Mary Wagstaff, came to 'live with me one year and I payd her two pound five shillings being...one years wages'. D331/23 [Brailsford Society for the Prosecution of Felons] defines crimes relating to farm life but also that of 'listening in ye night at his Neighbour's Doors and Windows', 18 Feb. 1755. D331/12/25 is Gilbert's appointment as tax collector, 1776; D331/12/26/4 is addressed to Mr Soarsby, Constable, 2 Feb. 1743.

59. DRO D5202/10/2/ii, Bundle of writing exercises and poems [early 18th cent.].

60. DRO D5202/10/i–xiii.

61. DRO D5202/10/2/ii. A letter is copied about a man who 'maniged the Half dusoon [girls] and pleased them to the hart the puled out shilings...but I would not have one peny tho thanked me for my Love of them'.

62. DRO D331/12/1–6, receipts, 1733–67.

63. DRO D331/12/26/1, 11 May 1726, written on the back.

64. DRO D331/12/26/1, draft letter, n.d. [1726?].

65. DRO D331/12/19/1–2; D331/14/1–2 has questions in red, answers in black. D331/14/38, Will of Gilbert Soresbie, 13 Mar. 1829.

66. DRO D331/14/1/3, Notebook, 1773–92.

67. DRO D331/12/19/1–2 (1), Gilbert Sorsby's book, 1763.

68. DRO D331/12/18/3, Account Book, 1760–89.

69. DRO D331/14/15–17, Copybooks with printed covers; D5202/10/5/i, John Charlton, *The English Language*, n.d. See also William Jackson, *Book-Keeping in the True Italian Form* (Dublin, 1792); D331/18/11, *The Parents' Best Gift: A new spelling book* [18??].

70. DRO D331/24/1–6, Cox Family; Glover and Noble, *The History of the County of Derby*, ii, 138; Bagshaw, *History, Gazetteer, and Directory of Derbyshire*, 110, 125, 279; *Jane Mosley's Derbyshire Recipes* (Matlock, 1979), vii–viii.

71. Aileen Douglas, 'Maria Edgworth's writing classes', *Eighteenth-Century Fiction*, 14 (2002), 372.

72. Harold Love, *Scribal Publication in Seventeenth-Century England* (Oxford, 1993), 40–1; Margaret Ezell, *The Patriarch's Wife* (1987), 65–8.

73. Lisa Jardine, *Erasmus, Man of Letters* (Princeton, NJ, 1993), 59.

74. Johnson, *Derbyshire Village Schools* does not list a Brailsford School. In 1739, Gilbert Sr made a list of his books. In his own words, they included: 'An ould Bible, a Large one; A call to ye uncovered; Christ's first Sermon; The Lamentations of jeremiah; The author & meanes of faith, the first leafe figured gay; The first Sermon of Mr Hughe Latimer, which he preached before ye Kinges Majesty with six more sermons; The Litany & psalmes; and The Explanation of the Church Catechism' in which his children wrote their names. See John Hart, *Christ's first sermon*, 22nd edn (Newcastle on Tyne, 1730–69); Hugh Latimer, *The Fyrste Sermon of Mayster Hughe Latimer, which he preached before the kyges grace* [1549]; *The Church Catechism, Analysed, Explained, and Improved* (Norwich, 1703). See also D331/12/18/1.

75. DRO D5202/10/2/xi, Letter to a 'Lovinge ffreind' with arithmetic sums on the back, n.d; D331/26/12 is a lease for a free school in Radbourne dated 1718. D5557/16/6 notes the Muggington school founded in 1746 for poor children by the Chandos-Pole family. D5202/10/8 is a notice for a later Brailsford School in 1865.

76. DRO D331/12/18/2, Account books, 1746–64. For notes of Ann and Gilbert's births see D331/12/28, n.d. For Frances's copybooks see D331/12/32–3, 1765 [1750s–60s].

77. DRO D331/13/11/1–2, 5, 24, 26–31, 36. Papers relating to Charles Soresbie's will, 1762–4.

78. DRO D331/13/11/2, 5.

79. DRO D5202/10/3. This copybook contained forms for drawing up a will on the last page. Someone copied legal documents into it, probably for

reference. Whoever did so was becoming familiar with legal papers and was learning Latin. D331/12/20/2.

80. All references are to copies in the Cumbria Record Office (CRO), Kendal. For the originals see National Library of Scotland, MS 10789, fos. 1–33. CRO WDY 75, fo. 4, Joseph Morton/Thomas Morton, 4 Jan. 1770.

81. Jonathan Healey, 'Agrarian social structure in the central Lake District *c.*1574–1830', *Northern History*, 44 (2007), 73–91; Arthur Duxbury, 'The decline of the Cumbrian yeoman Ravensdale', *Transactions of the Cumberland & Westmoreland Antiquarian & Archaeological Society*, 94 (1994), 201–13; Angus Winchester, 'Regional identity in the Lake Counties', *Northern History*, 42 (2005), 29–48; J. V. Beckett, 'The decline of the small land owner in eighteenth- and nineteenth-century England', *Agricultural History Review*, 30 (1982), 97–111.

82. For domestic travel see Malcolm Andrews, *The Search for the Picturesque* (1989). For the wider world see Katherine Turner, *British Travel Writers in Europe 1750–1800* (Aldershot, 2001); Jean Viviés, *English Travel Narratives in the Eighteenth Century* (Aldershot, 2002); Percy G. Adams, *Travel Literature and the Evolution of the Novel* (Lexington, KY, 1983).

83. J. D. Marshall and Carol Dyouse, 'Social transition in Kendal & Westmorland, *c.*1760–1860', *Northern History*, 19 (1983), 128–57; M. A. Gordon, *A Short History of Kendal* (Kendal, 1950).

84. Matthew Greenhall, 'Cattle to claret', *History Today*, 56 (2006), 22–7.

85. T. Pennant *A Tour in Scotland 1769* (1774).

86. CRO WDY 75, fo. 1, Joseph Morton/James Morton Sr, 18 Feb. 1765.

87. Ibid., fos. 3–4, Joseph Morton/Thomas Morton, 9 July 1769, 4 Jan. 1770.

88. Ibid., fo. 1, Joseph Morton/James Morton Sr, 18 Feb. 1765.

89. Ibid., fo. 2, Joseph Morton/James Morton Sr, 9 Jan. 1767.

90. Ian Whyte, ' "Wild, Barren and Frightful": Parliamentary enclosure in an upland county', *Rural History*, 14 (2003), 21–37.

91. CRO WDY 75, fo. 3, Joseph Morton/Thomas Morton, 9 July 1769.

92. Ibid., fo. 4, Joseph Morton/Thomas Morton, 4 Jan. 1770.

93. Ibid., fo. 4.

94. CRO, Barrow, MS BD HJ290/8, Lease 28 Sept. 1772. Joseph Morton, 'gardnener' was tenant of the field called the Farmery behind the Church.

95. CRO WDY 75, fo. 5, Joseph Morton/Thomas Morton, 27 Jan. 1770.

96. Ibid., fo. 6, Joseph Morton/Thomas Morton, 20 Apr. 1770.

97. Ibid., fos. 7–8, Joseph Morton/Thomas Morton, 9 July 1770, 18 July 1777.

98. Ibid., fo. 8.

99. Ibid., fo. 9, Joseph Morton/Thomas Morton, 2 Feb. 1778; John F. Curwen, *Historical Description of Levens Hall* (Kendal, 1898), 33, 'A Map of Leavens Garding', *c.*1720, 38, 'A Plan of the Park'; Thomas West in *A Guide to the Lakes, in Cumberland, Westmorland, Lancashire*, 7th edn (1799), 26, calls its deer park 'one of the sweetest spots that fancy can imagine' (181). Morton

and other staff were occasionally given venison, but he was disappointed in the tips he received from garden visitors.

100. CRO WDY 75, fo. 9.

101. Ibid., fo. 10, Joseph Morton/Thomas Morton, 28 Mar. 1778.

102. Ibid., fos. 9–10.

103. Angus Winchester, 'Regional identity in the Lake Counties', *Northern History*, 42 (2005); Paul Nunn, 'Aristocratic estates and employment in South Yorkshire 1700–1800' in Sidney Pollard and Colin Holmes (eds.), *Essays in the Economic and Social History of South Yorkshire* (Sheffield, 1976), 28–45.

104. CRO WDY 75, fo. 14, 18 Feb. 1779. Early rumours of the Earl's death noted in fo. 13, 3 Jan. 1779 may have affected his employment. The Earl died that year. Curwen, *Historical Description of Levens Hall*, 7–8.

105. CRO WDY 75, fo.15, Joseph Morton/Thomas Morton, 5 July 1779.

106. Ibid., fo. 16, 5 Oct. 1779. J. D. Marshall (ed.), *The Autobiography of William Stout of Lancaster 1665–1752* (Manchester, 1967), 71, 247–8. Stout noted in 1678 that Heversham was 'reputed the best schoole and master in these north Parts'. It was founded in 1613 by Edward Wilson. See R. P. Brown, *Edward Wilson of Nether Levens and his Kin* (Kendal, 1930); *A Short History of Heversham School* (reprinted from the Westmorland Gazette, 1, 8–10); John F. Curwen, *History of Heversham with Milnthorpe* (Kendal, 1930).

107. CRO WDY 75, fo. 16, 5 Oct. 1779. See also Kenneth Harper, 'John Atkinson, 1773–1857, yeoman schoolmaster', *Transactions of the Cumberland & Westmorland Antiquarian & Archarological Society*, 83 (1983), 157–60.

108. CRO WDY 75, fo. 17, Joseph Morton/Thomas Morton, 15 Nov. 1779.

109. Ibid., fo. 18, Joseph Morton/Thomas Morton, 12 Feb. 1780; Cornelius Nicholson, *The Annals of Kendal* (Kendal, 1832), 127.

110. CRO WDY 75, fo. 18

111. Ibid.

112. Ibid.

113. My italics. Ibid., fo. 19, 2 Nov. 1786. Morton and his family appear in Revd Johnson Baily (ed.), *The Registers of Ryton, In the County of Durham* (Sunderland, 1902), 154–7. N. Smith, *Addison: The Rise and Fall of a Pit Village, 1864–1962* (Ryton and Houghton, 1991) has a map of the mines in the area. Wood, *The Politics of Social Conflict*, 155.

114. North Yorkshire County Record Office (NY) Z 640 (originals); NY MIC 1958, 1976 (microfilm), Letters & Papers of John Fawdington of Asenby (1757–1817) & his family, (c.1698–1896); NY MIC 1976/2013, 1 May, 1698; 7 July 1720.

115. NY MIC 1976/2013, 2024, 2214, 2227, 2234, 2241, 2251, 2259, 2269, 2285, 2288, 2303. Letters are cited by date.

116. NY MIC 1976/2013, 19 Mar. 1759.

117. NY MIC 1976/2024, c.1781.

118. Thomas Langdale, *A Topographical Dictionary of Yorkshire* (N. Allerton, 1822). There were two respected schools in Great and Little Budworth, but Bubwith

was a small place in Yorkshire. See Derek Robson, *Some Aspects of Education in Cheshire in the Eighteenth Century*, no. 13 in the 3rd series of *Remains, Historical and Literary, connected with . . . Lancaster and Chester* (Manchester: Chetham Society, 1966), 107.

119. NY MIC 1976.

120. Ibid.

121. NY MIC 1976/2024, n.d., 'Wednesday Morn Early'.

122. NY MIC 1976/2203, 8 Jan. n.y.

123. NY MIC 1976/2024, Thursday morn.

124. Ibid., Thursday morn.

125. NY MIC 1976/2404, Tuesday 29 May 1786.

126. NY MIC 1976/2214, Saturday 3 Mar. 1787.

127. NY MIC/1976/2227, Tuesday 17 Apr. 1787.

128. NY MIC 1976/2288, n.d. It was written 'while on the banks of Swale I musing sat'. The poet hears a bell and knows that it will toll for him.

129. See Ch. 6.

130. NY MIC 1976/2234, Wed. 31 Oct. 1787.

131. NY MIC 1976/2227, Monday 14 May 1787.

132. NY MIC 1976/2241, 15 Oct. 1789.

133. Ibid., 21 Oct. 1789.

134. NY MIC 1976/2251, 14 Oct. 1794.

135. NY MIC 1976/2259, 9 Oct. 1796.

136. NY MIC 1976/2241, 15 Oct. 1789.

137. Ibid., 2 Oct. 1790.

138. NY MIC 1976/2234, 31 Oct. 1787.

139. Ibid., 30 Oct. 1787.

140. NY MIC 1976/2269, 12 Oct. 1798.

141. NY MIC 1976/2285, 16 Oct. 1803. By 1814, his son is in the West Indies. NY MIC 1976/2286, 21 Jan. 1804.

142. NY MIC 1976/2234, 31 Oct. 1787, 4 Oct. 1791.

143. NY MIC 1976/2286, 21 Jan. 1804.

144. Ibid., 16 Aug. 1818.

145. I thank the Arkwright Mill, Cromford, for a private tour, 25 May 2002. For Richard Arkwright's family letters see DRO D5991/1–4; R. S. Fitton, *The Arkwrights* (Manchester, 1989).

146. M. Berg and P. Hudson, 'Rehabilitating the Industrial Revolution', *Economic History Review*, 2nd series, 45 (1992), 24–50; Roderick Floud and Paul Johnson, *The Cambridge Economic History of Modern Britain*, 2nd edn (Cambridge, 2004).

147. But see R. S. Fitton and A. P. Wadsworth, *The Strutts and the Arkwrights 1758–1830* (Manchester, 1958) (hereafter Fitton, *Strutts*).

148. For Elizabeth Woollat Strutt see *ODNB*/54677.

149. Derbyshire Record Office (DRO) D5303, Correspondence, *c.*1748–20th cent.; D2943, Personal letters, diaries and travel journals, *c.*1814–61; including D2943/F9/1 and 2, The Strutts of Derbyshire: Being the Records and Biographical Memoirs of Jedediah Strutt, his son William Strutt 1756–1830, and Joseph Strutt, First Lord Belper by Frederick Strutt, edited and arranged by R. Harold Paget, typescript (hereafter Paget, Memoirs); D3772 Deeds, estate, and family papers; DRO, *The Strutts: Industry and Paternalism* (1998) (hereafter DRO, *The Strutts*). Abstracts of many original letters are printed in Fitton, *Strutts*; ODNB/26683. See Strutt's portrait in J. C. Cox, *Memorials of Old Derbyshire* (1907), 371–85.

150. DRO D5303/1–5, Apprenticeship indenture, 1740.

151. DRO, *The Strutts*, 1.

152. Paget, Memoirs, 1–2; Fitton, *Strutts*, 164, Jedediah Strutt/Eliza Strutt Evans, 23 Mar. 1786.

153. DRO D3772/E/32/82; DRO, *The Strutts*, 1.

154. DRO, *The Strutts*, 1; H. McLachlan, 'Ebenezer Latham and the Academy at Findern', *Essays and Addresses* (1950), 147–66; *English Education under the Test Acts being the History of the Non-Conformist Academies 1662–1820* (Manchester, 1931).

155. The school was established in 1714 by John Allsop. William Page (ed.), *The Victoria County History of Derbyshire*, ii (1907), 276.

156. H. McLachlan, 'Ebenezer Latham', 147–66; Fitton, *Strutts*, 3; Frederick Strutt, 'Jedediah Strutt' in Cox, *Memorials of Old Derbyshire*.

157. DRO, *The Strutts*, 1. The minister was George Benson.

158. T. C. Smout, 'Born again at Cambuslang', *Past and Present*, 97 (1982), 114–27 (126).

159. DRO D3772/E45/3. In 1767 he still described himself as a wheelwright in a patent registration. DRO, *The Strutts*, 1–2. Blackwell is near Alfreton.

160. DRO D5303/5/2, A. Dethick/Elizabeth Strutt, 5 Nov. [1755]; Fitton, *Strutts*, 23.

161. D5303/1–5; Paget, Memoirs, 2, 7–19.

162. DRO D5303/4/1, Jedediah Strutt/Elizabeth Strutt, 3 Feb. 1755; D5303/4/11, note on bottom signed by Jedediah.

163. DRO D5303/4/1.

164. DRO D5303/4/6, Jedediah Strutt/Elizabeth Strutt, 28 June [1755] is the letter sent; 4/7 is the draft.

165. DRO D5303/1/1, Jedediah Strutt/Elizabeth Strutt, n.d; Fitton, *Strutts*, 9.

166. DRO D5303/1/2 (iii), Elizabeth Strutt/Jedediah Strutt, 3 Mar. 1748; D5303/1, Elizabeth Strutt/Jedediah Strutt, n.d; Fitton, *Strutts*, 4.

167. DRO D5303/1/2 (iii), Elizabeth Strutt/Jedediah Strutt, 3 Mar. 1748.

168. DRO D5303/1/3, Jedediah Strutt/Elizabeth Strutt, 25 Feb. 1751; Fitton, *Strutts*, 7–8.

169. DRO D5303/4/3, Elizabeth Strutt/JedediahStrutt, 1 Apr. 1755.

170. DRO D5303/1/2 (iii), Elizabeth Strutt/Jedediah Strutt, 3 Mar. 1748. (Juba is a character in Addison's Cato.)

171. DRO D5303/4/6, Jedediah Strutt/Elizabeth Strutt, n.d, fragment on the back of a draft.

172. DRO D5303/1/2 (ii), Elizabeth Strutt/Jedediah Strutt, n.d, fragments on both sides.

173. DRO D5303/1/2 (ii), Elizabeth Strutt/Jedediah Strutt, n.d.

174. DRO D5303/4/1, Jedediah Strutt/Elizabeth Strutt, 3 Feb. 1755; Fitton, *Strutts*, 13.

175. DRO D5303/1/1, Jedediah Strutt/Elizabeth Strutt, n.d; Fitton, *Strutts*, 9–10; Carolyn Steedman, *The Radical Soldier's Tale* (1988), 79.

176. DRO D5303/4/6, Jedediah Strutt/Elizabeth Strutt, 28 June [1755]; Fitton, *Strutts*, 19.

177. Frank Musgrove, 'The exact men of the North from toll makers to historians', *Northern History*, 44 (2005), 55–74.

178. DRO, *The Strutts*, 2–3; *ODNB*.

179. DRO, *The Strutts*, 3; BL MS Add. 78476, Sidney Evelyn/Sir John Evelyn, 19 Feb. 1739, 13 Sept. 1738.

180. DRO, *The Strutts*, 3, 6; *ODNB*; Fitton, *The Arkwrights*. He later dissolved ties with Arkwright.

181. Fitton, *Strutts*, 111.

182. Daniel Defoe, *A Tour Thro' the Whole Island of Great Britain*, ii (1927), 563; Fitton, *Strutts*, 110; Stephen Glover, *The History and Directory of the Borough of Derby* (Derby, 1992).

183. Fitton, *Strutts*, 112; David Jeremy, *Business and Religion in Britain* (Aldershot, 1988).

184. DRO D5303/9/14, Jedediah Strutt/Elizabeth Strutt, 26 Nov. 1765; D5303/9/11, Jedediah Strutt/Elizabeth Strutt, 3 Apr. 1765; Fitton, *Strutts*, 109.

185. DRO D5303/9, Jedediah Strutt/Elizabeth Strutt, 1765; Fitton *Strutts*, 109–10; John Seed, 'Theologies of power' in R. J. Morris (ed.), *Class, Power, and Social Structure in British Nineteenth-century Towns* (Leicester, 1986), 108–56; David Hey, 'The changing patterns of nonconformity 1660–1851' in Pollard and Holmes, *Essays in the Economic and Social History of South Yorkshire*, 204–18.

186. Martin Nystrand and John Duffy (eds.), *Towards a Rhetoric of Everyday Life* (Madison, WI, 2003).

187. DRO, *The Strutts*, 5–6.

188. DRO D5303/15/5, George Strutt/Jedediah Strutt, 27 July 1774; DRO, *The Strutts*, 8; Fitton, *Strutts*, 111.

189. DRO D5303/13/9, Eliza Strutt/Jedediah Strutt, 9 July 1774; Fitton, *Strutts*, 138.

190. DRO D5303/20, George Benson Strutt/William Strutt, 5 Sept. 1778.

191. DRO D5303/15/2, William Strutt/Jedediah Strutt, 4 July 1775; Fitton, *Strutts*, 155.

192. Fitton, *Strutts*, 156, Martha Strutt/William Strutt, July 1775.

193. DRO D5303/9/10, Jedediah Strutt/Elizabeth Strutt, 28 Mar. 1765; Fitton, *Strutts*, 334. His unease about London fashion was apparent: 'I have made it some of my business to observe the taste about Coats & find some with Collars & some without, Some with buttons at the Sleeves & some with none...I thot it was necessay to tell you this.'

194. Philip Stanhope, Earl of Chesterfield, *Letters* (1774); DRO D5303/10, Jedediah Strutt/William Strutt, 17 Aug. 1774, Paget, Memoirs, 61–6; Fitton, *Strutts*, 144–8.

195. DRO D5303/10, Jedediah Strutt/William Strutt, 17 Aug. 1774; D5303/13/14, William Strutt/Jedediah Strutt, 14 Sept. 1774.

196. DRO D5303/21/i, Jedediah Strutt/Eliza Strutt, 23 Mar. 1786; Fitton, *Strutts*, 163, 165.

197. DRO D5303/15/5, George Strutt/Jedediah Strutt, 27 July 1774; DRO, *The Strutts*, 6–7.

198. Fitton, *Strutts*, 166–7, Eliza Strutt Evans/Joseph Strutt, 24 Oct. 1793. After reading Godwin's *Enquiry* Elizabeth avowed: 'The grand desideratum in Politics is the diffusion of knowledge and morals amongst the poor. This the manufacturer has it in his power considerably to promote & is culpable in the neglect of it.'

199. DRO D5303/15/3, Eliza Strutt/Jedediah Strutt, 24 July 1775; Fitton, *Strutts*, 157, 163–6; Don Peters, *Darley Abbey* (Buxton, 1874), 88.

200. DRO, *The Strutts*, 8–9. Strutt's children socialized with the Arkwrights.

201. Quoted in Stuart Andrews, *Unitarian Radicalism* (Houndmills, 2003), 120–1.

202. R. A. Houston, 'The development of literacy', *Economic History Review*, new series, 35 (May, 1982), 199–216 (214). For a more negative view see Cressy, 'Social status and literacy in north east England 1560–1630', *Local Population Studies*, 21 (1978), 19–23. Baker and Billinge (eds.), *Geographies of England*; Edward Hughes, *North Country Life in the Eighteenth Century* (Oxford, 1952); Norman McCord and Richard Thompson, *The Northern Counties from AD 1000* (1998).

203. Walter Ong, *Orality and Literacy* (2002); Jack Goody, *The Logic of Writing and the Organization of Society* (Cambridge, 1986).

204. David Cressy, *Literacy and the Social Order* (Cambridge, 1980); Keith Thomas, 'The meaning of literacy in early modern England' in Gerald Baumann (ed.), *The Written Word* (Oxford, 1986), 97–133; Keith Wrightson, *English Society 1680–1680* (1982), ch. 7; W. B. Stephens (ed.), *Studies in the History of Literacy* (Leeds, 1983).

205. Barry Reay, 'The context and meaning of popular literacy', *Past and Present*, 131 (May 1991), 89–129; Jacqueline Grayson, 'Literacy, schooling, and industrialization' in Stephens (ed.), *Studies in the History of Literacy*, 54–67; Stephens, 'Literacy in England, Scotland and Wales, 1500–1900', *History of Education Quarterly*, 30 (1990), 545–71 (570). Writing primers used in schools

did not mention name signing, for it did not fit in with their prescriptive rules.

206. Cressy, *Literacy and the Social Order*, 176–7; W. B. Stephens, *Education, Literacy, and Society, 1830–70* (Manchester, 1987), 514. In 2003, Cressy defended his statistics in *Society and Culture in Early Modern England* (2003), 305–19 (314). For careful statistical evidence see R. S. Schofield, 'The measurement of literacy in pre-industrial England' in Jack Goody (ed.), *Literacy in Traditional Societies* (Cambridge, 1968), 311–25, 'Dimensions of illiteracy', *Explorations in Economic History 1750–1850*, 10 (1973), 437–54.

207. Stephens, *Education, Literacy, and Society, 1830–70*; V. A. Hatley, 'Literacy at Northampton, 1761–1900', *Northamptonshire Past and Present*, 4 (1971), 379–81.

208. Alysa Levene and Steven King (eds.), *Narratives of the Poor in Eighteenth-century Britain*, 5 vols. (2006); Thomas Sokoll (ed.), *Essex Pauper Letters* (Oxford, 2001); Deidre Palk, *Prisoners' Letters to the Bank of England 1781–1827*, London Record Society, xlii (2007).

209. Margaret Spufford, 'First steps in literacy', *Social History*, 4 (1979), 407–35; *Small Books and Pleasant Histories* (Athens, GA, 1982); Jonathan Rose, *The Intellectual Life of the English Working Classes* (New Haven, CT, 2001).

210. David Vincent, *Literacy and Popular Culture* (Cambridge, 1989); *The Rise of Mass Literacy* (Cambridge, 2000); R. A. Houston, *Scottish Literacy and the Scottish Identity* (Cambridge, 1985); *Literacy in Early Modern Europe*, 2nd edn (Harlow, 2002); Jonathan Payne, 'Review', *Labour History Review*, 67 (2002), 365–73.

211. Houston, 'The development of literacy', 204, 214.

212. David Levine and Keith Wrightson, *The Making of an Industrial Society* (Oxford, 1991), 326.

213. Wood, *The Politics of Social Conflict*, 155–6 (64% males, 26% women).

214. McCord and Thompson, *The Northern Counties from AD 1000*, 166.

215. Vincent, *Literacy and Popular Culture*, 53.

216. In the last decade, studies announcing a 'new literacy' have been written by scholars in different disciplines. Those that stress narrative and cognition are particularly relevant to arguments presented here.

217. Sylvia Harrop, 'Literacy and educational attitudes as factors in the industrialization of north-east Cheshire, 1760–1830', in Stephens (ed.), *Studies in the History of Literacy*, 52; Stephens, *History of Literacy in England*, 564.

218. Houston, 'The development of literacy', 212–14.

219. Mark Billinge, 'Divided by a common language', 94.

220. David Hey, *Packmen, Carriers and Packhorse Roads* (Leicester, 1980); J. Radley and S. R. Penny, 'The turnpike roads of the Peak District', *The Derbyshire Archaeological Journal*, xcii (1975), 93–109; Geoffrey Wright, *Roads and Trackways of the Yorkshire Dales* (Ashbourne, 1985), 165; David Ripley, *Postal History of North West Derbyshire* (Stockport, 1994); Harold S. Wilson, *History of the Post in Derby 1635–1941* (1990).

221. Sheffield Archives, MS TR 292/3, 446/4–7.

222. Jerome Bruner, 'Narrative distancing' in Jens Brockmeier et al. (eds.), *Literacy, Narrative, and Culture* (Richmond, Surrey, 2002), 86–98; G. D. Fireman et al. (eds.), *Narrative and Consciousness* (Oxford, 2003); Ronald T. Kellogg, *The Psychology of Writing* (NY and Oxford, 1994), 43; David Herman (ed.), *Theory and the Cognitive Sciences* (Stanford, 2003). For a different opinion see Galen Strawson, 'Against narrativity', *Ratio*, xvii (4 Dec. 2004), 428–52.

223. David Vincent, *Bread, Knowledge, and Freedom* (1981); Thomas, *The Meaning of Literacy*, 106–8. I thank Jane Humphries for ideas on this point.

224. There is a huge literature on this issue. For two different views see [Bernard Mandeville], *An Essay on Charity and Charity Schools* (1923) and Isaac Watts, *An Essay Towards the Encouragement of Charity Schools . . . with Some Apology for those Schools which instruct them to write a plain Hand* (1728).

225. Johnson, *Derbyshire Village Schools*, 16, 27.

226. Spufford, *Small Books and Pleasant Histories*; Robson, *Some Aspects of Education in Cheshire in the Eighteenth Century*; Lawrence Stone, 'The educational revolution in England 1560–1640', *Past and Present*, 28 (1964), 41–80; J. H. Moran, 'Literacy and education in northern England 1300–1550', *History*, xvii (1981), 11–23, map 19; Doreen Smith, 'Eighteenth-century literacy levels in West Sussex', *Sussex Archaeological Collections*, 128 (1990), 177–86; Glover and Noble, *The History of the County of Derby*. See J. S. Hurt, *Bringing Literacy to Rural England* (1972) for nineteenth-century schools in Hertfordshire.

227. Visitation returns in East Yorkshire in 1743 show 'schools were recorded in nearly 40% of the parishs and chapelries which sent in returns'. Baker, *Parish Registers and Illiteracy in East Yorkshire*, 9, 14.

228. Wrightson and Levine, *Making of an Industrial Society*, 325.

229. Spufford, *Contrasting Communities*, 213.

230. In Smout, 'Born again at Cambusland', 25, T. C. Smout noted that 'supplementary home education was reserved for girls because it was cheap'.

231. Robert Mayer, 'Literacy in a rural community', *Staffordshire Studies*, 15 (2003/4), 1–25; Smout, 'Born again at Cambusland', 125; Doreen Smith, 'Eighteenth-century literacy levels in West Sussex', 77–9.

232. DRO 5303/4/3, Elizabeth Strutt/Jedediah Strutt, 1 Apr. 1755; Fireman et al. (eds.), *Narrative and Consciousness*, 33.

233. David R. Olson, 'Towards a psychology of literacy', *Cognition*, 60 (1996), 83–104; Ronald Kellogg, *Cognitive Psychology*, 2nd edn (Thousand Oaks, CA, 2003), 322; DRO D5303/4/6, Jedediah Strutt/Elizabeth Strutt, 28 June [1755]. Handwriting is typically about 1/10th of the speed of oral speech.

234. David R. Olson and Deepthi Kamawar, 'Writing as a form of quotation' in Brockmeier, *Literacy* (Richmond, 2002), 187–98 (189); Vincent, 'The decline of the oral tradition in popular culture' in R. D. Storch (ed.), *Popular Culture and Custom in 19th-century England* (1982), 20–47; Carolyn Steedman,

'Poetical maids and cooks who wrote', *Eighteenth-Century Studies*, 39 (2005), 1–27.

235. Robert Pattison, *On Literacy* (Oxford, 1984), 5, 9.

236. Vincent, *Rise of Mass Literacy*, 22.

CHAPTER 4

1. H. R. French, 'Social status, localism and "the middle sort of people" in England 1620–1750', *Past & Present*, 166 (2000), 66–99; 'The search for the "middle sort of people" in England 1600–1800', *Historical Journal*, 43 (2000), 277–93; 'Ingenious & learned gentlemen', *Social History*, 25 (2000), 44–66; J. Barry and C. Brooks (eds.), *The Middling Sort of People* (Houndmills, 1994); Penelope Corfield, *Language, History and Class* (Oxford, 1991), 'The rivals' in N. Harte and R. Quinault (eds.), *Land and Society in Britain 1700–1914*; Perry Gauci, 'Finding the middle-ground', *History Compass*, 4 (2006), 1–6; John Smail, *The Origins of Middle Class Culture* (Ithaca, NY, 1994); John Seed, 'From "middling sort" to middle class in late eighteenth- and early nineteenth-century England', in M. L. Bush (ed.), *Social Orders and Social Classes in Europe since 1500* (1991), 114–35; Dror Wahrman, *Imagining the Middle Class* (Cambridge, 1995).

2. Margaret Hunt, *The Middling Sort* (Berkeley, 1996); Peter Earle, *The Making of the Middle Class* (1989); Paul Langford, *A Polite and Commercial People* (Oxford, 1989).

3. French, *The Middle Sort of People in Provincial England 1600–1750* (Oxford, 2007).

4. See Appendix II: Arkwright, Baker, Bateman, Bowers, Bowrey, Cannon, Conyers, Cotesworth, Dawson, Farmer, Follows, Hubbertsy, Langton, Lucas, Maister, Muggle, Newton, Payne, Pease, Smith, Spencer, Story, Strutt, Tucker, and Wilson collections.

5. Craig Muldrew, *The Economy of Obligation* (Basingstoke, 1998); Margot Finn, *The Character of Credit* (Cambridge, 2003).

6. Penelope Corfield, 'Class by name and number in eighteenth-century Britain', *History*, lxxii (1987), 36–61; Keith Wrightson, *English Society* (1982); Richard Wendorf, 'Abandoning the capital in eighteenth-century London' in Kevin Sharpe and Steven Zwicker (eds.), *Reading, Society and Politics* (Cambridge, 2003), 72–98.

7. Beinecke Library, Yale University (BLY) MS OSB 32/3, William Armitage/Rebekah Bateman, 20 Dec. 1783.

8. Michael Mascuch, *Origins of the Individualist Self* (Cambridge, 1997); Anthony Giddens, *Modernity and Self Identity* (Stanford, 1991).

9. Robert More, *Of the First Invention of Writing* [1716]; James O'Donnell, *Avatars of the Word from Papyrus to Cyberspace* (Cambridge, 1998); Alvin Harlow, *Old Post Bags* (1928).

10. David Hancock, *Citizens of the World* (Cambridge, 1997), 98–100; Ceri Sullivan, *Merchants in Early Modern Writing* (Madison, NJ, 2002), 29.

11. Richard Steele, *The Trades-man's Calling* (1684), 40, quoted in Keith Thomas, 'The meaning of literacy in early modern England' in Gerald Baumann (ed.), *The Written Word* (Oxford, 1986), 116.

12. Natasha Glaisyer, *The Culture of Commerce in England 1660–1720* (Woodbridge, 2006), 112.

13. HCA DFP/1–33368; Gordon Jackson, *Hull in the Eighteenth Century* (Oxford, 1972); Hugh Calvert, *A History of Kingston upon Hull* (1978), 101; Seed, 'From "Middling Sort"', 119.

14. Thomas Watts, *An Essay on the Proper Method for Forming the Man of Business*, 3rd edn (1717); Glaisyer, *The Culture of Commerce*, 111–12.

15. J. William Frost (ed.), *Records and Recollections of James Jenkins* (New York, 1984).

16. For the Spencers, see Sheffield Archives (SA), MSS 60528, 60531; for Baker, Guildhall (GH) MS 16,927, fo. 34v, Edward Baker/William Lowndes, [1782]; for the Hubbertsys, Cumbria Record Office (CRO) WDX 744, Letters to Zachary Hubbertsy, 1749–58.

17. C. G. Bolam et al. (eds.), *The English Presbyterians* (1968); Davidoff and Hall, *Family Fortunes* (1987), 76.

18. Nicholas Rogers, 'Review: Paul Langford's *Age of Improvement*', *Past and Present*, 130 (1991), 203.

19. N. H. Keeble, *The Literary Culture of Nonconformity in Later Seventeenth-Century England* (Athens, GA, 1987), 137–8; Michael Watts, *The Dissenters* (Oxford, 1978), 269–73; G. M. Ditchfield, 'A Unitarian view of English Dissent in 1807', *Transactions of the Unitarian Historical Society*, 18 (Apr. 1984), 1–16.

20. Marjorie Reeves, *Pursuing the Muses* (1997), 5.

21. Edward Royle, *Modern Britain* (1997), 330, 332; Alan Gilbert, *Religion and Society in Industrial England* (1976), 82–5.

22. *Quaker Faith and Practice* (1995); BL Add. MS 60168, Muggletonian Archive; William Lamont, *Last Witnesses* (Aldershot, 2006).

23. See Appendix II.

24. Bodl MS Don. b. 18, fos. 156–7, John Tucker/Richard Tucker, 24 Feb. 1737.

25. Edward III's letters date mainly from the 1750s and 60s. MS Don. c. 128, fo. 13, Will of Rebecca Steward, pr. 12 June 1812; MS Don c. 130, Letters to Rebecca from her children.

26. Catalogue of the Tucker Papers in the Bodleian Library, Oxford (Typescript, 1971), Bodl MSS Don. a. 10; b. 16–28; c. 101–34. The Bodleian Library, Oxford University is the location of all references to the Tucker collection in this chapter.

27. MS Don. b. 16, fos. 2–3; MS Don. c. 130.

28. Ibid., fo. 12, Richard Tucker/Edward Tucker Sr, 15 Feb. 1689.

29. Circular letter, MS Don. c. 112, fo. 183, John Tucker/Joseph Radcliffe, 9 July 1740. Holes cut in letters show need for safety.

30. David Parsons (ed.), *Stone* (Chichester, 1990); Akira Satoh, *Building in Britain* (Aldershot, 1995).

31. MS Don. c. 125–6; c. 111, fo. 1, Richard Tucker/John Tucker, n.d.; c. 111, fo. 21, 21 Apr. 1753; c. 110, fo. 130, 15 Dec. 1748; c. 110, fo. 140, John Tucker/Richard Tucker, 28 Dec. 1748.

32. MS Don. c. 111, fo. 4, Richard Tucker/John Tucker, 9 Apr. 1753; c. 103, fo. 54, Henry Steelman/John Tucker, 15 Jan. 1747; c. 126, fo. 15, Sam White/Richard Tucker, 15 July 1758.

33. MS Don. b. 20, fos. 13–81; MS Don. c. 128, fo. 12.

34. MS Don. a. 10, fo. 2; Bob Harris and Jeremy Black, 'John Tucker MP and mid-eighteenth-century British politics', *Albion*, 29 (1997), 21.

35. MS Don. c. 125–6; Thomas Francklyn, *Serious Advice and Fair Warning to All that Live upon the Sea-coast . . . particularly . . . Weymouth and Portland* (1756); Peter Raban, 'The profits of privateering', *The Mariner's Mirror*, 80 (1994), 298–311.

36. Henry Moule, *Descriptive Catalogue of . . . Documents of the Borough of Weymouth and Melcombe Regis 1252–1800* (Weymouth, 1883), 83.

37. MS Don. b. 16, fo. 16, Richard Tucker/Edward Tucker Sr, 8 July 1691; b. 18, fo. 133, Richard Tucker/John Tucker, 5 Mar. 1733.

38. MS Don. b. 18, fo. 62, Richard Tucker/John Tucker, 2 Oct. 1728; Moule, *Descriptive Catalogue*, 119, 125, 139, 202; MS Don. b. 18, fos. 138–9, Richard Tucker/John Tucker, 3 July 1733.

39. MS Don. b. 16, fos. 32–3, Edward Tucker Jr/Mr Pope, n.d.

40. Ibid., fos. 47–68.

41. Pedigree of Gollop family in J. Hutchins, *History and Antiquities of the County of Dorset*, ii. 3rd edn (East Ardsley, Wakefield, 1973), 111–13, 281, 326; Dorset Record Office, MS Ref. D/ASH Marriage settlement; MS Don. b. 23, fos. 105–39; MS Don. c. 110, fo. 37, John Tucker/Richard Tucker, 11 Aug. 1748; Moule, *Descriptive Catalogue*, 66.

42. MS Don. c. 128, fo. 1 Marriage settlement, Martha Gollop, 15 Sept. 1731, fo. 2, Sarah Gollop, 18 Dec. 1734.

43. MS Don. b. 16, fo. 57, Edward Tucker Sr/Richard Tucker, 17 June 1700; b. 16, fo. 63, Edward Tucker Sr/Rebecca Gollop, 1 Jan. 1701.

44. MS Don. b. 16, fo. 65, Edward Tucker Sr/Rebecca Gollop, 15 Jan. 1701; Samuel Butler, *Hudibras* (1770), part 1, 52, ll. 429–30.

45. MS Don. b. 16, fo. 65, Edward Tucker Sr/Rebecca Gollop, 15 Jan. 1701; b. 17, fo. 49, Inventory of Elizabeth Gilbert, 29 June 1705; Sir Matthew Hale, *Contemplations Moral and Divine* (1699).

46. *ODNB*/7752; L. Namier and J. Brooke (eds.), *The House of Commons 1754–90*, ii (1964), 327–8; Charles Sanders, *Patron and Place-hunter* (1919);

H. Wyndham (ed.), *The Diary of the Late George Bubb Dodington* (Dublin, 1784); John Carswell and Lewis Dralle (eds.), *The Political Journal of George Bubb Dodington* (Oxford, 1965).

47. *ODNB/*28601.

48. Romney Sedgwick (ed.), *The House of Commons 1715–54*, i (1970), 238–9; ibid., ii, 484–5; Namier and Brooke, *The House of Commons 1754–90*, iii, 565; ibid., i, 272–3; John Carswell, *The Old Cause* (1954), 188–9.

49. John was Mayor of Weymouth in 1726, 1732, 1754, 1763, and 1772, alternating terms with Richard. T. H. B. Oldfield, *An Entire and Complete History, Political and Personal, of the Boroughs of Great Britain*, i, 2nd edn (1794), 189–91; *The Copy of the Poll at the Last Election, as delivered by Mr. Tucker, the Mayor* (1727). For Weymouth see *The Weymouth Guide* (Weymouth, 1792); T. Lockett, *The New Weymouth Guide* (Dorchester, 1798); The *Weymouth Guide* (Weymouth, n.d.); *Weymouth and Melcombe Regis* (Weymouth *c.*1834); [R. Graves], *A New Weymouth Guide* [*c.*1800]; John Harvey, *Harvey's Improved Guide* (Dorchester, [1800?]); William Page (ed.), *Victoria County History of the County of Dorset* (1908); H. R. French, 'The creation of a pocket borough in Clitheroe Lancashire, 1693–1780', *Northern History*, xli (2004), 301–26.

50. MS Don. b. 16, fos. 80, 176–7, 188; Sedgwick, *The House of Commons 1715–54*, i, 238; ibid., ii, 484; *Calendar of Treasury Books*, xxix (1714–15), xxxii (1718). He was not legally allowed to hold both posts.

51. TNA ADM 106/1140/37, 1765; ADM106/1142/70 1765; ADM 106/1160/357, 1767.

52. Carswell, *The Old Cause*, 188.

53. MS Don. b. 18, fo. 90, Edward Tucker/JohnTucker, 8 Apr. 1729.

54. Ibid., fo. 75, Edward Tucker Jr/JohnTucker, 27 Oct. 1728 and fos. 81–2, Edward Tucker Jr/JohnTucker and Richard Tucker, 18 Nov. 1728.

55. MS Don. b. 17, fos. 140–58, Edward Tucker Jr, Will, 25 Jan. 1736/7; TNA PROB 11/696, 1739.

56. MS Don. b. 18, fo. 127, Edward Tucker Jr/Richard Tucker and John Tucker, 28 Jan. 1733.

57. Ibid., fo. 147, Edward Tucker Jr/Dear Son, 19 Apr. 1734.

58. Ibid., fo. 145, Richard Tucker/Edward Tucker Jr, 2 Feb. 1732.

59. MS Don. b. 17–18, c. 105–12. They cost 4d. when sent from London and took 2 days to reach Weymouth.

60. Carswell and Dralle (eds.), *The Political Journal of George Bubb Dodington*, xii; MS Don. c. 110, fo. 83, John Tucker/Richard Tucker, 20 Oct. 1748.

61. MS Don. c. 110, fo. 83, 20 Oct. 1748.

62. Ibid., fo. 119, John Tucker/Richard Tucker, 1 Dec. 1748.

63. Ibid., fo. 33, Richard Tucker/John Tucker, 4 Aug. 1748.

64. Ibid., fo. 53, John Tucker/Richard Tucker, 6 Sept. 1748; MS Don. c. 111, fo. 9, Richard Tucker/John Tucker, 14 Apr. 1753; TNA D1843/1/6/3, 1729.

65. MS Don. b. 18, fo. 133, Richard Tucker/John Tucker, 5 Mar. 1733.

66. [R. Graves], *A New Weymouth Guide* [*c.*1800], 17.
67. MS Don. b. 23, fo. 53, Richard Tucker/John Tucker, 30 Aug. 1758.
68. MS Don. c. 110, fo. 72, John Tucker/Richard Tucker, 12 Apr. 1742.
69. MS Don. c. 111, fo. 6, Richard Tucker/John Tucker, n.d.
70. MS Don. c. 105, fo. 72.
71. MS Don. c. 110, fo. 119, John Tucker/Edward Tucker Sr, 1 Dec. 1748.
72. MS Don. c. 105, fo. 101, John Tucker/Richard Tucker, 4 May 1742.
73. MS Don. c. 110, fo. 119.
74. Young was a regular member of the Dodington household at Eastbury and Tucker probably knew him. Carswell, *The Old Cause*, 131–268 (159–61, 201, 204–5, 210, 214–15, 235).
75. Edward Young, *Night Thoughts* (1751); MS Don. c. 111, fo. 21, John Tucker/Richard Tucker, 21 Apr. 1753.
76. MS Don. b. 23, fos. 43–6, Richard Tucker/Edward Tucker III, 30 Nov. 1757.
77. MS Don. b. 18, fo. 6, Mary Tucker/John Tucker, 24 Nov. 1724; ibid., b. 18, fo. 6, Mary Tucker/John Tucker, 14 Nov. 1724.
78. MS Don. c. 105, fo. 64, Martha Tucker/Richard Tucker, 7 Apr. 1742.
79. MS Don. c. 130, fo. 19, Letter to Rebecca Steward, 24 Apr.
80. Ibid. 130, fos. 4–5, Dorothy Tucker/Rebecca Steward, 10 Apr. 1780.
81. Ambrose Heal, *The English Writing-Masters and their Copy-books 1570–1800* (Cambridge 1931), xvi.
82. MS Don. c. 111.
83. MS Don. b. 18, fos. 81–2, Edward Tucker Jr/John Tucker, 18 Nov. 1728.
84. Ibid., fo. 62, Richard Tucker/John Tucker, 4 Oct. 1728.
85. Ibid., fo. 70, Richard Tucker/John Tucker,16 Oct. 1728.
86. MS Don. c. 105, fo. 51, John Tucker/Richard Tucker, 30 Mar. 1742; MS Don. c. 110, fo. 97, John Tucker/Richard Tucker, 5 Nov. 1748.
87. MS Don. b. 18, fo. 85, Edward Tucker Jr/John Tucker, 20 Nov. 1728.
88. Martin Clare, *Youth's Introduction to Trade and Business*, 4th edn (1735), 69; George Brown, *The New English Letter-Writer* (1779), b2r–v; Ann Fisher, *A New Grammar* (1757).
89. MS Don. b. 17, fo. 29, Richard Tucker/John Tucker, 2 Dec. 1724.
90. MS Don. b. 18, fos. 104–5, Richard Tucker/John Tucker, 20 Oct. 1729.
91. Ibid., fo. 35, Richard Tucker and Edward Tucker Jr/John Tucker, 2 Jan. 1725.
92. Ibid., fo. 22, Richard Tucker/John Tucker, 9 Dec. 1724; fo. 33, John Robins/John Tucker, 30 Dec. 1724; fo. 62, Richard Tucker/John Tucker, 4 Oct. 1728; Lynne Magnusson, *Shakespeare and Social Dialogue* (Cambridge, 1999), 131.
93. MS Don. c. 105, fos. 55–6, John Tucker/Richard Tucker, 1 Apr. 1742.
94. Black and Harris, 'John Tucker MP', 15–38.
95. Sedgwick, *The House of Commons 1715–54*, 485.
96. For merchant MPs see Namier and Brooke, *The House of Commons 1754–90*, i, 131–8.

97. Bodl G. Pamph 1574 (7), Great Britain, House of Commons, *A Further Report . . . to enquire into the conduct of Robert E. of Orford* (1742), 17–20.

98. Sedgwick, *The House of Commons 1715–54*, ii, 484–5; Namier and Brooke, *The House of Commons 1754–90*, iii, 565.

99. My italics. MS Don. c. 110, fo. 43, John Tucker/Richard Tucker, 18 Aug. 1748.

100. For example MS Don. c. 112, fos. 117ff.

101. Carswell and Dralle (eds.), *The Political Journal of George Bubb Dodington*, 129, 147.

102. MS Don. b. 20 fo. 11, Dashwood letters and papers 1761–3; *ODNB*/7179, Namier and Brooke, *The House of Commons 1754–90*, ii, 300–1; Carswell and Dralle (eds.), *The Political Journal of George Bubb Dodington*, 473; Carswell, *The Old Cause*, 188–90; Donald Mc Cormick, *The Hell-Fire Club* (1958), 199–201 lists members including John.

103. Bodl MSS D. D. Dashwood, R. 11/8, Twelve letters from John Tucker to Sir Francis Dashwood, 1754–67, especially 11 Aug. 1764 and 22 March 1766; Carswell, *The Old Cause*, 253.

104. Carswell and Dralle (eds.), *The Political Journal of George Bubb Dodington*, 334–5.

105. Ibid., 95.

106. Ibid., 155.

107. MS Don. c. 105, John Tucker/Richard Tucker, 1 Apr. 1742.

108. Carswell, *The Old Cause*, 188–9; Carswell and Dralle (eds.), *The Political Journal of George Bubb Dodington*, 114.

109. Carswell and Dralle (eds.), *The Political Journal of George Bubb Dodington*, 355, 439.

110. My italics. Ibid., 439.

111. French, *The Middle Sort of People in Provincial England 1600–1750*, 263–4.

112. MS Don. b. 18, fo. 60, Dorothy Gollop/John Tucker, 28 Sept. 1728.

113. MS Don. b. 23, fo. 83, Richard Tucker/John Tucker, 15 Feb. 1760.

114. MS Don. b. 17, fos. 104–5, Richard Tucker/Edward Tucker Jr, 9 Apr. 1729. Only in London when addressed as MP is he sometimes called Esq.

115. MS Don. c. 128, fos. 1–2, 1731, 1734.

116. MS Don. c. 111, fo. 52, Richard Tucker/John Tucker, 9 May [1753]; fo. 65, 19 May [1753].

117. Maule, *Catalogue*, 146.

118. MS Don. c. 127, fo. 126, Will of John Tucker, merchant, 2 Dec. 1728; fo. 127/1, Will of John Tucker, Esquire, 1 Mar. 1777; TNA PROB 11/1059; MS Don. c. 127, fo. 28, Will of Richard Tucker, 6 Jan. 1775; TNA PROB 11/1028.

119. MS Don. b. 18, fo. 68, Richard Tucker/John Tucker, 14 Oct. 1728.

120. MS Don. c. 106, fos. 12–13, John Tucker/Richard Tucker, 25 Jan. 1742.

121. MS Don. c. 111, fo. 15, Richard Tucker/John Tucker, 18 Apr. 1753.

122. MS Don. c. 105, fo. 185, John Tucker/Samuel White, 19 July 1740.

123. MS Don. b. 18, fos. 135−6, Richard Tucker/John Tucker, 28 Mar. 1733.

124. MS Don. c. 106, fos. 18−19, Richard Tucker/John Tucker, 29 Jan. 1742.

125. Ibid., fos. 14−15, John Tucker/Richard Tucker, 27 Jan. 1742.

126. MS Don. b. 18, fos. 153−4, Richard Tucker/John Tucker, 25 Feb. 1736.

127. MS Don. c. 106, fos. 14−15.

128. MS Don. c. 110, fo. 110, John Tucker/Richard Tucker, 24 Nov. 1748.

129. Black and Harris, 'John Tucker MP', 24, n. 42; MS Don. c. 105, fo. 55.

130. MS Don. c.105, fos. 14−15, 27 Jan. 1742.

131. French, *Middle Sort*, 21, 25−7, 266−7; David Postles, 'The politics of address in early modern England', *Journal of Historical Sociology*, 18 (2005), 99−121.

132. French, *Middle Sort*, 229, 234.

133. Helen Berry, 'Sense and singularity', in H. R. French and Jonathan Barry (eds.), *Identity and Agency in England, 1500−1800* (Houndmills, 2004), 178−99 (181).

134. Bath Central Library (BCL), R69/12675 B920, Edmund Rack, 'A Desultory Journal of Events &c at Bath, Dec. 22 1779', Typescript.

135. Vera Nunning (Koln), 'The invention of the (superiority of the) middling ranks in eighteenth-century England', *Journal for the Study of British Culture*, 2 (1995), 25−35.

136. MS Don. c. 106, fos. 18−19, Richard Tucker/John Tucker, 29 Jan. 1742.

137. MS Don. b. 18, fos. 138−9, Richard Tucker/John Tucker, 3 July, 1733; b. 18, fo. 145, Richard Tucker and John Tucker/Edward Tucker Jr, 2 Feb. 1734.

138. Ibid., fo. 137, Richard Tucker/John Tucker, 30 June 1733.

139. Ibid., fo. 131, Edward Tucker Jr/John Tucker, 16 Feb. 1733.

140. Ibid., fo. 145, Richard Tucker and John Tucker/Edward Tucker Jr, 2 Feb. 1734.

141. Black and Harris, 'John Tucker MP', 33.

142. Ibid., 26, n. 52.

143. MS Don. b. 18, fos. 138−9, Richard Tucker/John Tucker, 3 July 1733.

144. Ibid., fo. 140, Richard Tucker/John Tucker, 5 July 1733.

145. MS Don. c. 110, fo. 79, John Tucker/Richard Tucker, 13 Oct. 1748; c. 106, fos. 20−1, Richard Tucker/John Tucker, 31 Jan. 1743; c. 110, fo. 115, John Tucker/Richard Tucker, 29 Nov. 1748; c. 111, fo. 12, Richard Tucker/John Tucker, 18 Apr. 1753.

146. MS Don. c. 111, fo. 15, Richard Tucker/John Tucker, 18 Apr. 1753.

147. Joyce Ellis, *The Georgian Town, 1680−1840* (Basingstoke, 2001), 68.

148. MS Don. c. 111, fo. 15, Richard Tucker/John Tucker, 18 Apr. 1753.

149. Ibid., fo. 87, Richard Tucker/John Tucker, 30 May 1755.

150. Ibid., fo. 54, Richard Tucker/John Tucker, 12 May 1753.

151. MS Don. b. 18, fos. 156−7, John Tucker/Richard Tucker, 24 Feb. 1737.

152. David Gerber, 'Epistolary ethics', *Journal of American Ethnic History*, 19 (2000), 3−24 (3).

153. E. P. Thompson, *The Making of the English Working Class* (NY, 1966).

154. S. Wallech, 'Class versus rank', *Journal of the History of Ideas*, 47 (1986), 409–31; Mike Savage, 'Social mobility and class analysis', *Social History*, 19 (1994), 169–79; Robert Erikson and John H. Goldthorpe, *The Constant Flux* (Oxford, 1992); Seed, 'Argument: Capital and class formation in early industrial England', *Social History*, 18 (1993), 17–30.

155. BLY MSS OSB 32, Bateman Family Correspondence with Box 1/5 Inventory and will, 1/7 poem, 1/12 misc poetry, prayers, school exercise, accts 1777–91. Unfoliated. MS OSB 32/36, Elizabeth Wilson/Rebekah Bateman, 12 Dec. 94. The Beinecke Library, Yale University is the location of all references to the Bateman collection in this chapter.

156. MS OSB 32/9–10, are from Rebekah, starting 11 Oct. 1780; OSB 32/23–5, 31–2, 34–5 are to Rebekah at Mrs Trinder's school, Northampton.

157. MS OSB 32/10, Rebekah Bateman/Mary Jane Hodson, 7 Aug. 1781.

158. Ibid., 31 Nov. 1781.

159. Congregational Library at Dr Williams's Library (hereafter CL DWL), Handlist of Manuscripts, Nov. 2004; MS OSB 32/25, 17 Feb. 1778. Sarah Clegg died at Higher Ardwick and was buried in the Independent Meeting House at Gatley near Cheadle, Chester. Fletcher Moss, *A History of the Old Parish of Cheadle... the Hamlet of Gatley* (Didsbury, 1894); BLY MS OSB 32/24, Letters of Sarah (Pearson) Clegg; Bodl MS Top Derbyshire d. 1 (hereafter MS Top D), Materials for a History of the Bateman Family, fos. 315, 321, 403; CL DWL MS II c. 36, Sarah Clegg/Elizabeth Wilson, 19 Sept. 1798; Manchester Central Library (MCL), Archives and Local Studies, MS M162, o.s., Moseley St Chapel Membership Rolls 1800–1, 1803, 1806–19; CL DWL Hd 4/9, Jonathan Scott Arthur Clegg, 13 Aug. 1781.

160. MS OSB 32/25, 17 Feb. 1778, Arthur Clegg died age 85; 32/25, Arthur Clegg/Rebekah Bateman and Elizabeth Wilson (neé Clegg), 1777–8; Charles Leach, *Manchester Congregationalism* (Manchester, 1989); Benjamin Nightingale, *Lancashire Nonconformity* (Manchester, 1893), 53; MSS Derbyshire d. 1, fos. 237–9, 242, 403; W. H. Thomson, *History of Manchester to 1852* (Altrincham, 1967), 183; CL DWL MS II c. 34, Arthur Clegg/Thomas Wilson, 20 Jan. 1808; MCL M162 o.s., Moseley St Chapel Minutes, 1800–1, 1804, 1812–14, 1818; MCL M162 Box 5, Church Minutes, 1797–8; M162 Box 24, Moseley Street Subscription and Building Accounts 1787–95; M162 Box 6, Church Minutes, 1798–1827 with members list 1798–1800; Deeds: M/C1–1379, M/C579, M/C742, MC1524; Elizabeth Raffald, *Directory of Manchester and Salford* (1772–3, 1781); Edward Holme, *Manchester and Salford Directory* (1788); Scholes, *Manchester and Salford Directory* (1794, 1797); G. Bancks, *Directory* (1800).

161. Raffald, *Directory of Manchester and Salford* (1788) but not earlier; Scholes, *Manchester and Salford Directory* (1794, 1794, 1797, 1800). By 1794, their house and work were separate at 2 Cromford Court and 116 Levers Row. By

1797 their son William had joined the company. Bodl MS Top D, fos. 72, 74, Register of Marriages, Thos. Bateman, Cotton Merchant and Rebekah Clegg, Spinster, 13 Apr. 1786, Register, Collegiate and Parish Church. He was the eldest son of Richard Bateman of Hartington. Later he returned to Yorkshire.

162. CL DWL MSS II c. 34–5, Letters and papers of Thomas Wilson; CL DWL MSSII c. 88, Collection of Documents relating to Thomas Wilson (1764–1843), his wife Elizabeth, their children Rebekah Stratten (d. 1870); Elizabeth Coombs (d. 1878), and their son Joshua (1795–1874). MS II c. 88/7, Marriage Settlement of Rebekah, 6 May 1819; c. 88/8, Marriage Settlement of Elizabeth, 9 Jan. 1823; c. 88/9, Settlement of Thomas Wilson, 7 Apr. 1838; c. 88/10, Probate of Will and codicil of Thomas Wilson, with copy, 9 Apr. 1838 and codicil, 20 Apr. 1842.

163. Seed, 'Theologies of power' in R. J. Morris (ed.), *Class, Power, and Social Structure in British Nineteenth-century Towns* (Leicester, 1986), 117. By 1831 there were about 2,000 congregations and by 1851 over 3,200. I thank David Wykes for these figures.

164. Michael Watts, *The Dissenters*, 34–6, 55–61; Royle, *Modern Britain*, 319; Gilbert, *Religion and Society*, 53; Deryck Lovegrove, *Established Church, Sectarian People* (Cambridge, 1988), 30–1, 44–8, 63–77.

165. Gilbert, *Religion and Society*, 89.

166. MS OSB 32/36, Elizabeth Wilson/Rebekah Bateman, Apr. 1794.

167. Kenneth Brown, 'The Congregational ministry in the first half of the nineteenth century', *The Journal of the United Reformed Church History Society*, 3 (1983), 6.

168. Lovegrove, *The Rise of the Laity in Evangelical Protestantism* (2002), 7; Clive Field, 'Adam and Eve', *Journal of Ecclesiastical History*, 44 (1993), 63–79.

169. Keeble, *The Literary Culture of Nonconformity*, 10; Alan Sell, *Dissenting Thought and the Life of the Churches* (San Francisco, 1990), 29.

170. Sell, 'The worship of English Congregationalism' in Lukas Vischer (ed.), *Christian Worship in Reformed Churches Past and Present* (Grand Rapids, MI, 2005), 83–106; Michael Watts, *The Dissenters*, 241.

171. MS OSB 32/31, Ann Rutt/Rebekah Bateman, 30 Dec. 1777.

172. R. T. Jones, *Congregationalism in England 1662–1962* (1962), 140–70.

173. George Wilson McCree, *Thomas Wilson, the Silkman* (1879), 14.

174. Bernard Manning, *Essays in Orthodox Dissent* (1939), 185.

175. Jones, *Congregationalism in England 1662–1962*, 109.

176. Clyde Binfield, *So Down to Prayers* (1977), 11, 26–9.

177. Jones, *Congregationalism in England 1662–1962*, 184; Shani d'Cruze, *Our Time in God's Hands* (Chelmsford, 1991), 26; Davidoff and Hall, *Family Fortunes*, 97; David Wykes, 'A finished monster of the true Birmingham breed' in Sell (ed.), *Protestant Nonconformists and the West Midlands of England* (Keele, 1996), 57.

178. Sir Thomas Baker, *Memorials of a Dissenting Chapel . . . in Manchester* (1884).

179. R. Slate, *A Brief History of the Rise and Progress of the Lancaster Congregational Union* (1840), 15–21; C. E. Surman, 'Roby's Academy', *Transactions of the Congregational Historical Society*, 13 (1937–9), 41–53; F. A. Bruton, *A Short History of Manchester and Salford*, 2nd edn (Wakefield, 1970), 118, 158.

180. Leach, *Manchester Congregationalism*, 47; MS OSB 32/30, Sarah Clegg/Rebekah Bateman and Elizabeth Wilson, n.d.

181. MCL M162 Box 5, Confession of Faith, 22 Mar. 1795 and Church Minutes, Thomas Kennedy 1798; Leach, *Manchester Congregationalism*, 49; MS OSB, 32/36, Elizabeth Wilson/Rebekah Bateman, 10 Feb. 1796.

182. MS OSB 32/36, Elizabeth Wilson/Rebekah Bateman, 6 May [1791].

183. MCL MS M162 Box 5, 1, 12, 18 Mar. 1797.

184. W. H. Shercliff, *Gatley United Reformed Church . . . 1777–1977* (1976), 15; Nightingale, *Lancashire Nonconformity*, 138.

185. MCL M162 Box 5, 11 Mar. 1798; CL DWL MS II c. 36, Sarah Clegg/Elizabeth Wilson, 19 Sept. 1798.

186. MCL M162 Box 24, Moseley Street Subscription and Building Accounts, 1787–95, 2, 4–5.

187. MCL M162 Box 6; M162 o.s., Member list, 1800 includes chart of tickets used.

188. There were 178 members in 1800, 240 in 1820, 260 in 1832. Many more attended services. CL DWL MSS II c. 34, Revd Samuel Bradley of Manchester/Thomas Wilson, 28 Nov. 1821.

189. Alan Kidd, *Manchester*, 3rd edn (Edinburgh, 2002), ch. 1; Thomson, *History of Manchester to 1852*, 203, 213, 235, maps, 122, 182–3; CL DWL MSS II c. 34, Samuel Bradley/Thomas Wilson, 28 Nov. 1821.

190. Anna Walker, *Diary*, 30 Mar. 1788, quoted in Thomson, *History of Manchester to 1852*, 237. Lever's Row was a prolongation of Market Street, afterwards called Picadilly Street; Bancks, *Directory* (1802), 14, notes William Bateman, cotton merchant, house at 16 Levers Row.

191. Samuel Curwen quoted in Thomson, *History of Manchester to 1852*, 222. See also J. Seed, 'Commerce and the liberal arts' in J. Wolff and J. Seed (eds.), *The Culture of Capital* (Manchester, 1988), 45–82.

192. George Evans, comp., *Record of the Provincial Assembly in Lancashire and Cheshire* (Manchester, 1896), 128. William Hawkes was minister.

193. MS OSB 32/6, Rebekah Bateman/Thomas Bateman, 13 Dec. 1792; CL DWL MSS II d. 5, fos. 13–14; Thomson, *History of Manchester to 1852*, 240–9. Davidoff and Hall, *Family Fortunes*, 97.

194. MS OSB 32/24, Sarah Clegg/Rebekah Bateman, 21 Sept. 1780. For political comments see: 32/6, Rebekah Bateman/Thomas Bateman, 20 July 1791; 32/36, Elizabeth Wilson/Rebekah Bateman, 18 July 1791, 30 Oct. 1793, 17 Dec. 1793, 13 Jan. 1793, 26 Feb. 1794, 10 May 94, 1 Dec. 1795, 5 Jan. 1796, 3 Mar. 1797; 32/39 Mary Wilson/Rebekah Bateman, 11 Feb. 1793.

195. MS OSB 32/25, Sarah Clegg/Rebekah Bateman and Elizabeth Wilson, 17 Nov. 1777, 20 Jan. 1778, 18 May 1792.

196. MCL L1/56/1/1, Clegg family pedigree; Bodl MS Top D, fo. 313; Raffald, *Directory of Manchester and Salford* (1772) cites Arthur Clegg, Timber-Merchant, Great Turner St. His partner was James Wild; MCL M/C 579, 1786; M/C 772, 1799; M/C 1524, 1792.

197. Leach, *Manchester Congregationalism*, 49.

198. MS OSB 32/36, Elizabeth Wilson/Rebekah Bateman, 20 Oct. 92.

199. Ibid., Elizabeth Wilson/Rebekah Bateman, 6 May 1791; 32/10, Rebekah Bateman/Mary Jane Hodson, [1782]; 32/11, Rebekah Bateman/Elizabeth Wilson, 1 Mar. 1781.

200. MS OSB 32/34, Ann Wilson/Rebekah Bateman, 1 Apr. 1781.

201. MS OSB 32/10, Rebekah Bateman/Mary Jane Hodson, 31 Nov. 1781.

202. Ibid., Rebekah Bateman/Mary Jane Hodson, [19 Jan. 1782].

203. MS OSB 32/6, Rebekah Bateman/Thomas Bateman, 12 Oct. 1788 ('ye words of Saul in ye Samuel 24 Chapter').

204. Ibid., Rebekah Bateman/Thomas Bateman, 27 Aug. 1788.

205. Ibid., Rebekah Bateman/Thomas Bateman, 4 Mar. 1789.

206. Ibid., Elizabeth Wilson/Rebekah Bateman, 21 Dec. 1792.

207. MS OSB 32/8, Rebekah Bateman/Arthur Clegg, 19 May 1797 with 2 copies in another hand and 32/6, n.d.

208. MS OSB 32/36, Elizabeth Wilson/Rebekah Bateman, 3 Dec. 1787.

209. MS Top D, fo. 74, 25 July 1787; MCL, Local studies news clippings file: Thomas Bateman GOR 10–21–71. Letter 25 Aug. 1881; MS OSB 32/7, Rebekah Bateman/Thomas Bateman II at Mr Littlewoods school, 2 Dec. 1796; 32/19, William Bateman/Thomas Bateman, 29 Jan. 1801 with Revd Simon at St Paul Cray School, Kent; John W. Brown, comp., *Hasted's History of St. Paul's Cray* (1797, repr. 1997).

210. MS Top D, fos. 74–6 notes Thomas Bateman in Everton near Liverpool, 1810 and died there. MS OSB 32/16, 22 Apr. 1810.

211. MS Top D, fo. 110. Rebekah married Samuel Hope of Liverpool (a broker in 1781, a banker in 1824) in 1816. She lived at Everton. OSB MS 32/14, Thomas Bateman Jr/Rebekah Bateman Jr, Jan. 1810; MS OSB 32/4; CL DWL MSS II c. 36.

212. MCL 5106 ch. 68, Records of Gatley Congregational Church; W. Urwick, *Historical Sketches of Nonconformity in Cheshire* (1864); *Congregational Church, Elm Road Gatley* (n.d.), n.p. 'Gatley was then no more than a collection of cottages grouped round the village green. It was a small centre of hand-loom weaving in linen and later in cotton.' Thomas was a trustee and benefactor of the congregation.

213. MS OSB 32/6, Rebekah Bateman/Thomas Bateman, 9 July 1791; Shercliff, *Gatley*; CL DWL MSS II c. 36, M. L. Maurice/Elizabeth Wilson, 14 Aug. 1809.

214. MS OSB 32/20, Indenture, Thomas and William Bateman, 31 Aug. 1807.
215. CL DWL MSS II c. 34/1, Thomas Bateman/Thomas Wilson, 29 Jan. 1836. Thomas Bateman's letters are found in DWL New College MSS, for example 302/5, 308/8, 343/3–4.
216. MS OSB 32/6, Rebekah Bateman/Thomas Bateman, 20 June 1787.
217. MS OSB 32/36, Elizabeth Wilson/Rebekah Bateman, 17 Sept. 1793.
218. Ibid., Rebekah Bateman/Thomas Bateman, 13 Dec. 1787.
219. MS OSB 32/6, Rebekah Bateman/Thomas Bateman, 22 May 1788.
220. Ibid., Rebekah Bateman/Thomas Bateman, 10 Sept. 1792.
221. MS OSB 32/37, Elizabeth Wilson/Thomas Bateman, 20 Oct. 1798.
222. MS OSB 32/6, Rebekah Bateman/Thomas Bateman, 7 Dec. 1786.
223. Ibid., Rebekah Bateman/Thomas Bateman, 20 June 1787.
224. Ibid., Rebekah Bateman/Thomas Bateman, 7 Dec. 1786.
225. Ibid., Rebekah Bateman/Thomas Bateman, 7 May 1790.
226. Ibid., Rebekah Bateman/Thomas Bateman, 3 Feb. 1789.
227. Ibid., Rebekah Bateman/Thomas Bateman, 12 Apr. 1788.
228. Ibid., Rebekah Bateman/Thomas Bateman, 27 Aug. 1788.
229. Ibid., Rebekah Bateman/Thomas Bateman, 1 Sept. 1792.
230. Ibid., Rebekah Bateman/Thomas Bateman, 12 Sept. 1792.
231. MS OSB 32/36, Elizabeth Wilson/Rebekah Bateman, 21 Dec. 1792.
232. MS OSB 32/26, John Hope/Thomas Bateman, 24 June 1797.
233. Bodl MS Top D, fo. 406, Newspaper article, 22 Mar. 1823; CL DWL MS II d. 5, fos. 56–7, 1 Aug. 1823. Wilson notes he visited 'my relation Thos Bateman Esq High Sheriff for the County at Middleton'. DRO D258/54/3, 6, Derbyshire volume, Daniel and Samuel Lysons' *Magna Britannia*; D6755/2; Q/AT/1/12, Files of Assize cases, 1750–8; DRO D258/23/8/16, Delivery to Thomas Bateman, present sheriff, of the County Court books, 1823.
234. NTA PROB 11/2063, 2070; DRO D2323/11/2, Correspondence and accounts for Bateman's Charity, 1897–1950; DRO F511, Bateman of Middleton by Youlgreave estate correspondence, 1791–1867; DRO D6755, Accounts by Thomas Bateman; Will of Thomas Bateman of Youlgreave, Derbyshire, 19 Oct. 1847. I thank Clyde Binfield for data about Bateman's activity in chapels at Gatley, Buxton, and Middleton.
235. CL DWL MSS II c. 88/11, Copy of will, Elizabeth Wilson, 31 Jan. 1844.
236. Joshua Wilson, *Memoir of the Life and Character of Thomas Wilson, Esq, Treasurer of Highbury College* (1849), 83, 8 Nov. 1790.
237. Ibid., 74. Compare with David L. Wykes, 'The reluctant businessman', *Transactions of the Leicestershire Archaeological and Historical Society*, lxix (1995), 71–85.
238. CL DWL MSS II d. 5, fo. 1, Thomas Wilson, *Autobiographical Notes . . . to which are added several letters received by him 1799–1840*; Clive Binfield, 'Business paternalism and the Congregational ideal' in David Jeremy (ed.), *Business and Religion in Britain* (Aldershot, 1988), 118–41.

239. Wilson, *Memoir of the Life and Character of Thomas Wilson*; DWL New College MSS 125/1, Hoxton Academy Minute Book, Letter of Thomas Wilson to Ministers, 10 Mar. 1797; Rules of the Academy, 137/1–2; Copy letter book of Thomas Wilson Apr. 1833–May 1837, 225; Letters to Thomas Wilson relating to Hoxton Academy, 1794–1807; McCree, *Thomas Wilson, the Silkman*, 9–10.

240. Wilson, *Memoir of the Life and Character of Thomas Wilson*, ch. 6.

241. CL DWL MS II d. 5, fo. 9.

242. Clyde Binfield, *So Down to Prayers*, 10.

243. John Creasey, *The Congregational Library* (1978), 1.

244. Robert Halley, 'Recollections of old Dissent', *The Congregationalist*, iv (1875), 94.

245. CL DWL MSS II c. 88, fo. 11.

246. MS OSB 32/36, Elizabeth Wilson/Rebekah Bateman, 6 May 1791.

247. CL DWL MSS II c. 88, fos. 7–8.

248. Wilson, *Memoir of the Life and Character of Thomas Wilson*, 84–5.

249. Ibid., 83.

250. Ibid.

251. MS OSB 32/36, Elizabeth Wilson/Rebekah Bateman, 29 Sept. 1795.

252. Ibid., Elizabeth Wilson/Rebekah Bateman, 10 Apr. 1792.

253. Ibid., Elizabeth Wilson/Rebekah Bateman, 9 Feb. 1782.

254. Ibid., Elizabeth Wilson/Rebekah Bateman, 10 Feb. 1796.

255. Wilson, *Memoir of the Life and Character of Thomas Wilson*, 480.

256. Ibid., 482.

257. MS OSB 32/36, Elizabeth Wilson/Rebekah Bateman, 30 Oct. 93; DWL MSS II d. 5, Thomas Wilson, autobiographical notes, fos. 11–14.

258. She waited three years to have Joshua.

259. MS OSB 32/36, Elizabeth Wilson/Rebekah Bateman, 17 Dec. 1793.

260. Ibid., Elizabeth Wilson/Rebekah Bateman, 25 June 1792.

261. Ibid., Elizabeth Wilson/Rebekah Bateman, 9 Feb. 1792.

262. Ibid., Elizabeth Wilson/Rebekah Bateman, 2 Oct. 1792.

263. MS OSB 32/10, Rebekah Bateman/Mary Jane Hodson, 29 Apr. 1784.

264. Ibid., Rebekah Bateman/Mary Jane Hodson, 7 Mar. 1782.

265. MS OSB 32/36, Elizabeth Wilson/Rebekah Bateman, 25 Oct. 1791.

266. Ibid., Elizabeth Wilson/Rebekah Bateman [1791].

267. Ibid., Elizabeth Wilson/Rebekah Bateman, 26 Feb. 1794.

268. Ibid., Elizabeth Wilson/Rebekah Bateman, 3 Sept. 1787.

269. MS OSB 32/39, Mary Wilson/Rebekah Bateman, 10 Dec. 1792.

270. MS OSB 32/36, Elizabeth Wilson/Rebekah Bateman, 20 Oct. 1794.

271. Ibid., Elizabeth Wilson/Rebekah Bateman, 20 Nov. 1792.

272. Ibid., Elizabeth Wilson/Rebekah Bateman, 17 Sept. 1792.

273. Ibid., Elizabeth Wilson/Rebekah Bateman, 12 Dec. 1794.

274. Davidoff and Hall, *Family Fortunes*, 76–106.

275. CL DWL MSS II c. 34, Samuel Bradley/Thomas Wilson, 6 Nov. 1821.

276. R. H. Campbell, 'A critique of the Christian businessman and his paternalism' in David Jeremy (ed.), *Business and Religion in Britain* (Aldershot, 1988), 27−46.

277. Leach, *Manchester Congregationalism*, 49.

278. CL DWL MSS II c. 34, Samuel Bradley/Thomas Wilson, Oct. 1805.

279. Wilson, *Memoir of the Life and Character of Thomas Wilson*, 82.

280. Margaret Jacob and Matthew Kadane, 'Missing, now found in the eighteenth century', *American Historical Review*, 29 (2003), 29.

281. Davidoff and Hall, *Family Fortunes*, 450.

282. MS OSB 32/2, Anna Maria Alwood/Rebekah Bateman, 4 Sept.

283. MS OSB 32/36, Elizabeth Wilson/Rebekah Bateman, 7 Mar. 1793.

284. MS OSB 32/3, William Armitage/Rebekah Bateman, 20 Dec. 1783.

285. MS OSB 32/1, Anna Maria Alwood/Rebekah Bateman, 4 June 1787; 32/1, Anna Maria Alwood/Rebekah Bateman, 19 Sept. 1786.

286. Samuel Stansfield (ed.), 'Memoirs of Ruth Follows', *The Friends' Library*, iv (Philadelphia, 1840), 29.

287. Library of the Religious Society of Friends in Britain (LSF), Temp MSS 127, Follows Papers. Temp MS 127/3/39, Samuel Follows/Ruth Follows and George Follows, 1 Jan. 1782. The Library of the Religious Society of Friends is the location of all references to the Follows collection in this chapter. Dates in the Quaker style are converted throughout to match the style of other letter-writers.

288. Temp MS 127/3/40, Ruth Follows/Samuel Follows, 19 Aug. 1782.

289. Temp MSS 127, Follows Papers *c.*1723−1851; Dictionary of Quaker Biography (DQB), typescript; Indexes to Testimonies 1700−1925; Typed Register Extracts; Letters indexed in MS catalogue; Temp MS 127/2 handwritten dates of children and TNA registers.

290. Stansfield, 'Memoirs of Ruth Follows', 22.

291. Ibid., 25. Ruth was the daughter of Richard and Ruth of Weston, Notts; Temp MS 127/2/1, R. Alcock/Ruth Follows, 24 Oct. 1738; 127/6/3, Testimony of Ruth Alcock.

292. Leicestershire Record Office (LRO) PR/T/1804/86, Will of George Follows, basket maker, 1804; David Butler, *The Quaker Meeting Houses of Britain*, i (1999), 354−5; *ODNB*/9797; Stansfield, 'Memoirs of Ruth Follows', 24; Nottingham Record Office (NotRO), List of Quaker Holdings; R. H. Evans, 'The Quakers of Leicestershire 1660−1714', *Transactions of the Leicestershire Archaeology Society* (1992), 121−35; E. Quine, *Quakers in Leicestershire* (1968).

293. Temp MS 127/4/14, Ruth Follows/Joseph Fellowes, 5 Feb. 1775.

294. Stansfield, 'Memoirs of Ruth Follows', 26.

295. Butler, *The Quaker Meeting Houses of Britain*, i, 354. Quaker ministers were not ordained. The practice of acknowledging them in monthly meeting developed in the eighteenth century. See E. Milligan and M. Thomas, *My Ancestors were Quakers* (1998), sec. 40.

296. LSF DQB; Temp MS 127/6, Ruth Alcock's journeys 1723; Testimony, 1738. For women ministers see Margaret Hope Bacon, *Mothers of Feminism* (San Francisco, 1986), ch. 2; Su Fang Ng, 'Marriage and discipline', *The Seventeenth Century*, 18 (2003), 113–40.

297. Temp MS 127/10.

298. Norfolk Record Office (NFRO) Marriage Certificate, SF303/38 302 × 1, 29 Aug. 1769; Temp MS 127/3/3, 17, 22, Samuel Follows/Ruth and George Follows, 12 Mar. 1769; 127/7, 23 Aug. 1771, 27 Jan. 1778. Richard was a Norwich basket-maker.

299. TNA IR 26/375; LRO PR/T/1809/46, Will of Joseph, 1809; NotRO Q312/107, Certificate of Consent George and Ruth Follows on the marriage of their son Joseph and Rebecca Kent, 3 Mar. 1800. I thank Jess Jenkins for help with wills.

300. TNA PROB 11/1527, pr. 11 Nov. 1811 may be Samuel's will.

301. *Journal of the Life, Labours, and Travels of Thomas Shillitoe*, i (1839), 53; *Memoirs of the Life and Travels . . . of Sarah Stephenson* (Philadelphia, 1807), 545.

302. *Some Account of the Life and Religious Experience of Mary Alexander* (York, 1822), 40.

303. Frost, *Records and Recollections of James Jenkins*, 469.

304. Temp MS 127/3/28, Ruth Follows/Samuel Follows, 27 Aug. 1779.

305. Temp MS 127/3/23, Ruth Follows/Samuel Follows, 24 July 1778. Relief would have come from Quakers, not public sources.

306. Joseph is called yeoman in his will. TNA IR 36/375; Temp MS 127/7, Letters of George and Emily Hyatt, 1827–47, MS 127/5, Letters of Joseph and Rebecca Follows, 1814–36. Joseph's property included a bookcase and 'handsome' furniture, tea trays, looking glasses etc. *Catalogue of the Real & Usfull Household Furniture . . . To be sold by Auction. upon the Premises of the Late Joseph Follows of Castle Donington* (8 June 1810).

307. Adrian Davies, *Quakers in English Society 1665–1725* (Oxford, 2000), 108–16; Rebecca Larson, *Daughters of Light* (NY, 1999), 33.

308. Gil Skidmore (ed.), *Strength in Weakness* (Walnut Creek, CA, 2005), 11–12. I thank Skidmore for assistance.

309. Temp MS 127/2/2, Ruth Follows/George Follows, 21 Mar. 1748.

310. Temp MS 127/4/4, Ruth Follows/Joseph Follows, 20 Mar. 1774.

311. Temp MS 127/3/4, Ruth Follows/Samuel Follows, 4 Apr. 1769.

312. Stansfield, 'Memoirs of Ruth Follows', 59.

313. Temp MS 127/2/42, Ruth Follows/George Follows, 7 July 1794.

314. Temp MS 127/3/27, Ruth Follows/Samuel Follows, 29 Oct. 1779.

315. Temp MS 127/2/2, Ruth Follows/George Follows, 21 Mar. 1748; 127/2/3, Ruth Follows/George Follows, 18 Aug. 1760.

316. Stansfield, 'Memoirs of Ruth Follows', 43.

317. Temp MS 127/9/7, Elizabeth Follows/Ruth Follows, 5 Apr. 1783.

318. Temp MS 127/4/8, Joseph Follows/Ruth Follows 30 July 1773.

319. Larson, *Daughters of Light*, 167–8.

320. LSF Temp MSS 745/44/44–8, Robson Papers, Richard and Elizabeth Shackleton/Ruth Follows, 25 Dec. 1773.

321. Temp MS 127/3/19, Ruth Follows/Samuel Follows, 1 Aug. 1777.

322. For another Quaker epistolary network see Sandra Holton, 'Family memory, religion and radicalism' *Quaker Studies*, 9 (2005), 156–75.

323. Richard C. Allen, 'An alternative community in north-east England' in Helen Berry and Jeremy Gregory (eds.), *Creating and Consuming Culture in North East England 1660–1830* (Aldershot, 2003), 107; James Walvin, *The Quakers* (1997), 48–50.

324. Temp MS 127/3/1, Ruth and George Follows/Samuel Follows, 2 Feb. 1769; 127/3/5, July 14 1771.

325. I thank Sylvia Stevens for invaluable advice. LSF DQB, Arthur J. Eddington (ed.), *Minutes of the Norwich Monthly Meeting 1701–1800*, 2 vols. (Norwich, 1935); *The First Fifty Years of Quakerism in Norwich* (1932); Clyde Binfield, 'The pleasures of imagination', *Durham University Journal*, 86 (1994), 227–40; LSF Temp MSS 963/2/1–11; 'American letters of Edmund Peckover of Wisbech', *Journal of the Friends' Historical Society*, 4 (1907), 17–23; J. William Frost, *The Quaker Family in Colonial America* (NY, 1973), 134; East Riding of Yorkshire Archives, DHB/20/51, 147; Madeline McReynolds, *The Peckovers of Wisbech* (Wisbech, 1994).

326. Perry Gauci, *Politics and Society in Great Yarmouth 1660–1722* (Oxford, 1996), 88–91.

327. NFRO, The Records of the Society of Friends in Norfolk, SF1–334; Butler, *The Quaker Meeting Houses of Britain*, i, 437, 462–3.

328. Minutes of monthly meetings show sums set aside for schooling and apprenticing children. See Suffolk RO FK6/3/15, 8 May 1776.

329. Temp MS 127/3/1, Ruth and George Follows/Samuel Follows, 3 Feb. 1769.

330. Temp MS 127/3/3, Samuel Follows/Ruth Follows and George Follows, 12 Mar. 1769.

331. Temp MS 127/3/9, Samuel Follows/Ruth Follows and George Follows, 29 Nov. 1772.

332. Temp MS 127/3/3.

333. Temp MS 127/3/6, Samuel Follows/Ruth Follows, 2 Mar. 1771.

334. He tried to help his brother, Joseph become an under-clerk. Temp MS 127/3/5, Samuel Follows/Ruth Follows and George Follows, 14 July 1771.

335. *Woodbridge . . . The Official Guide* (Woodbridge [1953]); *Orders . . . for . . . the Free School in Woodbridge* (Woodbridge, 1784); *The Terrier of Woodbridge* (1784); Butler, *The Quaker Meeting Houses of Britain*, ii, 567, 580; William White, *White's Suffolk* (Plymouth, 1844, repr. 1970); Dudley Symon, *Woodbridge in Suffolk* (Ipswich, 1934); *Particulars and Conditions of Sale of a Commodious Mansion House . . . sold by auction, Tues 20th of June 1786* (Woodbridge, 1786); Suffolk Record Office (SFRO), 'List of Friends lately come into or gone'; SFRO QS Woodbridge 058, *Woodbridge Directory 1782* lists Quaker tradesmen.

336. SFRO FK6/3/15, Woodbridge Monthly Meeting Minutes 1770–92, 5 Aug. 1776: 'Simon May presented to this Meeting a Certificate of removal from the Mo. Meeting of Yarmouth on behalf of Samuel Followes signifying that during his apprenticeship he was of sober Life and conversation; which was here read to Satisfaction and He recd a Member of this Meeting.'

337. Temp MS 127/3/15, Samuel Follows/Ruth Follows, 13 June, 1776. Samuel's address is 'Dudley and Maw, Grocers'.

338. *Particulars and Conditions of Sale of a Commodious Mansion House . . . sold by auction, Tues 20th of June 1786.*

339. For insights into apprenticeship in Woodbridge see Frost, *Records and Recollections of James Jenkins.* Jenkins was apprenticed to Hannah Jesup, Mary Maw's sister shortly before Samuel. SFRO Q9, fo. 173, John Glyde, Materials for a Study of Woodbridge. The Woodbridge Ipswich Post Coach in 1774 left at 5 a.m. for Gracechurch St Cross Keys London and arrived early the same evening. It cost 3d. per mile.

340. Temp MS 127/3/15, Samuel Follows/Ruth Follows, 13 Dec. 1775; Frost, *Records and Recollections of James Jenkins*; SFRO FK6/3/14, 8 June 1787; SFRO FK6/3/3, 7 May 1787.

341. SFRO, Index of Records Deposited by the Society of Friends; SFRO FK6/3/14–16; FK6/2/3, Accounts of Sufferings, Woodbridge Monthly Meeting, 1793–1833; FK6/3/36, Women's Monthly Meeting, 1779–92; FK 6/3/3, Minutes of Suffolk Quarterly Meeting, Sufferings, Yearly Meeting; FK6/1/1, Lists of members of the Woodbridge Monthly Meetings, Sufferings, 1793–1823; Norma Virgoe and Tom Williamson (eds.), *Religious Dissent in East Anglia* (Norwich, 1993), 17–18; SFRO HD472/7, ii, fo. [47], James, Ford, MS Collection of Materials towards a History of Woodbridge.

342. Frost, *Records and Recollections of James Jenkins*, 33–4.

343. Temp MS 127/3/15, Samuel Follows/Ruth Follows, 13 Dec. 1775.

344. Royle, *Modern Britain*, 319; Gilbert, *Religion and Society*, 34, 41; M. Watts, *The Dissenters*, 263, 269–70, 276, 285, 298. Quaker temperance at this time meant moderation, not total abstinence.

345. Temp MS 127/3/4, Ruth Follows/Samuel Follows, 3 Apr. 1769; Jane Desforges, 'Satisfaction and improvement', *Publishing History*, 49 (2001), 5–48.

346. SFRO FK6/3/15, 3 July 1775, 7 Aug. 1775, 4 Sept. 1775.

347. Frost, *Records and Recollections of James Jenkins*, 33.

348. Temp MS 127/3/20, Samuel Follows/Ruth Follows and George Follows, 5 Sept. 1777.

349. Temp MS 127/9/6, Samuel Follows/Elizabeth Follows, 25 Sept. 1782; Temp MS 127/3/20, Samuel Follows/Ruth Follows and George Follows, 5 Sept. 1777.

350. SFRO FK6/3/15, 3 Feb. 1777, 6 Jan. 1777, 2 Feb. 1777.

351. SFRO FK6/3/15, 2 Aug. 1779.

352. Temp MS 127/3/21, Samuel Follows/Ruth Follows and George Follows, 5 Oct. 1777. His friend appears to be John Gurney of Brooke (1718–79). Verily Anderson, *Friends and Relations* (1980), 12; Arthur J. Eddington, comp, *List and Index of Gurney Manuscripts*, ii (1973), 113–14 (1777).

353. Temp MS 127/3/43, Samuel Follows/Ruth Follows and George Follows, 4 Sept. 1783.

354. Temp MS 127/3/44, Samuel Follows/Joseph Follows, 29 Jan. 1784.

355. Temp MS 127/3/26, Samuel Follows/Ruth Follows and George Follows, 17 Oct. 1779.

356. Eddington, *Minutes of Norwich Monthly Meeting 1766–1800*, i (Norwich 1936), 150, 2 Dec. 1799, 16 Apr. 1799.

357. TNA PROB 11/1527.

358. Temp MS 127/4/21, Joseph Follows/Samuel Follows, 1 Nov. 1780; 127/4/3, Samuel Follows/Joseph Follows, 19 Mar. 1773.

359. Temp MS 127/4, 1772–98, Account of voyage to Newfoundland and Nova Scotia; 127/4/11, Account of journey to the Island of St John in the Gulph of St Lawrence North America; 127/1/31, M. Routh/Ruth Follows, 9 Aug. 1782.

360. Temp MS 127/4/7, Ruth Follows/Joseph Follows, 5 Apr. 1774.

361. Temp MS 127/4/9, Samuel Follows/Joseph Follows, 5 Apr. 1775.

362. Temp MS 127/4/15, Joseph Follows/Samuel Follows, 29 Oct. 1775; 127/4/18, Samuel Follows/Ruth and George Follows, 20 Oct. 1776; 127/4/14, Ruth Follows/Joseph Follows, 5 Feb. 1775.

363. Temp MS 127/4/14, Ruth Follows/Joseph Follows, 5 Feb. 1775.

364. Temp MS 127/4/21, Joseph Follows and Elizabeth Follows/Samuel Follows, 1 Nov. 1780; 127/9, Letters to and from Ruth Fellows and her daughter-in-law Elizabeth Fellows, 1780–4; 127/11, Elizabeth Rogers Fellows and Ruth and George Fellows, 1770–9; 127/3/29, Ruth Follows/Samuel Follows, 18 June 1779; LRO PR/T/1825/81/1, 2, Will of Elizabeth Follows, 1825.

365. Temp MS 127/4/24, Joseph and Elizabeth Follows/Ruth Follows, 14 Nov. 1784; 127/7, Letters of George and Emily Follows, 1827–47 include George's Copy Exercise Book and children's polite letters.

366. Temp MS 127/7, Indenture, 30 Oct. 1814; Sam Kent/George Follows Jr, 18 Dec. 1827; Stamped paper with advertisement for, 'Geo Follows's Tea Warehouse, 51, Byrom Street, Opposite Richmond Row, Liverpool', n.d; Letter from New York, 5 May 1834, George Follows Jr/John Archard, Aug. 1838.

367. *Extracts from the Minutes and Advices of the Yearly Meeting of Friends held in London* (1783), 81, 201; *Quaker Faith and Practice*; Thomas Corns and David Lowenstein (eds.), 'The emergence of Quaker writing', *Prose Studies*, 17 (1994).

368. For Quaker language see George Fox et al. (eds.), *A Battle-Door for Teachers and Professors to Learn Singular and Plural* (1660); Giovanni Iamartino, *Linguistic*

and Religious Polemics (1988); T. E. Harvey, *Quaker Language* (1928); Maurice Creasey, *'Inward' and 'Outward'* (1962); E. Maxfield, 'Quaker "Thee" and its History', *American Speech*, 1 (1926); Thomas Lansbury, 'Pronouns of address', *Harpers Monthly Magazine*, 752 (1913), 200−6; William Comfort, *Just Among Friends* (New York, 1941); Jackson Cope, 'Seventeenth-century Quaker style' in Stanley Fish (ed.), *Modern Essays in Criticism* (NY, 1971), 200−35; Luella M. Wright, *The Literary Life of the Early Friend 1650−1725* (NY, 1932); Richard Bauman, *Let Your Words Be Few* (Cambridge, 1983).

369. Skidmore (ed.), *Strength in Weakness*, 5−9. For Payne see SA MS MD 5856/1−50 48; for Story see LSF Temp MSS 388, Letters of Thomas and Ann Story; LSF MS vol. 340, 'Journal of the life of Thomas Story with letters'; Emily Moore, *Travelling with Thomas Story* (Letchworth, 1947).

370. Temp MS 127/3/5, Samuel Follows/Ruth Follows and George Follows, 14 July 1771.

371. Temp MS 127/1/35, John Davis/Ruth Follows, 12 Apr. 1783.

372. Temp MS 127/3/7, Samuel Follows/Ruth Follows and George Follows, 23 Aug. 1771; 127/9/6, Samuel Follows/Elizabeth Follows, 25 Sept. 1782.

373. Carolyn Downs, 'The business letters of Daniel Eccleston of Lancaster', *Northern History*, xli (2004), 130.

374. Temp MS/127/3/5, Samuel Follows/Ruth Follows and George Follows, 14 July 1771.

375. Stansfield, 'Memoirs of Ruth Follows', 50.

376. Temp MS 127/4/6, Ruth and George Follows/Joseph Follows, 28 Mar. 1774; 127/3/41, Samuel Follows/Ruth Follows, 9 Jan. 1783.

377. Temp MS 127/3/11, Ruth Follows/Samuel Follows, 26 Apr. 1773.

378. LSF, Guide 6, 'The Quaker Calendar'; Valerie Norrington, 'The first month Called March', *Suffolk Review*, new series, 27 (1996), 14−18.

379. Davies, *Quakers in English Society 1665−1725*, 51−7, calls this 'Holy Language'.

380. Temp MS 127/3/1, Ruth and George Follows/Samuel Follows, 3 Feb. 1769.

381. Temp MS 127/3/3, Samuel Follows/Ruth Follows and George Follows, 12 Mar. 1769.

382. Temp MS 127/3/5, Samuel Follows/Ruth Follows and George Follows, 14 July 1771.

383. Temp MS 127/9/6, Samuel Follows/Elizabeth Follows, 25 Sept. 1782.

384. Temp MS 127/1/41, John Abbott/'My dear Friend', 10 May 1807.

385. Temp MS 127/1/31, M. Routh/Ruth Follows, 9 Aug. 1782.

386. Temp MS 127/9/2, Elizabeth Follows/Ruth Follows, 27 Mar. 1782.

387. Stansfield, 'Memoirs of Ruth Follows', 48.

388. Ibid., 29.

389. LSF MS Temp 127/1/31.

390. Skidmore (ed.), *Strength in Weakness*, 12−13; Helen Plant, 'Subjective Testimonies', *Gender & History*, 15 (2003), 297−318.

391. LSF Spriggs MSS I, vol. 156/132, Hanna Evans/Ruth Follows, 26 Aug. 1796.

392. LSF Temp MSS 745/44/32–4, Robson Papers, Sarah Taylor/Ruth Follows, 28 Sept. 1770.

393. Stansfield, 'Memoirs of Ruth Follows', 38.

394. Skidmore (ed.), *Strength in Weakness*, 1.

395. Temp MS 127/3/28, Ruth Follows/Samuel Follows, 27 Aug. 1779; Stansfield, 'Memoirs of Ruth Follows', 49.

396. Stansfield, 'Memoirs of Ruth Follows', 118.

397. Temp MS 127/3/12, Ruth Follows/Samuel Follows, 4 Jan. 1774.

398. Stanley Morison 'The development of hand-writing: An outline' in Ambrose Heal, *The English Writing-Masters* (Cambridge, 1931), xvi, xxvii, xxxix, xxx, xxxviii–xl; John Ayres, *Tutor to Penmanship* (1698) Preface; George Bickham, *The Universal Penman* (1733–41). For aristocratic letters written by a secretary see BL Add. MS 61449, vol. 349, Correspondence of the Duchess of Marlborough, early eighteenth century.

CHAPTER 5

1. Bodleian Library (Bodl), Catalogue of the Papers of Jane Johnson of Olney, Buckinghamshire and her Family, 17th–19th cent.: MSS Don. b. 39–40, c. 190–6, d. 202, e. 193–200. See also Johnson papers at the Buckinghamshire, Lincolnshire, and Staffordshire Record Offices.

2. Mary Clapinson, 'Jane Johnson', *ODNB*/61151, and 'Notable Accessions', *Bodleian Library Record* 16 (1997), 165–8.

3. For Woolsey see 'Pedigree of Johnson of Witham-on-the-Hill', *Miscellanea Genealogica et Heraldica*, ii, new series (1877), 123 (contains errors); TNA image 503, PCC, Will of Woolsey Johnson, 13 May 1756; Bodl MS Don. b. 40/1–2; *The Clergyman's Intelligencer* (1745), 106; Centre of Buckinghamshire Studies (CBS), Johnson family papers, D-X827/1–2; Staffordshire Record Office (Staffs RO) D742/9/1–3; D742/G/9/1, Dartmouth Survey of Olney, 1676; Lincolnshire Record Office, 3ANC1/15; 3ANC7/1–2. Woolsey was at Clare College, BA (1717), MA (1721), appointed Deacon at Peterborough (1720), Rector of Wilby, Northants (1729–56), Deacon in the Bishopric of London (1728), and Curate of St Andrew's Holborn (1724–7?). Natalie Rothstein (ed.), *Barbara Johnson's Album of Fashions and Fabrics* (1987), 9.

4. T. C. D. Eaves and Ben D. Kimpel, *Samuel Richardson: A Biography* (Oxford, 1971) (hereafter E&K, *Richardson*), 98, 213–14; Margaret Doody, *Concise Dictionary of British Literary Biography*, ii (Detroit, 1991), 369–99; William Sale, *Samuel Richardson* (New Haven, CT, 1937); Allan McKillop, *Samuel Richardson, Printer and Novelist* (Chapel Hill, NC, 1936); Elizabeth Brophy, *Samuel Richardson* (Knoxville, TN, 1974); Carol Flynn, *Samuel Richardson* (Princeton, NJ, 1982); Harold Bloom (ed.), *Samuel Richardson* (NY, 1987); Margaret Doody and Peter Sabor (eds.), *Tercentenary Essays* (Cambridge, 1989); Albert Rivero (ed.), *New Essays on Samuel Richardson* (NY, 1996).

5. John Feather, 'The country trade in books' in R. Myers and M. Harris (eds.), *Spreading the Word* (Winchester, 1990), 165–83; *The Provincial Book Trade in Eighteenth-century England* (Cambridge, 1985).

6. Ian Watt, *The Rise of the Novel* (Berkeley, CA, 1957); 'Reconsidering the rise of the novel', *Eighteenth-century Fiction*, 12(2–3) (2000); Robert Folkenflik, 'The heirs of Ian Watt', *Eighteenth-Century Studies*, 25 (1991), 203–17.

7. Catherine Gallagher, *Nobody's Story* (Berkeley, CA, 1994); J. Paul Hunter, *Before Novels* (NY, 1990), xx; Paula McDowell, *The Women of Grub Street* (Oxford, 1998); Michael McKeon, *The Origins of the English Novel, 1600–1740* (Baltimore, 2002); John Richetti (ed.), *The Cambridge Companion to the Eighteenth-century Novel* (Cambridge, 1996); Patricia Meyer Spacks, *Novel Beginnings* (New Haven, CT, 2006); Janet Todd, *The Sign of Angelica* (1989); William Warner, *Licensing Entertainment* (Berkeley, CA, 1998).

8. Barbara Benedict, *Making the Modern Reader* (Princeton, NJ, 1996).

9. Elspeth Knights, 'Daring to touch the hem of her garment', *Women's Writing*, 7 (2000), 221–45; Charles Wallace Jr, 'Some stated employment of your mind', *Church History*, 58 (1989), 354–66; Patricia Howell, 'Women in the reading circle', *Eighteenth-century Life*, 13 (1989), 59–60; Charlotte Sussman, 'Women's private reading and political action, 1649–1838' in Timothy Morton and Nigel Smith (eds.), *Radicalism in British Literary Culture* (Cambridge, 2002), 133–50; Maire Kennedy, 'Women and reading in eighteenth-century Ireland' in Bernadette Cunningham and Maire Kennedy (eds.), *The Experience of Reading* (Dublin, 1999), 78–98; Peter H. Pawlowicz, 'Reading women' in Ann Bermingham and John Brewer (eds.), *The Consumption of Culture, 1600–1800* (1995), 42–53; James Raven et al. (eds.), *The Practice and Representation of Reading in England* (Cambridge, 1996); Marjorie Reeves, *Pursuing the Muses* (1997); Jan Fergus, 'Women readers' in Vivien Jones (ed.), *Women and Literature in Britain, 1700–1800* (Cambridge, 2000), 155–78; 'Provincial servants' reading in the late eighteenth century' in Raven, *Practice*, 202–25; Stephen Coclough, *Reading Experiences 1700–1840* (Reading, 2000).

10. Bodl MS Don. c. 192, fos. 20–1, Ann Ingram/Barbara Johnson, 5 May 1762.

11. MS Don. e. 198 contains two columns of letters sent and received by day and month of the year inside the back cover of the journal.

12. MS Don. c. 192, fo. 60, Ann Smyth/Barbara Johnson, 26 April 1764; c. 191, fo. 61, Harriet Johnson/Barbara Johnson, 22 Feb.; c. 191, fos. 18–19, Robert Johnson/Barbara Johnson, 31 July 1788; c. 192, fo. 73, W. Smyth/Barbara Johnson, 27 Feb. 1804.

13. E&K, *Richardson*, 98, 213–14.

14. For example, Janet Todd, 'Fatal fluency', *Eighteenth-century Fiction* 12(2–3) (2000), 417–34; Ros Ballaster, *Seductive Forms* (Oxford, 1998); Margaret Doody, *A Natural Passion* (Oxford, 1974).

15. E&K, *Richardson*, 1–55.

16. E&K, 9–11, 94, 568–89.

17. Sir Thomas Roe, *The Negotiations of Sir Thomas Roe*, S. Richardson (ed.) (1740); Sale, *Samuel Richardson*, 6–9; E&K, *Richardson* 81–3.

18. William Slattery (ed.), *The Richardson-Stinistra Correspondence and Stinistra's Prefaces to 'Clarissa'* (Carbondale, IL, 1969), no. 5, 2 June 1753; Anna Barbauld (ed.), *Samuel Richardson's Correspondence*, i (1804, repr. 1966), xxxviii–xlii; Peter Sabor, 'Such extraordinary tokens' in Rivero (ed.), *New Essays*, 1–16.

19. Samuel Richardson, *The Apprentice's Vade Mecum or, Young Man's Pocket Companion* (1734); E&K, *Richardson*, 50–1.

20. [Samuel Richardson], *Letters Written to and for Particular Friends, on the Most Important Occasions* (1741), Preface, A2v; Barbauld (ed.), *Samuel Richardson's Correspondence*, i, lii; E&K, *Richardson*, 93.

21. John Hill, *The Young Secretary's Guide*, 22nd edn (1734) was printed for Richardson's brother-in-law, Allington Wilde. E&K, *Richardson*, 90, 92–3; [Samuel Richardson], *Pamela: or, Virtue Rewarded*, 4 vols. (1741–2).

22. Jacqueline Pearson, *Women's Reading in Britain, 1750–1835* (Cambridge, 1999); Lynne Pearce, *Feminism and the Politics of Reading* (1997); Martha Koehler, *Models of Reading* (Lewisburg, PA, 2005); Lucy Newlyn, *Reading, Writing, and Romanticism* (Oxford, 2000); Kate Flint, *The Woman Reader, 1837–1914* (Oxford, 1993).

23. Samuel Richardson, *Clarissa. Or, the History of a Young Lady*, 7 vols. (1748).

24. Barbauld (ed.), *Samuel Richardson's Correspondence*, i, lviii; Thomas Keymer and Peter Sabor, *Pamela in the Marketplace* (Cambridge, 2005); Warner, *Licensing Entertainment*, 76–230.

25. Thomas Keymer, *Richardson's* Clarissa *and the Eighteenth-century Reader* (Cambridge, 1992); *Clarissa*, The Clarissa Project (1751; repr. NY, 1990), Introduction, i; Carol Flynn and Edward Copeland (eds.), *Clarissa and Her Readers* (NY, 1999), Introduction, 1–17; Knights, 'Daring to touch the hem of her garment', 222–9, 240; Hunter, *Before Novels*, 142.

26. John Carroll (ed.), *Selected Letters of Samuel Richardson* (Oxford, 1964), 199–206, 311–12, Samuel Richardson/Hester Mulso, 21 Aug. 1754, Samuel Richardson/Sarah Chapone, 2 Mar. 1752.

27. For a summary, see Keymer and Sabor, *Pamela in the Marketplace*, Appendix: A chronology of publications, Performances and related events to 1750, 216–25, and *Richardsoniana* (1974).

28. *Samuel Richardson's Published Commentary on Clarissa, 1747–65*, 3 vols. (1998); *Meditations Collected from the Sacred Books 1750* (repr. 1976); *Richardsoniana* (1974).

29. Carroll (ed.), *Selected Letters of Samuel Richardson*, 126, Samuel Richardson/Aaron Hill, 12 July 1754; Pawlowicz, 'Reading women', 48.

30. A conference on Jane's nursery library, 'Scrapbooks and chapbooks: Reading, writing, and childhood 1700–1850' was held at Homerton College,

University of Cambridge, on 4–5 Apr. 1995 with an exhibition, 'Handmade readings: Jane Johnson's nursery library (c.1738–48)' at the Fitzwilliam Museum. The contents of the shoebox in the Lilly Library, MSS, Johnson 1740–59, Indiana University, Bloomington have been digitized. They are found at <http://www.dlib.indiana.edu/collections/janejohnson>.

31. MS Don. c. 190, fos. 5–6.

32. MS Don. c. 190, fos. 34–5. The two wooden boards are located after fo. 118.

33. The story was found in 1995. See MS Don. d. 198, fos. 19–44 and Gillian Avery, *A Very Pretty Story*, A Facsimilie of the MS held in the Bodleian Library (Oxford, 2001), fos. 19–42. Jane's tale was written in the same year that John Newbery published *A Pretty Little Pocket-Book*. See the 1767 facsimile edited by M. F. Thwaite (1966); Victor Watson, 'Jane Johnson' in Mary Hilton et al. (eds.), *Opening the Nursery Door* (1997), 31–46; Ruth Boettigheimer, 'An important system of its own', *Princeton University Library Chronicle*, 4 (1998), 191–210; *Early Children's Books in the Bodleian Library* (Oxford, 1995).

34. [Samuel Richardson], *Pamela: or Virtue Rewarded . . . in Genteel Life*, iv (1742), 451, Letter 64. Compare with Marie Catherine La Mothe, Baronne d'Aulnoy, *Diverting Works*, 2d edn (1715), and *The History of the Tales of the Fairies Newly Done from the French* (1716), 1–23; Charles Perrault, *Histories, or Tales of Passed Times*, 3d edn (1741).

35. Evelyn Arizpe and Morag Styles, *Reading Lessons from the Eighteenth Century* (2006), and ' "Love to Learn your Book" ', *History of Education*, 33 (2004), 337–52; Kenneth Charlton, *Women, Religion, and Education in Early Modern England* (1999).

36. Literature Online (LION) and Eighteenth-century Collections Online (ECCO) were used to research this article.

37. MS Don. c. 190, fos. 1–118, with comments on fo. 72v.

38. For another modest woman author, see Whyman, 'The correspondence of Esther Masham and John Locke', *Huntington Library Quarterly*, 66 (2003), 275–305.

39. MS Don. c. 190, fos. 64–9, Marriage licence, 1735; Will, TNA PROB 11/844/97, 1758.

40. Sir William Dugdale, *The Antiquities of Warwickshire*, ii (1730), 784; L. F. Salzman (ed.), *The Victoria History of the County of Warwick*, ii (1904), 131. Jane's mother was Lucy Rainsford. MS Don. c. 192, fos. 180–9. For Jane's father and mother, see Arizpe and Styles, *Reading Lessons*, viii–xxiii, 17–24.

41. Oliver Ratcliff, *The Register of the Parish of Olney, Co. Bucks. 1665–1812* (Bucks Parish Register Society, n.d.), 275, 284, 292, 297, 305; Bodl MS Don. b. 40/1.

42. Thomas Wright, *The Town of Cowper* (1886); D. Bruce Hindmarsh, *John Newton and the English Evangelical Tradition between the Conversions of Wesley*

and Wilberforce (Oxford, 1996), 170; James Storer, *The Rural Walks of Cowper* (1835); Oliver Ratcliff and N. Brown, *Olney Past and Present* (Olney, 1893).

43. Elizabeth Knight, *William Cowper's Olney* (Olney, n.d.) I thank Knight for sharing her notes and her valuable knowledge of Olney. The exact location of the house was recently determined when droughts revealed the foundation of the house.

44. D. Demaray, *The Innovation of John Newton* (Lewiston, 1988); Ratcliff and Brown, *Olney*, 33–4; Wright, *The Town of Cowper*, 26–7, 33; Storer, *Rural Walks*, 11. The house where Jane lived is often confused with the vicarage, rebuilt by William Johnson. The house gradually fell into decay. See 'Sunday at Home', newspaper clipping, 29 Oct. 1857 for a woodcut and description.

45. MS. Don. c. 192, fos. 88–9, Barbara Johnson's papers, n.d.

46. Wright, *The Town of Cowper*, 18.

47. Ratcliff and Brown *Olney*, 32, Knight, *William Cowper's Olney*, 4; 'A quick tour around Olney' (Olney, n.d).

48. John Martin, *John Newton* (1950), 238.

49. Ratcliff and Brown, *Olney,* 43.

50. William Page (ed.), *The Victoria History of the County of Buckingham* (1927), 429; George Lipscomb (ed.), *The History and Antiquities of the County of Buckingham*, iv (1847), 298.

51. Wright, *The Town of Cowper*, 15; Knight, *William Cowper's Olney*, 21.

52. Michael Haykin, *One Heart and One Soul* (Durham, 99); Knight, *William Cowper's Olney*, 17, 22; Cowper and Newton Museum (CNM) 3797, History of the Congregational Church At Olney; CNM, pamphlet, P. B. Gravett, *Sutcliff Baptist Church.*

53. Martin, *Newton*, 263, Knight *William Cowper's Olney*, 26.

54. Hindmarsh, *John Newton and the English Evangelical Tradition*, 171.

55. William Cowper, *The Correspondence of William Cowper*, Thomas Wright (ed.), ii (1904), letter to Revd William Unwin, 18 Nov. 1782; Knight, *William Cowper's Olney*; CNM 1390, Olney Parish Account Book, 1744–60; Knight and the Olney History Workshop, 'Olney Feoffee Charity', n.d.; CNM 786/1–2, Olney Workhouse Books, 1746–82; Staffs RO D742/G/2/1–3, Poor Rate Assessments 1713, 1735, 1742.

56. CBS D-X827/1, Johnson family correspondence items 38, 40, and 46 mention lace buyers carrying letters and money from Olney to London. Jim Styles, *Let's Talk about Olney's Amazing Curate* (Olney, 1983), 16; Demaray, *The Innovation of John Newton*, 124; Haykin, *One Heart*, 100; Elizabeth Wilson, *Olney and the Lace Makers* (Bethnal Green, 1864).

57. Martin, *Newton*, 211; Thomas Wright, *The Romance of the Lace Pillow* (Olney, 1919).

58. Haykin, *One Heart*, 101; Thomas Wright, *Buckingham and Northamptonshire Ballads*, 3rd edn (Olney, 1925); Wilson, *Olney and the Lace Makers.*

59. Hindmarsh, *John Newton and the English Evangelical Tradition*, 211; Wilson, *Olney and the Lace Makers*, 58, 62, and *Bygone Olney*, (n.d.).

60. Wright, *The Town of Cowper*, 12–13; Ratcliff and Brown, *Olney*, 244; Wilson, *Olney and the Lace Makers*, 65, 69. An example is: 'The plums are so scarce, the flour so dear, I cannot get married till after next year.'

61. Wright, *The Town of Cowper*, 235.

62. The first workhouses date from *c.*1597–8, *ODNB/*66535. Tim Hitchcock, 'Paupers and preachers' in Lee Davison and Tim Hitchcock (eds.), *Stilling the Grumbling Hive* (Stroud, 1992), 145–66.

63. Ratcliff, *Parish Register*, Extracts from a book without a title page (*c.*1726), 501.

64. CNM 786/1–2, Olney Workhouse Books, 1746–82. By 1754, levies on 12d. in the pound produced revenues of over £304 with disbursements of £288.

65. Dissenting ministers in the area included John Gibbs 1627–99, Newport Pagnell; Richard Davis d. 1714, Rothwell and Wellingborough; Matthias Maurice 1684–1738. John Drake, an Independent of Yardley Hastings, preached every Sunday in Olney from 1738 and lived there 1759–75. William Walker, a Baptist, d. 1793, preached in Olney 1735–75. John Wesley and George Whitefield also preached in the area. See CNM booklets.

66. John Broad (ed.), *Buckinghamshire Dissent and Parish Life, 1669–1712*, Buckinghamshire Record Society no. 28, xlvi (1993), 180–1; Hindmarsh, *John Newton and the English Evangelical Tradition*, 177.

67. *The History of the Congregational Church at Olney* (Olney, 1929).

68. Geoffrey Nuttall, 'Baptists and Independents in Olney to the time of John Newton', *The Baptist Quarterly*, 30 (1983), 26–36; Hindmarsh, *John Newton and the English Evangelical Tradition*, 179.

69. Obituary of Mrs Drake notes, 'this venerable woman', *Evangelical Magazine* (1799), 466; CNM, Day Book of Dr Samuel Teedon, 14 May 1759.

70. George Whitefield, *The Two First Parts of his Life, with his Journals, Revised* (1756), 187–9. On 23 May 1739 he noted Johnson turned him away: 'Being denied the pulpit, I preached this morning in a field near the town, to about two thousand people.'

71. Woolsey built a house and enclosed the land in 1752. Arizpe and Styles, *Reading Lessons*, 21.

72. Ratcliff, *Parish Register*, v–vi; Hindmarsh, *John Newton and the English Evangelical Tradition*, 170–84; Nuttall, 'Baptists and Independents in Olney'.

73. Hindmarsh, *John Newton and the English Evangelical Tradition*, 177.

74. Staffs RO D742/G/3, Order for induction of Moses Browne as Vicar of Olney; B. S. Schlenther, *Queen of the Methodists* (Durham, 1997). Legge was a protege of Selena, Countess of Huntingdon (1707–91).

75. For Browne in Olney see Ratcliff, *Parish Register,* 365; CNM 1391, Workhouse Book, 24 Nov. 1753; CNM 1390, Parish Account Book, 21 Jan. 1758.

76. Moses Browne, *The Nativity . . . A Sermon preached on Christmas-Day in the Parish Church of Olney* (1754); Wright, *The Town of Cowper*, 34–7; Hindmarsh,

John Newton and the English Evangelical Tradition, 183; Demaray, *The Innovation of John Newton*, 124; Nuttall, 'Baptists and Independents in Olney', 33.

77. Quoted in Marylynn Rouse (ed.), *The Life of John Newton by Richard Cecil* (Fearn, 2000), 265–6 from a letter to Robert Jones. Browne tried to hinder Jane's sale of the vicarage to the future Countess of Dartmouth. Staffs RO D742/G/9/3, letter from Moses Browne, 14 Nov. 1754; D(W)1778/V/711, 1759, Copy Case and Answers, *Churchwardens of Olney v Vicar of Olney and his Bonds* (1753).

78. Lipscomb, (ed.), *The History and Antiquities of the County of Buckingham*, iv, 131–2. Staffs RO, D742/B/22/1–5, D742/B/7/1–23, D742/9/1/1, D742/B/22–1–5, and D742/B/7/17–23 confirm Jane's sale of her house and land to Dartmouth despite Browne's interference.

79. For Woolsey's properties and sale see Staffs RO D742/G/6, Notes on the the History of Parsonage Estate Olney, 18th cent.; D742/G/9/1–3, Two Surveys of the Estate of Woolsey Johnson, 1753–4; D742/B/7/1–23, Deeds 1753–4, including articles of agreement between Jane Johnson, widow of Woolsey Johnson and the Earl of Dartmouth; D742/B/22/1–5, Deeds with letter from Woolsey Johnson, 6 Aug. 1754; D742/9/1, General Survey of Olney, 17th cent., with note: 'Rec'd from Mrs Jane Johnson soon after completing Lord Dartmouth's purchase of the Vicarage of Olney and Lands there, Saml Reynardson'; Copy of the Dartmouth Survey of Olney, Warrington, and Bradwell Abbey, 1796 with maps.

80. MS Don. c. 190, fo. 72, note in commonplace book, 6 Mar. 1756.

81. Ibid., fo. 37r.

82. MS Don. c. 196, fos. 68–9. See Jane's note on the envelope.

83. Ibid., 196.

84. For a study in silences see Whyman, 'Esther Masham', 275–305.

85. MS Don. c. 190, fos. 11–24, Letters to Mrs Brompton and Mrs Garth, 1739–55.

86. For the history of reading see the work of Robert Darnton and Kevin Sharpe, *Reading Revolutions* (New Haven, CT, 2000); Guglielmo Cavallo and Roger Chartier (eds.), *A History of Reading in the West*, trans. Lydia G. Cochrane (Oxford, 1999); Alberto Manguel, *A History of Reading* (1997); Wolfgange Iser, *The Implied Reader* (Baltimore, 1974).

87. Kevin Sharpe and Steven Zwicker, *Reading, Society, and Politics in Early Modern England* (Cambridge, 2003), 23.

88. Searches on LION and ECCO databases show this process.

89. MS Don. c. 190, fo. 72; Giovanni Marana, *The Eight Volumes of Letters Writ by a Turkish Spy*, 13th edn (1753–4) and 24th edn (Dublin, 1754); In fo. 93, see *Letters of Mr Alexander Pope and Several of his Friends* (1737); fo. 96, see John Shebbeare, *Letters on the English Nation: by Batista Angeloni, a Jesuit* (1755); fo. 91, see *Persian Letters . . . from Selim at London, to Mirza at Ispahan*, 3rd edn (1736); Samuel Richardson, *Clarissa*.

90. Barbauld (ed.), *Samuel Richardson's Correspondence*, i, 133–5, W. Warburton/ Samuel Richardson, 28 Dec. 1742; Richardson, *Published Commentary*, i, 25; E&K, *Richardson*, 148, 568.

91. Jane made 38 extracts. From Marana, 24th edn, see fo. 97v and vol. iv, 125; In fo. 101r, see vol. v, 63–4. William Mc Burney, 'The authorship of the Turkish Spy, *PMLA*, 52 (1957), 915–35.

92. MS Don. c. 190, fo. 89r.

93. MS Don. e. 193, fo. 2v.

94. MS Don. e. 198, fos. 12–13, An Hymn for Good Friday. See *The Psalm-Singer's Pocket Companion*, 2nd edn (1758), 144.

95. MS Don. c. 190, fo. 88r.

96. Ibid., fo. 70r. Barbara edited Jane's notebook, calling it 'Extracts by my Mother from different Authors'. On fo. 95r she added '+Bab: Johnson' in the margin next to Jane's list of favourite authors. Apparently, Jane wrote the list and Barbara added her name too. Since their handwriting is similar, it is sometimes hard to determine authorship. Barbara's writing is generally more angular than Jane's rounder hand, but when Jane writes hastily the hands are alike. For Laetitia Pilkington's similar list of favourite authors see Pearson, *Women's Reading*, 127.

97. See especially Warner, *Licensing Entertainment*.

98. MS Don. c. 190, fo. 75v. 'Read Homer once & you need read no more/For all things else appear so mean & Poor/Verse will seem prose, yet often on him look/You will hardly need another book.' Jane's quotation is almost like one by the Duke of Buckingham in *From an Essay on Poetry* (1682), 20. For extracts from Pope's translations see MS Don. c. 190, fo. 83: 'All this page out of Pope's Homer's Odyssey', and fo. 84v: 'All this page from Pope's Homer's Iliad'. Extracts from fo. 83 are found in Alexander Pope, *The Odyssey of Homer* (1725–6), vol. ii, book 7, and vol. iii, book 11. More quotations from Pope on fo. 73v, appear in his 'On the Monument of the Hon. Robert Digby', *Epistles and Satires*, ii (1736), 157.

99. MS Don. c. 190, fos. 83r, 87r, 90r. References are to Milton's *Paradise Lost* and *Il Penseroso*.

100. Ibid., fos. 84r, 87v, 92r.

101. Ibid., fos. 79r, 84v, 92r, 93v. The Quotation in fo. 79r is from Juvenal's 5th Satire, line 48.

102. Ibid., fo. 93v is about a black swan.

103. Jane's maxims bear remarkable likeness to Richardson's *A Collection of the Moral and Instructive Sentiments* (1755) that is appended to the 3rd edn of *Clarissa*. His awareness of the needs of readers like Jane is apparent.

104. MS Don. c. 190, fo. 92r. See *Plutarch's Lives in Six Volumes*, v (1758), 435.

105. Henry Fielding's *Miscellanies in Three Volumes*, 2nd edn (1743) is a typical example. Jane may have used it to satirize the black swan in Fielding's *Part of Juvenal's Sixth Satire, Modernized in Burlesque Verse*, i (1743), 97, 252–6.

106. MS Don. c. 190, fos. 40r, 88r.

107. Donald F. Bond (ed.), *The Spectator*, i (Oxford, 1965), Introduction, xxxviii; Richmond P. Bond, *The Tatler* (Cambridge, MA, 1971), and *New Letters to the Tatler and Spectator* (Austin, 1959).

108. Gilbert D. McEwen, *The Oracle of the Coffee House* (San Marino, CA, 1972); Helen Berry, 'An early coffee house periodical and its readers', *London Journal*, 25:1 (2000), 14–33; Natasha Glaisyer, 'Readers, correspondents, and communities' in Alexandra Shepard and Phil Withington (eds.), *Communities in Early Modern England* (Manchester, 2000), 235–51; Kathryn Shevelow *Women and Print Culture* (1989).

109. Eve Bannet, 'Epistolary commerce in *The Spectator*' in Donald J. Newman (ed.), *The Spectator* (Newark, DE, 2005), 219–47; *Original and Genuine Letters Sent to the Tatler and Spectator . . . None of Which have been Before Printed*, 2 vols. (1725).

110. MS Don. c. 190, fos. 11–14, 17–20.

111. Ibid., fos. 7–8, Jane Johnson/Robert Johnson, 15 Nov. 1753. See also Lincolnshire Record Office, Johnson/1/1–2 for additional letters to her children.

112. See similar sentiments in Richardson, *Meditations*, nos. 27, 30 (repr. 1976), 59, 65–6.

113. MS Don. c. 190, fos. 9v and 86r. The last two lines of Jane's poem can be found in Frederick Boas (ed.), *Giles and Phineas Fletcher: Poetical works* (Cambridge, 1909). See 'The Purple Island or the Isle of Man', ii, 76, canto vi: 34 and in 'Upon the Contemplations of B. of Excester', ii, 247, lines 26–7.

114. MS Don. c. 190, fos. 11–25.

115. Ibid., fo. 81.

116. Carroll, *Selected Letters*, 67–9, Samuel Richardson/Sarah Westcomb, 15 Sept. 1746. For Richardson's letters see Carroll (ed.), *Selected Letters of Samuel Richardson*; Barbauld (ed.), *Samuel Richardson's Correspondence*; Peter Sabor, 'Publishing Richardson's correspondence' in Doody and Sabor (ed.), *Tercentenary Essays*, 237–50; Beinecke Library MSS, Yale University (BLY): Gen MSS MISC 1335/F1–6; Chauncey Brewster Tinker Gen MSS 310, Box 4/F; Gen MSS MISC Group 541/F; OSB MSS File R, FO. 12574–7, 135550; Princeton University Library (PUL), Robert H. Taylor Collection, MS RTC01; 'Original letters of Miss E. Carter and Mr Samuel Richardson', *Monthly Magazine*, 228, vol. 33 (1 July 1812), 533–43.

117. E&K, *Richardson*, 11, 198–204, 342–8; Rivero (ed.), *New Essays*, 142.

118. E&K, *Richardson*, 349–54.

119. PUL, Robert H. Taylor Collection MS 18th–446, Lady Bradshaigh's annotated copy of *Clarissa*, 1748, with answers from Richardson; E&K, *Richardson*, 447–50; Lady Elizabeth Echlin, *An Alternative Ending to Richardson's Clarissa*, D. Daphinoff (ed.) (Bern, 1981).

120. E&K, *Richardson*, 343, 365; Carroll, *Selected Letters*, 24; Ingrid Tieken-boon van Ostade, 'Samuel Richardson's role as linguistic innovator' in Matts Ryden et al. (eds.), *A Reader in Early Modern English* (Frankfurt, 1998), 407–19.

121. MS Don. c. 190, fos. 13–14, Jane Johnson/Mrs Brompton, 28 Feb. 1756; Pamela Espeland, *The Story of Arachne* (Minneapolis, 1980).

122. MS Don. c. 190, fos. 13–14. For hoar frost see Richardson, *Meditations*, no. 32, p. 69.

123. Ibid., fo. 14, 28 Feb. 1756; (Margaret) Georgiana Spencer (1737–1814), *ODNB*/39563.

124. G.E.C., *The Complete Peerage*, xii, part 1 (1953), 153–4; George Baker, *The History and Antiquities of the County of Northampton*, i (1822–41), 108–12; John First Earl Spencer (1734–83), *ODNB*/38713.

125. MS Don. c. 190, fo. 14, 28 Feb. 1756.

126. Ibid., fos. 17–20, Jane Johnson/Mrs Garth, 3 June 1742, fos. 21–2, 8 July 1742. Mrs Garth was the wife of John Garth, MP for Devizes, Wiltshire and first cousin to Jane. See R. Sedgwick (ed.), *The House of Commons 1715–54*, ii (1970), 59.

127. MS Don. c. 190, fo. 21, Jane Johnson/Mrs Garth, 8 July 1742.

128. Richardson, *Meditations*; Thomas Keymer 'Richardson's *Meditations*' in Doody and Sabor, *Tercentenary Essays*, 89–109.

129. MS Don. c. 190, fo. 21r. Jane's italics.

130. Ibid., fo. 21r-v.

131. Ibid., fo. 18, Jane Johnson/Mrs Garth [1742] continued on fos. 19–20, 3 June 1742; Ibid., fo. 83 and *Spectator*, no. 626, viii, 231, 29 Nov. 1714; MS Don. c. 190, fo. 92 and *Spectator* no. 75, i, 284–7, 26 May 1711.

132. MS Don. c. 190, fo. 19.

133. Jane's capitalization. Ibid., fos. 17–18, Jane Johnson/Mrs Garth [1742]. See Gallagher, *Nobody's Story* for the effects of women's dispossession of property.

134. Samuel Richardson, *Pamela: or Virtue Rewarded*, 3rd edn, i (London, 1741), title page; E&K, *Richardson*, 206.

135. MS Don. c. 190, fos. 11–12, Jane Johnson/Mrs Brompton, 17 Oct. 1749.

136. Richardson, *Clarissa*. In MSDon. c. 190, fo. 85, Jane makes extracts from Richardson's *The History of Sir Charles Grandison*, 7 vols. (1754).

137. John Peck and Martin Coyle, *Literary Terms and Criticism*, 3rd edn (Basingstoke, 2002), 114.

138. MS Don. c. 190, fo. 11; Richardson, *Clarissa*, vii, letter XL, Mrs Norton/Miss Clarissa Harlowe, 165.

139. See Lady Bradshaigh's annotated copy of *Clarissa,* 1748.

140. MS Don. c. 190, fos. 11v–12r.

141. Richardson, *Clarissa*, vi, letter LXVI, Miss Clarissa Harlowe/Miss Howe, 240; Ian Watt, 'Richardson as novelist' in Harold Bloom (ed.), *Samuel Richardson* (1987), 9.

142. Richardson, *Clarissa*, iv, letter XXVIII, Miss Clarissa Harlowe/Mr Lovelace, 165; Christopher Hill, 'Clarissa Harlowe and her times' in *Puritanism and Revolution* (1958), 102–23.

143. Quoted in Dale A. Johnson, comp., *Women in English Religion, 1700–1925* (1983), 61–4, 70–1 from Wesley's 'On Visiting the Sick'.

144. Schlenther, *Queen of the Methodists*, 1–2, 163.

145. MS Don. c. 190, fo. 88r.

146. Ibid., fo. 86r.

147. As noted, this phrase was used by Richardson on *Pamela*'s title page.

148. MS Don. c. 190, fo. 12r.

149. Ibid., fo. 12r–v.

150. Richardson, *Letters Written to and for Particular Friends*, Preface, A2v.

151. Flynn and Copeland (eds.), *Clarissa and Her Readers*; Warner, *Reading Clarissa* (1979). Volume 16 of the Clarissa Project will record reactions of men and women to the novel throughout the eighteenth century. Other volumes will include responses from the nineteenth century to the present day. There is a vast literature about Richardson's effect on British and continental novelists and novels, for example, Thomas O. Beebee, *Clarissa on the Continent* (University Park, PA, 1990).

152. Keymer, *Richardson's* Clarissa *and the Eighteenth-century Reader*, 96; Ruth Perry, 'Clarissa's daughters' in Flynn and Copeland (eds.), *Clarissa and Her Readers*, 121.

153. E&K, *Richardson*, 351–2, 287 quoting a letter of 20 June 1759.

154. Shari Benstock, 'From letters to literature', *Genre*, 18 (1985), 257–95.

155. Keymer, *Richardson's* Clarissa *and the Eighteenth-century Reader*, 48.

156. Penelope Wilson, 'Classical poetry and the eighteenth-century reader' in Isabel Rivers (ed.), *Books and Their Readers in Eighteenth-century England* (Leicester, 1982), 69–96.

157. J. Paul Hunter, 'Couplets and conversation' in John E. Sitter (ed.), *The Cambridge Companion to Eighteenth-century Poetry* (Cambridge, 2001), 15; Kennedy, 'Women and reading in eighteenth-century Ireland', 89.

158. In MS Don. c. 190, fo. 95 see, for example, extracts from *Tompsons Poems*.

159. Ibid., fos. 26–8 and d. 198, fos. 1–2.

160. *A General Index to the Spectators, Tatlers, and Guardians* (1757) may be searched online for references to poetry.

161. MS Don. e 198, fo. 1; *Psalms*, xix:1; *Spectator*, no. 465, vi, 253–4, 23 Aug. 1712.

162. Ibid., fos. 1–2. The asterisk is Johnson's.

163. John Hughes, *The Ecstasy, An Ode* (1720), and *The Poetical Works*, i (Edinburgh, 1779), 92–100 (99).

164. Maciej Kazimierz Sarbiewski, *The Odes of Casimire*, trans. G. Hils (1646; repr. 1953), Ode 5. Lib. 2, 16–25.

165. William Stevenson, *Original Poems on Several Subjects*, ii (Edinburgh, 1765), 126, 128.

166. Moses Browne, *Sunday Thoughts* (1753), 'To Stella', in *Poems on Various Subjects* (1739), 260.

167. In MS Don. c. 190, fo. 95, Johnson copied a description of heaven from *Sunday Thoughts*.

168. MS Don e. 198, fo. 17 contains extracts from Hervey's 'On Reading the Inscription on Mrs Stonhouses's Monument', *Meditations and Contemplations*, 11th edn, i (1753), 36. His 'Contemplations on the Starry Heavens' is found at ii, 89–91.

169. MS Don. e. 198, fo. 2; c. 190, fo. 26; James Bridie, *Tobias and the Angel* (1961), xxi. Tobias is found in the book of Tobit in the Apocrypha. The angel Raphael accompanied him on his travels.

170. MS Don. e. 198, fo. 5; Gordon Phelps, *A Short History of English Literature* (1962), 74–5, 82.

171. See Reeves, *Pursuing the Muses*, 21–2, about Elizabeth Rowe's reading. Fergus, 'Provincial servants', 213; Kennedy, 'Women and reading in eighteenth-century Ireland', 78–98; Felicity Nussbaum, 'Eighteenth-century women's autobiographical commonplaces' in Shari Benstock (ed.), *The Private Self* (Chapel Hill, NC, 1988), 147–71.

172. In *Provincial Readers*, Fergus argues convincingly that booksellers' records do not confirm the stereotype of the woman novel reader.

173. *The Critical Review*, 533 (Sept. 1761), 203–11, compares the impact of the novels of Richardson and Rousseau. See also Bodl MS Edwards 1011, fo. 94, Thomas Edwards/D. Wray Esq., 16 Jan. 1748; Janet Todd, *Sensibility* (1986), 4. On reading letters aloud see Barbauld (ed.), *Samuel Richardson's Correspondence*, i, clxxxvii; and O. M. Brack, 'Bibliographical essay' in *Richardson's Published Commentary*, ii (1998), 313.

174. E&K, *Richardson*, 199; Carroll (ed.), *Selected Letters of Samuel Richardson*, 64–7, Samuel Richardson/Sarah Westcomb, [1746].

175. Margaret Reeves, 'Telling the tale of the rise of the novel', *CLIO* 30:1 (2000), 25–49; Thomas Keymer and Jon Mee, *The Cambridge Companion to English Literature, 1740–1830* (Cambridge, 2004), xi.

176. *Clarissa*, The Clarissa Project (1751, repr. NY, 1990), 37.

177. Pawlowicz, 'Reading women', 46.

178. Bernard Scholz, 'Self-fashioning by mail' in Amanda Gilroy and W. M. Verhoeven (eds.), *Prose Studies: Correspondences: A Special Issue on Letters*, 19(2) (1996), 140.

CHAPTER 6

1. Bodl MS Don. c. 191, fos. 1–2, Robert Johnson/Barbara Johnson, 26 Apr. 1776. The Bodleian Library, Oxford University is the location of all references to the Johnson collection in this chapter.

2. Lady Anna Riggs Miller, *Letters from Italy*, 3 vols. (1776).

3. MS Don. c. 191; c. 193, fos. 1–41. Barbara was born at Warwick Court, Holborn, baptized 19 June Olney, died aged 87, and was buried in Thenford Church, Northants. TNA PROB 11/1695; George Baker, *History and Antiquities of the County of Northampton*, ii (1822–30), 711–17; MS Don. b. 40/1, 'Pedigree of Johnson of Wytham-on-the-Hill', *Miscellanea Genealogica et Heraldica*, vol. 2, new series (1877) 125. Natalie Rothstein (ed.), *Barbara Johnson's Album of Fashions* (1987). Both have genealogical errors.

4. MS Don. c. 193, fos. 42–117; e. 194–8. Robert was baptized at Olney and died at Bath. I thank Mr C. A. Johnston of the Bath and North East Somerset Record Office (BNSRO), Arthur Burns, and Mary Clayton for searching records about Robert. See The Clergy Database, ID 120159.

5. *ODNB*/18720; Ruth Hesselgrave, *Lady Miller and the Batheaston Literary Circle* (New Haven, CT, 1927); B. Dobbie, *An English Rural Community* (Bath, 1969), 88; Christopher Anstey, *An Election Ball* (Bristol, 1997), 39. See Bath Central Library (BCL) card and newspaper clipping files.

6. Johnson pedigrees and genealogical sources give educational data for other males, but not Robert. The Wistanstow Parish Register cites education for every vicar except Robert. Robert does not appear in admissions records for Oxford or Cambridge. Only MS Don. e. 197, fo. 2, 17 Nov. 1776 notes his attending church in Bath. Otherwise, the church is not mentioned.

7. John Money, *Experience and Identity* (Manchester, 1977), 99. Peter Jones, Birmingham University confirms that Robert attended the Lunar Society intermittently and sent apologies on 1 Apr. 1793. The Boulton and Watt Archive and the Matthew Boulton Papers from Birmingham Central Library. Part 1, Lunar Society correspondence reel II, incoming letters 1787–95; Part 10 Matthew Boulton, correspondence A–J: Box 240: 163–7; William Page (ed.), *Victoria History of the County of Warwick*, vii (1904–69), 213.

8. MS Don. c. 191, fo. 20, Robert Johnson/Barbara Johnson, n.d.; c. 192, fo. 91, 1773; c. 192, fo. 92, May 1778.

9. *ODNB*/29818. Catherine's portrait by Zoffany hangs in the Tate Britain Museum, London.

10. TNA PROB 11/1587; *ODNB*/29818; BL Egerton MSS 3784–5; Brasenose College, Oxford University, Library Catalogues; Beinecke Library, Yale University (BLY), X34S, 1886/1/11, Sale Catalogue.

11. Hesselgrave, *Lady Miller and the Batheaston Literary Circle*, xi–xii. Anna is mentioned in the dedication of Sheridan's *The School for Scandal* and suggested as an inspiration for Mrs Leo Hunter in Charles Dickens's *The Pickwick Papers*, ch. 15, and the Duchess of Fitz-Fulke in Byron's *Don Juan* (stanza 50 of canto XVI). Gavin Turner, 'Bath 1775: An election ball', *Archives*, xxvii (2002), 23–30.

12. Quoted in Hesselgrave, *Lady Miller and the Batheaston Literary Circle*, 5.

13. Austin Dobson (ed.), *Diary & Letters of Madam d'Arblay*, i (1904), 382; Elizabeth Child, '"To Sing the Town"', *Studies in Eighteenth Century Culture*, 22 (1997), 155–72 (171, n. 40).

14. *ODNB/*64753; John Collinson, *The History and Antiquities of the County of Somersetshire*, ii (Bath, 1791), 103–5; Namier and Brook (eds.), *The House of Commons, 1754–90*, iii (1964), 138. From 1784–90, Miller was MP for Newport, Cornwall. He was known in London as a gossip and newsmonger.

15. Hesselgrave, *Lady Miller and the Batheaston Literary Circle*, 9.

16. Quoted in ibid., 5; A. Barbeau, *Life and Letters in the XVIIIth Century* (NY, 1904), 225.

17. Mrs Paget Toynbee, *Lettres de Mme Du Deffand á Horace Walpole*, ii (1912), 355; Hesselgrave, *Lady Miller and the Batheaston Literary Circle*, 7–8.

18. Hesselgrave, *Lady Miller and the Batheaston Literary Circle*, 7.

19. Anstey, *An Election Ball*, illus. no. 7; BCL files.

20. Thomas Whalley, *Journals and Correspondence*, Revd Hill Wickham (ed.), ii (1863), 315, 3 Nov. 1780; BCL, J. Craddock, *Literary Memoirs and Correspondence*, i, (n.d.), 77.

21. Whalley, *Journals*, ii, 312–13, 30 Oct. 1779.

22. Ibid., 314–15, 20 Nov. 20.

23. Swami Avyaktananda, *The Story of Batheaston Villa* (Bath, 1965), 4–5; R. V. Lucas, *A Swan and her Friends* (1907), 194, 3 Nov. 1780.

24. Tobias Smollett, *The Expedition of Humphry Clinker* (1771); [Laurence Sterne], *A Sentimental Journey Through France and Italy* [1771]; Malcolm Andrews, *The Search for the Picturesque* (Aldershot, 1989); Jean Viviès, *English Travel Narratives in the Eighteenth Century* (Aldershot, 2002); Percy Adams, *Travel Literature and the Evolution of the Novel* (Lexington, KY, 1983).

25. Katherine Turner, *British Travel Writers in Europe 1750–1800* (Aldershot, 2001), 1–2, 17–19.

26. MS Don. c. 193, fos. 19–20, Barbara Johnson/George Johnson, 17 Aug. [1776].

27. Ibid., fos. 90–1, Robert Johnson/George Johnson, 5 June 1779.

28. Ibid., fo. 21, Barbara Johnson/George Johnson, 13 Feb. 1777; Henry Penruddocke Wyndham, *A Gentleman's Tour through Monmouthshire and Wales* (1775), A2r, *Letters from Snowdon* (1770), A2v. Robert also read Giuseppe Baretti's *An Account of the Manners and Customs of Italy* (1769).

29. MS Don. c. 191, fos. 53–4, Robert Johnson/Barbara Johnson, n.d.; John Eglin, *Venice Transfigured* (NY, 2001).

30. Katherine Turner, *British Travel*, 121, 128, 131; *Critical Review*, 43 (1777), 439; *Monthly Review*, 80 (1789), 209. Robert's sister-in-law, the notorious Elizabeth, Lady Craven, published *A Journey through the Crimea to Constantinople in a Series of Letters* (1789, 1814). I am indebted to Katherine Turner's analysis.

31. *ODNB/*7671; Sylvester H. Bingham, 'Publishing in the eighteenth century with special reference to the firm of Edward and Charles Dilly', Ph.D., Yale

University, (New Haven, CT, 1937); W. Denham Sutcliffe, 'English book reviewing 1749–1800', D.Phil., University of Oxford (Oxford, 1942).

32. Miller, *Letters from Italy*, vii.

33. Ibid., vi.

34. Ibid., x–xi.

35. Ibid., iii, 155–6.

36. Ibid., i, 2–3.

37. Quoted in Hesselgrave, *Lady Miller and the Batheaston Literary Circle*, 6.

38. *Monthly Review*, 55 (Aug. 1776), 105.

39. *Critical Review*, 41 (May 1776), 355.

40. Katherine Turner, *British Travel*, 129.

41. For the rise of women writers see Janet Todd, *The Sign of Angelica* (1989); Margaret Ezell, *Writing Women's Literary History* (1993); Jane Spencer, *The Rise of the Woman Novelist* (Oxford, 1986); Cheryl Turner, *Living by the Pen* (1992); Roger Lonsdale (ed.), *Eighteenth-century Women Poets* (Oxford, 1993); Susan Staves, *A Literary History of Women's Writing in Britain, 1660–1789* (Cambridge, 2006); Jane Bowdler, *Poems and Essays*, 2nd edn (1786).

42. Women also left London due to financial and health problems. See Elizabeth Child, '"Virtuous Knowledge Woman's Truest Pride"' in Nicole Pohl, *Female Communities, 1600–1800* (Basingstoke, 1999), 219–37 and '"To Sing the Town"', 156; Susan Wiseman, 'Catherine Macaulay' in E. Eger et al. (eds.), *Women, Writing, and the Public Sphere, 1700–1830* (Cambridge, 2001).

43. Norma Clarke, *The Rise and Fall of the Woman of Letters* (2004), 3, 7–12.

44. Hesselgrave, *Lady Miller and the Batheaston Literary Circle*, 18; Chauncey B. Tinker, *The Salon and English Letters* (NY, 1915), 116–22.

45. See BCL newspaper files and Local Studies Pack for articles on the vase; BCL Boodle Collection, ii, 8, 9, 13; BCL Hunt Collection, fo. 89; F. Kilvert, *The Batheaston Vase* (Bath, 1858); MS Don. c. 191, fo. 12.

46. MS Don. c. 191, fos. 20–1, Robert Johnson/Barbara Johnson, n.d.

47. Ibid., fos. 18–19, Robert Johnson/Barbara Johnson, 22 Feb.

48. Revd R. Graves, *The Triflers* (1806), 12.

49. Dobson, *Diary & Letters of Madam d'Arblay*, i, 381–2.

50. William Lowndes, *They Came to Bath* (Bristol, 1983). For some members see BL L.R.269. b–1/3, *The Register Book of the Parish of Batheaston*; BLY, David Garrick Collection. General MSS 282 #32, 'The pleasures of May at Batheaston', MS poem endorsed by Garrick [1775].

51. Bodl MS Montagu d. 2, f. 132v, 13 June 1777.

52. MS Don. e. 197, fos. 12, 19 Dec. 1776; Gavin Turner, 'Bath 1775', 23–30.

53. [Anna Miller], *Poetical Amusements at a Villa near Bath*, 4 vols. (Bath, 1775–81), and *On Novelty: and on the Trifles and Triflers* (Bath, 1778); Tinker, *The Salon and English Letters*, 119; 'Review', *Gentleman's Magazine*, (Mar. 1775), 136–7; Hesselgrave, *Lady Miller and the Batheaston Literary Circle*, 77–88; Dobbie, *English Rural Community*, 88; 'Obituary', *Gentleman's Magazine* (1781); BLY,

OSB MS Shelves c. 509, Original Poems by Henry Skrine, fos. 12–31. Fos. 38–44 are 'A Familiar Epistle from an Oxonian to Lady Miller'. Miller encouraged Anna Seward, Harriet and Jane Bowdler, and Mary Alcock, ODNB/40631.

54. Anne Borsay, *Medicine and Charity in Georgian Bath* (Aldershot, 1999), 276, and 'A middle class in the making', *Journal of Social History*, 24 (1999), 269–86; *A State of the Casualty-Hospital in the City of Bath* [Bath, 1791]; Collinson, *The History and Antiquities of the County of Somersetshire*, ii, 42–50 (48); Crutwell, *New Bath Guide* (Bath, 1778), 32.

55. MS Don. e. 197, fo. 12, 19 Dec. 1776.

56. MS Don. e. 198, fo. 6, 22 Jan. 1777; e. 198, fo. 16, 3 Feb. 1777; e. 197, fo. 12, 20 Dec. 1776.

57. *Poem to the Memory of Lady Miller by Miss [Anna] Seward* (1782); E. Troide (ed.), *The Early Journals and Letters of Fanny Burney*, i (Oxford, 1988), 37. See BCL, Abbey Memorials, 385; Collinson, *The History and Antiquities of the County of Somersetshire*, ii, 69 for the inscription in Bath Abbey.

58. *Poem to the Memory of Lady Miller*, 5.

59. Peter Borsay, *The English Urban Renaissance* (Oxford, 1989).

60. MS Don. c. 193, fo. 58, Robert Johnson/George Johnson, 4 Nov. 1774.

61. Penelope Corfield, *The Impact of English Towns 1700–1800* (Oxford, 1982), 15, 59; R. S. Neale, *Bath 1680–1850* (1981), 44–6.

62. John Feather, 'The country trade in books' in Robin Myers and Michael Harris (eds.), *Spreading the Word* (Winchester, 1990), 165–84 (171), and *The Provincial Book Trade in Eighteenth-century England 1650–1800* (Cambridge, 1985); Elizabeth Child, ' "Virtuous Knowledge Woman's Truest Pride" ', 220.

63. Dobson, *Diary & Letters of Madam d'Arblay*, i, 381.

64. Hesselgrave, *Lady Miller and the Batheaston Literary Circle*, 13. For intimate thoughts of a middling-sort man attempting to break into Bath society see BCL, Edmund Rack, 'A Desultory Journal of Events &c at Bath' (22 Dec. 1779), typescript.

65. Janet Todd, *Sensibility* (1986), 14–15; Jonathan Barry, 'Provincial town culture 1640–1780' in Joan Pittock and Andrew Wear (eds.), *Interpretation and Cultural History* (NY, 1991).

66. Dena Goodman, *The Republic of Letters* (Ithaca, NY, 1994).

67. Marilyn Butler, *Romantics, Rebels, and Reactionaries* (Oxford, 1981), 32, 34.

68. I thank Elaine Chalus for discussions.

69. My italics. Letter to Mrs Robertson in Bath, 17 June 1779, quoted in Anstey, *An Election Ball*, 64.

70. For satire see MS Don. c. 191, fos. 9–10, Robert Johnson/Barbara Johnson, 16 Jan. 1777; c. 192, fo. 82–3, Catherine Wodhull/Barbara Johnson, 26 Feb. 1774; c. 193, fo. 23, Barbara Johnson/George Johnson, 13 Sept. 1777; c. 191, fo. 26, Robert Johnson/Barbara Johnson, 26 Mar. 1778.

71. Anne Borsay, *Medicine and Charity in Georgian Bath*, 272–5.

72. For Allen in Bath see BCL B383 Acc. 44543, Ralph Allen correspondence and accounts; Postal History Society, *Memorial to Ralph Allen* (1955); Marcia De Jersey, *Ralph Allen* (Bath, 1951); Leslie Ray, *The Society's Visit to Bath* (Bath, 1947); Elsie Russ, *Ralph Allen* (1948); *The Post Office and Bath* (Bath, 1936); Jerome Murch, *Ralph Allen* (1880).

73. Neale, *Bath*, 44, table of coach service 1700–1851; E. Emonet and P. Hobbs, 'Ralph Allen's new branch from Bath to Salisbury 1753', *Postal History*, 292 (n.d.), 117–19.

74. [Richard Cruttwell], *The Strangers Assistant and Guide to Bath, etc.* (Bath, 1773), 90–7. See the BCL's collection of Guidebooks and Directories: Thomas Boddely, *The Bath and Bristol Guide* (1753); Richard Cruttwell, *The New Bath Guide or Useful Pocket Companion* (1770); William Gregory, *A Bath Directory of 1783 … 1792 … 1797*; Messrs Bailey, *British Directory*, 1784, 336–41; *Universal British Directory*, 1793, 86–116.

75. MS Don. c. 191, fos. 110–11, Robert Johnson/George Johnson, n.d.; c. 192, fo. 61, Ann Smyth/Barbara Johnson, [7 May 1770].

76. For Charles and George see MS Don. c. 190, fos. 2–6; c. 191, fos. 57–8; c. 193–4.

77. MS Don. c. 192, fo. 48, [1788?].

78. MS Don. c. 193, fos. 13–14, Barbara Johnson/George Johnson, 2 Mar. [1776?].

79. Ibid., fos. 25–6, Barbara Johnson/George Johnson, 12 Dec. 1778.

80. TNA PROB 11/1695; MS Don. c. 195, fo. 82, 'Correct copy of my aunt's will'.

81. MS Don. c. 195, fo. 47, Barbara Johnson/William Johnson, 12 Apr. 1814.

82. Ibid., fo. 82.

83. For Barbara's papers see MS Don. c. 191; c. 192; c. 193, fos. 1–41; c. 195, fos. 3–4, Birth records with notes, fo. 82.

84. MS Don. c. 192, fos. 82–3, Catherine and Michael Wodhull/Barbara Johnson, 16 Feb. 1774.

85. Ibid., fo. 64, C. Smyth/Barbara Johnson, 12 Nov.

86. MS Don. c. 191, fos. 57–8, Charles Johnson/Barbara Johnson, 28 Feb. 1814; c. 191, fo. 96, Hugh Inglis/Barbara Johnson, 19 Feb. 1803.

87. MS Don. c. 192, fo. 59, Ann Smyth/Barbara Johnson, 22 Mar. 1762.

88. MS Don. c. 195, fo. 47, Barbara Johnson/William Johnson, 12 Apr. 1814.

89. MS Don. e. 198, fo. 29, 17 Apr. 1777; c. 191, fos. 20–4, Robert Johnson/Barbara Johnson, n.d.

90. MS Don. c. 191, fos. 49–50, Robert Johnson/Barbara Johnson, May 2.

91. MS Don. c. 191, fo. 22, Robert Johnson/Barbara Johnson, n.d.

92. Wodhull inherited Northamptonshire estates. His library at Thenford grew to over 4,000 books. MS Don. c. 192, fos. 7–10, Robert Harry Inglis/Barbara Johnson, 2 Apr. 1808; Bodl MS Eng. Lett. c. 370/2, fo. 132, Michael

Wodhull/John Nichols, 24 May 1780, fo. 133, 20 May 1786; fo. 134, Mar. 1787; Bodl MS Eng. Lett. b. 19, fo. 45, Michael Wodhull/John Nichols, 5 Nov. 1808.

93. Ms Don. c. 191, fos. 41–2, Robert Johnson/Barbara Johnson, 25 Oct.

94. E. J. Clery, *The Feminization Debate in Eighteenth-century England* (Houndmills, 2004), 140; BL Add. MS 39311, Berkeley Papers, Letters of Catherine Talbot, 1756–69.

95. Butler, *Romantics, Rebels, and Reactionaries*, 12, 15–16; Howard Weinbrot, *Britannia's Issue* (Cambridge, 1993).

96. For helpful statistics see William St Clair, *The Reading Nation in the Romantic Period* (Cambridge, 2004), 3, 10–11, 36, 122, 466–74.

97. Feather, *Provincial Book Trade*, 12, 23, 28, 37, Appendix IV.

98. James Raven, 'From promotion to proscription' in Raven et al. (eds.), *The Practice and Representation of Reading in England* (Cambridge, 1996), 175–201; Jacqueline Pearson, *Women's Reading in Britain 1750–1835* (Cambridge, 1999), 160, 163.

99. A. Crawford, *A Description of Brighthelmstone and the Adjacent Country* (Brighthelmstone, [1788]).

100. P. Garside et al. (eds.), *The English Novel 1770–1829*, i. (Oxford, 2000), 17; Child, ' "Virtuous Knowledge Woman's Truest Pride" ', 220.

101. MS Don. e. 197, fo. 2r, 15 Nov. 1776.

102. Jan Fergus, *Provincial Readers in Eighteenth-century* England (Oxford, 2006).

103. H. J. Jackson, *Romantic Readers* (New Haven, CT, 2005), 33–41, 52.

104. MS Don. c. 193, fos. 11–12, Barbara Johnson/George Johnson, 3 Feb. 1776.

105. MS Don. c. 192, fo. 71, C. Smyth/Barbara Johnson, n.d.

106. Ibid., fo. 93, Clara Quidnunc [Barbara Johnson]/Mr Baldwin, n.d.

107. Ibid., fos. 52–3, J. Russell/Barbara Johnson, 22 Mar. 1788.

108. MS Don. c. 191, fo. 89, S. Childers/Barbara Johnson, 16 Jan.

109. MS Don. c. 193, fos. 15–16, Barbara Johnson/George Johnson, 12 Mar. [1776].

110. Ibid., fos. 17–18, Barbara Johnson/George Johnson, 9 July 1776.

111. G. S. Rousseau, 'Science books and their readers in the eighteenth century' in Isabel Rivers (ed.), *Books and their Readers in Eighteenth-century England* (Leicester, 1982), 197–237 (223).

112. MS Don. c. 191, fos. 27–8, Robert Johnson/Barbara Johnson, 2 May 1788; c. 193, fos. 11–12, Barbara Johnson/George Johnson, 3 Feb. 1776; c. 193, fos. 15–16, Barbara Johnson/George Johnson, 12 Mar. [1776]; e. 195, fo. 26, 8 Oct.

113. MS Don. c. 191, fo. 89, S. Childers/Barbara Johnson, 16 Jan.

114. MS Don. c. 193, fos. 25–6, Barbara Johnson/George Johnson, 12 Dec. 1778.

115. Ibid., fos. 17–18, Barbara Johnson/George Johnson, 9 July 1776.

116. Bodl, The Craven Deposit [MSS], especially 282, 296, 378; MS Don. c. 195, fos. 97–136, Craven Family Papers, 1793–1838; e. 195, fo. 31, [30 Jan. 1773].

Anna Rebecca was the sister of William, sixth Baron Craven, daughter of John Craven, and widow of Ludford Taylor Esquire. See G.E.C. *Complete Peerage* (1913), 502–4.

117. *Miscellanea Genealogica*, 121–6 describes Robert as 'formerly a Captain in the Army'. His in-laws described him as a lieutenant in A. M. Broadley and L. Melville (eds.), *The Beautiful Lady Craven: The original memoirs*, i (1914), 45. In 1766, Robert visited his old regiment in Wells. MS Don. c. 191, fos. 1–2, Robert Johnson/Miss Barbara Johnson, 26 Apr. 1776. In c. 193, fos. 44–5, Robert Johnson/George Johnson, [5 Dec. 1772?], Robert admitted Mrs Taylor intended to marry without a settlement, but he fancied 'Ld Craven would not think it proper for her to marry without one.'

118. MS Don. c. 195, fo. 41, n.d.

119. Ibid., fos. 1–2, copy of Robert's Will, 1797. His children were Harriet, Maria, Georgiana, William Augustus, Robert Henry, and Charles Thomas.

120. Broadley and Melville, *The Beautiful Lady Craven*, i, 45.

121. MS Don. c. 193, fos. 83–4, Robert Johnson/George Johnson, 7 Feb. 1779.

122. Michael Wodhull, *Poems*, i (1772), 125–32.

123. MS Don. c. 191, fos. 31–2, Robert Johnson/Barbara Johnson, 8 Aug. [1778?].

124. Robert's son, Robert Henry, MA Brasenose College, assumed his father's Wistanstow living in 1806 and had an active career as a minister. W. Fletcher (ed.), *Shropshire Parish Registers, Diocese of Hereford, Wistanstow*, Shropshire Parish Register Society, xvii (1920), Part iii, 154, 184, 189. He was born in Kenilworth, 1782, died Oct. 1880. *Miscellanea Genealogica* states he was also Vicar of Claybooke and Rector of Lutterworth.

125. Robert's street may be seen in BNSRO, *A New and Correct Plan of the City of Bath with the New Additional Buildings*, *c*.1775. BNSRO, Bath City Rates Index; Walcot Poor Rates, 1780–1; Neale, *Bath*, 41.

126. Bodl, The Craven Deposit, MSS 282, 26 July 1805.

127. MS Don. e. 195, fo. 5, 17 Feb. [1772]; e. 194, fo. 201, Dec. [1771].

128. MS Don. e. 195, fo. 7, 12 Mar. [1772].

129. I thank Peter Jones of Birmingham for consulting 'Persons relating to the Archives of Soho' and providing information about Robert from his card index.

130. MS Don. c. 195, fos. 1–2.

131. MS Don. e. 198, fo. 4, 20 Jan. [1777]; fo. 22, 11 Mar. [1777]; fo. 28, 21 Mar. [1777]; Joseph Hunter, *The Connection of Bath with the Literature and Science of England* (Bath, 1853); BNSRO, Georgian Newspaper Project: for example, *Bath Chronicle*, 22 Feb. 1770, 21 Mar., 6 Apr., 14 Apr. 1774; *Weekly Chronicle*, 18 Jan. 1779.

132. MS Don. c. 193, fos. 81–2, Robert Johson/George Johnson, 14 Jan. 1779.

133. MS Don. e. 198, list of letters sent and received in back of notebook for 1777.

134. MS Don. c. 191, fo. 11, Robert Johnson/Barbara Johnson, 15 Oct. [1777].

135. MS Don. c. 191, fos. 9–10, Robert Johnson/Barbara Johnson, 16 Jan. 1777.

136. MS Don. c. 193, fos. 17–18, Barbara Johnson/George Johnson, 9 July 1776.

137. MS Don. c. 191, fo. 47, Robert Johnson/Barbara Johnson, n.d.

138. MS Don. c. 192, fos. 33–4, Henrietta and Bab Ingram/Barbara Johnson, 28 Dec. [1761].

139. MS Don. c. 191, fo. 16, Robert Johnson/Barbara Johnson, n.d.

140. MS Don. e. 194, fo. 19r, 27 Sept. [1771].

141. MS Don. c. 191, fos. 9–10, Robert Johnson/Barbara Johnson, 16 Jan. 1777.

142. Ibid., fo. 22, Robert Johnson/Barbara Johnson, n.d. 'It is not in the power of our language to convey in other words that sublime idea of the "Valley of the shadow of death".'

143. Ibid., fos. 20–1, Robert Johnson/Barbara Johnson, n.d.

144. Roger Chartier, *Inscription and Erasure*, trans. Arthur Goldhammer (Philadelphia, 2007), 114.

145. For examples see MS Don e. 194–8.

146. MS Don. e. 198, fos. 6–10 [1777]; e. 195, fo. 10, n.d.

147. MS Don. c. 193, fos. 44–7, Robert Johnson/George Johnson, [1772?].

148. For Adam Smith's, *Theory of Moral Sentiments*, David Hume's *History of England*, and Adam Ferguson's *An Essay on the History of Civil Society* see MS Don. e. 194, fo. 7 [1771]; e. 194, fos. 4–5, Apr. [1771]; c. 193, fos. 46–7, Robert Johnson/George Johnson, 10 Dec.; e. 196, fo. 14 [1775].

149. Steven Zwicker has argued that reading became passive in the eighteenth century in Kevin Sharpe and Steven Zwicker, *Reading, Society and Politics in Early Modern England* (Cambridge, 2003). The Johnsons' experience indicates a different conclusion.

150. MS Don. c. 191, fos. 41–2, Robert Johnson/Barbara Johnson, 25 Oct; Susan Staves, ' "Books without which I cannot write" ' in Jennie Batchelor and Cora Kaplan (eds.), *Women and Material Culture* (Houndmills, 2007), 192–211.

151. MS Don. c. 193, fos. 33–4, Barbara Johnson/George Johnson, 21 Mar. [1781].

152. MS Don. c. 191, fo. 40, Robert Johnson/Barbara Johnson, n.d.

153. Antonia Forster, *Index to Book Reviews in England 1749–74* (Carbondale, IL, 1990), Preface, ix, 4.

154. Ibid., 11; John Brewer, *Party Ideology and Popular Politics at the Accession of George III* (Cambridge, 1976), 154–5; Derek Roper, *Reviewing before the Edinburgh 1788–1802* (Newark, DE, 1978), 19–48.

155. Marilyn Butler, 'Culture's medium' in Stuart Curran (ed.), *The Cambridge Companion to British Romanticism* (Cambridge, 1993), 120–47; Roper, *Reviewing before the Edinburgh 1788–1802*, 126.

156. *Monthly Review*, 55 (Aug. 1776), 104–12 (105).

157. Feather, *Provincial Book Trade,* 51.

158. Katherine Turner, *British Travel,* 11.

159. Butler, 'Culture's medium', 125.

160. MS Don. c,191, fos. 18–19, Robert Johnson/Barbara Johnson, 22 Feb.

161. MS Don. e. 195, fo. 4, 1 Jan. [1772]; William Hay, *Religio Philosophi*, 3rd edn (1760).

162. MS Don. c. 191, fos. 27–8, Robert Johson/Barbara Johnson, 2 May 1788.

163. MS Don. c. 192, fos. 52–3, J. Russell/Barbara Johnson, 22 Mar. 1788.

164. MS Don. c. 193, fos. 64–5, Robert Johson/George Johnson, 24 July 1777.

165. MS Don. e. 198, fo. 18, 20, Feb. [1777].

166. MS Don. c. 191, fos. 20–1, Robert Johnson/Barbara Johnson, n.d.; Barbeau, *Life and Letters in the XVIIIth Century*, 224–41; in BLY OSB MSS File M 10273, Anna Miller/Dr William Kenrick, 4 July 1777 Anna denies choosing poems for publication on the basis of flattery.

167. MS Don. c. 191, fos. 10–11, Robert Johnson/Barbara Johnson, 16 Jan. 1777.

168. Ibid., fos. 7–8, Robert Johnson/Barbara Johnson, n.d.

169. For Anstey see *The New Bath Guide*, 10th edn (1776); *Envy: A Poem addressed to Mrs Miller at Batheaston Villa* (1778); *An Election Ball*, 3rd edn (Bath, 1776); *The Batheaston Paranassus Fairs* (San Francisco, CA, 1936).

170. MS Don. c. 191, fos. 23–4, Robert Johnson/Barbara Johnson, n.d.

171. *Ibid.*, fos. 20–1, Robert Johnson/Barbara Johnson, n.d.

172. Jerome McGann, *The Poetics of Sensibility* (Oxford, 1996); G. Barker-Benfield, *The Culture of Sensibility* (Chicago, IL, 1992); Chris Jones, *Radical Sensibility* (1993).

173. Roger Lonsdale (ed.), *The Penguin History of Literature, Dryden to Johnson* (1993), 255–7; Pat Rogers, *The Augustan Vision* (1974), 298.

174. Bodl MS 1011, fo. 97, Thomas Edwards/Mr Yorke, 19 Jan. 1748.

175. MS Don. e. 194, fo. 19, 27 Sept. [1771]. Sometimes extracts from particular books are identified; other times they are not.

176. Katherine Turner, *British Travel*, 121.

177. Philip Carter, *Men and the Emergence of Polite Society* (Harlow, 2001); Janet Todd, *Sensibility*, 6; Daniel Wickberg, 'What is the history of sensibilities?', *American Historical Review*, 112 (June 2007), 661–84.

178. Markman Ellis, *The Politics of Sensibility* (Cambridge, 1996), 5, 8; Robert Jones, 'Ruled passions: Re-reading the culture of sensibility', *Eighteenth-century Studies* 32 (1999), 395; Deirdre Lynch, 'Personal effects and sentimental fictions', *Eighteenth-century Fiction*, 12:2–3 (2000), 346–68.

179. John Locke, *An Essay Concerning Human Understanding* (1690).

180. MS Don. c. 191, fo. 11, Robert Johnson/Barbara Johnson, 15 Oct. [1777].

181. Jonathan Lamb, *The Evolution of Sympathy in the Long Eighteenth Century* 2009); Janet Todd, *Sensibility*, 3, 59; Ellis, *The Politics of Sensibility*, 13; Adam Smith, *The Theory of Moral Sentiments*, Knud Haakonssen (ed.) (Cambridge, 2002), 11–16.

182. MS Don. e. 194, fo. 2, 6 Mar. [1771] and throughout Robert's notebooks.

183. MS Don. e. 194, fo. 3, 30 Mar. [1771].

184. MS Don. c. 193, fo. 50, Robert Johnson/George Johnson, 30 Oct. [1773].

185. MS Don. e. 196, fo. 24, 25 Apr. [1775]; fo. 28, 9 May [1775].

186. MS Don. e. 195, fo. 17, 2 Aug.

187. MS Don. e. 198, fo. 2, 4, Jan. [1777]; c. 191, fo. 11, Robert Johnson/Barbara Johnson, 15 Oct. 1777.

188. MS Don. e. 194, fo. 4, 5 Apr. [1771].

189. MS Don. e. 195, fo. 9, 19 Mar.

190. MS Don. e. 194, fo. 2, 6 Mar. [1771].

191. Ibid., fo. 4, 5 Apr. [1771].

192. MS Don. e. 196, fo. 6, 6 Jan. [1775].

193. MS Don. e. 195, fo. 2, 1 Jan. [1772], fo 9, 19 Mar. [1772].

194. A computer search produced over a hundred instances where 'head' and 'heart' were expressed in relation to each other.

195. MS Don. c. 191, fo. 11, Robert Johnson/Barbara Johnson, 15 Oct. 1777.

196. Ibid., fo. 96, Hugh Inglis/Barbara Johnson, 19 Feb. 1803.

197. MS Don. e. 195, fo. 30, 1 Jan. 1773.

198. MS Don. e. 194, fos. 11–12, 30 June [1771].

199. MS Don. c. 192, fo. 71, C. Smyth/Barbara Johnson, n.d.

200. Ibid., fo. 17, C. Smyth/Barbara Johnson, 14 July [1794?].

201. MS Don. c. 192, fo. 71. C. Smyth/Barbara Johnson, n.d.

202. Ibid., fos. 39–40, Palm: Jenings/Barbara Johnson, n.d.

203. Wodhull, *Poems* (1772); MS Don. c. 192, fos. 84–5, Michael Wodhull/Barbara Johnson, 9 May 1803.

204. MS Don. c. 192, fos. 87–8, n.d.

205. Jean Jacques Rousseau, *Julie, or the New Heloise,* Part One, Letter XXVI, trans. P. Stewart (1761, repr. Hanover, NH, 1998) 12; R. Howells, *Julie, ou La Nouvelle Héloïse* (1986).

206. Nicola Watson, *Revolution and the Form of the British Novel 1790–1825* (Oxford, 1994); Mary Favret, *Romantic Correspondence* (Cambridge, 1993). By the 1790s, the perceived dangers of sentimental literature lead to critical publications with titles like *The Illusions of Sentiment* (1788); *Arubia: The Victim of Sensibility* (1790); *Errors of Sensibility* (1793); *Excessive Sensibility* (1787). See also Hannah More, *Strictures on the Modern System of Education* (1799); Iain Mc Calman (ed.), *An Oxford Companion to the Romantic Age* (Oxford, 1991), 111, 114.

207. Garside et al. (eds.), *The English Novel,* i, 30–32; Thomas Beebe, *Epistolary Fiction in Europe, 1500–1850* (Cambridge, 1999).

208. Jones, *Radical Sensibility*, 3.

209. Susan Manning, 'Sensibility' in Keymer and Mee, *Cambridge Companion* (Cambridge, 2004), 84–5.

210. Ellis, *The Politics of Sensibility*, 3.

CONCLUSION

1. I thank Shirley Brice Heath for discussions.

2. W. E. Gladstone (ed.), *Sermons by Joseph Butler*, ii (Oxford, 1897), 295, 9 May 1745.

3. Susan Skedd, 'Women teachers and the expansion of girls' schooling in England *c.*1760–1820' in Hannah Barker and Elaine Chalus (eds.), *Gender in Eighteenth-century England* (1997), 101–25.

4. For example, Bodl MS. Fairfax 35, fo. 65, Catherine Fairfax/Thomas Fairfax, 15 Dec. 1711; GH MS 3041/4, fo. 11, Mary Bowrey/Thomas Bowrey, [3 Feb. 1697?].

5. For example, [A. Behn], *Love-Letters Between a Noble-man and his Sister* (1684); E. Goldsmith (ed.), *Writing the Female Voice* (Boston, 1989), xii; P. M. Spacks, *Boredom* (Chicago, IL 1995), 83–109; Sandra Gilbert and Susan Gubar, *The Madwoman in the Attic* (New Haven, CT, 1979); Melissa Mowry, '(Re)productive histories', unpublished Ph.D. thesis, University of Delaware (Newark, DE, 1993); Jane Spencer, *The Rise of the Woman Novelist* (Oxford, 1986); Domna Stanton (ed.), *The Female Autograph* (NY, 1984); Nancy Armstrong, *Desire and Domestic Fiction* (NY, 1987); Claire Brant and Diane Purkiss (eds.), *Women, Texts and Histories 1575–1760* (1992).

6. Susan Whyman, 'The correspondence of Esther Masham and John Locke', *Huntington Library Quarterly*, 66 (2004), 275–307.

7. David Olson, 'Towards a psychology of literacy', *Cognition*, 60 (1996), 83–104; Ronald Kellogg, *Cognitive Psychology*, 2nd edn (Thousand Oaks, CA, 2003), 322.

8. Jane Desforges, '"Satisfaction and improvement"', *Publishing History*, 49 (2001), 5–48 (31).

9. John Rylands Library English MS 703, Diary of George Heywood, 7. I thank Hannah Barker for this reference.

10. Ronald Kellogg, *The Psychology of Writing* (NY, 1994), 16, 34.

11. BL Add. MS 78462, fo. 695, Sir John Evelyn/John Evelyn, 2 Oct. 1699.

12. David Carr, *Time, Narrative, and History* (Bloomington, Indiana, 1986), 52.

13. Julian P. Bond, *The Papers of Thomas Jefferson*, i (Princeton, NJ, 1950), xi.

14. E. P. Thompson, *The Making of the English Working Class* (NY, 1966).

15. Shari Benstock, 'From letters to literature', *Genre*, XVIII (1985), 263.

16. Nicola J. Watson, *Revolution and the Form of the British Novel 1790–1825* (Oxford, 1994), 15–16.

17. Dorothy Sheridan et al. (eds.), *Writing Ourselves* (Cresskill, NJ, 2000), 7; Romy Clark and Roz Ivanič, *The Politics of Writing* (1997), 275.

18. MS Don. c. 191, fo. 40, Robert Johnson/Barbara Johnson, n.d.

19. R. S. Fitton and A. P. Wadsworth, *The Strutts and the Arkwrights 1758–1830* (Manchester, 1958), 166–7, Eliza Strutt Evans/Joseph Strutt, 24 Oct. 1793.

Index